How Does It Sound Now?

How Does It Sound Now? features 32 interviews with top engineers and producers who have contributed to hundreds of millions of albums and CDs throughout their combined careers, including a new interview with Leslie Gaston-Bird for this second edition.

Winner of the 2010 Association for Recorded Sound Collections' Award for Excellence in Historical Recorded Sound Research, the second edition of *How Does It Sound Now?* allows readers to benefit from the collective experience of 32 industry heavyweights, whose interviews provide a comprehensive overview of the changes in methodology and equipment over the last 60 years. The collection focuses on engineers who made the transition through different technologies—analog to digital, wire to tape, and CD to mp3—and explores the methodology they employed when confronted with new and evolving technology. With a wide range of interviewees, from Phil Ramone to Geoff Emerick, discussions are centered around how producers and engineers retain quality and continue to create a product that conforms to their own high standards in the face of changing technologies.

The techniques described will be valuable to students of audio history or theory and recording courses, and will also be of interest to audio professionals, including home recordists and studio owners, who can use this book to educate their staff and offer to clients.

Gary Gottlieb is a long-time engineer, producer, writer, photographer, and music business professional, who refers to himself as a music generalist. As a recording engineer and music producer in New York, Gottlieb's long and distinguished career includes numerous Grammy Award winners and Rock & Roll Hall of Fame inductees. After earning his Master of Audio Aesthetics & Technology from Marlboro College, Gottlieb accepted a full-time faculty position at Webster University, where he created and chaired their Department of Audio Aesthetics & Technology. During his 15 years at Webster he published three books. He has remained active in Audio Engineering Society leadership for over 20 years. He is currently the President of AES and resides in Ukiah, California with his daughter, their dog Bean, and their cat Silver, who makes frequent appearances during Zoom calls.

How Does It Sound Now?

Legendary Engineers and Vintage Gear

Second Edition

Gary Gottlieb

Routledge
Taylor & Francis Group
LONDON AND NEW YORK

Designed cover image: Pimonova via Getty Images

Second edition published 2025
by Routledge
4 Park Square, Milton Park, Abingdon, Oxon, OX14 4RN

and by Routledge
605 Third Avenue, New York, NY 10158

Routledge is an imprint of the Taylor & Francis Group, an informa business

All photos by Gary Gottlieb unless otherwise indicated

First edition published by Course Technology 2010

British Library Cataloguing-in-Publication Data
A catalogue record for this book is available from the British Library

Library of Congress Cataloging-in-Publication Data
Names: Gottlieb, Gary, 1956 – author, interviewer.
Title: How does it sound now? : legendary engineers and vintage gear / [interviews by] Gary Gottlieb.
Description: Second edition. | Abingdon, Oxon; New York, NY: Routledge, 2025. | Includes index.
Identifiers: LCCN 2024058541 (print) | LCCN 2024058542 (ebook) | ISBN 9781032857893 (hardback) | ISBN 9781032857091 (paperback) | ISBN 9781003519829 (ebook)
Subjects: LCSH: Sound engineers—Interviews. | Sound recordings—Production and direction. | Sound—Recording and reproducing—Equipment and supplies.
Classification: LCC ML3790 .H698 2025 (print) | LCC ML3790 (ebook) | DDC 781.49092/2—dc23/eng/20241204
LC record available at https://lccn.loc.gov/2024058541
LC ebook record available at https://lccn.loc.gov/2024058542

ISBN: 978-1-032-85789-3 (hbk)
ISBN: 978-1-032-85709-1 (pbk)
ISBN: 978-1-003-51982-9 (ebk)

DOI: 10.4324/9781003519829

Typeset in Sabon
by codeMantra

This book is dedicated to the engineers and professionals who shaped our passion and have passed on:

Tom Dowd
Les Paul
Wally Heider
Alan Blumlein
John Eargle
Larry Levine
Bob Fine
William Hoekstra
To name a few

And to those among the audio professionals who were interviewed in the First Edition of this book, who have since passed away:

Phil Ramone
Al Schmitt
Geoff Emerick
Ed Cherney
Danny Leake
Marc Aubort
Jim Malloy
Glenn Snoddy
Cowboy Jack Clement
Gene Eichleberger
Bil VornDick
And most recently
Mark Rubel, who I did not have the opportunity to interview.

And to those they have mentored. Their memories, their skills, and their commitment to quality live on through those they have mentored who have, in turn, mentored us all.

Contents

About the Author

Long-time engineer, writer, photographer, and music business professional **Gary Gottlieb** refers to himself as a music generalist. A professional musician since age 13, he worked in radio on and off for 25 years and was a music critic, journalist, and photojournalist for a decade. As a recording engineer and music producer in New York, Gottlieb's long and distinguished career includes numerous Grammy Award winners and Rock & Roll Hall of Fame inductees. During this time, he was associated with some of the top studios in the city, including Sigma Sound, Right Track Recording, Counterpoint, and National Edison. His credits as a sound designer include numerous off-off-Broadway productions, community theater productions throughout New England, and college productions at Marlboro College and Plymouth State College. Along with his history as a music critic and entertainment writer for the Deerfield Valley News in West Dover, Vermont, and disc jockey for WEQX, a major modern rock station in Manchester, Vermont, Gottlieb owned and operated a mobile DJ service. An avid snowboarder and member of Mount Snow's ski patrol, he received his undergraduate degree from the Temple University School of Communications and Theatre and received his Master of Audio Aesthetics & Technology from Marlboro College. Following a few years as adjunct faculty at UMass Lowell, Castleton State College, Marlboro College, and Plymouth State College, Gottlieb accepted a full-time faculty position at Webster University, where he created and chaired their Department of Audio Aesthetics & Technology. During his 15 years at Webster, Gottlieb published three books. He has remained active in the AES Education and Historical Committees for over 20 years. He has consistently worked toward enlarging the scope of our audio community. To ensure that all are welcome, Gottlieb has served as the Chair of the Conference Policy and Events Coordination Committees, Regional Vice President on the BOG, and on the section level as a Chair, Secretary, Faculty Advisor, and Liaison. He is currently the President of the Audio Engineering Society and resides in Ukiah, California with his daughter, their dog Bean, and their cat Silver, who makes frequent appearances during Zoom calls.

About the Author

[illegible]

Foreword

It is the music that attracts us to learn how to record better than reality while making the player trust us to release their recording. I have listened to recordings that were made throughout the century. The common feeling I got, whether the engineer wore a lab coat or jeans, was inner passion and pride. The gear changes constantly. For me, immediacy and spontaneity drive my drive. Cleaner and purer is always the hope, but the rough and imperfect audio must be addressed for the engineer to be more prepared and to try new gear when they can evaluate it on their own time. This book, with all its interviews, gives you insight into the souls of the players. Read into the depths and realize the heart of this book.

Phil Ramone

Acknowledgments

I thought an interview book would be easier to write than any of the others I've written. After all, I'm just thinking up a list of questions and people to interview. Easy, right?

Little did I know just how difficult this project would be, and the resources and personnel I would need to complete the project.

Speaking of resources, I would like to express my gratitude to Webster University for providing me with a generous research grant. This funding allowed me to travel to perform the necessary interviews and also permitted me to pay for transcriptions. Without this support, the goals I set for this project would not have been realized.

I would like to thank those transcriptionists who toiled to decipher the jargon-heavy ramblings of my 32 interviewees and myself. Some of these were in environments with high ambient noise levels. Their task should not be underestimated: Thank you Larry Mollard, Andrea Sisney, Roger Landreth, and Laura Sarsen.

Obviously, I cannot begin to express the contribution made by the 32 engineers and producers I interviewed for this book. To state the obvious, this book would not be here without them. These are all incredibly busy people who took time out of their personal and professional lives to sit down with me. The only reason they did so was to advance your knowledge. None of them were paid or will receive any personal gain from this, other than the satisfaction of knowing that they have helped the next generation of engineers and producers.

Along with the 32 I interviewed, there are hundreds of recording engineers, maintenance engineers, producers, and inventors over the last century or so who contributed indirectly to this book. When you read it, you will see some of the same names repeated—Tom Dowd, Wally Heider, Roy Halee, Bill Porter, Frank Laico—alongside lesser-known names, people who also had a tremendous influence on me, the people I interviewed, and everyone in our business. I would like to thank all the teachers and mentors in our business—the ones who shaped it into whatever it is today. We may complain about this business, but we are all here, drawn into it, and we're not going anywhere else anytime soon.

Lastly, I would like to thank my family and friends for putting up with my travels to perform interviews, punctuated by weeks locked in my home office to get this book written. Miranda, Cassie, I love you and could not do this without your support. Thank you.

Acknowledgments

Introduction

While conducting the research for this project, a friend suggested that I start the introduction by talking about the hundreds of millions—probably billions—of copies of albums and CDs that the engineers and producers interviewed in this book contributed to throughout their combined careers – and since we now live in the age of streaming that number could reach into the billions!

While I am confident that his math was correct, this project is about quality, not quantity. The original concept was simply interviews with engineers who made the transition through different technologies—analog to digital, wire to tape, and CD to MP3. I sought to explore the methodology employed by the most successful among us when confronted with new and evolving technology. In the course of these conversations, we can't help but talk about the gear, but the real discussion that emerged focused on how we retain quality and continue to create a product that conforms to our own high standards. This, of course, led to many other side conversations about the musicians we work with, the consumers we serve, and the differences and similarities between their standards and our own. There's a lot of good, timeless advice in these pages regarding how high your standards could be. Having said that, I need to point out that some of these interviews dating back to 2008 may include outdated terminology. In order to preserve the integrity of the interview I retained those terms to stay true to the interviewee's intent. I have the utmost respect for everyone I interviewed for this project, and I gave them a great deal of latitude. I asked some questions specific to the transitions I mentioned earlier, but I also gave them a forum to speak to any aspect of the music business they chose. The discussions were very interesting and insightful, and some of them were very long. (Imagine that—an engineer who likes to ramble on!).

The title of the book may need an explanation if you are unfamiliar with the story. I discussed possible titles with some students and colleagues and was reminded of this Chet Atkins story. Chet was playing his guitar when a woman approached him. She said, "That guitar sounds beautiful." Chet immediately quit playing. Staring her in the eyes, he asked, "How does it sound now?"

The quality of the sound in Chet's case clearly rested with the player, not the instrument, and the quality of our product ultimately lies with us as engineers and producers, not with the gear we use. I was also drawn to the dual significance of the line, "How does it sound now?" because it addresses the changes we have seen and heard as our business and methodology have evolved through the decades.

The interviewees range in age from their 40s through their 80s, and many of them have passed away since the early interviews. Some of them started in the business as far back as World War II, so the range of experiences revealed is wide. I hope you find these opinions and thoughts, sometimes widely divergent and sometimes in complete opposition with each other, as interesting as I did. The common thread of quality is inherent in the work we all performed then and continue to perform now.

Introduction

Chapter 1

Alan Parsons

Born in England, Alan Parsons is a world-famous musician, engineer, and producer. Although his most famous associations are with Pink Floyd's The Dark Side of the Moon and the Beatles' Abbey Road, fans know him through his own band, the Alan Parsons Project, and various solo recordings.

Parsons started as an assistant engineer at Abbey Road Studios when he was 18, in 1967. The first project he worked on was Abbey Road, and he went on to engineer projects for Paul McCartney, the Hollies, Al Stewart, and Pink Floyd. He was nominated for his first Grammy Award for his groundbreaking work on The Dark Side of the Moon.

In 1975, he founded the Alan Parsons Project with Eric Woolfson. At different times, the band featured members of Pilot, members of Ambrosia, and a variety of studio musicians. The Alan Parsons Project generated ten albums between 1975 and 1987; since then, Parsons continues to release albums and tour. Parsons has garnered 11 Grammy Award nominations for engineering and production, and in 2007, he was nominated for Best Surround Sound Album for A Valid Path.

Parsons lives in Santa Barbara, California.

My name is Alan Parsons. I was born in London on 20th December, 1948, not 1949 as a lot of websites seem to think. My first beginnings in audio were as a result of the fact that there was, unusually for somebody my age, a tape recorder in the house. My father bought a Ferrograph to record me as a baby in the bathtub singing and playing and splashing and whatever. And I got to know how to use it, literally at the age of seven or eight. I had a cousin who was interested in radio drama and stuff like that; we used to make radio plays with sound effects and stuff. It was all good fun, but a serious interest in audio recording came soon after I learned to play guitar, which was at about the age of 12, 13.

My first job in audio was at EMI in West London, in Hayes, where they were making 1/4-inch reel-to-reel commercially available records. The department was called Tape Records, and I was appointed to maintain the BTR2 tape machines, as a kind of trainee. But I also got into a department that was doing the transfers, the copying for that process,

DOI: 10.4324/9781003519829-1

Figure 1.1 At Abbey Road, everything was pretty much big racks of valve chassis; the BTR2 was still the sort of de rigueur recording standard machine; valve consoles, of course; the big, gray 4-track consoles were in all the studios when | arrived; the 8-track Solid State console arrived a year after | got there. Of course, the microphone collection even then would've been the envy of every engineer of today. It was just countless M 49s, M 50s, U 47s, 48s, all manner of dynamic mics, AKG condenser mics. Great, great collection...But we were fighting with the somewhat primitive consoles and unreliable tape machines.

Figure 1.2 I was actually against compressing a whole mix, although when Chris Thomas came in to supposedly mixing supervise The Dark Side of the Moon album, he did ask for compression across the desk. Obviously, he was in charge, so made that happen, but I| did at least make a request that the drums didn't get so compressed and limited. So we had two stems, one for the drums and one for everything else. The "everything else" stems got limited by the Fairchilds. The sound of the drums came from Nick and from the miking and then from the remote that we used. It certainly didn't result from any compression or limiting.

and also doing copying work for international branches of the alliance. So, you know, one of the jobs early on was making countless copies of the Sergeant Pepper album for different countries to manufacture their vinyl discs from.

In the tape duplication place, it was all BTR2s. There were a couple of TR90s in the copying area—quite a rare machine these days, a huge, green EMI machine that you don't see very often. The BTR2s were the classic mono 1/4-inch machines that Abbey

Figure 1.3 The mixer, the EMI TG Solid State mixer—the basic design remained in use for probably 20 years after that time, and then much sort of revered, valued by the people who now own them. Mark Knopfler's got one, for example. There's another one in Los Angeles, where people go through the various modules that are lying around. It's one of those funny things; nobody would've ever thought that they'd be hugely revered and that people would want to use them as a central piece of gear to go through. But that's what it's all about these days—everything's down to Neve modules SSL modules, EMI modules, and consoles seem to have almost disappeared. People just use plug-in channel strips these days. That seems like a slight contradiction in value to me, to be in the digital domain and then try and emulate a very much analog mic pre inside the digital domain. I don't see how that can possibly work.

Figure 1.4 At Abbey Road, the first digital delay line was the Eventide. And then, the huge development from that was the pitch card. It was a thing that you could modify the pitch and incoming signal through an electronic version of the Doppler Effect. And it was that that the harmonizing was developed from. That was an extraordinary development, I think—the harmonizer. That was big news at the time. That must have been '75.

Road had a huge number of. So that was a useful experience, to have worked all those machines before I got to Abbey Road, which was three years later or so.

At Abbey Road, everything was pretty much big racks of valve chassis; the BTR2 was still the sort of de rigueur recording standard machine; valve consoles, of course; the big, gray 4-track consoles were in all the studios when I arrived; the 8-track Solid State

Figure 1.5 Interestingly, that concept is still very much alive and well in Nashville. And it's not just country music—there's rock music being made in Nashville that involves people playing together. And I think that the whole organic sound that produces is wonderful, and I think too much music these days doesn't have that magic that you get with musicians playing together.

Figure 1.6 I think the Universal Audio classic reproductions sound great. I have an Aphex mic pre that I like very much. I've got a Studer tube mic pre that | like. There are so many choices. It actually has become quite difficult because there are so many manufacturers selling so many different units out there, all doing essentially the same job. And you could also argue that one box isn't necessarily right for everything. It's not one size fits all. It's down to your experience and your desire to experiment along with everything else.

console arrived a year after I got there. Of course, the microphone collection even then would've been the envy of every engineer of today. It was just countless M 49s, M 50s, U 47s, 48s, all manner of dynamic mics, AKG condenser mics. Great, great collection... But we were fighting with the somewhat primitive consoles and unreliable tape machines.

There was actually some outboard because the standard format for recording pop was through Altec compressors, and Fairchild limiters, and so on. So, yes, there was outboard. But no outboard reverb—the only reverbs available were echo chambers and

EMT echo plates, which were housed upstairs on the roof. Not on the roof, really— on the highest floor of the building. That was in 68.

I think my title was assistant engineer or second engineer. But it was essentially a trainee process. I did all kinds of stuff; I even worked in the tape library for a short period of time, which was a good experience. Learning how badly things got logged and how important it was...at least when I started logging stuff, I knew how important it was to give as much information as possible. There are an awful lot of tapes out there that nobody knows what they are because they just weren't marked properly.

There was a great feeling at the time when I got the job, that here I was working in the same studio where all these great records were being made. You know, all the way from Sir Edward Elgar in the 30s and right through to The Beatles, and everything that was going on at the time I joined. And it was obviously very fulfilling at the time when I did actually get a job working with The Beatles, which was to start with not at Abbey Road—it was at their studio, Apple, a short bus ride away down in central London.

I'd been at Abbey Road several months, and I went to Apple courtesy of Abbey Road as a second engineer; Glynn Johns was the engineer. At Apple, they had a mixer made by the now infamous Magic Alex, and it didn't work, so Abbey Road was brought in to solve problems, and we moved two of the valve desks down there and two of the 4-track desks—one to record on 8-track, and one essentially was for monitoring. It was a good setup; it was actually much easier than The Beatles had ever had the luxury of having at Abbey Road, because there just wasn't the space. So, it was actually quite a good system to record on one desk and monitor on the other. The only other work at Apple was the rooftop session.

It really was pretty slow at Abbey Road in terms of outboard gear until the digital revolution. I suppose '75 to '76 that started happening. When I was working on The Dark Side of the Moon, virtually the only outboard gear we had was external limiters. There were the Kepex noise gates; they appeared in about '72. So, they got good use on The Dark Side of the Moon. But there really wasn't much in the way of external gear because digital electronics were still a few years away.

The Fairchilds were part of the Abbey Road stock. We also used the Allison Research Gain Brains, which fit in the same racks as the Kepexes. I favored those; I thought they worked quite well.

Anyway, we were talking about some of the different limiters and when they got used. All vocals and virtually every time I recorded a band, I would stick a limiter on. I'm one of these people who actually is anti-limiting and compression as a general rule; I'm a staunch non-supporter of the level war that is going on now. And I do not, generally speaking, compress on mixes. I just like to hold onto dynamic range as much as possible. I think the best limiter and compressor are the human fingers on the faders.

I only compressed individual elements. I was actually against compressing a whole mix, although when Chris Thomas came in to supposedly mixing supervise The Dark Side of the Moon album, he did ask for compression across the desk. Obviously, he was in charge, so I made that happen, but I did at least make a request that the drums didn't get so compressed and limited. So, we had two stems, one for the drums and one for everything else. The "everything else" stems got limited by the Fairchilds. The sound of the drums came from Nick and from the miking and then from the remote that we used. It certainly didn't result from any compression or limiting.

The EMI TG desk did have limiters and compressors on every channel. And a lot of people are buying those modules as channel strips or using the mixers in new locations. But the fact is that a lot of the engineers at Abbey Road actually hated those things; they never used them. They'd much prefer to use an Altec compressor or a Fairchild limiter in most cases. And I was one of them. I didn't like the fact that you could hear the things working. A Fairchild was a much more natural, much more pleasing to the ear-limiting effect.

The mixer, the EMI TG Solid State mixer—the basic design remained in use for probably 20 years after that time and then much sort of revered, valued by the people who now own them. Mark Knopfler's got one, for example. There's another one in Los Angeles, where people go through various modules that are lying around. It's one of those funny things; nobody would've ever thought that they'd be hugely revered and that people would want to use them as a central piece of gear to go through. But that's what it's all about these days—everything's down to Neve modules, SSL modules, EMI modules, and consoles seem to have almost disappeared. People just use plug-in channel strips these days. That seems like a slight contradiction in value to me, to be in the digital domain and then try and emulate a very much analog mic pre inside the digital domain. I don't see how that can possibly work.

I suppose vintage commonly starts in the '80s for the purposes of audio. Yeah, I think maybe they'll start calling the '50s and '60s stuff antique rather than vintage.

I think cut-and-paste audio is a remarkable timesaver. Not much else... Just thinking in a nonlinear fashion has changed the way everybody works. You don't even give it a second thought that you can edit between two takes or take a vocal from one take and put it in the backing track of another take. All that stuff was possible, but by enormously convoluted means in the analog days. So, it's just a means to think in a nonlinear fashion that I think has changed all that. And digital reverb is easy, and effects are good and easy to set up. But I think there was a certain element of discovery that we went through when we used effects or when we developed special effects or used combinations of outboard gear or tape delays or whatever to achieve something. It's a little bit easier now to have a black box with 500 settings on it and just choose one. We really had to work hard to get anything different, and that's borne out by the fact that we used to have cables running down the corridors between studios, using every tape machine in the building. You just don't need to do that anymore.

There are all kinds of pieces of gear from then that I would love to have in my studio now, microphones.... 1 don't possess a Fairchild limiter because they cost an arm and a leg these days, and they tend to end up in quantities in single places by collectors. There's a guy called John McBride who runs a studio in Nashville called Blackbird and he's got rooms full of vintage mics and Fairchilds and all kinds of stuff. So, in a funny way, he's commonly contributing to the high price because they're becoming less and less available. And there are lots of emulations people are building, plug-in versions of old gear. Which is fine; it's the next best thing. But I would like to have a Fairchild limiter in my collection. And I would also like to have a Neumann U 47.

At Abbey Road, the first digital delay line was the Eventide. And then the huge development from that was the pitch card. It was a thing that you could modify the pitch and incoming signal through an electronic version of the Doppler Effect. And it was that that the harmonizing was developed from. That was an extraordinary development, I think—the harmonizer. That was big news at the time. That must have been '75.

It was interesting that the predecessor to the harmonizer was this delay line box that I can't remember the serial number of or the model number, but I remember distinctly that it was an add-on card that fitted into the middle of the panel—it did the pitch control.

I can't say I have a vivid memory of what devices came in at Abbey Road. The digital revolution also brought rapid developments in musical instrument technology as well as recording technology—I think perhaps that was more noticeable. The Fairlight, for example, and the DX7 all coming in around the 1980 to '81 period... But there were several companies that were born out of the hunger in the industry for digital processing.

Some of the changes in the business? Well, if the answer was about business, the answer is nothing's changed—you always get ripped off. The changes.... well, I think the industry just grew up. It just turned from very much a process that only record labels could afford to have, and their margin depends on studios, and it's now become within the reach of every Tom, Dick, or Harry with a laptop. So there's the change. It's just the fact that technology came within reach of the man on the street. Whereas when I started, it was very much a goal to attain, to get signed by a label, and to have the luxury of walking into a recording studio for the first time and actually making a record. The sense of occasion is gone now, which is a little lamentable. But having said that, a lot of talent has appeared that might otherwise not have.

As I approach the edge where I'm going to hang up my hat, I think there's so much music being made now because there are so many budding songwriters and recording artists doing stuff on laptops. So it's tough to wade through it all and then discover the stuff that has value. But you know, along with it comes the Internet, along with the ability for the man on the street to make a record. Along with it comes the Internet, so it will reach the masses no matter what. And the masses have a habit of picking up on a large scale and narrowing what has value down to a smaller scale, and then the people who make it through that mire of listeners will eventually win out, eventually find a home, and talent eventually gets recognized. But I think it's a longer process these days.

There are no tape machines in my studio. I'm a sort of digital audio workstation convert. I think I still would always try to keep the analog chain alive and use the best mics, the best mic pres, the best analog processing that I could before I went into the digital domain. But once I'm in the digital domain, I'm pretty much in the box. I haven't had the luxury of having a full-blown, large-scale console. I have a Yamaha digital mixer, an O2R96, which works great. But, it's more often than not just simply controlling the levels inside the box. It's not actually being used to process audio.

I think the Universal Audio classic reproductions sound great. I have an Aphex mic pre that I like very much. I've got a Studer tube mic pre that I like. There are so many choices. It actually has become quite difficult because there are so many manufacturers selling so many different units out there, all doing essentially the same job. And you could also argue that one box isn't necessarily right for everything. It's not one size fits all. It's down to your experience and your desire to experiment along with everything else. But I think the so-called classic mic pres and the so-called classic equalizers—everybody loves the Massenburg parametric EQ, for example. It's still very much held in high esteem, I think. Pultecs are lovely gear. And you know, again, countless emulations of those as plug-ins. Do the emulations as plug-ins come close? You know, you could write a book on that subject. Sometimes yes, sometimes no.

As an aside, because modern recording has become so much of a one-input multi-output process, I think we're losing the idea that musicians can form this thing called a band and play together. And it just seems it's getting lost in the general attitude to recording. The songwriter has his laptop or his little home studio with his few processing devices and keyboard and guitar and bass guitar, and he's quite likely to play everything himself, or maybe he has a friend who comes in and helps him. I do have this wish that more people would form bands and then go and record as bands, and it's becoming difficult because the budgets aren't there anymore with the industry being in the state it's in. And that's just a general comment on the idea of computer recording. The computer recording has somewhat destroyed the general idea that you can have multi-inputs going on at once, and the systems are capable of it. What seems to be happening now is you start with a click and then you add a keyboard and you add a bass, then you add this, you add that, and it's just a little sad that you don't really hear the attraction between musicians often enough in the modern, digital, in-the-box DAW (Digital Audio Workstation) world.

Interestingly, that concept is still very much alive and well in Nashville. And it's not just country music—there's rock music being made in Nashville that involves people playing together. And I think that the whole organic sound that produces is wonderful, and I think too much music these days doesn't have that magic that you get with musicians playing together.

Chapter 2

Chuck Ainlay

Along with four Grammy's, two CMA's, two TEC Awards and ten ACM Awards, Producer/Engineer, Chuck Ainlay has well over 3,500 credits to his name, including work with legendary and defining country music artists such as; George Strait, Miranda Lambert, Lee Ann Womack, Steve Earle, Lyle Lovett, Emmylou Harris, and The Chicks.

Chuck has placed his distinctive production and engineering stamp on projects with more mainstream artists such as Dire Straits and nearly the entire solo career of Mark Knopfler as well as Peter Frampton, Taylor Swift, Lionel Richie, Ann Wilson, James Taylor, Jewel, Bob Seger, Pentatonix, and Sheryl Crow.

His work in immersive mixing has resulted in groundbreaking projects such as the 25th anniversary remix of Peter Frampton's *Frampton Comes Alive* and the Grammy Award-winning 20th anniversary remix of the Dire Straits album *Brothers In Arms.*

He is currently serving as a Trustee of the Recording Academy after serving numerous terms as Governor. He has chaired the Nashville P&E Wing and is currently co-chairing the Recording Academy P&E Wing National Steering Committee, along with serving on the Nashville Section of the Audio Engineering Society.

Chuck has been a coauthor of the majority of the P&E Wing Guidelines and recommendations and is currently on the board of directors for the Country Music Association. Belmont University awarded him with the Robert E. Mulloy Award of Excellence. Chuck is also a founding member of METAlliance Inc., which launched in January of 2005.

My name is Chuck Ainlay, originally Charles W. Ainlay, known as "Ollie" when I was in high school. I grew up in northern Indiana about 10 miles from Michigan, in a small farm town where you had a choice of two things to do as a kid: One was to be into sports, and the other was to be into music. And, although I loved sports and still am an avid water-skier, I chose the music end of it because it had more fun people to hang out with.

The earliest beginning in audio for me was that my uncle had a studio in his house about half an hour away from our hometown. He was a really interesting guy—actually,

DOI: 10.4324/9781003519829-2

Figure 2.1 It was because of the SSL and the 3M out there at Castle Studios that Nashville became the leader in digital, and I think really worldwide, because the producer, Jim Bowen, came out to work with me, and I introduced him to working on digital tape. He realized very quickly the benefits of being able to comp and no signal generation loss, and having more than 24 tracks was intriguing to him. So he pretty much insisted that all the studios that were to get his work—and he had 70-plus percent of the market; he brought that much work in—so if a studio was going to get his business, he required a Mitsubishi X850 and an SSL 4000 desk. That's why I think Nashville progressed in that direction a lot quicker than other places.

Figure 2.2 We had a couple of really nice echo chambers and an EMT stereo plate. We also had a box that had a tube inside of it, a Cooper Time Cube. You had two outputs: One was a five-millisecond delay, and the other one was 35 milliseconds or something like that. But that was a great little delay device; it had a really interesting sound. I wish I could find one now, and somebody needs to build a plug-in. It had a really unique EQ to it; it was basically a garden hose with the transducer in one end and a pickup at the other end. You've got sound going down a tube, so it's going to sound weird, and then it had its EQ to try and flatten it out. A lot of times we put the time cube in front of the plate or on the chambers to pre-delay, which had a great sound to it. It was just a different-sounding box, you know? Nobody's done a plug-in of it yet.

Figure 2.3 I haven't seen anything come along that allowed me to get my job done more quickly. If anything, there are just more options, and the job takes longer. Or people just don't make decisions, and they put it off. So obviously, for me, primarily mixing, now I'm the one making the choices of which tracks are going to stay in a record and what stuff needs to get cut out because there are three solos playing at once and comping vocals because they just left it all for you to figure out.... We've obviously seen the ability to create even better digital recordings, and we've had for a time a consumer format where we could give those really high-resolution recordings to the public.... The technology keeps changing, but I don't know that we're making any better records. You can go back to a Led Zeppelin record or a Beatles record—those records still sound wonderful, even by today's standards. They're so creative and they're warm and they're musical. Having all these plug-ins and the capacity to tune things, I think it just makes the performers weaker. They don't actually strive to get a take from one end to the other.... There should be a lot of benefits to the changes in technology, but they're actually not making anything better. I wouldn't stretch and say we're not making as good of records as back then, but you would think with what's available we should be making even better records.

Figure 2.4 I've been forced to work on Pro Tools maybe three times. Otherwise, I actually find it a real advantage because the clients come in, reach over my shoulder, grab the mouse, and start doing stuff themselves. They look: and they go, "Oh, that's Nuendo," and they just leave me alone to do my own thing.

Figure 2.5 You never stop learning; that's the main thing. Every day I go into the studio, and I'm happy to go to work every day. I love going to work every day. I don't mind spending 13, 14 hours—however long it takes. Every day I go in I learn something, and even working on projects that aren't going to have any kind of critical acclaim or aren't even going to make it in the marketplace, I still do my absolute best to make the best record I possibly can for that person. For one, it's their record— that's what they're going to have to live with. Also, I know that I'm going to learn something from that experience, if nothing else just to keep myself fine-tuned for the next project where it does matter. The other thing is that, obviously, to be able to dedicate yourself to your work as much as that, it requires a really special wife, and I've finally found a really great one.

Figure 2.6 I never, ever thought that I would make my residence in Nashville. I wasn't a big country fan or anything. I liked sort of what was country music to me at the time—like Poco, The Flying Burrito Brothers, The Band, stuff like that. But Conway Twitty or something like that just didn't make sense. Now I have a huge appreciation for country music, and I'm very happy that I live in Nashville because it's one of the still-prospering recording cities.

he probably had a lot of influence on why I chose to be an engineer—but he was a ventriloquist, and a really good one…he had the dummies and everything. And at Christmas he was Santa Claus, you know, had the costume…. He played banjo, but he also was really into audio and built a studio in his house with a real control room with a studio, and he built his own display until he could afford to buy a real one. He had the Ampex open-reel machines and RCA microphones and everything.

So, when I was in fourth grade I had a little band, and we actually went to the studio and recorded our first 45. So, you know, there was kind of that beginning and introduction to recording, but in my bands and so forth I was just avidly into music. I listened to music all of the time, read the Hi-Fi magazines and everything, did whatever I could until I could buy my first open-reel tape machine, which was a Tandberg. I would do tons of sound-on-sound types of recordings, just experimenting and trying to create the same kinds of sounds I was hearing on records. And then a friend of mine got a Teac 4-track. I had some aptitude and was the guy who ran it. From there I went to Indiana University. There was a studio in Bloomington, Indiana, called Gilfoy Sound Recorders, and I took a little six-month program there, which really made me realize that this was what I wanted to do, so I dropped out of Indiana University and found out that summer about Belmont College in Nashville—that they had a recording program and music business degree. This made my parents happy—that there was actually a degree, and with business in it—so I went to Belmont in 1975 and enrolled in that program. I stayed there for about a year and a half before I decided to kind of go on my own. Not so much anything other than I wanted to get out from underneath my parents' wings, and I was able to get a job.

Well, my first job was working for Opryland as the live sound for one of the shows they had there. Then I got a job at a tourist studio, where they run a hundred at a time through the studio, and I was the engineer. We had a Langevin console and a Scully 8-track machine, and we'd record this performance for the audience and then play it back—make them clap or sing along or something. They all filed through the control room, and I'd explain recording, you know? But that kind of was my earliest beginnings. I got a job from there back up in Fort Wayne, Indiana. I had a girlfriend going to school in Michigan, so I thought, "Well, I could get a job in a real studio, a chief engineer...." But that didn't last long. She died of an aneurysm in class. Also in that same week, somebody hit-and-run and totaled my car, and someone else walked into the studio and stole my Martin guitar. So it was like all these signs that this was not the right place for me, and I went back to Nashville. Been there ever since, really.

I never, ever thought that I would make my residence in Nashville. I wasn't a big country fan or anything. I liked sort of what was country music to me at the time—like Poco, The Flying Burrito Brothers, The Band, stuff like that. But Conway Twitty or something like that just didn't make sense. Now I have a huge appreciation for country music, and I'm very happy that I live in Nashville because it's one of the still-prospering recording cities.

The first studio when I went back to Nashville had a Flickinger console, which was a really unique console. They've only made a few consoles, but this console had a switching assignment matrix, so it was a really interesting console for the time—it actually sounded great. But no automation—we're talking a manual console. We had an MM 1100 16-track, an MM 1100 24-track, and some HE 440 2-tracks. We eventually upgraded to a Studer A80 24-track and an ATR-100 2-track. And that's pretty much what you found; there were Harrison consoles, API consoles, Neve consoles, Quad Eight, MCI....

After that job I got a chief engineering job at Castle; we had a Harrison console there. Quickly, I talked them into going digital, and we bought the 3M 32-track digital machine, so we were the first studio in town to be digital. Shortly after that, we got rid of the Harrison and got the first SSL. It was because of the SSL and the 3M out there at

Castle Studios that Nashville became the leader in digital, and I think really worldwide, because the producer, Jim Bowen, came out to work with me, and I introduced him to working on digital tape. He realized very quickly the benefits of being able to comp and no signal generation loss, and having more than 24 tracks was intriguing to him. So he pretty much insisted that all the studios that were to get his work—and he had 70-plus percent of the market; he brought that much work in—so if a studio was going to get his business, he required a Mitsubishi X850 and an SSL 4000 desk. That's why I think Nashville progressed in that direction a lot quicker than other places. I've been working with digital since pretty much the beginning of my time, other than the early years.

When I started it was really before digital. We had a couple of really nice echo chambers and an EMT stereo plate. We also had a box that had a tube inside of it, a Cooper Time Cube. You had two outputs: One was a 5-millisecond delay, and the other one was 35 milliseconds or something like that. But that was a great little delay device; it had a really interesting sound. I wish I could find one now, and somebody needs to build a plug-in. It had a really unique EQ to it; it was basically a garden hose with the transducer in one end and a pickup at the other end. You got sound going down a tube, so it's going to sound weird, and then it had its EQ to try and flatten it out. A lot of times we put the time cube in front of the plate or on the chambers to pre-delay, which had a great sound to it. It was just a different-sounding box, you know? Nobody's done a plug-in of it yet. And tape, of course—we had a mono machine that we just used on tape loops and another stereo machine that was a tape-loop machine. So all your FX were based around that.

We had 1176s and LA-2As, that kind of compressor. The studio is blessed to have a gazillion U 87 microphones, a bunch of Neumann microphones—you know, a few EVs and Shures, and stuff like that. It was really a fun studio to work at because it wasn't doing a lot of country. We did all the Dr. Hook records and Helen Reddy and that sort of stuff. It kind of had a reputation for the local rock. And the cool thing I think about in those days as opposed to once we moved into having fader automation—it required a lot of people to be on the console to mix a record. You'd have the chief engineer who was kind of in charge of the main section and directed everybody about what to do. But as an assistant… really I don't think we were thought of as an assistant—we were thought of as a second engineer. We'd take home portions of the mix as well and do all the editing and all the setup and getting mic levels and preliminary EQ for tracking before the track would begin. Then the chief engineer would sit down and run the session. So if a client couldn't pay for the full rate, they'd get us. We got a lot of engineering work rather than nowadays, when the assistants pretty much just document the session there's not a lot of real hands-on experience.

There weren't many options, so you pretty much used everything you had. Like I said, the chambers and the plate were always utilized. I wouldn't say the time cube was used all the time, but in one way or another, it was probably utilized to delay either the plate or the chamber. Tape slap was always used, flanging…we'd do that kind of stuff, too. I remember hearing gated reverb for the first time on a record, and it was never explained to me what it was. But I heard this really huge reverb and then it cut off really quickly, and I was like, "How'd they do that?" About the same time, this kid had invented a gate. We had Gain Brains and Keypexes. But the gate this guy invented had a really fast on and a really controllable release, and I remember thinking, "I wonder if I put that on the reverb and then keyed it off the snare drum if I could get that sound?" And it worked, and it was like, "Wow, gated reverb." And that kind of made me popular with all the rock guys, that I knew how to do that. I also remember going off to LA to mix this project with this little rock band that wanted to go to LA to mix their record.

So I went out there, and that was where I was first introduced to Yamaha NS-10s. I bought a pair immediately because up until then all we had were the little Auratone speakers. That was your near-field, an Auratone—mono Auratone. And then we had these horrible JBL speakers in the wall there. They were JBLs, and they had this lens over the horn because it was so directional. You find them in a lot of studios because it was the first sort of full-range compact speaker. After the Voice of the Theatres, the competition I guess would've been the Big Red, but that hadn't really shown up in Nashville as much as it did in LA. So you saw a lot of those JBL speakers, and they really weren't very great-sounding. So the Yamaha, the NS-10—I think a lot of what was great in them and why they got started was there weren't a lot of alternatives at the time.

Among my favorites, obviously things like LA-2As and 1176s, I still use all the time. The EMT plate—I still like a real EMT plate. There isn't a digital reverb that's really captured it, although I will say the UA plug-in is actually a really good plate emulation. And I really like the new Lexicon PCM96—the plates that they're doing are just really, really good. It's hard to come across a studio that's got a great chamber anymore. But there are some. I was just working over at the old RCA Studio B studios on this Elvis Presley project, and they've still got the original plates and chamber from those days. Sound Emporium's still got their plates happening, but the chamber is the hard thing to come by, something that was really done well. Tape slap I don't really use anymore. At Castle, the booth started getting into digital by this time, like the EMT 250. I remember when that was first brought by. You know, the one that looks like R2-D2? I still love that; it's still my favorite reverb.

It's a completely different thing than an EMT 140. I still use an EMT 250 a lot, all the time. I think it's just that kind of generic reverb that nobody really quite captured the same, although the TC 6000s have a good emulation of it. But I actually still have the "R2-D2" version. Sony came out with a really great digital reverb, the DRE-2000. It had the little flat controller, a little flat box and remote, and it had one reverb that was the small-room sound thing that became really popular. But you can hardly find any of those working anymore. At Castle, I remember Lexicon came out with the PCM 42 delay—now that's still my favorite mono-delay. I mean, I've got a couple of those, and there's something about the Lo-Fi-ness.... It kind of sounded like tape delay, but you didn't have to just run a tape back and forth. And it's got a little limiter on it, so if you hit it too hard, it kind of limits like tape; it's got a real crunchy sound when it does distort. I love that thing. It's still my favorite sort of delay I use on vocals.

I also never stopped using analog tape. I mean, I still love 16-track 2-inch analog. I've got a Studer 800 with a really pristine 16-track head stack on it. As often as I can, when I do tracking, I track through that to Nuendo and capture it, and I just love the sound. Particularly now, with the new ATR analog tape, which sounds amazing. Speaking of ATR, it's probably been 10 or 12 years since, at AES (Audio Engineering Society), I ran into John Spitz at ATR services, and he was showing his 1-inch 2-track ATR-100, and I said, "Oh my god, this is way cool." You know, "I got to hear this." He said, "Well, I'll send you one." So I bought two: It's just an amazing thing. We've since sold one, but I still use that on all my mixes. It's an amazing sound. I can run it at 15 inches per second (IPS), so you get that really great low end. You know, it lowers the head bump down to kind of a really nice musical place, whereas at 30 IPS, the head bump got up there to 180 and kind of filled things out a little too much. The top end is nice, but you kind of lost a little bit of the way low end. So, I love it. I mean, it's got next to no noise because of that much tape, and just a beautiful vocal range. I mean, the voice just seems to pop out even better than my mix. I have artists all the time going, "What did you do to my vocal?" and I go, "Oh, this tape machine over here."

Clients come to me for a culmination of everything that I do. I do use compression; I'm trying to make a modern and competitive record, but I don't think I over-compress as much as a lot of other engineers. Instead, I do a lot of manual riding of instruments. I can make a mix more interesting, get things to really pop out and be dynamic, and yet fill out a mix really well if I manually ride things. I also like bottom end. For so many of the young guys it's all about top end, making things as bright as they possibly can. They're always grabbing the brightest microphone, crankin' on the EQ, and compressing the shit out of everything. I like to keep the warmth in there and let the music reach more to your heart. It pulls on the heartstrings a little better. And analog, I think, is a big part of that because it is a nice, warm musical medium—it tends to take the harshness off the drums.

There's been loads of analog gear that's come my way that I've just tossed; I don't really pay any attention to it once it's come and gone. I do remember one time, these Japanese fellows came into my studio, and they had this speaker that they wanted me to check out. And basically, it was a sphere. And it had speakers all the way around it. All the way around it. I guess it was about 2 feet in diameter, this sphere with speakers all the way around. And the guy had devised some DSP to work with this, and he said, "The great thing about this speaker is that no matter where you sit, you're going to hear the music as though there weren't a sweet spot." The great thing in the studios—that a producer sitting off to the side or in the back of the room or whatever was going to hear it exactly the way you were hearing it. And in a way he was right, because there was no sweet spot. There was no concept of directionality, no concept of where anything was coming from. It was just this big omni sound—it was horrible!

I tend to like the quirky things. Like the Cooper Time Cube or the Echoplex—you know, little guitar pedal things. I like those sorts of things. And those, to me, could be considered vintage, quirky gear. The stuff that really stands out is the 1176, LA-3A and LA-2A, Fairchild, and, obviously EMT plates. I don't think I'd ever call a Mitsubishi X-850 "vintage gear," because it was a piece of crap at the time, and they don't run anymore. So it's kind of one of those things that came and went. I recall the 3M digital machines sounding unbelievable compared to the 3324 or the Mitsubishi. But, it was just a piece of junk. The tape transport sounded like a jet taking off when you were rewinding it or fast-forwarding it. And you'd have to put a digital analyzer on it every day before the session. We actually had to install a new air-conditioner system just to keep it cold.

One of the things that I really love that I have now is my main monitors in my control room. I've got the ATC 300A main speakers. And I just love them—I mean, I think they're great-sounding full-range loudspeakers. If I need to hear real bottom end I can hear it, and yet they're subtle enough speakers that you can listen at a low volume on a large speaker. I like what I'm currently using for mid-field or near-field speakers, which are the Adam 3As. I think they're great monitors; you really can't do anything unless you can hear. I love, as I brought up already, the ATR-100—the 1-inch 2-track—which I think is a great-sounding machine. I also use an SSL 9000 at my studio, and I've become so familiar with that console over the years of working on it that it's just second nature to me. I'd be hard-pressed to really get on anything else and love it as much.

There are some great microphones now that I really enjoy that I didn't have back then, like the DPA 4011. I love that microphone. I love the Royer microphones. We didn't have those. The ribbons that we did have in the day—the RCAs—were just kind of dark and didn't have a lot of output. So I never really had a big appreciation for ribbon microphones until the Royers. And now I've been introduced to some others, like the Coles, that we just didn't have. I know that they were very popular in the U.K., but we just didn't have them in Nashville. I never saw them before. And like I said, the RCAs were generally either beat up or ruined. I've never heard one that I've really loved anyhow. I'd love to have a Cooper Time Cube now!

One thing I'm glad I don't have anymore is Dolby. As much as I loved analog recording, once we left 16-track and went to 24-track, there was always a lot of noise. And we didn't have the really high-output tapes then. So really, you had to use Dolbys to drop the noise, and we're talking Dolby A's, not SR. Just the alignment time that it took to go through a rack of Dolbys…I mean, in Nashville, we were based on sort of three-hour sessions. So, we'd have one session start at 10 a.m., and we'd have to get set up and work on that three-hour session. Then we'd have a one-hour turnover for the 2 o'clock. And it may be a totally different tape alignment, which meant a different Dolby alignment, a different setup in the studio, and a different engineer, so that hour was frantic, and it was rare that I ever got to go to the bathroom or eat anything until the day was over. The assistants today really don't know how good they have it with hard-disk recording.

I was talking to Phil Ramone last night, and he was saying how in his studio, at one point the cloth he had on the walls covering the fiberglass was getting pretty rank, and he decided to take it down and put up new fiberglass in the walls and recover it. He took it all down, and he said, "Everybody was complaining that the sound had changed in the studio." So he went back out to the dumpster and pulled out all this old linen and fiberglass and put it back up. You know, there's magic in them walls.

As far as changes in the business, obviously the move toward digital tape and now hard-disk recorders… Digital signal processing and now plug-ins… Automation, fader automation, and now total control in the DAW… Those are all really huge changes that have happened. When I was a kid, we had the Teac 4-track. To me, that was really the beginning of the home studio, where you could really kind of multi-track at home. So, it was right about that time I knew there were smaller tape formats and sort of homesumer recording gear for 8-track, and then A-DATS and all that that came along. I've kind of grown up with the home studio explosion, but it's really gotten to the point now where somebody can build a home studio and get the same kinds of results that the major studios can, with the exception of the acoustics of a really large room. I've also seen the change in people who were really qualified to be running those knobs go from people who came up under the tutelage of engineers who have been doing it for a life career, to now just a computer music dude or a guitar player who thinks that he can make his own record, mix his own record, and not have to pay a qualified person who has got years of experience and understands how to mix a record. I guess those are pretty profound changes.

I haven't seen anything come along that allowed me to get my job done more quickly. If anything, there are just more options, and the job takes longer. Or people just don't make decisions, and they put it off. So obviously, for me, primarily mixing, now I'm the one making the choices of which tracks are going to stay in a record and what stuff needs to get cut out because there are three solos playing at once and comping vocals because they just left it all for you to figure out. Tuning, too—people come to you, and you're the one who has to fix that in the time that you're meant to be mixing. Fixing mistakes later, a lot of options to leave too many takes, and the necessity to make choices while recording is also taken away.

We've obviously seen the ability to create even better digital recordings, and we've had for a time a consumer format where we could give those really high-resolution recordings to the public—and also in surround, which was really a promising thing for a while. Obviously, that's gone away. At the moment there are no record companies supporting those releases. Really, we're looking at Internet delivery, so compressed audio, which is—as we all know or should know—really a postage-stamp picture of what the real record is. The technology keeps changing, but I don't know that we're making any better records. You can go back to a Led Zeppelin record or a Beatles record—those records still sound wonderful, even by today's standards. They're so creative and they're warm and they're musical. Having all these plug-ins and capacity to tune things, I think it just makes the performers weaker. They don't actually strive to get a take from one end to the other. I just recorded a band, they all have their own little Pro Tools LE systems or whatever that they grew up with. They're all used to performing a verse and stopping and then performing a chorus and stopping—they can't actually play the song. They're great musicians, don't get me wrong... but to play the song from top to bottom as a band, really listening to each other and not just isolating themselves, and playing off of each other, was really difficult for them. There should be a lot of benefits to the changes in technology, but they're actually not making anything better. I wouldn't stretch and say we're not making as good of records as back then, but you would think with what's available we should be making even better records.

I think some of the most creative and learning things that I did in a studio were when I first went to Belmont College, and all we had was an 8-track tape machine to record on. We had to get everything on that 8-track that we had in our heads, and that meant putting three or four things on one track and EQing or whatever processing you were going to do with FX—you'd print that, too. Basically, when it's done it's done; you just put all of the faders flat, and there's your mix. That was a really creative time. I'd hate to listen to it now, but in my mind's eye, I learned so much from that process. I think all schools should be required to make their students do their first recordings that way.

When I started working with Mark Knopfler in Dire Straits on the On Every Street album, he had a Synclavier Direct-to-Disk system, so at the time we were doing all of this hard-disk editing, pitching of stuff and all that with that system. I won't even go into how integrated it was, but it did sound good. And then the first Pro Tools systems came around, and we grabbed one of those because we could do certain things on it that we couldn't do on the Synclavier, but it really sounded like dog meat. I was tempted to the hard-disk system. Then I heard about Nuendo, and obviously there were some great converters around, but you couldn't use them with Pro Tools. With Nuendo I could use any converter that I wanted to. So I got a Nuendo Version 1 system, and I have the Mytek converters—they still sound great. From there I kind of just stuck with Nuendo. I got to learn it and know it, and now I'm still working on Nuendo. A lot of people are afraid to go the Nuendo way because they feel like they may not be able to get the work that's coming from the Pro Tools clients, but it hasn't been a problem for me.

I've been forced to work on Pro Tools maybe three times. Otherwise, I actually find it a real advantage because the clients come in, reach over my shoulder, grab the mouse, and start doing stuff themselves. They look and they go, "Oh, that's Nuendo," and they just leave me alone to do my own thing. Everybody who comes to me wants what I do; they don't really care what format I work on. Ever since we did the NARAS document on deliverables, people understand what it means to consolidate projects, so that's not a problem either. I get consolidated files from a Pro Tools session and import them into a Nuendo session and work from there.

I use basically a hybrid approach. Like I said, I still like to record on analog tape and dump it into Nuendo. I think it sounds great, but even if I don't, 96k/24-bit is pretty good-sounding. I always work at least 96k. If I do a project that comes in on 48k, I up-sample it to 96k and then I convert it. I've got Apogee 16X converters A to D and D to A and 48 channels at the moment. Then I've got a 60-channel SSL 9000 console, so I do my mixing on that. Then I mix back to the Nuendo at 96k, or I also mix to the 1-inch ATR-100 for my final mixes. And generally, the mastering gets done from the analog.

I just bought a pair of DPA 4011 microphones, which I love. Yeah, I mean, I love those. Bruce Myers at DPA…I ran into him at a microphone panel that I was on; it was an AES panel in Nashville that we did. There were a bunch of engineers on the panel. I ran into Bruce Myers outside the studio there, and he said, "You're Chuck Ainlay." I said, "Yeah, that's right," and he said, "You know, I really like your work. I really admire what you do, but your work would be so much better if you used my microphones." I wasn't quite sure how to take that. I guess about a year later I had a project that I knew I'd have a chance to try some stuff on, so I called up Bruce, and he ended up sending me a bunch of his microphones, and I absolutely fell in love with them. That's probably the last analog piece of gear I bought other than the Adam speakers. I'm actually pretty happy with the stuff that I've got. I've got four channels of Neve 1081s and four channels of Neve 1073s. I've got 1176s. I've got these really killer prototype mic preamps from this company called UpState Audio. It's going to start delivering soon. I think that it's the best mic preamp I've ever used, and I'm only saying that because I think that it's going to be a really great product. Al Schmidt loves them as well. He says it's his favorite mic preamp, and Michael Bishop of Telarc Records says it's his favorite mic preamp, and we're this guy's beta testers. So, it's a really high-quality zero phase shift—it's down .5 at 200k. I mean, it's an amazing mic preamp.

You never stop learning; that's the main thing. Every day I go into the studio, and I'm happy to go to work every day. I love going to work every day. I don't mind spending 13, 14 hours—however long it takes. Every day I go in I learn something, and even working on projects that aren't going to have any kind of critical acclaim or aren't even going to make it in the marketplace, I still do my absolute best to make the best record I possibly can for that person. For one, it's their record—that's what they're going to have to live with. Also, I know that I'm going to learn something from that experience—if nothing else, just to keep myself fine-tuned for the next project where it does matter. The other thing is that, obviously, to be able to dedicate yourself to your work as much as that, it requires a really special wife, and I've finally found a really great one.

Chapter 3

Ed Cherney

Grammy and TEC award-winning producer/engineer Ed Cherney was especially known for his work with a wide array of artists, among them Iggy Pop, Bob Seger, Bette Midler, Bonnie Raitt, Wynonna, Eric Clapton, Jann Arden, Jackson Browne, Keb' Mo', Bob Dylan, and the Rolling Stones, to name just a few. Cherney was also highly respected by his peers. Over the course of his career, he amassed six Grammy nominations and four wins. He took home the coveted Best Engineered Album award for Bonnie Raitt's Longing in Their Hearts in 1994—a year in which he, remarkably, recorded and mixed three out of the five albums nominated in that category. He has also been honored with seven TEC award nominations and five wins, as well as three Emmy nominations for his work on Bonnie Raitt's broadcast of Road Tested, The Rolling Stones Live from Madison Square Garden on HBO, and Eric Clapton's 2004 Crossroads Guitar Festival.

A founding member of the Music Producers Guild of America (now the Producers and Engineer's Wing of the Recording Academy), Cherney was also Governor of the L.A. chapter of the Recording Academy. Some projects include Buddy Guy's Grammy-winning Blues Singer, Susan Tedeschi's Hope and Desire, and the Grammy-nominated Best Soundtrack Hairspray. He also recorded and mixed the Rolling Stones' acclaimed HBO special and live box set four Flicks, and he recorded and mixed the Grammy-nominated soundtrack and score for the hit film A Mighty Wind. Ed also was a music producer and engineer for the Rolling Stones' The Biggest Bang DVD.

A native of Chicago, Ed started at the prestigious Paragon Studios before moving to Los Angeles to work for Westlake Audio, and then subsequently worked in a private room in The Village, a top recording studio in L.A. Ed Cherney passed away in October 2019.

My name is Ed Cherney. I was born in Chicago, Illinois.

I started in audio in third grade, when I got my first Wollensak. It was a reel-to-reel machine that they had in AV at school, and somehow it got my attention. For a while in the late '50s, reel-to-reel tape machines were pretty popular. My dad got one, and

DOI: 10.4324/9781003519829-3

Figure 3.1 I know many people want to talk about gear, and there are great-sounding microphones, preamps, and other things that help you make great recordings, but the most important thing is your perspective. That's where the magic is; it's not in the gear. And if you have that perspective, you'll find a way to get what it is you hear and see in your imagination. And you may find a specific piece of gear, or you'll invent some way to do it, but it's your perspective that the magic is, it's not the gear.... That debate about digital versus analog, I don't want to hear it. That debate is over. Yes, we still love that analog sound and still may cut to tape sometimes...but it's a digital world, and it's not going back. If you know what you're doing, there are the tools to achieve what you want. You can make a great-sounding recording digitally in the box; I hear people do it all the time. And I hear people doing a really crappy job of it, too. And again, it's not all about the gear; it's the nut behind the wheel.

Figure 3.2 Every day, new gear was being released, and Westlake had it all. I remember when I was recording something, I was thinking, "Well, all of this gear is here; you have to use it all." It took me a long time to learn that stuff would sound better if I didn't use it all.

I started doing make-believe radio shows, and sound effects, and making feedback loops, and just doing all kinds of goofy things with it.

That's when I first started messing with audio, although I didn't really know that's what I was doing. I got into audio professionally when I was going to college. I was about to graduate, and I was home for summer. I was thinking about law school. I had friends that I had played music for, and they had a band and were going on tour. They were going

Figure 3.3 Some engineers came through who didn't have those great abilities, but for whatever reason they were working—their stuff didn't sound great, and they did a lot of things wrong. So it was an opportunity to learn what worked and what didn't work, what you should do and what you shouldn't do. There were a lot of good lessons in what you shouldn't do.

Figure 3.4 One of the reasons why I've been successful and I've been able to maintain a career is that I got to sit behind great engineers and great producers, great arrangers and great musicians, and I got to hear through their ears and their techniques and got to experience what great-sounding records sounded like. And more importantly, what great-feeling records sound like. If you do that enough, it becomes part of your DNA, it becomes part of you. If I'd never had that opportunity, I don't think I would be as good as I am now.

to play at clubs, and they asked me if I would drive their truck. I put myself through school working for my uncle, so I knew how to drive a truck. And I said sure. I started driving their truck and humping gear for them. In those days, live sound was quite rudimentary. I just started paying attention to it, and one day a few weeks in, the soundman didn't show up. They pointed to me and said, "You're mixing the band tonight." That's how I started, around 1972.

And I had a natural affinity for balancing music, especially vocals. So instead of going to law school and finishing college, I traveled and did live sound for them and started to learn more and more. The bass player was really into electronics and taught me. I got more into the signal chain and how things worked. I didn't know much about electronics, but I did know about music, and that summer the band went into a recording studio. I didn't even know that recording studios existed. They invited me along, and I went. When I walked in, with the console and the speakers and the music going and flashing lights, I absolutely knew that that's what I was supposed to do.

When I first started doing live sound for my friends, equipment was rudimentary—Crown amplifiers, SM5S7 microphones; that's probably about all you had. I remember the mixing desk; it was really advanced. It was a Tapco, and it had eight channels. It had some built-in reverb. I didn't know it at the time, but it really sounded like shit. But I was trying things, adding speakers. They had some custom speakers—I built a box and ended up getting a tweeter and doing the soldering. I don't think we had a compressor or anything like that.

There was a company called EBW, Euphoria Blimp Works, that became Neotek, and they came out with this desk. It had 12 inputs, graphic equalizers, and some EQ, and I thought that was the greatest thing, and we checked it out and bought one. I started using it, and at that time I was self-taught. So I just figured it out. At that time, I was also just mixing monitors. Altec had something called an Altec 1220, and that was a 12-input mixer, and it had built-in reverb, but it was a fairly simple console. At the time it looked like the most complicated thing in the world to me. I looked at it and said, "How am I gonna figure this out?" but I eventually did.

After that, I figured I really needed a lot more information and really wanted to know how electricity worked. I enrolled in DeVry and studied electronics. I went to DeVry for a year, learned Ohm's law, built my own multimeter, learned how transistors worked and tubes worked, learned how to read a schematic, and learned electronics. Around that time, I started working. I got a job at a local sound company in Chicago doing monitors for local bands. There were a handful of professional recording studios in Chicago, so I started making the rounds, applying for jobs, and of course there were none. So it could be a little discouraging, but I saw in a paper somewhere that there was a recording class offered. And at that time there were no recording schools.

It was being taught at a studio by Bruce Swedien in Chicago. I didn't know who he was, but I went and paid my money and enrolled in this recording class. I took this class and learned a bit on how microphones work, polar patterns, signal flow, consoles, and even things like studio etiquette—everything that he had to offer. He was a very generous man with his knowledge, and I became friendly with him. We lived kind of in the same place, and I used to see him on the train going into Chicago; I'd see him around different places. And he let me carry his briefcase around for him and go to some sessions. During that time, I was still doing live PA and hauling equipment and loading it, but still going every month, making the rounds of all the recording studios in Chicago.

And one day, three years later, in 1976, the day Jimmy Carter was elected President, I went into Paragon Studios. Paragon Studios in Chicago is a famous place; they did a lot of jingles and a lot of rock records, and it was an independent studio. And they had an apprenticeship. The owner of the studio was Marty Feldman. The apprenticeship was a way for him to get cheap help, certainly, and you would go there and start cleaning the bathrooms and working at the very bottom. But you would learn as you were going. And somebody had just gotten fired, and I showed up, and coincidentally, Bruce Swedien was doing a session. They gave me a test to take. I couldn't tell you what any of the answers were, but it was about recording, signal flow, electronics, et cetera. Bruce kept coming down to the lobby where I was taking the test, and I said, "Bruce, what's the answer to this?" and he would tell me an answer and chuckle and go back into the studio. He gave me all the wrong answers just to mess with me. I got hired, and I started the next day as an apprentice engineer at Paragon. It was the happiest day of my life. I was happy that Jimmy Carter got elected President, too, although that really didn't work out, but it was a really great day for me. It would've been November 4, 1976.

When I got a job at a studio, I didn't work on live sound as much, but I was still working for my friends when there was a local club they'd work at and I was available. They had a lot of vocals, a lot of harmonies, and I was pretty good at it. I actually got a reputation for being able to balance voices—people would say, "Hey, they sound really great tonight!" So I knew that I could do it.

Paragon was based on an English studio—it might have been Olympic—and they had a Flickinger console that had the first parametric equalizers in it. It was a 20-input, 16-bus console, and I thought it was fairly complicated. It took me a bit to figure out how that worked, but there were people there who would teach you. They had one of the first digital delays—it was a Lexicon 102, and it could go all the way to a 100-millisecond delay. Certainly, 1176s, LA-2s, LA-3s, LA-4s, mostly Urei, because all that stuff was designed and built by Bill Putnam, who was at Universal Audio, which is in Chicago. So we had all of his gear.

As an apprentice at Paragon, I started at the very bottom. I remember the day after they hired me, I showed up at five in the morning. I cleaned the bathrooms, scrubbed the floors, wiped down the headphones, ran for food, and other things.... And you had to do everything by the book—the way you held a microphone on a mic stand, the way you did everything was on a list that prescribed this as the way you did it. And if you didn't do it right, you were fired.

It was a total apprenticeship, and some of the best engineers in the world were working at Paragon at the time. There was Bruce Swedien. There was Barry Mraz, who was one of the first independent producer/engineers, and he was producing and engineering the Ohio Players and Styx—he brought a lot of projects in. And Mercury Records was in Chicago at the time, so we did a lot of artists that were on Mercury.

They brought me up. They taught me how to make dubs. When you do a jingle, you'd have to go to the dubbing machine, where you would take the master and deliver 7-1/2 IPS tapes to all the radio stations. So you might have to do 100 dubs or 150 or 200 dubs, and they taught me how to do that—how to make copies and transfers and do quality control. And then you'd go up to the copy room, where we did transfers for libraries from Mercury Records, backing up their library to tape, getting old tapes that were falling apart, making new tapes. In addition to that, there would be morning sessions for jingles, and it could be a jazz trio, it could be a rock band, it could be an orchestra, it could be a polka band, it could be anything.... So you would help the assistants, help the engineer, bring in the microphones, move mic stands, run cables, set up headphones, and help them that way. And certainly, run to get everybody lunch or dinner. You would work your way up. You would assist the assistant, and then after a period of time, you really had to excel at each thing you did before they moved you up to the next thing.

When I was there, they had just gone from 8-track to 16-track. They had just bought their first 16-track machine. It was a 3M, an M56. Everybody was really excited about that, although people were going, "Well, if you can't get it on 8-track, then what do you need a 16-track for? Can't get it on 8, you can't do it." So there were always people who were resisting it, but then they would fully embrace it. And then I remember within six months or eight months, we had a 24-track.

It was also a 3M. We were pretty much a 3M shop. Although Ampex went from an 8-track to 16-track to 24-track pretty quickly… And at that time, Dolby noise reduction was introduced, too. And soon after that dbx came in with noise reduction, too.

Plus, we had a chamber in the basement. There were two EMT 140 plates; Jim Cunningham from Chicago had invented the EMT plates. There wasn't any digital reverb yet. Digital was starting; I think the Delta T 102 was the first digital delay line that offered 100 milliseconds, maybe 120 milliseconds. People were using tape slap. People were doing tape flanging, which was really cool. They learned that from an English engineer. I was just reading about him last night, as a matter of fact—Ken Townsend. And Gary Kellgren, here in Los Angeles at the Record Plant, was starting to mess with tape flanging.

In terms of effects, it was pretty rudimentary. You had to invent them. Everybody would invent them themselves. Eventide had an instant phaser/flanger, which kind of worked, and that was a big deal: "Ooh, look at that, try that." And then there was the Kepex. Valley People came out with Kepex, which was a noise gate and a pretty radical compressor. So we had those, but basically, in terms of limiters, compressors, it was 1176s, LA-2s; there were some Fairchilds around, but that was about it. And the EQ—basically, we used the EQ that was on the console. It was a three-band parametric EQ. And you basically had a tone control. You could have some high-end or you could filter, high pass, and filter some low-end, and maybe have one midrange frequency that you could boost or cut. We did have Pultecs, too.

At Paragon I moved through the ranks and moved up to assistant engineer. I assisted in a lot of jingles; I assisted Barry Mraz, who was just a fabulous engineer and producer and a really great and generous guy. Barry unfortunately passed away about ten years ago. When I got into it, it wasn't about money or fame or anything, it was just like, "They invented this job just for me; here's this thing I want to do." The joke was that a recording engineer was too dumb for school and too cool for life. And I was lucky enough to find this job; there weren't a lot of them. Engineers were just starting to get credit on albums, but nobody really knew who they were or what they did.

So I started assisting, and then I assisted Steve Kusiciel—very generous and knowledgeable and a wonderful teacher. Unfortunately, he also passed away a few years ago. There was Bill Bradley, who was a very skilled and successful engineer in Chicago. There were a handful of these guys who were really great and really generous with sharing their knowledge. Standing behind them, you could really get a sonic perspective and learn about different techniques, microphone choices, and placement. There were 251s, KM 86s, MSOs, all the Neumann microphones, 67s…a lot of large-diaphragm tube microphones were being used.

I started to do some first engineering and doing some overdubs and filling in on smaller and simpler sessions, but I was really mostly assisting. I remember a time when they tried to identify some guys who they thought would be really great engineers, and the owner and the general manager brought up a tape and gave each one of us a chance and said, "Here, mix this thing," to see what we could do. And I did, and I wasn't very good. I thought that this was gonna be my big chance, and I wasn't very good. And the other guys who worked there, they were really good assistants, but they didn't do very well with it, either. It was then that I kind of figured out that engineers are born to want to do it—they have the desire to do it, but in order to learn how to do it, it's a long road, and it takes a lot of trial and error and a lot of experience.

A book I was recently reading, Outliers—the author did a study of geniuses and people who had excelled in their field. And basically, he found out that, first of all, they never did it alone, and second of all, none of them was born into it. It was what he called the 20-10 rule—20,000 hours over ten years of doing the same thing.... That's what made them great, and that's what made you a genius at it. And it turns out that in my case, it is definitely true.

And it's the kind of thing that I'm still getting better at and I'm still learning, and every time I do it, I'm better at it. And everyone I know in the business has the same story. So anyway, back at Paragon, I worked as an assistant engineer—I worked my way up to assistant, and I worked hard. There were 20-hour days, and I think the pay might've been $3 an hour. I think I was making $2.75 and then $3 and change an hour. That was really a big deal, and I was literally working 20-hour days. Sometimes you wouldn't go home for three days.

Eventually I got burnt out, and something happened, and I quit. I wasn't eating right, and I was really neglecting myself. I loved being in the studio and neglected the rest of my life—in those days there were a lot of drugs around, and you just didn't take care of yourself. Because we were young, you could recover from it. I got pissed off one long and late night about some perceived slight. I was exhausted, and most likely not thinking too clearly, and I may have said some things that I didn't really mean to my boss, Marty Feldman, but I quit. Unfortunately, he also passed away, and I never got a chance to make things right with him. He was also a great teacher and a wonderful influence, and he certainly paved the way for my success and many others', too. Anyway, I went home to my girlfriend at the time, and said, "Let's go to California." Because I'd just heard some records that were made out there. It was Boston, and I'd never heard guitars like that.

We packed up our stuff—I think we had $200 in our pockets—and we got this drive-away van and loaded it up. Our stuff that wouldn't fit, we left it on the curb, and we drove to Los Angeles. And the second day that we got to Los Angeles, I went and got a Billboard directory. The Billboard directory listed all of the recording studios, and it was a thick book. There were a lot of recording studios at the time. I started backwards—I went to the end of the book, and the first one I saw was a place called Westlake Audio, and coincidentally, that was the place that the first Boston record was mixed. And I went in there, and no kidding, they hired me on the spot.

They needed someone, and the day after that I was an assistant engineer at Westlake. And the training that I had gotten in Chicago really helped me. I was really ready and eager, and I got in there and just flowered—I got to assist Tommy Vicari on a George Duke record, and Georgio Moroder, who was producing Donna Summer, and many others. At that time, Westlake was one of the happening studios in L.A., maybe in the world. The rooms were really advanced, and Westlake was also selling gear and designing and building studios around the world. They had all the newest and coolest gear—all the gear in the world you could mess around with. That was my first experience with having as much gear as you can mess with. Harrison consoles, 3M tape machines, all of the most advanced equipment of the day. And then coincidentally, Bruce Swedien moved to California, and he was working with Quincy Jones. Within the first six months or the first year that I was working there, they came to Westlake, and I was assisting Bruce and Quincy Jones on Michael Jackson's Off the Wall album. That may have been the first thing I worked with them on when I was an assistant engineer, and I ended up working for them for six years. And standing behind them and working behind them, and believe me, I was paying really close attention.

I just loved them, and they put up with me. I hustled for them—I ran, and I know they appreciated it. I was just in the game all the time. My ear was on whatever they were doing, and I could always look five minutes into the future and be prepared for what was going to happen next. Bruce was doing very advanced things for that time. He was one of the first guys to lock up multitrack machines. I remember Bruce was one of the guys who said, "If you can't get it on 8-track, you can't get it." At Westlake he started making work tapes. He called it the Acusonic recording process. He would record stereo pairs and fill up one 24-track and then lock up a second. And at the very beginning, it was very difficult and tricky to do. I was the guy in charge of keeping the machines locked up. So we started locking up two 24-tracks, then three 24-tracks, sometimes four 24-tracks, and that was a full-time job, just keeping those in sync. Bruce was always a pioneer; he was always reaching for the new technology at that time, so it was a great opportunity for me to learn it right behind him.

I assisted at Westlake for six or seven years. Westlake was a really great place because when there weren't sessions, they would let us use the studios. So I'd make new friends with musicians, and there were always musicians around. So you could make friends at the clubs or whatever and meet a band and say, "Hey, come on in. Let's do a demo. I've got the studio all night." So sessions would end, and we would go in at one or two in the morning and work until seven or eight in the morning, and then I'd be assisting on whatever I was working on the next day. And the other guys who worked there... Dave Rideau has become a very successful engineer, and Eric Zobler has also become very successful, and Brian Reeves and Steve Hodge...all very skilled and successful...a lot of great guys. But that's what we did—we were so into it that we didn't sleep, so you'd use every opportunity to be in the studio and try different things, different microphones, trying to make great music...and we shared information. It was a great place to be.

Also, a lot of times, if you were sharp as an assistant, your clients would begin to trust you. If the engineer would get sick or had another gig, they would let me record O/Ds. It would start out that you were operating the multitrack machine; you had to do punch-ins and punch-outs. You had a limited number of tracks, so the ins and outs would be tight. If you screw up, performances could be lost forever. So as they trusted you more, you would get to do more and more, operate the machine, do the punching in and out, record some things. And that could be 8, 12, 15 hours of punch-ins and outs, and believe me, you'd better not screw that up or erase something. Because you couldn't get it back—there was no undo function back in those days. If they trusted you, you'd work your way up, and then maybe they were doing vocals, and they would let you do the punch in through the vocals, or the engineer at that time would have a sound on something, and he was busy or sick, and you would get in and sit behind the console and do the balances and be the engineer on the session. So you would build your chops really slowly over a period of time. But as you proved yourself, you would get invited to do more and more.

The digital age came in while I was there. I remember seeing the first automated fader system at Westlake. It wasn't moving faders; it was Allison automation on the Harrison console. Having automation on faders was a big deal because, traditionally, you would do a mix, and it would be a performance, and everyone in the band would have a fader and have a move, or you would mix something 4, 8, 16 bars at a time and then edit them together. It started getting more complicated. And having a limited number of tracks, sometimes you would have a vocal on a track and then a guitar solo on that track; there would be four or five different elements on the same track that you would have to split out or change the EQ or change the reverb on as you were doing a mix.

Also, bigger and more complicated consoles were introduced. They just started getting bigger and bigger. I saw the first digital machine, the 32-track digital 3M machine—we were the first studio to have that. And that was the beginning of the digital age with recording digitally. Digital delay lines, digital reverbs, and effects, plus all kinds of different compressors and gates and all kinds of wonderful boxes.

Every day, new gear was being released, and Westlake had it all. I remember when I was recording something, I was thinking, "Well, all of this gear is here; you have to use it all." It took me a long time to learn that stuff would sound better if I didn't use it all.

With all of the analog and digital gear, you would start to develop your palette, develop the tools that you would go to, and typically the tools I would go to were the things that were being used by the engineers I was working behind. I used to assist the greatest engineers in the world; Tommy Vicari was one of the guys, Mick Guzauski, Paul Grupp... These were guys who had been there for a while and were really great engineers, and by osmosis you would take on their techniques in a lot of ways. And you would sit behind them and say, "Oh, listen what they did with that." And you would kind of liberate some of their techniques. So it would start that way—this works for him; this is the set of mics he uses for kick drum; this is what he used for snare, guitars, and vocals...and how they did it—and I would do it that way depending on the engineer I was working with. So it was an opportunity to learn what worked and what didn't work, what you should do and what you shouldn't do. There were a lot of good lessons in what you shouldn't do.

What I have now that I wish I'd had back then? Perspective and good mental health. The ability to recognize opportunity. Emotional and intellectual tools can be more important than equipment. I can't attribute it to gear. I've always been a proponent of a guy like Al Schmitt—he could make a better record with a two-by-four than a guy who has every piece of gear in the world but doesn't have those abilities. I always joke, it's the nut behind the wheel, it's not the gear—it's absolutely not the gear. That being said, there are some things that sound better than others, and the right piece of gear can be immensely helpful... but people using a tin can and a string who are talented and know what they're doing could make a great-feeling recording, something that will affect you emotionally and make you feel something. Like Bruce Swedien said, "Nobody leaves the studio dancing to the console, it's the music."

I think it's important to talk about mental health, and I don't think they teach that in schools: psychology and mental health. I think one of the things that makes you successful in this is growing up and having good mental health, having your ego in check, being able to get the most out of musicians and artists. And also getting the most out of yourself, not tricking yourself, and not sabotaging yourself. And a lot of times, I've seen people who are really talented sabotage their careers and make their experience in the studio completely miserable because they can't control their emotions.

So many times I've just seen people be stupid and unyielding in the studio. I've seen artists and writers, and even as an engineer and producer.... Standing up for something that they believe in and having artistic integrity, that's one thing. But just being needlessly stubborn and egotistical is something else, and I think sometimes it stands in the way of the music; it especially stands in the way of your happiness and your success in your career and your life.

Something that I see lacking a lot of times in younger engineers is perspective. Audio perspective and sonic perspective... And I think one of the reasons why I've been successful and I've been able to maintain a career is that I got to sit behind great engineers and great producers, great arrangers, and great musicians, and I got to hear through their ears and their techniques and got to experience what great-sounding records sound like. And more importantly, what great-feeling records sound like. If you do that enough, it becomes part of your DNA; it becomes part of you. If I'd never had that opportunity, I don't think I would be as good as I am now. I'm pretty good at it, but if I was just sitting there by myself, I never would've gotten a sonic perspective and something to measure against.

I get sent a lot of things now recorded by graduates of schools and people who came up who never had the opportunity to serve an apprenticeship or to assist anyone in a studio, and they never got that sonic perspective. And the stuff they send usually is not just broken-sounding, but broken-feeling. I get sent lots of things to mix that are both hard and dark by kids who haven't had that opportunity to sit behind somebody great in the studio. When I say hard and dark, I mean something that's dull and lifeless, but if you add the slightest bit of upper midrange or high end, then it tears your head off. Most of these things are just over-compressed and over-EQed going in. I think that sonic perspective is something that Swedien always used to encourage me to do. I went to the symphony; I'd go hear live music, live instruments being played in a great space. That was something that served me well, and other people I know who have done it; it's served them well, too.

It's a problem, and I feel bad for these kids who haven't had that opportunity. There's little opportunity for students to learn critical listening. We talked about this with George [Massenburg], Al [Schmitt], Frank [Filipetti], and all those guys—where do you learn how to listen critically? And how do you teach it? Traditionally, it was taught by osmosis—you would be in the room with people who were striving to make the best-sounding records they possibly could. Things that were dynamic and wide-range and true, and sounds that you could almost step into. And sitting behind these guys, you would get that perspective, and you would learn how to listen critically. I don't know how you find another way to teach it in a classroom. You could try comparative listening, like you do comparative literature. Put things on a button, listen to that: there's an MP3, there's full range. We did some of that, and George was able to separate an MP3 out of all the things they pull out of there. Being aware of those things, I fear for our business, for the art and science of doing this. How do you get that ability to get that sonic perspective?

I have a studio here in The Village, and there are a lot of assistants who work here. I love it when I'm mixing—they come in my room, and I love to blow their socks off, and I like to see them go back to their room and work on their demos or whatever they're doing and trying to emulate the depth that I'm able to get because I sat behind guys like Bruce Swedien, Paul Grupp, Tommy Vicari, Mick Guzauski, and those kind of people. That's how you get it—you compare what you're doing to what these really great guys did.

It's a challenge, but I know everyone wants that perspective; they want to find a way to do it. It's funny how this career finds people. Maybe you stumble on it, but it finds people. I know so many people for whom it saved their lives; it gave them their special purpose in life that they never, ever would have found. And it's a very special thing that they do. And I know every one of them—they're very into audio and music, and they would like nothing more than to have the opportunity to be great at it. Everyone I know strives for it; nobody's trying to make anything sound bad. Everyone I know who does it goes way above and beyond the call of duty. I've never met anyone doing it who was doing "good enough" productions. I've never met anyone like that. Everyone struggles and sacrifices to excel. Everyone who I know who's done it and is doing it or wants to do it...every kid, every apprentice, every person who's in his bedroom or garage with a laptop on a card table...

I know many people want to talk about gear, and there are great-sounding microphones, preamps, and other things that help you make great recordings, but the most important thing is your perspective. That's where the magic is; it's not in the gear. And if you have that perspective; you'll find a way to get what it is you hear and see in your imagination. And you may find a specific piece of gear, or you'll invent some way to do it, but it's your perspective that the magic is, it's not the gear.

You know what I miss from back then? Having great-sounding analog consoles, great-sounding studios, great musicians, using great microphones—those days for the music business, for making timeless music, that stuff certainly diminished. I'm not being an old guy, an old dinosaur remembering the old days, because I continue to look forward, not back. But having a band in a studio that could really play their instruments, having a large-format analog console and a big analog machine with the red record lights on, and these guys had to play a complete take through the song—that is what I wish I had now.

Those are skills. It was just fun, being with the cats and making music like that. And it was always a case of the whole being greater than the individual parts—everybody brought something to the party. And we would make these really great, timeless, great-sounding, and especially great-feeling records. The way you typically do it now, it starts with a loop in a machine and ten minutes of somebody recording something and ten hours of a guy sitting in front of a computer screen. That's how records are made now. That being said, I've got my own studio. I've got a digital console, I've got a big Pro Tools rig, I've got some analog things, I've got every plug-in in the world, I've got great-sounding speakers, and basically I mix in there, but I can make great records for a fraction of the price that it used to cost. And I can do my own hours, and that's pretty cool. And with an investment of $100,000 to $150,000 instead of a $5,000,000 investment, I'm in business and I have a studio.

I still have a piece of gear that I got then that I thought was the greatest thing in the world, and it was a Publison. It was one of the first digital delays and digital reverberators, and it had sampling. It was one of the first samplers, and it had 20 seconds of sampling time. It had 40 seconds on a single channel, and it had 20-seconds stereo, and that was a really great thing to have. All of a sudden, you could fly choruses around, and you could replace kick drums, and you could sample things and start playing some games, and it was the gateway to the modern age of digital recording. I still have it—kept it after all these years. And when I got it, it was about $15,000, which was all the money in the world at that time. So I kept that, and it doesn't sound that great, but now I use it for a digital delay like a tape slap because it's kind of dark, and that's what was nice about a tape slap. So I use it just for that.

I still use other analog gear. I've got a Night Technology NTI Equalizer; it's a very broad EQ that's phase-coherent that I use on the stereo bus, and I also have a Tube-Tech SM3-2A. It's a three-band tube compressor. I really like that three-band compressor on the stereo bus, too; I think it helps improve the sound of the mixes. The cliché of it warming up the digital world—it does. That debate about digital versus analog, I don't want to hear it. That debate is over, and analog lost and digital won, and never the twain shall meet. So if you know what you're doing, there are the tools. You can make a great-sounding recording digitally in the box; I hear people do it all the time. And I hear people doing a really crappy job of it, too. And again, it's not all about the gear; it's the nut behind the wheel.

In analog, there were a lot of things that gave you a certain sound. There was a dbx 160 compressor that was kind of fuzzy sounding, but it was a brick wall, and it was really effective for some things. It's really a good box to have, but there are other things that do that. Obviously, Fairchild's helped make some records sound really great. There was a warmth and a depth that you could get using some of the tube compressors that were spectacular sounding. But the myth of "I gotta have this piece of gear or that piece of gear"—it's less about the gear. It's about the music and about the emotion that you can ring out of it, no matter what tools you have.

If somebody came to you and said, "I just got this piece of gear, and now all of my mixes are going to sound great," I would nod my head and say, "Yeah, sure." That being said, you get your skill set together, you find things that are part of your palette that work for you. Plus, you need the imagination and the licks in the first place to recognize what you want to do with it. Just running your music through some piece of gear will not necessarily make your recordings better. A great performance of a great song and finding the formula that gets the emotion and beauty of that across… that's the magic.

Chapter 4

Marc Aubort

Born in Switzerland, Marc Aubort first came to the United States in 1955 and worked as an assistant producer for Vanguard Records in New York City. In 1958, Aubort became chief engineer for the company. It was also during these early years that he worked together with Ray Dolby to develop the Dolby Sound System we know today. Aubort's years at Dolby Labs were a groundbreaking era for noise reduction technology and high-definition sound. They remained dear friends until Dolby's death in 2013.

Branching out on his own in 1965, Aubort founded his own company, Elite Recordings, producing iconic classical recordings of major orchestras and musicians all over the world. In the 1970s, he was joined in his company by the late Joanna Nickrenz, and together they recorded and produced the bulk of the company's releases. Winning six Grammys as the Aubort/Nickrenz team, he won two for himself, including Classical Producer of the Year in 1983. Aubort's countless recordings were revered for their clarity and richness of sound. He was known in the industry as the minimalist sound engineer, often using only two Schoeps microphones strategically placed to get optimal sound and balance. For big orchestral works, he maintained his belief that a minimal amount of miking was ideal and sometimes, much to a conductor's chagrin, he reorganized sections within an orchestra for certain symphonic repertoire to achieve a homogenous orchestral sound. He did little post-production mixing to preserve sonic purity and raw musical expression. He also became known for his "piano sound" due to mic placement and balancing levels before recording.

Music training began in his early years in Switzerland. As a teen he became fascinated by sound engineering; he first trained in Zurich and began his career in the late 1940s working initially with wire recordings and later with tape. Aubort's first engineering and producing job was recording for Vanguard Records in Vienna.

Once in the US, Aubort continued to record classical performances but was also involved in the recordings of American folk music in the early 1960s. He recorded and produced Joan Baez's Vanguard debut album, following her around the country

DOI: 10.4324/9781003519829-4

during her rise to produce "Joan Baez in Concert." He recorded other great American folk artists such as Bob Dylan and The Weavers at the Newport Folk Festival. Among some of the more unusual recordings that Aubort released was the spoken album "Moses" with Charlton Heston, and live recordings of Frank Zappa's concert tributes to then recently fallen Beatle, John Lennon. Aubort also did a series of preservation recordings of dying global traditional music for National Geographic in the early 1970s.

As the use of multiple microphones became more popular in the 1970s, Aubort and his producer, the late Joanna Nickrenz, remained consistent in their technique of using fewer microphones and placing them with great care and attention to detail, creating a spacious, natural sound that became the signature of their production company, Elite Recordings. As other recordists and record labels abandoned these techniques, recordings created by Aubort and Nickrenz stood out. Over the 32 years of their collaboration, they averaged more than 20 recordings per year, always consistent with the highest standards of quality.

He proudly became an American citizen in 1972. Marc Aubort passed away in March 2023, at the age of 93.

My name is Marc Aubort. I was born in Switzerland in 1929. I started in audio in 1949. I was interested in audio recorders. I remember giving papers in high school about the whole process of fixing records and recording records and all that. I was really fascinated. Even as a child, I remember trying to turn the record backward so the grooves would come back into the record.

As a professional, it all started with an amplifier that didn't work. I went to see a local guru. He was doing recordings as well as building amplifiers for movie theaters, and he showed me where I had goofed up on this amplifier. We became friends, and that's how the whole thing started. Then one day he got a Magnacorder from New York, and that was after we had started recording on wires with the wire recorder. We unpacked this Magnacorder and looked at it and figured out how it worked and started using that.

Then of course came the problem with editing. We had a crude editing process with the wires.... We knocked the wires together, but of course, it didn't work too well because the speed was different. There was a pickup reel—there was no capstan; the speed was given by the pickup reel. So when a piece was missing in between, suddenly the pitch changed. So we figured out how to edit and developed a system and found out years later that in Vienna there was a totally different system. We can talk about that later, but that's how it all started.

And this guy, my mentor in Switzerland, was doing recordings for an American outfit called MMS—Musical Masterpiece Society. They broke the barrier of the expensive classical records in Europe by having it like a book club and bringing out recordings at a third of the price of the full-price records. In the beginning, the industry was fighting that, and then they were very grateful because they sold a lot of turntables and subsequently their expensive records. Meanwhile, we recorded all over Europe—people who were not

Figure 4.1 We had wire recorders when I started...well, there was nothing else before that. There were steel bands—enormous spools that were used at broadcast studios. They were essentially the same thing; they were ribbons of steel, huge drums.

Figure 4.2 I have sessions with Zuckerman, for instance, and with the Tokyo Quartet: "It just doesn't sound right; it's kind of dull and tough." And so I just raise the monitor volume, and, "Oh, that's perfect! That's the way it should sound." Just make it a little louder because your ears are not flat; use the Fletcher-Munson Curve. You make it a little louder, and it gets more linear. Fine. You don't need any EQ.

as well known maybe as the big names, but they had valued musical performances, and that's how it all started.

We had wire recorders when I started...well, there was nothing else before that. There were steel bands—enormous spools that were used at broadcast studios. They were essentially the same thing; they were ribbons of steel, huge drums. And then came the wire recorder, which was a breakthrough at that time.

Then came the Magnacorder. Where I was working, they called it a lab. It was a small factory that made amplifiers, but the owner had always been involved in recording and lathes, and that was one of his hobbies, to record things. And he was approached then by this Musical Masterpiece Society to do the recordings in Europe for this American

Figure 4.3 At that time the Ampex machines came out—the 350s and 300s and all that—but I would still tape and use the technology. The technique remained the same—the whole approach of how to record and how to have the perspective on the stage, not just bringing all sorts of microphones into one plane, then mixing it together to keep the distance to the back. That hasn't changed ever since, as far as I'm concerned. That's why I never really adopted the multichannel, multi-miking technique.... I'm using flash recording now, but it's the same technique. There's one thing that this guru, this friend of mine, told me, which I never forgot. He said, "When you set a balance, don't just sit there and say, 'Oh, that's great, that's nice.' Compare what you hear to what you think you should hear and then go and adjust it if it doesn't conform to the sound picture that you have in your head of what this particular piece should sound like." And I've been trying to live up to that.

Figure 4.4 I have been using the same microphones for practically 40 years. Whatever else is the media is actually a pain in the neck because you accumulate an archival trove of analog tapes and then F1 tapes and then JVC 900 tapes, and then the stuff is obsolete. After a few years, I just threw out all this JVC 900 equipment for which I paid $65,000 because I hadn't fired it up in years.... And I had about 400 original U-Matic tapes from all over that were just sitting there, and I couldn't even play them. But each CD that was out on the market was a backup mastered to these original tapes. So eventually I just threw out the whole thing lock, stock, and barrel, including the equipment. But for archival purposes, there is still nothing better than analog tape.

Figure 4.5 To me today, recordings are done much, much too close up. Your ears are not designed for that. They're not programmed to have a fiddle right next to you; you're supposed to have some distance to it. And a lot of recordings today are recorded so close for the sake of high fidelity or whatever that you completely lose the aesthetic interaction between different instruments. My idea of recording is to have a mix before it reaches the microphone. So not to mix afterward, because if you do that, you can never achieve the satisfaction of the audio picture or a tapestry or whatever you call it that sounds natural... No matter how much you can remix later, it doesn't solve the problem of distance and depth of stage and width of stage on an orchestral recording. That's what I'm trying to preserve—that the horns are not in front, the horns are in the back.... It takes guts not to use a microphone, but to place the instrument within an orchestra where it's for your purpose sounding best.

company, and that's how we started teaming up. I was doing most of the musical part of it, and he was doing the technical part of it. But both things overlapped.

I was using practically the same microphones I'm still using today, the Schoeps tube microphones—221B. I've tried many other microphones, but so far I haven't found one that has the warmth and the reach of these old tube microphones. They need a lot of babying and tender loving care, but they're worth it.

We had several microphones. We had the Altec microphones. We had the Neumann, the old bicycle-lamp type thing. And then came the Schoeps, all microphones of that time. And we had several types of microphones at that time, but more or less, the Schoeps microphones would be used on a main performance.

For a console, we had home-built stuff that my mentor had designed. At that time there were no real consoles—certainly not portable ones—and we needed that because we traveled all over Europe in a car, and brought everything with us.

I worked for him for almost ten years, I think. The technology started just with the LP. It was still pressed on red vinyl. But it was just at the tail end of the 78s, and the LP just started there. And that was one of the launching reasons for these records—there was the big breakthrough that you had 25 minutes on the side instead of only 4½.

After that, upper management wanted to put me in my boss's place, and I refused. I said, "This is not only my boss, he's also my friend." They were after me, signing contracts, and out of sheer desperation, I called Vanguard in New York. I didn't know Seymour Solomon then, but I liked the way they were recording. They were very similar to our recording. At first, I wrote, but I didn't get any answer. Then they called on the phone, and Seymour said, "Well, join me in Vienna. I'll be there in spring, and if it works out, then you'll have a job." By that time, they were doing everything in mono, and we had already started doing stereo recording. I already had some experience in stereo recording, and I immediately started doing stereo recordings for Vanguard in Vienna. So that's how I got into this whole thing. And so it worked out, and until I got my immigration papers, I worked two years in Vienna for Vanguard and then I came here.

Now, Vanguard had the Ampex—at that time the Ampex machines came out—the 350s and 300s and all that—but I would still tape and use the technology. The technique remained the same—the whole approach of how to record and how to have the perspective on the stage, not just bringing all sorts of microphones into one plane, then mixing it together to keep the distance to the back. That hasn't changed ever since, as far as I'm concerned. That's why I never really adopted the multichannel, multi-miking technique.

I stayed with two-channel, not that I use only two microphones. But I use two main microphones and then, if I need it, an accent here and there. Then I had an additional microphone, considered each additional microphone to the main microphones—sort of a crutch to make up for the distances in the hall or the orchestration or individual outputs of instruments, mixing celli and bassoons together, things like that.

I'm using flash recording now, but it's the same technique. There's one thing that this guru, this friend of mine, told me, which I never forgot. He said, "When you set a balance, don't just sit there and say, 'Oh, that's great, that's nice.' Compare what you hear to what you think you should hear and then go and adjust it if it doesn't conform to the sound picture that you have in your head of what this particular piece should sound like." And I've been trying to live up to that. His name was Wettler, Freddie Wettler. My mentor, friend, boss, whatever. When he died I was in Berlin. We drove like mad from Berlin to Zurich in one nonstop stretch to get to his funeral.

I use compressors, limiters, and EQs only as a last resort. My philosophy is, "If you have a good microphone that is flat that gives you little sound picture, don't go and change it." For the sheer thrill and effect of it, like making brass much brighter than they actually sound, making it hi-fi... never adopted that idea.

I use EQ if, for instance, the hall is not up to snuff, and it's too dry a hall or it's too wet of a hall. If it's too dry, obviously at that time there were reverb systems with springs that were really deficient. They sounded very artificial and very metallic. Today, we're doing new reverb techniques with digital; you can actually get pretty decent results with good equipment. I'm using it in Toronto, which is a fairly dry hall. I add a certain amount of reverb, and it suddenly becomes a good hall. It's a Sony. It's a Sony piece of equipment you can couple.

In those days, there was one little trick that we used when the choir was too thin or too puny. We used to do a graphic equalization of 400 and 1,000 Hz...slightly push that up, and that's how we made the choir bigger. Things like that to enhance the picture, not to artificially boost the bass.

At that time there was virtually nothing else but the Pultecs, which were nice. Good warm sound; they did the trick. And later on, I used limiting, but only when I did cutting. That was here. When you cut a record, you use vertical limiting so that the groove doesn't thin out. And that's the only time I used the limiter—to prevent the groove from thinning or out-of-phase bass information. But not for sound reasons, for technical reasons.

I was doing mastering as sort of a side job because a friend of mine was quite ill, and I kept his outfit going off-hours and cut a lot of stuff for Westminster, Vanguard, and other clients that were his clients.

One of the reasons that I needed to adopt a good Dolby system was because it gave me the 10-dB latitude that I needed for full dynamic range. And I practically pulled the prototype out of Ray [Dolby]'s hand when it came. He was looking for the studio to demonstrate to Ampex. And he brought two suitcases—Dolby A301—and when I heard what it did, I bought it right out of his hand because it was great, and subsequently, I started importing these things and selling them, demonstrating, and I became vice president of Dolby. I was a very good friend of Ray's, and that's why I had to hire somebody—because I couldn't drive both horses. That's why I hired Joanna Nickrenz for editing, and then subsequently she was producing as well as editing. We worked 32 years together, and we figured out once that we made more than 800 records together.

I left Vanguard in 65. They told me, "There's no place to go for you because we are the boss, and you have reached the ceiling, so we recommend that you do your own thing." And I was scared stiff that I would never find enough customers to record classical music, but I was wrong. I immediately had more than I could handle. And that hasn't changed except for the last two or three years. With outsourcing and downloading and all that, it's been pretty dismal.

Orchestras are still playing, but the pop and rock business is the one that financed the classical recordings. This is a prestige item for recording companies because they didn't ever make money with classical music, except Vox. Mendelssohn... Vox is the only one in classical music who made it back.

Vanguard did folk and jazz. Like the Weavers and Joan Baez. That pulled the engine for the classical label. And when that income started to fail because of downloading and other reasons, I slumped into folk music recording. All of that contributed to the slowdown in the income from the pop and rock fields that were financing classical music. Then came outsourcing. Today, orchestras are busiest in Slovakia, Romania, and Bulgaria because they can offer a $5,000 flat rate including orchestral costs, conducting—everything for $5,000. I can't do that. There's no way I can do that.

I was in a situation where I went to Slovakia to record a Mozart clarinet concerto, and they had never played a Mozart clarinet concerto. They're an hour away from Vienna, and that orchestra had never played that concerto. They had to learn it on the spot. It came out all right, but it took a lot of work. Whereas here, if you have an orchestral recording, the orchestra is absolutely prepared. They have been on tour, they have played it several times in concert, and they know it inside out.

They are professional there, but what happens in these places is that you'll rehearse something in the morning, and in the afternoon you'll have a recording session that's another orchestra. So that everybody gets a piece of the pie, they send out the people who're recording, and you have a rehearsal with part of the orchestra, and the other half is not the same.

That happened in Vienna at that time I was working for Vanguard, who had to insist that the same people would come to the recording session that came for the rehearsal. It was not self-understood at all. Whereas here, the problem is that the orchestral costs for recordings are so high that you can never make your investment back, even after 20 years. That's why Mendelssohn had this phenomenal idea with a media guarantee—that he would finance one session per LP, and the orchestra had to come up with the rest of it, and he would pay them back within, let's say, eight years or ten years for that part of it.

A lot of orchestras were put on the map, because before that, there was virtually no recording. And this media guarantee thing kick-started a lot of orchestras in this country.

That was true for Baltimore, for Atlanta, for Cincinnati, for St. Louis, for San Francisco… It came to the point where St. Louis was called the second-best orchestra in the country. It was a good orchestra to begin with, but it was not represented on recordings. It was a good touring orchestra, and they couldn't really buy any recordings in St. Louis.

As far as anything that I have now that I wish I'd had then, I have been using the same microphones for practically 40 years. Whatever else is the media is actually a pain in the neck because you accumulate an archival trove of analog tapes and then F1 tapes and then JVC 900 tapes, and then the stuff is obsolete. After a few years, I just threw out all this JVC 900 equipment for which I paid $65,000 because I hadn't fired it up in years. It was just sitting there because, in the meantime, there came workstations like Sadie or Pro Tools and all that. And the whole idea at that time was to use broadcast 3/4-inch U-Matic tape, and you copied from one machine to the other, and as you rehearsed your splice, you copied from one machine to the next. In other words, you could not make inserts either. You had to recall the whole thing to the end. It took weeks to edit something that should have taken only hours.

So not only did I throw out all that equipment, but I moved. I moved into a smaller place because my rent was going up. And I had about 400 original U-Matic tapes from all over that were just sitting there, and I couldn't even play them. But each CD that was out on the market was a backup mastered to these original tapes. So eventually I just threw out the whole thing lock, stock, and barrel, including the equipment. But for archival purposes, there is still nothing better than analog tape.

It hasn't changed. I play recordings I made in the '50s and '60s. They play like they were, provided they were stored properly and the emulsion didn't peel off. But I guarantee you the older formats, these subsequent steps have happened, and some recordings are already obsolete. DAT. I mean, DAT was a very handy format for professionals, but now it's obsolete. Nobody's using it anymore.

And even CDs are not archival. I mean, I have CDs that after three to four months don't play anymore, especially the ones with the silver and gold surface. The ones with the dye—with the green and blue dyes—last much longer, but they're not good for 100 years, as they claim. No way. But analog tape, properly stored, is good for 100 years.

Optical is going to be as obsolete as all the other formats. It's the equipment. It's not there to play this stuff anymore, and you can't get spare parts for the equipment. You're sunk. Then you end up with hundreds of tapes sitting on your shelves, but you can't play them.

There's nothing that I had then that I wish I had now. It has made working much simpler, the whole digital revolution. You don't have to align the machines; you don't have to test tape and phasing problems with heads and so on and so forth. This used to take a lot of time. Before the recording session, with each reel, you had to put on 1,000 cycles or 10,000 to be sure that the machine was still working properly. All of that is gone. You just push a button today. It's zero or nothing. Zero once. You can get great or just zilch. Also, any kind of tape format, digital, is doomed to fail. For instance, I have a whole library of Exabyte tapes as a backup. These Exabyte tapes are already obsolete; the machines are not available, or they cannot be repaired. If you touch the tape, it's gone. The whole cassette is kaput. So it's just a very fickle archival system. As long as you make CDs and all that, you have backups.

I've recorded tons of stuff with Beta. I still have Beta machines, and I baby them because I have to scavenge from one machine to the next now. And at that time it was convenient, it was small, it was portable...it was not the greatest quality, but it was 16-bit. Interweaves, sure...nevertheless, it was digital, and it did the trick. Each Beta tape had two hours on it, which was great. You didn't have to change tape every half hour. That's all it took.

Let's talk about the approach to recordings. To me today, recordings are done much, much too close up. Your ears are not designed for that. They're not programmed to have a fiddle right next to you; you're supposed to have some distance to it. And a lot of recordings today are recorded so close for the sake of high fidelity or whatever that you completely lose the aesthetic interaction between different instruments. My idea of recording is to have a mix before it reaches the microphone. So not to mix afterward, because if you do that, you can never achieve the satisfaction of the audio picture or a tapestry or whatever you call it that sounds natural... No matter how much you can remix later, it doesn't solve the problem of distance and depth of stage and width of stage on an orchestral recording. That's what I'm trying to preserve—that the horns are not in front, the horns are in the back. I've seen it from the CBC, Canada. They hang their microphones over the orchestra. There are about 10 or 12 microphones hanging over the orchestra. How the hell can you get a perspective that way?

It's not the way you hear it in the best seat in the house. It takes guts not to use a microphone, but to place the instrument, within an orchestra, where it's for your purpose sounding best. What if I need to put harps between first and second violins, to the horror of the people behind who can't see the conductor? It's solvable—you can just move people around a bit until they can see the conductor—but at least you get a natural sound.

Most conductors go along with it once you convincingly explain what you're trying to do. You still have a natural mix, and each microphone is a crutch compared to the main pickup. It's even four microphones in front of the stage if it's the right stage, but ideally just two microphones. But for that you need microphones that have the depth and the reach to the back, and that's a funny thing with these Schoeps microphones. The sound pressure declines with the square of the distance, but if I use today's modern microphones right next to the ones that I've been using for years and years, you don't hear the back of the stage. There's a classic example, a recording in L.A., Johann Christian Bach concerto for harpsichord solo, but there's also harpsichord in the orchestra as a continual. With some Danish microphones that are considered to be the cat's last meow, you could not even hear the continuing harpsichord. With Schoeps only placed an inch away from each other, perfect balance. So physics is great, but sometimes it doesn't work.

Don't get lost in all of this technology and forget your steps. It's your ears that have to hear the recording, not the meters and the flashing lights and the console and all that. It's what you can translate from the orchestra for listening and be faithful to the composer. That's what counts, not the gimmicks. I remember a company in Vienna that whenever there was a triangle, you had marked a big fat circle around the triangle on the score, and every time the triangle came up, we were pushing the faders down. The whole damn thing sounded like a phone going off right next to you. This kind of thing to me is totally nonsense. There are lots of instruments that don't even have to be heard. They are part of the color, the fabric of an orchestra.

These days, sometimes the equipment and the gimmicks take precedence over the actual intent of recording. It is an aesthetic question. Don't forget that you're recording a Mozart piece and that Mozart had very simple lines, and they have to be heard as such and not as a sensational high fidelity. That's why I'm saying, as I said at the beginning, that things are recorded much too close together. It's not the way we hear an orchestra. The conductor is actually in a very bad spot to hear the orchestra because he hears first and second fiddles and the violas and cellos, the first few rows, and the back portion is lost. But if you had the fifth seat about 10 feet up, that's where an orchestra sounds best, and that's where I try to place the microphones.

If you set a balance and you use good headphones, you can compensate for the fact that it's binaural by thinking about the stereo picture, but you cannot do that in a real-world situation where people are walking around and talking and all that. And it takes much more time to set the proper balance in loudspeakers than in headphones. Each movement on a fader can instantly be heard on headphones, but on the loudspeakers, you need big movement, plus, minus, plus, minus, until you finally get to the point. You get so many of these variables. Whereas with headphones you take your whole ambience with you, no matter what the green room sounds like.

With each improvement in headphones, the microphone stayed the same, but each generation of headphones widened the whole perspective on the range of the microphone that you're using. I used to use BT 48s, which I thought were great headphones, but there have been so many good headphones since that today they sound like tin cans. But with the same microphones, your ears develop, and you get used to hearing something a certain way, and then you can't stand anything else. I remember having been weaned on Tannoy loudspeakers in Europe. Then I came here, and they had the LC-1As, and the RCA loudspeakers. How on earth can anybody listen to that? And I went back to Europe and heard the Tannoys again, and I thought, "How on earth can you listen to this?"

There's sometimes acoustics involved in there. I have sessions with Zuckerman, for instance, and with the Tokyo Quartet: "It just doesn't sound right; it's kind of dull and tough." And so I just raise the monitor volume, and, "Oh, that's perfect! That's the way it should sound." Just make it a little louder because your ears are not flat; use the Fletcher-Munson Curve. You make it a little louder, and it gets more linear. Fine. You don't need any EQ.

We did that with Stokowski. Stokowski was a nut for that. He thought he could mix things. So we gave him a mixer that was only mixing the monitor, but not the tape. And he was going up and down with the faders—"Oh, this is fabulous!"—and he thought it was him.

Chapter 5

Bob Ludwig

Thirteen-time Grammy-winning mastering engineer Bob Ludwig (with 34 nominations) graduated from the University of Rochester's Eastman School of Music. He holds a Bachelor of Music degree in music education and a Master of Music degree in performance (trumpet) and music literature. In May, 2006, Bob was honored by the University of Southern Maine with an Honorary Doctorate of Humane Letters degree.

While studying at Eastman, Bob worked several years in the school's recording department, as well as working for the local Century Records affiliate, recording many high school band/orchestra and choir concerts around western New York state. While Bob was finishing work on his master's degree during a summer session, engineer and producer Phil Ramone came to Eastman and conducted Eastman's first Summer Session recording workshop, where Bob assisted him. After the workshop, Phil hired Bob to work at his A&R Recording Studios in New York City. Bob began his professional career in 1967 at AR Recording as an assistant engineer working with Phil Ramone, Roy Halee (who worked there for a short time), Don Hahn, Roy Cicala, Shelly Yakus, Elliot Scheiner, and other A@R Recording staff engineers. Bob learned the art of vinyl record mastering at ACR. He moved to Sterling Sound, Inc., shortly after its incorporation in 1969 and became vice president. Bob cut many famous records at Sterling, including Led Zeppelin's II and Houses of the Holy, some Jimi Hendrix, and most of The Band's famous albums.

After seven years at Sterling Sound, he moved to Masterdisk Corporation, where he was vice president and chief engineer. He continued mastering many hit records, by such groups and artists as U2, Phil Collins, Sting, the Police, Bryan Adams, Barbra Streisand, and so on. As chief engineer, Bob continued to be involved with many firsts. Bob cut his first album from a Soundstream digital recorder for Telarc in 1978. He owned the second Sony portable: DAT machine in America. (Michael Jackson owned the first.) In 1993, Bob left Masterdisk and opened his own business, Gateway Mastering Studios, Inc., in Portland, Maine. The studio was an instant success, winning the 1994 TEC Awards for Mastering Facility and Mastering Engineer, the first full year it was eligible.

DOI: 10.4324/9781003519829-5

Bob Ludwig holds the largest number of mastering credits of all engineers employed in the industry. He won a Latin Grammy Award for Alejandro Sanz's Album of the Year and a Grammy Award for Best Surround Recording (Dire Straits' Brothers in Arms 20th anniversary edition). Bob has mastered countless gold and platinum records. He was the first person to be honored with the Les Paul Award when it was established in 1991 for "...individuals who have set the highest standards of excellence in recording and sound production over a period of many years." Bob won numerous Pro Sound News Mastering Awards and Mix Magazine's TEC Award for Outstanding Creative Achievement, Mastering Engineer, an unprecedented 13 times. Gateway Mastering Studios won the TEC Award for Mastering Studio nine times.

Bob is now co-chairman of the 5,000+ member Producers and Engineers Wing of the National Academy of Recording Arts and Sciences. He is active in the Audio Engineering Society and was a past chairman of the New York section. At the 2008 convention, Bob chaired a Grammy Award-winning panel of mastering engineers and was himself a speaker on panels covering surround sound artistry, HD-DVD, and Blu-ray. In 2009, he again chaired the Platinum Mastering Panel, and he is a judge for the AES student non-classical surround competition.

I'm Bob Ludwig. I was born in Savannah, Georgia. I grew up in northern New York City and Westchester County, and Mount Vernon, and South Salem, New York. I went to John Jay High School in Cross River, which was a fabulous high school. I had great music teachers there who convinced me to go to Eastman. It was always a toss-up whether to go into engineering or to go into music. I had this great music teacher who is still alive and who I am still in contact with, who convinced me to go to Eastman, and I'm so happy that he did. And, it was really great. This is a special high school; we had a humanities course that I took there that had me and one other kid. This is a public high school. I went to the Eastman School of Music and got a bachelor's and a master's there. I have an honorary doctorate from the University of Southern Maine, 13 Tech awards and Grammys, and Cinema Audio Society, all that stuff...

I was in the recording department at Eastman. Naturally, I went to the school, and I was playing principal trumpet with the Utica Symphony Orchestra while I was still at Eastman, but I also worked in the recording department recording countless student recitals. And I also did freelance work for Century Records, which was an outfit from California that would go and record high school bands, choirs, and orchestras and sell them vinyl] discs several weeks later. So it took him a while to process everything and cut it and all that stuff. So I've been to about every major high school in western New York state. I know that area of the world very, very well.

And, when I was finishing up my master's degree, they had the first recording workshop at Eastman they ever had. The person who came up to teach it was Phil Ramone, so I was Phil's de facto assistant during this class that he gave during the summer session. And at the end of it, he asked me if I wanted to come work for him in New York. I'd been in the Utica Symphony long enough by then that I knew what the life of a Grade B symphony

Figure 5.1 So Phil locked Aaron Baron and their maintenance man and myself in the room and said, "Don't come out until you can at least equal what they did." So he and I spent a lot of time looking at the lathe, trying to figure out, because it was a very different concept having an analog computer-controlled lathe compared to a fixed-pitch mono lathe, where if you had too much level, it truly would just cross into the next groove, that kind of thing. And so we finally figured out that the way they told you to set up the lathe wasn't quite right and that you needed to actually lower the preview signal going into the lathe.... It turned out the way that they told me to set up the lathe was a little too conservative, so we would lower the level of the preview system a couple of dB.... The thing was that, totally unknowingly, I began telling people that we knew how to "cheat" the preview. This is where it became a cachet. It's like, "Oh, at A&R they cheat the preview; they can cut hotter records." I wish in retrospect I could've enjoyed that, coined that phrase back then. So we started getting a lot of outside work that A&R would never have attracted.

Figure 5.2 We just had a major triumph. A major, major triumph. The new Guns N' Roses record—Caram Costanzo and Axl mixed it. There are some tracks that must have had hundreds of tracks of stuff on it, and they wanted to be able to hear all the layering and everything. And as soon as you put too much compression on it, it just flattens out. This record is mastered like a 1980s CD. You have to turn your playback line up in order to enjoy this record at a loud level. Its average level is quiet. It's quieter than anything I've done probably in 15 years. And believe me, they spent some ungodly amount of money on this record. They spent eight and a half years in the making, and to have the fortitude to put it out on the market without it being loud is pretty amazing. And over the air it sounds as loud as the things around it because the radio stations are all in competition with each other. It will not sound loud on an iPod Shuffle compared to other things or on the iTunes store. So, there you go. It's an amazing-sounding record.

Figure 5.3 When producers would work at Columbia and would want to work at Sterling, the union people bitched and wouldn't allow them to do that. And so the IBEW came up with this thing: if you need to use an independent studio you can, but the engineer from Columbia has to come and do it there just like they did with recording studios. And as far as I know, I was the first person to break that or to have anyone go outside Columbia. My friend Paul Rothchild, who did all the Doors stuff, had just produced Janis Joplin's record with "Me and Bobby McGee," so I cut her single at Sterling, and the union guy comes over—this guy named Ben Ernholt, cigar-smoking guy—and he says, "I was sup- posed to cut this on the lathe." And, well, this is a Neumann lathe. Scully lathes and heads are just fine, no issue with Scully, but at the time we felt the Neumann was better. Anyway, I said, "Ben, this cutter head is like $3,000." And this is like 1968. "Are you going to be responsible for that if anything goes wrong?" He said, "No, I ain't gonna touch that." So I'd cut, and he would sit there in the lounge, and he would scribe the records at the end, but he was getting paid to be there. And he was really—God bless him—he was one of these really union guys, like he could tell me how many years, months, and days he had until his retirement. He was just counting down.

Figure 5.4 So for the compact disc, we ultimately had to record through the 1610, which had these off-the-drawing-board, industrial-design A-to-D converters. And because the CD had taken off, all the research and development was in the digital-to-analog converters. And there was still very little research being done on the A-to-D part of it. So the A-to-D converters that were on the Sony 1600 and the 1610 were just not very good. But that was all they had at the time, so that's what we used. They were so bad that it was common practice on some really great-sounding digital records that were done, like the Rush Moving Pictures record—they were done monitoring through the Sony A to D and D to A. You'd monitor through the whole chain and mix through it like that, so that if it needed more reverb because of the crappy digital, you'd put more reverb, and it would come out good, right? It was bad enough so you'd listen to the entire chain, almost like it was the Dolby.

Figure 5.5 And having this lathe with this cutter head and the Solid State cutting amps, there was a period of about half a year or more where at Sterling we could cut a record that nobody else could cut. Maybe Doug had that same head in California, but there was a period of time when we had an advantage over every other studio in New York, where we could cut more high-frequency stuff than they could, and it was like that short period of time when America only had the atomic bomb and nobody else did. Everybody felt safe for half a year until Russia had it, too.

Figure 5.6 And so that's an "aha." That was the big "aha" moment for me. And I'd just started working with Scepter Records and Stanley Greenberg, who did all the great Dionne Warwick stuff. I had just started; he was kind of trying me out. I did this obscure Dionne Warwick record called The Magic of Believing—it was her answer to Aretha Franklin doing gospel stuff. And again, I was still in the head of trying to match what mixes I had gotten. And I had cut the thing, but we hadn't sent the references out at that time. I took the reference home with me and listened to it and said, "Nope, I've got to change it." And I went back and recut it with more compression, more midrange and everything, and they totally loved it. And I did all the Dionne Warwick hits from then on—"Do You Know the Way to San Jose," "Alfie," all that.

orchestra player was going to be like, and I knew from my other trumpet player friends at Eastman, who went right into first chair of the Cleveland Orchestra and places like that, that I was good, but I wasn't that good as a trumpet player. I was good enough to be in the Utica Symphony but not good enough to be first chair in the Cleveland. And so for a B orchestra like that and probably the A orchestras nowadays, I spent a lot of time playing afternoon luncheon fundraisers and played this pretty crap literature. The other side of the coin is you play some good literature in the regular concerts. My goal was always to play the Bach B Minor Mass on the piccolo trumpet, and one day it came up, so I did it. And at the end of it, I was like, "Now what do I do?"

So I worked there for about a year and a half and learned how to do mastering there, and Phil has always been and will always be my mentor. This was like 1967–68.

Mastering was all at Capitol, RCA, Columbia—all had union jobs, and union guys did all the work there, and any lathe that was around was associated with a recording studio because that was how you got a reference disk. Because you either got a reel-to-reel tape or you would get a vinyl cut of your mixes. That actually just preceded cassettes—even cassettes weren't quite around yet then. They'd been invented by Philips, but you couldn't use them for music yet. It was still voice quality back then.

At A&R, they had a lot of Scully 4-tracks. And in the mastering room, we had Ampex 300s, mono, because I started off in the mono cutting room. Probably the first thing I ever mastered was like a commercial for Sunoco or something like that, but my first number-one record was Neil Diamond doing "Kentucky Woman." And then the Amboy Dukes' Journey to the Center of the Mind...Ted Nugent, right?

So we had this really good ES-59 cutting head on the mono Neumann lathe, and then, A&R was the first independent facility to buy the first Neumann computerized lathe—the VMS-66. But, it was really 67, and we were at 112 West 48th Street, which was where the original A&R was. And Phil had just bought 799 7th Avenue from Columbia and was building the studio there, and they put in this brand-new stereo lathe in that building. And there was really no manual for it, and for every time we would cut, trying to compete with Columbia's Scully lathes, we couldn't get the same level on it.

So, Phil locked Aaron Baron, their maintenance man, and myself in the room and said, "Don't come out until you can at least equal what they did." So he and I spent a lot of time looking at the lathe, trying to figure it out, because it was a very different concept having an analog computer-controlled lathe compared to a fixed-pitch mono lathe, where if you had too much level, it truly would just cross into the next groove, that kind of thing. And so we finally figured out that the way they told you to set up the lathe wasn't quite right and that you needed to actually lower the preview signal going into the lathe.

With a variable-pitch lathe, where, when things are soft, the thing might cut 400 lines per inch, if you looked through a microscope, you'd count 400 lines within a period of an inch, and really loud stuff would be about 80 lines per inch. Huge difference. And the way the computer knew how far apart to set the grooves before the music hit was by preview head. So the music would hit this preview head, and the analog computer that was built into the Neumann lathe would say, "Aha, it's got this much voltage; it needs this." So it pre-opened up. It turned out the way that they told me to set up the lathe was a little too conservative, so we would lower the level of the preview system a couple of dB.

The thing was that, totally unknowingly, I began telling people that we knew how to "cheat" the preview. This is where it became a cachet. It's like, "Oh, at AXR they cheat the preview; they can cut hotter records." I wish in retrospect I could've enjoyed that, coined that phrase back then. So we started getting a lot of outside work that A&R would never have attracted.

For instance, because I came from Eastman, I knew how to read a score. Nonesuch Records, which was then headed by Tracy Sterne—this was Jac Holzman's classical label for Elektra—started using me for classical cuts, where they'd hand me a score and taught me to cut from that. Like with the Mahler Symphony, you need to know when these huge climaxes would come. So, we had started attracting clients like that, and then New World Records and Connoisseur Society, so we started doing cutting for projects that weren't part of A&R; things weren't recorded there.

And it started turning into its own nice little business, and one of his clients was Enoch Light. When stereo first came out in the late '50s, he had this label called Command Records. And they had a thing called "Persuasive Percussion"—one of these horrible arrangements, just cheesy elevator-music stuff—but it would feature first the bongos on the left channel and then the bongos on the right, to demonstrate your new stereo system. And Enoch had always recorded with Bob Fine at Fine Recording, where the Parker Meridian hotel is right now in New York, and Enoch left there to work with Phil. So I used to cut all of Enoch's stuff, and his daughter, Julie Klages, was one of the people who I really credit with teaching me how to hear. This woman, besides doing these cheesy elevator things, they'd also do classical music from time to time, and they recorded William Steinberg and the Pittsburgh Symphony. There's a story about them doing a session and him turning to the orchestra and saying, "That woman can hear the grass grow." And so she, when we were mastering this cheesy stuff, would really be tuned into things like mixes and ask me to do all these manipulations on the fly—you know, add a little EQ just for this one little line or all this stuff that we do now very routinely.

Pretty much the union guys at CBS and Capitol and RCA, they would put a tone up and just cut it from beginning to end, and if there were any changes, they'd go back in the mix room. If it was dull, they'd come back to the mix room and redo it, brighten it up. If the level wasn't right, they'd go back and re-tone it. It was a very mechanical kind of a process. So, a guy named Dominick Romeo—a guy I learned a lot from, although I never met him except once briefly… He worked in another independent studio called Bell Sound, and he too was into doing this. In fact, he's the guy who really gave me the context for being able to branch out and do kind of wild things in mastering that weren't commonly done then. And someone should trace Dominick down, because in the late 60s, before I got there, he probably cut more number-one records than anybody on the planet. I really mean that; he really did. He was definitely the guy in New York who everybody, all the indie labels, would go to. And justifiably—he did a great job. And he was the one who taught me.

Bob Crewe, the guy who did all the Four Seasons stuff… When I was learning at A&R, I would cut his reference mixes. He'd take them home and listen to them, and for a long time, when it came time to cut the final thing, he would go over to Dominick and cut it over there. And I did this one thing for him of Mitch Ryder, I think it was. I was on this reference; I was so careful to match exactly what he had on his mix. I did diameter equalization; I did whatever it took so that from the beginning to the end of this reference, it would sound just like what he had mixed. And so I knew that what I was handing him was exactly what he had mixed. And this goes to Dominick, comes back, and so I got a copy of what Dominick did. And it sounded nothing like his mix! You know, nothing—midrange boosted, this and that—and I said, "This doesn't sound anything like your mix." He says, "All I know is, when I go home and put it on my turntable at home, I get the same excitement I had when I mixed it in the control room."

And so that's an "aha." That was the big "aha" moment for me. And I'd just started working with Scepter Records and Stanley Greenberg, who did all the great Dionne Warwick stuff. I had just started; he was kind of trying me out. I did this obscure Dionne

Warwick record called The Magic of Believing—it was her answer to Aretha Franklin doing gospel stuff. And again, I was still in the head of trying to match what mixes I had gotten. And I had cut the thing, but we hadn't sent the references out at that time. I took the reference home with me and listened to it and said, "Nope, I've got to change it." And I went back and recut it with more compression, more midrange, and everything, and they totally loved it. And I did all the Dionne Warwick hits from then on—"Do You Know the Way to San Jose," "Alfie," all that.

We had the Fairchild limiter, the one that goes for $25,000–$30,000 on eBay now. And at the time, we couldn't wait to get rid of it. If you look at the manual for the Fairchild limiter, its specification for distortion is less than one percent. So if you have .9 percent distortion on it, that's fine. That's factory spec. So for mastering, we thought we needed something cleaner than that. EMT and Pi came out with limiters that were quite a bit cleaner, and we used those. As I say, at the time we were happy to get rid of it. But, in fact, to this day it still is probably a better recording limiter than it is a mastering limiter because of that.

They were originally built to be mastering limiters, and the one thing was if there was too much vertical modulation, you could use the summing difference knob on that, and we would use that to limit just the vertical mode for cutting. So that was helpful, but I think in reality we probably used a combination of that and the Pi limiter. Then, of course, we had Pultecs—we had the MEQ, the 1A, and the high- and low-pass filters. We had everything Pultec made.

And yeah, I remember those. Pultec stands for "pulse techniques," and they were in West Englewood, New Jersey. Later in life, I lived in Englewood, New Jersey, and there's no such place on the map anymore as West Englewood. Tried to find where they were, but I could never find them.

So, that was interesting. And then, Mr. Neumann—Georg Neumann in Berlin—got a whole development team making lathes, microphones, consoles, equalizers.... I guess there was a Neumann compressor back then. And cutting consoles, cutting amps, all that stuff. Mr. Neumann had his own little lab over there, and one day he came out with the SX-68, which was the first really great Neumann stereo cutter head, and it was like going from like 7 1/2 IPS to 30 IPS—it was a major leap forward in quality and the ability to handle level.

And Stephen Temmer, who was their distributor, Gotham Audio, brought it by and put it on the lathe. I was like, "Oh my god, this is great." For whatever reason, Art Ward, who was the president of A&R and handled all the money and things like that... he wasn't interested in getting that for me. So I knew that no matter what I did, I'd never be able to compete against such a smooth-sounding head. And this new company was opening up that not only was going to have the first SX-68, but they also had the new Neumann Solid State amps to go with it and a Neumann de-esser and all this great cutting gear that hadn't existed yet. It was called Sterling Sound, and when we opened Sterling, I was their first employee there.

They used the Telefunken M10A tape machine, which, unlike the Scully and the Ampex machines at the time, had motion sensing on the reel, so the thing was actually on speed from beginning to end of the reel. Before motion sensing on the reels, all the Ampex and Scullys would start slightly up in pitch or go faster, then be correct for most of it and run slow at the end. And we'd always spin a couple of minutes onto the tape so it would be a more consistent speed.

Bell Sound was also mastering, and there was Dick Charles Recording—they also had a lathe. And Gotham Recording, as opposed to Gotham Audio, had a lathe; in fact, the cutting engineer at Gotham Recording was using a non-computer AM 32-b. The person mastering at that facility was named Walter Carlos, who became Wendy later on, so I knew Wendy when she was a Walter.

But anyway, when Sterling opened up, Lee Hulko started it with his partner Joe Paschek. I believe they were the first corporation anywhere in the world to be incorporated as an independent mastering facility. Doug Sax started The Mastering Lab out in California quite shortly after that. And it's conceivable that Doug might have opened up before Sterling, but I don't think so. So anyway, they were the first company to really be incorporated as an independent cutting room in 68.

And having this lathe with this cutter head and the solid-state cutting amps, there was a period of about half a year or more where at Sterling we could cut a record that nobody else could cut. Maybe Doug had that same head in California, but there was a period of time when we had an advantage over every other studio in New York, where we could cut more high-frequency stuff than they could, and it was like that short period of time when America only had the atomic bomb, and nobody else did. Everybody felt safe for half a year until Russia had it, too. I was at Sterling Sound for seven years. I became vice president there; it was good.

Horst Redlich in Berlin invented a thing called the tracing simulator. This was a piece of gear that, basically, when you're cutting a disc, you're cutting with a chisel-shaped device and playing it back with a spherical-shaped device. Especially back then, before they invented the elliptical stylus...and because of that, the geometry could never meld exactly perfectly. So he invented this box that created a certain amount of harmonic distortion that pre-distorted the signal and corrected for this anomaly in the geometry. And you could do tests. There were tone generators on the thing—you'd listen to the playback, and you could hear the distortion getting less when you put it through this tracing simulator.

Its usefulness turned out to be fairly short-lived in that the elliptical stylus was invented, which more closely represented the chisel that you cut with and consequently wore out records quicker, which they did. But then they made cartridges lighter, so it didn't wear out quite as fast...back and forth, back and forth, back and forth.... Typical analog thing, where everything you touch changes the sound. So then we started recalibrating for elliptical styli, which meant you were putting just a smidgen of stuff into it. Pretty soon, for most stuff it didn't matter in the real world if you used it or not, once everybody started using elliptical styli.

We used a compressor made by EMT, the same people that did the chamber. And that had an analog computer in it as well. I remember the hype was that it divided the signal up and looked at all the little parts of it. It's been a while since I thought about that, actually. But it was the EMT limiter, and so for a long time that was used on all the big rock records. Early on at Sterling, I cut the Led Zeppelin IJ and Houses of the Holy records with Eddie Kramer and Jimi Hendrix's The Cry of Love and a bunch of other records after he passed away.

When producers would work at Columbia and would want to work at Sterling, the union people bitched and wouldn't allow them to do that. And so the IBEW came up with this thing: if you need to use an independent studio, you can, but the engineer from Columbia has to come and do it there, just like they did with recording studios. And as far as I know, I was the first person to break that or to have anyone go outside Columbia. My friend Paul Rothchild, who did all the Doors stuff, had just produced Janis Joplin's record with "Me and Bobby McGee," so I cut her single at Sterling, and the union guy comes over—this guy named Ben Ernholt, cigar-smoking guy—and he says, "I was supposed to cut this on the lathe." And, well, this is a Neumann lathe. Scully lathes and heads are just fine; no issue with Scully, but at the time we felt the Neumann was better. Anyway, I said, "Ben, this cutter head is like $3,000." And this is like 1968. "Are you going to be responsible for that if anything goes wrong?" He said, "No, I ain't gonna touch that." So I'd cut, and he would sit there in the lounge, and he would scribe the records at the end, but he was getting paid to be there. And he was really—God bless him—he was one of these really union guys, like he could tell me how many years, months, and days he had until his retirement. He was just counting down.

So that was fun, and then, after that single all the producers at Columbia wanted to use us or Doug, or Artisan had opened up in California by then. And it was Artisan and Doug with main the facilities out there, besides the Capitol union guys.

Sterling was bought by a public company called OCG Technology, which made computerized EKG machines; it was a medical company. And I never was privy to why they decided to buy Sterling; I don't know why. But Lee and Joe, who owned Sterling, wanted to sell it. And so they sold it to this public company, and then a little while later this OCG Technology bought Mercury Records' cutting facility at 110 W. 57th Street. Sterling at that time was also at 110 W. 57th Street, on the top floor, and the Mercury facility, with chief engineer John Eargle, was on the fifth floor. And then they also had a big recording studio in that building. And so OCG bought that and named it Masterdisk. So, OCG Technology owned both Sterling Sound and Masterdisk at the same time. And then John Eargle, when it was bought by OCG, left and went to JBL at that time.

So Lee and Joe were upset with the way the public company was dealing with Sterling and how they were managing it, so they decided they were going to buy it back from them, so they did. And they got, in my opinion, very paranoid, and they asked me and George Marino, who had come on by then, to sign this employment agreement that gave us no ownership, no nothing, no increase in salary, nothing, but if we quit or were fired, we couldn't work within like 500 miles of New York for five years. Something that would be blatantly illegal now, right?

I thought, "Oh my god, these guys have really lost their minds." So I started looking around. And the guys at Masterdisk said, "Well, you know, you've been working for us. Why don't you just work here?" So I did. And so I moved over to Masterdisk, and when I was there we tried a couple of different things. My first monitoring system there was a Mark Levinson HQD system. The HQD thing was as hi-fi a speaker as anybody had made at that point. It was the very revered quad electrostatic speaker that was used in all the classical rooms by Deutsche Grammophon. Philips used them, and they're very well regarded, but they didn't have low bass extension. So, Mark built this thing with a quad electrostatic on this top part of the frame and another one on the bottom part of the frame. So it had a lot more output, and then in the space between them, he put a Decca ribbon tweeter, which is a gorgeous tweeter, and he designed this great analog crossover. The only specification of it that I remember was that the tweeter part of it had a slew rate of 400 volts per microsecond, which even today is pretty damn fast for a piece of gear. So, we used that, and I liked it a lot, actually. Oh, and this thing crossed over into a 24-inch Hartley subwoofer that I heard either our government or the French or somebody bought a lot of them and did all these really low-frequency experiments to kill people. To see how the body responded to loud, low frequency.

Anyway, I really liked it a lot. And we used an Ortofon head, which had just come out, and so we were experimenting with that because that was supposed to be very smooth and hi-fi. And it was, but it didn't have the same level that the Neumann head did. So after a trial period with that, we went back to the Neumann head, and then, while I loved this HQD system, clients had a hard time relating to it because it was just too hi-fi and didn't have a barking midrange like the 604Es had. And I might add even when I was at A&R, in addition to the 604Es that everyone used back then—and certainly the last time there was pretty much a gold-standard monitor speaker—I brought in home speakers. I brought these Altec Boleros into the cutting room, and we also used Auratones…or it could have been Colbert back then, which preceded the Auratone.

So at Masterdisk, they built a much bigger room for me, and I switched over, I think, to Altec A 19s, but with a ribbon tweeter on it and a subwoofer. I had the Hartley subwoofer, the Altec A 19, so now I had barking midrange again, although I had it dialed down as much as possible. It was a sound producers could relate to, so it did really well.

I was at Masterdisk until I started Gateway, which was incorporated in 1992. And we opened our doors in January of '93. And it feels like yesterday in some regards. Masterdisk moved from that Mercury facility at 110 W. 57th Street to 16 W. 61st Street, which was across from the American Bible Society, and if you went out to our back fire escape, you could look across it to Atlantic Records' fire escape. And so we were in that facility for quite a while, cut a lot of hit records there. And then Masterdisk finally moved to their present location on West 45th Street.

I cut the very first CD that was published in America, which was Bruce Springsteen's Born in the USA. If you go to DADC in Terre Haute, Indiana, there's a little kiosk or a little monument out front that's got Bruce's Born in the USA on it. It's the first commercially pressed CD in America. And in fact, I just sent a copy of it to the Grammy Museum out in Los Angeles—one of those first pressings is going to be on display there. And the CD I did before that was the one that really helped establish the CD format, which was Dire Straits' Brothers in Arms. That was the first CD I ever mastered that was mastered completely with the CD in mind. And the vinyl disc cut that we did of it came second.

So it was definitely a change, because up until that point, CDs were such a minuscule part of the sales; we'd master everything for vinyl because record companies, just like now, didn't have the budget to do multi-formats. And because it'd be very close in sound, they would make the CD masters from the vinyl. But a good vinyl cut generally has got brighter equalization as it gets toward the center of the groove, so all these things would have a range of acceptability. They would tend to be on the bright side until they got to what was, say, like cut five on a ten-cut record. And then cut six on the CD would go back to the EQ that was used for cut one of the CD. Thus, another reason why the remasterings of old CDs can sound quite a bit better… But anyway, Brothers in Arms…they knew it was going to be a big record, and they wanted it, but it was also one of the first times that the CD was longer than the vinyl cut. I think the CD was an hour or 59 minutes something on that—more than you could put on a single disc. And the version we did on the disc was edited, so that became a really big-selling CD and really pushed the format and actually sold a lot of CD players to help get the format established. So I was very proud of both of those records.

When people speak about the early digital age, they talk about how horrible everything sounded, but ironically, that wasn't really true in my case, because CDs came out in 1982. But as early as 1978, I cut my first vinyl from a digital source for Telarc.

It was a Soundstream system. And then after that we did Donald Fagen's The Nightfly. The first digital systems I ever worked with were the Soundstream and then the 3M digital machine, both of which are fine-sounding digital machines—seemed great to us back then. And then, say you'd cut a vinyl disc—in the upper corner of it, there'd be a little banner that said "digital" on it. So at first with digital, we knew that there was no gear for it—there was nothing in the digital domain at first. Everything had to go in the analog domain to do anything. So we had to be very respectful of running out of bits, going into the overs…because as you know, when you go into the over, it distorts immediately.

We'd use analog compressors, but that would only do a certain amount compared to these look-ahead digital compressors that are out now. So the average level was way lower, because the digital was considered a device for capturing the existing dynamic range, not as a technology you could use to crush the dynamic range. But we would only be cutting vinyl, and then in the case of the 3M, like when Roger Nichols would come in with Gary Katz and Donald and Walter, we'd record back onto the 3M machine. We would make equalized cutting copies that were done on that machine just for safety's sake. But what ended up going to the pressing was a vinyl cut, and we would make a 15 IPS usually Dolby A cutting master for the cassette. And that was standard operating procedure for a long time, and so these cassette cutting masters were what the record companies then used for CD reissues for a long time.

At some point, I was working on one of Bruce's records—I think it was Tunnel of Love—by then Sony had the 3324, 24-track digital. It was still only 16-bit. Yeah, and I remember when we first started working with digital, they hadn't standardized sample rates yet. And the 3M machine was 50 kilohertz, I think, originally. And then the Mitsubishi was 50.4, and they finally standardized that. I remember the first piece of digital gear besides the Delta delay line—that Delta delay line was the first piece of professional digital gear, around '76.

So, the first piece of dedicated digital gear that wasn't recording was something Sony made that had an equalizer and a level control. They had loaned it to Bruce's recording team to try out, and I remember thinking, "Oh boy, good. We can start working in the digital domain and not have to go into the A to D and then the D to A."

Sony made the PCM-1600 and then shortly thereafter the 1610. With the 1600, they used a video editor, which means you could only edit to a thirtieth of a frame, which was not very satisfactory. But then, by the 1610, they had their first digital editor that worked. Although everything is still 16-bit, and the fades were just god-awful on it. You'd get to –50 or –60 dB, and the distortion was just horrendous because of not having any internal bit structure to work with. But it could make good edits.

So for the compact disc, we ultimately had to record through the 1610, which had these off-the-drawing-board, industrial-design A-to-D converters. And because the CD had taken off, all the research and development was in the digital-to-analog converters. And there was still very little research being done on the A-to-D part of it. So the A-to-D converters that were on the Sony 1600 and the 1610 were just not very good. But that was all they had at the time, so that's what we used. They were so bad that it was common practice on some really great-sounding digital records that were done, like the Rush Moving Pictures record—they were done monitoring through the Sony A to D and D to A. You'd monitor through the whole chain and mix through it like that, so that if it needed more reverb because of the crappy digital, you'd put more reverb and it would come out good, right? It was bad enough so you'd listen to the entire chain almost like it was the Dolby.

So that Rush record sounded great, and I've remastered that record two or three times in my career. And every time I'd put that 1600 tape up, and it has emphasis on it and everything—it sounds great; it really sounds great. So if you were a good engineer and knew the limitations of your gear, it's the same old story; you can still make a great sounding record.

So anyway, Sony made this equalizer, and it was one of these things where I was so excited, and I put it in the chain, and I listened to the midrange and thought, "Hmm... that's not that great." And then I put a couple of steps at 10k, and I was like, "Eww." It was so bad; the only thing that sounded good was Off. So I said, "Aw, no thank you. Let us know," but they were still in—there was always this need to have to work in the digital domain.

So Neve had come out with the first digital recording console. I think it was called CTS, and London had it, and the BBC had some. And WDR in Germany had it. And this was a viable console, although it kept breaking down, apparently. I remember CTS finally had to give it up. But I remember when they were working, the engineers seemed pretty happy with it. Although maybe it was 20 bit...I don't know.

So Masterdisk, Sterling Sound, and a company in Nashville—the three of us commissioned Neve to build a digital domain mastering console, the DTS-1. And I remember it was like $136,000 or something, and the terms that they gave us were two-thirds up front. And you have to wait a year. Yeah. But we wanted it, and nobody else seemed to be interested in it, and we thought if anybody could make something that sounded at least decent, it would be Neve.

But after they said, "Well, don't worry, we won't sell any. You guys will have the exclusive on it for six months" or something, and of course when the three of us finally got it, they sold the next one as fast as they could to the next person. That was Steve Marcussen at Precision Lacquer; he ordered one and got it right away.

But it was viable, and the compressor was good—you could make a hit record on that thing, and I mastered a lot of records in the digital domain on that. Daniel Weiss, who worked with Harmonia Mundi Acustica—Daniel used to work for Studer—and Roger Lagadec at Studer invented the first sample rate converter that was usable. And they also invented some other piece of gear, but anyway, Roger ended up working for Sony. And Daniel started his own engineering company—Daniel Weiss Engineering. But he also worked with this company called Harmonia Mundi, and they made the software called the Penguin. And when I was at Masterdisk, we had the very first CD-R writer in the Western Hemisphere. So I was one of the people that made one of the very first CD-Rs ever.

Philips commissioned it because there were CD interactives as another subset of the CD Red Book format, and in order to make a CD interactive, every time they needed to try it, they'd have to go and plate it and press it and make a small round just to see if the thing worked. And it became a drag very quickly, so they commissioned Yamaha to make a CD-R writer. And then, Yamaha did, but it was for ROMs, for CD interactive. And then Russ Hamm at Gotham Audio—who had bought it from Steve Temmer by then—Russ Hamm is still involved with Internet connection stuff in New York now.

He's a very bright guy, and he also worked at Gotham Recording. And he also recorded the Shags. Do you know that group, the Shags? That was in Revere, Massachusetts. My head's filled with all this weird stuff.

He talked to this company, Meridian, or someone in America that was using this: "Look, you've got to be able to make an audio CD out of this." And they said, "No, no," and so he hired Daniel Weiss and the guy who actually wrote the software for Harmonia Mundi to make this thing called the Penguin. And it worked with the Sony 1610 by then. And it was close to, I think, $90,000, because you had to have a BVU-800 for the video deck. You needed a 1610 for the digital part, you needed a Sony preview for the lathe, and you needed the Yamaha CD-R writer, which was in two large boxes. One was the actual CD-R writer, and the other entire box contained the 8–14 modulator, before they made a VLSI chip with it.

So then they had this computer. Personal computers had just come out—those were out by the late *70s, maybe 1980? They were Compaqs. Anyway, so you'd put this Penguin software on it, and the thing would automatically run the 1610 and cut the discs. It actually made very good-sounding CDs, by the way. And so that was the first CD-R, and the blanks, which were invented by Taiyo Yuden—the blanks were $80 apiece, and you'd typically blow a couple early on. So I remember the first CD-R references Masterdisk sold were in the $250 or $300 range per disc, and people bought them all the time. Because it was digital. And you could listen on your brand-new CD player. And compare apples to apples.

So that was quite something. We never had that at Gateway, though. We had the Penguin software, but we didn't have the Yamaha writer, because Sonic Solutions finally came out with the world's first workstation—the SoundDroid. It came out of the Droid Works, which Lucasfilm had commissioned. And the initial reason he commissioned it was to do noise reduction on old movies. So Sonic, as you know, were the people that invented NoNOISE, and the engineering team and the executives all came out of Droid Works when Lucasfilm lost interest in that. So at Masterdisk we had the very first Sonic Solutions workstation in New York City.

So we were able to do NoNOISE right away, so that was really cool. But then the other thing was Sony came out with the 9000 writer, the CD-R writer. When that first came out, those cost only $3,000 apiece. I forgot—that Yamaha writer was $25,000. I mean, they weren't $300 a ref for nothing. Yeah, I'd have to advertise it. It's like, now we have probably hundreds of thousands of IT stuff in our studio, and some people wonder why we charge for a digital download. Oh, we should just not advertise our system. The connection alone costs us probably $20,000 a year or more.

Anything I have now that I wish I'd had then? Oh my god! Everything! We're always looking for something better. And with mastering, if you're going to try to be the best mastering engineer you can be in the best facility, that means you've got to have the very best gear that's out there. There's no question about it, because in mastering, just like the doctor, the first rule is, "First do no harm." And if you think about it, in mastering, because you're re-recording something, even though the tradeoff 99.999 percent of the time is way worth it, nevertheless you are adding distortion and noise to the master recording. Always hard; there's no way of getting around that. So, naturally I'm happy when I have the gear that does the least damage and sounds the best.

The A80 Studer was the best machine used for cutting because of the preview head on it. They had the preview system worked out really well. Ampex made a preview system for the ATR, but it was kind of kludgy. It didn't have a very good reputation, to the point where Ampex made a product where they had a digital delay line, and they had that when Ampex introduced the 1/2-inch 30 IPS machine, which, by the way, was preceded by years and years by Connoisseurs Society, who had a custom-made 1/2-inch head made. Connoisseurs Society used to record at 30 IPS 1/2-inch and then cut discs at 45 RPM—12-inch discs at 45 RPM; they're very audiophile.

But anyway, I remember ATR came out with a 1/2-inch machine and suggested using this digital delay line. So here I'm using this 16-bit digital delay on a machine that sounds really good. And of course it's the delayed signal that goes to the cutter head, so hardly anybody with ears bought that system. Anyway, we used the Studer delay line with it. Studer A80 had Mark I, Mark II, Mark III, and Mark IV grade amplifiers on them, but the Mark I was pretty bad sounding. It had these really bad-sounding transformers, and the II had a better transformer, and the III might have had a Jensen transformer or something. And then they finally went through a transformer-less electronics with Mark IV. But nevertheless, I think they're all still Class AB amps in there.

So there's a certain Studer sound, whereas the ATR was discrete Class A electronics and sounded better. So I ended up going over to Ampex machines, and at Gateway we have many different kinds of analog machines to choose from. We have a stock ATR 102; we have an ATR 102 that has tube electronics in it; we have an ATR that has the Esoteric Audio Research tube electronics that Tim de Paravicini makes, which are marvelous sounding tube electronics; then, we have Mike Spitz's and Dave Hill's Crane Song Aria with the tube electronics. We have those, and we also have the Studer A820 machine. And some engineers, like Michael Brauer, like to record on the A820 and consider that part of their sound, so we always have to use that machine when we're doing projects for him, like the Coldplay record we just did.

And then the stock ATR also has an unbalanced output that avoids a lot of the electronics on it. So we've got one, two, three, four, five, six different ways of playing back analog tape at our place, and they all sound different; they all have their own sound. And I know in my head what they all sound like, so if something comes in on analog, I'll immediately think, "Oh, I'm sure it will sound better on these electronics." And I try that, and normally I'm pretty right. The one funny thing that happens is when we're comparing, we have a 1-inch machine, too—1-inch stereo—and that machine has two playback heads on it, one for the Esoteric Audio Research and also the Aria. We can AB back and forth between the two of them very easily. And almost without question, the client, without exception, will say, "Well, 'd like the midrange and top of the Solid State with the bass of the tube." Sure, not yet, we can't do that. Although Roger Nichols...I'm not sure what the whole story is with this Roger Nichols software right now. Because I know he's divorced from them, but that company came out with this linear phase thing they can divide up into the lows, mids, and highs, so maybe we could record the output of both electronics simultaneously using that. Oh my god.

I've got 13 Tech awards, and the studio's got 9 or 10 of them, and so we get all these awards for it. But I've always said—and I still agree with what I said years ago—that it's very difficult to give a mastering engineer an award for something. Because, suppose you listen to a year's worth or a career's worth of stuff, and every time you pick up a record that you like, it's got the same names on it. You could probably safely say, "That guy probably knows what he's doing." But as far as any individual project receiving an award like the way it is now for the Tech awards instead of the way it was—submitting a year's worth of work, and then you would compete on all the mastering engineers' year's worth of work—it's a horrible thing, in my opinion, that they went to the Grammy system, where an artist wins, and then whoever that recording team is wins the Tech award. And maybe I did nothing. Maybe it was one of those rare tapes like Geoff Emerick did the Elvis Costello All This Useless Beauty record. It was so perfectly engineered; all I could do is stay out of its way and just transfer it as good as I could transfer it, and it was perfect. Whereas nowadays, the average tape that comes in to us sounds the worst it's ever sounded in my whole career, because everybody has no budget and is recording with their friends in the basement. So there are more records that need to be bailed out nowadays than ever before.

And the good thing is a good mastering engineer can take something that sounds like dog meat and at least make it sound normal. So what we do could sometimes sound like we've added hundreds of thousands of dollars to their budget as far as sound quality goes. The records sound much better than they would've sounded. It's very difficult to know what the mastering engineer did—for instance, the latest Metallica record was mixed that way. In a case like that, it really isn't the mastering engineer's fault that it sounds distorted. It's what the producer and the group, I might add, wanted. And Lars is aware of all this controversy, and he's going on the website saying, "No, I just like it. And that's the way we want it, and shut up, guys."

And then, the other thing is: first, do no harm. And you can't know what the mastering engineer really contributes unless you've heard the master tape. Then you can tell.

We just had a major triumph. A major, major triumph. The new Guns N' Roses record—Caram Costanzo and Axl mixed it. There are some tracks that must have had hundreds of tracks of stuff on it, and they wanted to be able to hear all the layering and everything. And as soon as you put too much compression on it, it just flattens out. This record is mastered like a 1980s CD. You have to turn your playback line up in order to enjoy this record at a loud level. Its average level is quiet. It's quieter than anything I've done probably in 15 years.

And believe me, they spent some ungodly amount of money on this record. They spent eight and a half years in the making, and to have the fortitude to put it out on the market without it being loud is pretty amazing. And over the air it sounds as loud as the things around it because the radio stations are all in competition with each other. It will not sound loud on an iPod Shuffle compared to other things or on the iTunes store. So, there you go. It's an amazing-sounding record.

Chapter 6

Leanne Ungar

Leanne Ungar began her studio career working at Sound Ideas in New York, where she assisted on sessions with James Brown, Leonard Cohen, The Brecker Brothers, and Manhattan Transfer. After working at Le Studio, Canada, in 1975, Leanne returned to New York and joined the staff at A&R Recording, working on sessions with Cat Stevens, Loudon Wainwright, and Janis Ian.

Ungar's independent recording career began when she worked with the avant-garde artist, Laurie Anderson on Big Science, Mister Heartbreak, and a concert film, Home of the Brave. Her client list grew to include Temptations, Fishbone, Holly Cole, Joe Henderson, Adam Cohen, Guster, Joy Askew, Carlene Carter, Willie Nelson, Big Mountain, 3T, Billy Joel, Luther Vandross, Natalie Cole, Vonda Shepard, Aaron Neville, Tom Jones, Leata Galloway, David Van Tieghem, The Paul Winter Consort, Peter Criss, The Roches, Kate, and Anna McGarrigle. She has worked on various film scores with Mason Daring (Matewan, Passion Fish) and Cliff Martinez (Pump Up the Volume, Kafka, The Underneath, The Limey), to name a few.

In 1984, Ungar started working again with Leonard Cohen on Various Positions then I'm Your Man in 1987, The Future in 1993, and Cohen Live in 1994. Ungar is currently a professor in the Music Production and Engineering Department at Berklee College of Music.

I'm Leanne Ungar, and I was born in Western Massachusetts in 1952.

I started in audio in 1973 in New York City. I had moved to New York to be a dancer actually, and that lasted for about three months. Then I realized I wasn't quite that masochistic and didn't want to be that poor. So, I was looking around for something to do and I had friends who were musicians, and I happened to go into a studio with them one day and kind of fell in love. That's how it all began. And that studio was Richard Factor's studio, Eventide, and I had no idea that it was as cutting edge as it was. It was just a random studio, but it happened to be right in the middle of developing some of the first digital delay lines, and he was always a great mentor to me, very encouraging.

There was all kinds of experimental stuff that I had no idea was it was at the time, and he was always in the back room tinkering with it. He was inspirational, just with his enthusiasm for every aspect of engineering.

DOI: 10.4324/9781003519829-6

Figure 6.1 What I see happening is the business is shrinking and it's turning into a much more do it yourself process, and if that happens, I see a lot more women doing it because just like anybody else, they want to put their tracks down and they can't really afford to hire studios. They're using whatever they've got in their computer. And the whole shrinkage of the music business is leading to a kind of ironic democracy, putting the power in the hands of the people now…If I look at it from the point of view of the kind of great art that I thought I was making in the 70s and 80s it's not good because I don't think the sound is good and I have a real snobby, purist attitude about what I think good sound is. But I don't think that we can forget that sound is the servant of the music and music is the important thing. And there's a lot of music that doesn't sound good, but it still communicates incredibly effectively, and it doesn't necessarily have to sound good for it to be great music. Think of any Prince record. Photo by Javier Mas.

Figure 6.2 There was another engineer at A&R at the time named Don Hahn, I think he's on the West Coast now, and he was just an incredible engineer, and I watched him do a lot of sessions with large orchestras and big sweetening groups and he was just amazing. You would never catch him using any outboard or any EQ or anything, and it just always sounded incredible. I watched him intently trying to see what it was that he did that made him get that sound, and I really just think it's in the ears. You just have it in your brain to know that's right and everything else is wrong and you massage it gently until you get there. I've seen Al Schmidt do the same thing recently. He touched nothing, occasionally just angled the microphone an inch or two, it was amazing. Photo by Rafael Gayol.

Figure 6.3 I never really was a big fan of vinyl, and the reason for that was because you could never get a lot of level on the inner tracks of vinyl. I always felt like if you had a 33 1/3 rpm record, if you could just use the outer two or three cuts then it sounded really good, but the inner bands always sounded really crappy to me. After a few plays, the whole thing started to sound crappy. So I know that there's a romance with this age of vinyl, you know, a perfect stylus on the perfect record that has never been played before, yeah, it's sublime, but as a real delivery system for music that you may be getting addicted to and play it over and over and over again, you need a CD. Photo by Javier Mas.

Figure 6.4 ...the large studios, the beautiful control rooms, and all the attention that was put into the room, that people can't really afford to do anymore. To me, the listening space, the control room, where you're making your decisions, is a big, big component. If you don't know what you're hearing or you're not used to what you're hearing or you think you're hearing something different than what's really happening, it really throws you off. So people trying to work at home or trying to rent office space and set up a studio in it, it's just problem after problem in terms of just trying to get a good balance out of that. Photo by Javier Mas.

I never worked there. I only just went in the one time and kind of became friendly with him and realized that engineering was something that I could actually pursue. And what I did from there was take the Institute for Audio Research course, which was a ten week course at that time, all I could really find about engineering. And I was also working for

Figure 6.5 I remember working with Paul Winter, and we were recording at the Church of St. John The Divine up in Harlem, and so we set up in this massive cathedral and it came time to put the microphone on and he wouldn't let me put the microphone any closer than a yard, and I was like, "Paul, there's going to be no presence on you." And what we got was just the most amazing recording of the entire place with some close sections, but really a picture of the place, and that couldn't be faked. You couldn't take your convolution reverb for St. John The Divine and slap it on a close-miked sax and get that sound, it would never happen. Photo by Javier Mas.

an educational publisher, Harcourt Brace, and they had a department that did recordings for math lessons and things like that. So, they were actually the first people that taught me how to engineer, and after I'd done that for about a year and I'd taken my audio course, then I started putting in resumes at music studios.

The first music studio I worked for was Sound Ideas on 46th street. The chief engineer in there was a guy named Geoff Daking, and you might know the name Daking from the consoles that he made and the processors that he makes now. He was a very knowledgeable engineer and taught me a lot, and there was another guy at that studio named Rick Rowe, who had been a disciple of Eddie Kramer. I learned a lot of things from him as well.

They had an API console. That was in 75. Then, I left and I went to Le Studio at Morin Heights in Quebec. So, I worked up there for a year and they had the Trident A Range console up there, it was fabulous.

They were 24 tracks. When I first went to Sound Ideas, it was switching back and forth between 8 and 16 tracks. They did as many 8-track tapes as we did 16-track tapes. And then, late in my apprenticeship at Sound Ideas, they got a 24 track. And also the first noise reduction was coming in, and at the time they were experimenting with DBX. When I went up to the studio at Morin Heights, one of the first things I noticed was the difference between the Dolby that they had up there at Morin Heights and the DBX they had at Sound Ideas. And the Dolby was quite superior just in terms of high-end response.

They had all kinds of outboard gear in both places. In Sound Ideas, in addition to having all the API compressors and API EQs, which were fabulous, there were a lot of Pultecs, which were quite normal. You'd see them in every studio everywhere you went: Urei processing, LA2s, LA3s, 1176s. There were EMT plates, the normal go-to reverbs, and you would generally have a couple of the 140 plates.

Then, I came back to the states and ended up at A&R recording. I was there a couple years, and I went freelance after that. Phil was still engineering during the time when

I was there. He did Billy Joel's "The Stranger," did the movie Hair, the movie A Star Is Born with Barbra Streisand. He was in and out of there all the time; also, Elliot Scheiner was still working there all the time, and I watched Elliot do some of the mixing for Aja.

A&R was just transitioning from some homemade boards that they had there, I think they were called Suburban Sounds, to Neve. So, during the two years that I was there I watched them change out the consoles one by one, and I was a big fan of the Neve, I liked them a lot. Also around that time, they were just starting to sync two multi-tracks together with SMPTE, and the head of their maintenance department was an incredible genius named Dave Smith, who passed away recently, but kind of got Phil going with all the stuff like syncing multi-track machines together. He was a very bright guy, went on to work at Sony Classical for many, many years.

They had all kinds of fabulous outboard gear. I remember seeing maybe a pair of Fairchilds, and I don't remember seeing quite so many, but certainly never want for either microphones or outboard gear. A&R had lots of stuff.

I don't remember people using outboard preamps as much during that period of time, but then the boards that I was working on, API, the Trident, or the Neve, all had fabulous mic pre's so you wouldn't necessarily think about avoiding the board. When I would freelance and started working in lesser studios, then sometimes I would think about what I could do to get around some of the gear. I remember working, for instance, on Laurie Anderson's first album, and that was cut in her loft. She had a Soundcraft board, which are nice boards for monitoring, but we didn't want to put the sound through that board necessarily. Now what I'm asking myself what mic pre I used for that? It's almost 30 years ago. I just can't believe it was that long ago.

I know that we were using an 8 track, I know that on the second album we rented an MCI tape machine. It wasn't Sony yet, and we had it in the loft. Every session with Laurie was fantastically interesting… very interesting person. I had a great time working with her. She was a real hard worker, long, incredible days. And then we mixed Big Science at the Hit Factory.

I was freelance in 1977. I had a couple of records in the pipeline and I had just come through a horrible negotiation with one of the business people at A&R where a client of mine wanted to produce a Loudon Wainwright album, and I was dying to do it, and Loudon's manager and his manager couldn't quite agree on a studio price and I think they got within $5 an hour of each other, and they ended up taking the record someplace else. It just hit me all of a sudden that the studio's priorities had nothing to do with my priorities. So we parted ways after that.

I think the idea of freelance was starting to appeal to everybody, and I'm sure I watched Elliot do it; of course, Elliot was a much more established engineer and had a lot of clients all over the place, and he was spending half his time in Los Angeles anyway. So it didn't really make much sense for him to stay at one studio, but the way the studios were structured at the time, you were paid a salary and your salary was kind of based on how much billing you were doing, but it wasn't like you were getting paid X number of dollars per hour based on your sessions, you were just making a salary so you could make a lot more money even as a low paid freelancer, which is how I started.

Going around town to different studios, I did always look for a Neve console because I just felt that with my style of mixing it kind of gave me the warm, colored, curve that I liked. Although I have to say that the times that I did use other consoles, specifically SSL which I kind of avoided, but when I did use them I found that the sound was quite nice.

So it's more of a prejudice and more of being able to point it my way. I would say that in terms of picking that kind of gear, consoles and mic pre's, we're quibbling over the top maybe 2 or 3 percent of the details of the sound. Any good mic in any good audio chain is going to get you a good enough recording, but we had the luxury of kind of refining it beyond that.

I always liked to see 1176s. I always liked to see Pultecs. I guess the style of music or the style of recording I do, I don't use a ton of processing. So it's more about mic selection and mic placement.

There was another engineer at A&R at the time named Don Hahn, I think he's on the West Coast now, and he was just an incredible engineer, and I watched him do a lot of sessions with large orchestras and big sweetening groups, and he was just amazing. You would never catch him using any outboard or any EQ or anything, and it just always sounded incredible. I watched him intently trying to see what it was that he did that made him get that sound, and I really just think it's in the ears. You just have it in your brain to know that's right and everything else is wrong, and you massage it gently until you get there. I've seen Al Schmidt do the same thing recently. He touched nothing, occasionally just angled the microphone an inch or two, it was amazing.

Now almost everything is outboard. There may be a console that you don't want to use so you're using a lot of outboard mic pres. You don't want to necessarily use the digital compression so you're looking for analog compression. With the digital EQ, it sounds good, but sometimes what you want is something less clinical and more colored. And I tell my students now, have the philosophy that the analog gear makes things sound more different, it points things in different directions than the digital stuff does.

When things started going digital, when I was doing analog projects and digital projects, I was trying to analyze what the difference was between analog and digital. I always tried to not take a negative view of digital, I'm not a digital hater, and I said to myself, "Well, I'm going to be able to make it sound good either in the analog domain or the digital domain or some kind of hybrid." To me, recording analog was always a process of chasing highs. You'd put something down on analog tape and the transients would soften, and you'd put it through a couple of pieces of gear and the initial sparkly presence would often be receding, and you would be chasing that; you would be taking low midrange out of things and scooping mud out of things. Whereas recording in digital, you're chasing warmth, things are sounding kind of bright and crunchy and you're looking for ways to warm things up.

To get that warmth use a really good signal chain before you go into digital, and try to touch it as little as possible once you're in the digital domain, so you're really thinking hard about what your final outcome is going to be so you have the sound that you want to have before you commit to digital. And also choosing reverbs carefully because the sense of spaciousness and depth kind of goes away in digital, so you have to be very careful of hording that, having as much as you really want. I think that's why the current trend for sound is kind of dry and crunchy and in your face. Cause all the people that have done digital recording… just find it that way, it's hard to get that kind of depth and spaciousness in digital recording.

If I have a nice console in a big studio where I'm really used to the control room, I would tend to use what's on the board. It'll probably be a Neve board, I'll probably be happy with the signal chain, and I won't go searching so much. If I'm in somebody's Pro

Tools studio, I'll be looking around to see what kind of mic pre's I could bring and what kind of analog processing.

I never really was a big fan of vinyl, and the reason for that was because you could never get a lot of level on the inner tracks of vinyl. I always felt like if you had a 33 1/3 rpm record, if you could just use the outer 2 or 3 cuts then it sounded really good, but the inner bands always sounded really crappy to me. After a few plays, the whole thing started to sound crappy. So I know that there's a romance with this age of vinyl, you know, a perfect stylus on the perfect record that has never been played before, yeah, it's sublime, but as a real delivery system for music that you may be getting addicted to and play it over and over and over again, you need a CD.

People get very nostalgic for that crackling and they want to put in on records. People want things to feel old-timey. I've used some of those tape simulators as well. Sometimes I find myself reaching for that when something's too pointy, and it needs to be blurrier sounding. I think analog tape as an outboard device is really, really valuable right now.

At Berklee we've had to take analog recording completely out of the curriculum in terms of requiring every student to learn how to do it, which we did up until about a year and a half ago. And when they did do their analog recording, watching their faces when they'd hear their mixes getting played back was really, really fun because they really did hear how good it could sound when they would print a mix and then play it back. But since we've taken it out of the general program, we've started it as an elective. We have an analog tape elective, making tape, and it's filled up instantly. I'm happy to see that there's still a lot of interest among the students.

I have a lot of equipment left and I don't own a studio. So I'm always lusting after things. With digital, just the amount of processing that you're able to put on everything is a different way of working. I can remember planning a mix back in the analog days and kind of deploying outboard gear; well if I want to use this for that and I'm going to use this for that, then I have to find some other piece of gear to cover whatever, and now you can just kind of keep piling on the processors, so kind of an interesting difference.

What I had then that I wish you had now? That would fall under the category of the physical space, the large studios, the beautiful control rooms, and all the attention that was put into the room, that people can't really afford to do anymore. To me, the listening space, the control room, where you're making your decisions, is a big, big component. If you don't know what you're hearing or you're not used to what you're hearing or you think you're hearing something different than what's really happening, it really throws you off. So people trying to work at home or trying to rent office space and set up a studio in it, it's just problem after problem in terms of just trying to get a good balance out of that.

One thing that I always thought would change, but didn't change, was the number of females in the business. I really seriously thought in the early 70s the fact that there weren't a lot of women engineers was just part of some kind of old sexist regime that was over, and kind of waking up and looking around in 2009 and seeing that it's just about the same...

I guess there's the culture doesn't change as fast as we thought it would. To me it seems a wonderful job for a woman to do, and I guess there's still a perception that it's too technical or not feminine, I don't know. Then again, I think there are people in the music business who use it as a boy's club. You can go back to the origin of any rock n roll band and see that band of brothers thing going on, but that's not always the case, so I would've thought that whereas some people might not want to hang home and around, others would, and that different energy for different situations would prevail.

I don't think girls are really steered in school, but I think girls are steered in the culture, and I don't think the culture is really instilled in school as much as just people talking, your parent's attitude, your friends' attitudes, what you see people doing in the media. It would be very hard for school to counteract that. I didn't like math very much when I was in school, and I found that when I had a use for it, when I wanted to learn engineering and I really wanted to understand how things worked, then suddenly those equations got fascinating, but not until then. I thought that was pretty interesting. I was kind of excited that there was actually a use for math in the real world. I thought my time had been wasted.

What I see happening is the business is shrinking, and it's turning into a much more do it yourself process, and if that happens, I see a lot more women doing it because just like anybody else, they want to put their tracks down, and they can't really afford to hire studios. They're using whatever they've got in their computer. And the whole shrinkage of the music business is leading to a kind of ironic democracy, putting the power in the hands of the people now.

If I look at it from the point of view of the kind of great art that I thought I was making in the 70s and 80s, it's not good because I don't think the sound is good and I have a real snobby, purist attitude about what I think good sound is. But I don't think that we can forget that sound is the servant of the music and music is the important thing. And there's a lot of music that doesn't sound good, but it still communicates incredibly effectively, and it doesn't necessarily have to sound good for it to be great music. Think of any Prince record.

The two pieces of gear that I've mentioned that I still have a lot of use for in the studio are the compressors I like, 1176 and LA2 compressors, tube EQ, like the Pultec, and I have to say that some of the other brands of knock-off EQ that are trying to do that thing to me don't really do it, and neither do the plug-ins. And I've spent a lot of time sitting with plug-ins and the actual piece of gear since I have the luxury of doing that, and I was proving to my students that they're totally different animals, but a plug-in 1176, I get some nice compression with it and if you need a compressor you certainly might want to reach for it, but don't think that you're getting that sound, that you're getting a real black faced 1176. They're just different.

The settings are doing exactly the same thing and I think that for those of us that grew up with analog gear, we take all these pictures for granted and we know what they represent, but to somebody who's coming into recording in this century, they don't know what any of those pictures represent. And they don't understand why I think it's freaky that there are no buses inside of Pro Tools, there's auxes, but the whole basis of a console used to be a combining network and when I suggested to my students that they combine microphones before they record, they don't understand it at all.

They get the idea and also to think about how much faster the mix goes when you're not making decisions later, you just to have fewer elements to worry about. So, maybe you're going to take three microphones that are going to make your snare sound, but decide on the snare sound and record it to one place, that's what it is.

There's nothing like being forced to live with it and also live with your mistakes to reinforce what you've done wrong and what you're going to do better next time. As far as that goes, recording school is a great place for making those kinds of mistakes.

One thing that is interesting is signal flow, patch bays, the efficiency of how you set up a session and where things go. If you're working in your project studio with Pro Tools and you have a bunch of outboard gear, how do you string it together? How do you know what your level is? There's all kinds of problems, even changing your mind and trying to look through the spaghetti to re-patch something. So the positive effect of the patch bay and having everything organized so you can quickly change from one piece of gear to another, it's really, really important, and something we take for granted.

The reason mic placement is a dying art is because there's only one kind of choice these days and that is close-miked because we don't have a beautiful, acoustic environment to try to balance in to what we're doing. So we don't dare get the microphones further away than say 6 inches, something like that. I remember working with Paul Winter, and we were recording at the Church of St. John The Divine up in Harlem, and so we set up in this massive cathedral, and it came time to put the microphone on, and he wouldn't let me put the microphone any closer than a yard, and I was like, "Paul, there's going to be no presence on you." And what we got was just the most amazing recording of the entire place with some close sections, but really a picture of the place, and that couldn't be faked. You couldn't take your convolution reverb for St. John The Divine and slap it on a close-miked sax and get that sound, it would never happen.

It's certainly true that people can still travel to a church and do their recording there if that's what they want to do, to be willing to go and search around with their microphone and find that sweet spot, and also have a place where they can listen to their recordings so they know what they're getting. Another thing about setting up in the church is that I would have to run from a long, long way away to actually come close to hearing the recording, because I needed to get away to hear it.

It also requires that you have a group of musicians who are used to playing together and playing songs from beginning to end. That's been a change of attitude that I don't really quite understand because it seems like the place where the business is monetized right now is in live music. So people are going out, and they're playing together live, but then when they're recording, they're not recording that way. They're recording one piece at a time in their bedrooms, and I just can't believe that they don't hear the difference.

Another thing that I find amazing among my kids, we were talking about how they don't really understand the pictures that they're looking at on Pro Tools. One of the things that they don't seem to hear, in music, or at least they don't hear it acutely the way I used to hear it, is feel. I think that growing up with sequenced music, with looped music, with a lot of rap and a lot of sequencey stuff, they don't hear the tension that comes from a live drummer and a live bass player and a live guitar player making that thing, locking into that thing that I find to be the essence of music. They don't hear when it's there, and they don't hear when it's gone.

I remain shocked. I think that in Berklee a lot of them are focused very much on their own chops to get into school, and when you're young and you're learning how to play, you're trying things and you're stretching yourself. I don't think they ever auditions ensemble, they have to play in ensemble, but I don't think ensemble playing is criteria for them to get into school. And then when they get in and they kind of disseminate through the school, the really, really good players focus on performance. They don't come into the recording department, and the one's that come into the recording department, some of them are very good players, but mostly they can play, and they're interested in something else. And it might be producing other people, it might be songwriting, it might be recording one's self or getting their own songs out, but none of it really focuses that much on the dynamic of the rock ensemble. Even the feel that goes on in the Jazz ensemble is different than what I'm talking about. Because we're dealing more with rock and pop and the popular radio genres in my department. The funny thing is that a lot of them do like that R&B stuff and the funk stuff, but I don't notice them concentrating on that one aspect, which to me is huge, and yet it seems to be dying away.

I just recorded some poetry for my sister, who's a writer, and she was speaking some of her poems, and so we went into a studio and I recorded this reading of her, and I recorded it at 24 bit 48k and I bounced it down for her to a CD so that she could carry it around and play it for people. And then I bounced it down to MP3 so that she could put it up on her website, and then I wanted to start recording all over again because everything I loved about the sounds in 48k was gradually vanishing as it got closer and closer to MP3, and it seemed to require a lot of different EQs and a different mic placement, and I think if I was recording only for MP3, I probably would've done it a little differently. So, interesting that it needs to be super bright and super compressed to sound good in that format, which is not something that I generally tend to want to do.

Most things are not going out only as MP3s, which is kind of a problem. So I guess what it needs for MP3 is its own separate mix. And at the same time that I wish the format would just go away. I'm as thrilled as anyone else that I can just stick the poem on an email and send it to her, I mean, it's fantastic. So I'm hoping that over time maybe we can solve some more of the technical barriers that are keeping us from sending more data so that we can have better sounding data that we can email around in that fashion. And I think it'll happen. I think that all the kinds of modeling programs for convolution reverb and mic modelers and digital compression and all this stuff is getting better and better. And I have no doubt that it will continue to get better to the point where we'll like it eventually. But I don't think that music is driving the culture right now, and I think that as long as that's happening, there's not going to be that huge infusion of money and energy the way there was in the 60s.

I think games and computers are driving the culture. But something I don't know very much about. How to make stuff sound the best that it can sound in a game. But a lot of my students are going into it for sure.

We don't have crystal balls. It's hard to say where it's going to go, but I think that some of the best of the analog stuff that we have is still going to be able to contribute in the future as long as we don't let it totally disappear.

Chapter 7

Jim Malloy

Jim Malloy's career spanned 36 years in music, television, and movie recording. With beginnings at California's Radio Recorders in 1956 (still using wax lathes to cut 78 rpm records), Malloy moved to Nashville and worked with an amazing list of performers and entertainment events. He recorded over 1,000 major albums including some of Elvis Presley's biggest hits. With six Grammy nominations, Jim worked with some of the biggest artists of all time, including Johnny Cash, Roy Orbison, Hank Williams Jr, Ike & Tina Turner, Willie Nelson, Waylon Jennings, Dolly Parton, George Jones, Jerry Lee Lewis, Jim Ed Brown, Charley Pride, The Statler Brothers, Homer & Jethro, Henry Mancini, Al Hirt, Louis Armstrong, Benny Goodman, Chet Atkins, Miles Davis, Floyd Cramer, Boots Randolph, Duke Ellington, Bruno Walter, Nelson Riddle, Duane Eddy, Neil Diamond, Gary Burton, Linda Ronstadt, Eddy Arnold, Doris Day, Frank Sinatra, Mahalia Jackson, Ray Stevens, Bing Crosby, Sammy Davis Jr, Paul Anka, Hugo Montenegro, Igor Stravinsky, Ricky Nelson, Dean Martin, The Carter Family, The Stoneman Family, Jack Benny, Perry Como, Anita Kerr, Bobby Gentry, Norman Luboff, Lefty Frizzell, Lightnin' Hopkins, Johnny Tillotson, Mitch Miller Singers, Billy Joe Walker Jr, Jack Clement, Billy Vaughn, Jake Hess, Tennessee Ernie Ford, Herbie Mann, and The Beach Boys.

Malloy was also one of the most successful music publishers in Nashville, signing writers like Ray Stevens, David Malloy, Richard "Spady" Brannan, Paul Overstreet, Thom Schuyler, Dan Tyler, Rick Polumbi, Steve Jones, Johnny Cymbol, Anthony Crawford, Karen Brooks, Bill & Kim Nash, Jeff Knight, John Smith, J. Gary Smith, Frank Meyers, Dolly Parton, Kris Krisstofferson, and Billy Joe Walker.

In 2005, Jim published his memoir, "PlayBack: A Collection of Stories and Musical Memories." He passed away in July, 2018.

My name is Jim Malloy, and I was born in Dixon, Illinois. Ronald Regan was born about four blocks from me, and we were both poor as hell. He was born about 19 years before me, and he already got a job at a radio station in Des Moines, Iowa. That was his first job. I started in audio by accident, actually. I got a job with NBC. I met the foreman and he hired me. And I was one of the people that put in the first two color sound stages in the United States. That's when General Sarnoff was still alive. In fact, I met him two or three

DOI: 10.4324/9781003519829-7

Figure 7.1 What I had was a bunch of friends. Al Schmidt and all of those people. Went out of their way to be sure I was good. They were great. I've always admired people like Alan Emmick and Al Schmidt and all of those people I used to know and work with.

Figure 7.2 I only ever used one compressor in my life and that was an LA2A. That's the only one I've ever used. All of the rest of them sounded like they were grabbing to me, and they just didn't sound right. Cowboy Jack Clement, one of my best friends, Jacks got a studio. Well he's a great guy, real good friend of mine. Jack's got a couple little compressors that are in one of the bays up there. I've turned all of those on and I didn't like the sound at all—sounded like they were grabbing. You know how on television, a lot of times the announcer will say "AND…this is so and so"… it's too late. That's the way these compressors that Jack had. So the cowboy, the way he is, went out and bought a couple of LA2A's. I don't do any sessions anymore for anybody, but Eddie Arnold was always a pretty good friend of mine because I got a lot of hits for him. The last thing in the world I want to do but anyway, Jack talked me into it and I talked Eddie into it and I'm damned glad I did. We talked him into doing one more album. He was 87 I think.

times doing this work. And we built those two studios, and then in doing that I was more interested in the audio than I was in the video part of it all. And, so afterward I went down to the IBM, everything was union out there, I went down to IBM headquarters, and asked if they had any kind of jobs that dealt with audio. And they sent me to the Radio Recorders. And so I become a tech for Radio Recorders because I had had 18 months of

Figure 7.3 Yeah it was real fun stuff. Especially when you had to get it all, and especially with a guy like Hank standing behind you, because Mancini really knew his stuff. And listened to every bit of it. He always called me the hillbilly engineer because I was from the Midwest. He'd say "well what do you think about it?" He was the A&R man; he'd say "What's the hillbilly engineer think about it?" He was always kind of digging me with all of that crap.

Figure 7.4 I did the LA Symphony for three years. I just did it in the summer time, something about the way they work. I did Wagner's Tannhäuser with 90 musicians and 65 singers. Did it on 3 track, all mixed live. We did all of Beethoven's symphonies with Bruno Walter. I did a lot of classical stuff.

electronics, circuitry, and everything. Of course, it was altogether different then than it is now, we had to deal with tubes and everything, whereas now it's different.

That was around the end of '55 and the beginning of '56. Radio Recorders was the biggest on the West Coast; they did everybody. They did one session with Colombia and then you do RCA. We had five studios and fifty engineers. And it was very competitive. The people that taught me, 'cause there was no schools, gotta remember that, and the guy that taught me was the head of Colombia Records. He had been an engineer. And he was a really good one. So he was gay, and of course, I was from the farm in the Midwest. I didn't even know what the hell "gay" meant. You know, I know it was dumb. But, that's the way it was.

Figure 7.5 I did the very first stereo record done in the United States. It was mastered in Germany. I got a call from a guy named Sid Frye from New York and said he's got some little label. He said, "I understand the Germans have just done a stereo record. I want to be the first one to do one in the United States." So, he booked Radio Recorders because it was about the most technical you could get, we had a guy that did nothing but build consoles, the interior, not the console itself, but the wood work and all that. It was amazing the amount of people we had, anyway he called about that and he told me he wanted to do a stereo album.

Figure 7.6 When I started it was all mono. They still had a 78 lathe in the control room in Studio B. It probably took 'em, several months to get it out of there. That place was really busy, that was a great school. That's what it was. The consoles were all handmade, in fact I built one of the consoles myself. The one that we used on remotes. It was a 12 in and 3 out. By that time, we had 3 tracks. And I had EQ. I only had three EQs, one for each track. And then the rest was just all for volumes. I did Benny Goodman with that console and Miles Davis. Oh a lot of them, a lot of those people, Lena Horne. All those were live shows.

But anyway, none of the maintenance people would go, fix the studio for him or anything? And I said, "Well, hell I don't care if he's gay or not, I'll go in there and do it." So, I did. And, in doing that why, he said, "Every time I book a Colombia, session in here", because he's the head of Colombia on the West Coast, he said, "I'm going to ask for you to stand by." And so I got to know him a little more and more and more, my wife and

I, and we used to go over to his house all the time. And so then, he started teaching me mixing. And that's where I did people like Percy Faith, Mahalia Jackson, all those kind of people. And he would stand over me, so I learned from a really good teacher to start. And then, of course, I ended up with Al Schmidt who is probably the best engineer in the world, or at least to me.

I only engineered for ten years. And I went into publishing, I still engineered a little bit, I didn't just quit altogether, but when they brought out all the [multi-track track stuff, I lost interest in it. I didn't care about it, about hearing all those tracks. I wanted to do it and get it done with, like I did Mancini and Frank Sinatra, and Dean Martin, and all those people, you know, we fit 30, 40, 50 people in the room. Everybody plays and everybody sings and it's done! So I just lost interest in it. The only real thing I ever did on a 16 track was Ray Stevens, we cut a monster hit with him. That was my introduction. It went 3 tracks, 4 tracks, 8 tracks, 16 tracks, 24 tracks. That's the way the machines ran.

When I started it was all mono. They still had a 78 lathe in the control room in Studio B. It probably took 'em, several months to get it out of there. That place was really busy, that was a great school. That's what it was. The consoles were all handmade; in fact, I built one of the consoles myself. The one that we used on remotes. It was a 12 in and 3 out. By that time, we had 3 tracks. And I had EQ. I only had three EQs, one for each track. And then the rest was just all for volumes. I did Benny Goodman with that console and Miles Davis. Oh a lot of them, a lot of those people, Lena Horne. All those were live shows.

In the studio, we had equalization in the consoles. When I left RCA, for example, we had 22 in and 3 out. And, I tell you what was interesting. When I did the Johnny Cash show, I had Wally Heider build me a console. And, it was 50 in and 1 out. That's what it took, and I did that whole show by myself. I had guys out in the studio to move mics for me and stuff, but as far as mixing it and everything, I did all of his episodes. Yeah, it was quite an adventure because the Ryman Auditorium was not made for recording.

It was made for live sound, except you know that I've had probably more compliments on that sound of that show than almost anything other than the albums I did. I had to take the room echo into consideration, and could I add any echo, could I not, all that stuff. It was quite a chore. It took a day and a half a week of my time to do that show. Because by that time I was an independent engineer. I just worked for whoever, whenever. In fact, I was the first independent engineer. I went independent; let's see, it would have been about '69. But that was when I was already in Nashville.

In LA, Chet Akins came out, and we needed a pair of singers. Did an album with him 'cause they wanted to use a bunch of strings and stuff. And Chet asked Duane Eddy, "Who should I use to do this?" Because he obviously needed to use RAC—back in those days, if you were on RCA you had to do RCA so on and so forth. I did a lot of independents besides RCA, but anyway, Duane Eddy said, "Use Jim Malloy," he said, "No two ways about that," he said, "You'll get what you want." So, anyway, Chet booked me, and I did it, of course, and every time we would get done, Chet would say, "Why don't you move to Nashville?" And he just kept it up the whole time, you know.

So anyway, Charlie Pizanski, the studio manager in Los Angeles, always kind of let me do as I pleased because everybody came to me. Some people book a year in advance. Like Paul Anka, Paul Anka had to book a year in advance. I was very busy out there, and when I came to Nashville, I did four, three, four, three, four every week—those are sessions. That's about as many as I could do. I did about a 1,000.

So when I came to Nashville, I did a lot of stuff in Studio B, but Chet wanted me to come down because he wanted to start doing some big stuff in Studio A. So that's why, as soon as they got that done, I didn't work too much in Studio B. I did Elvis in Studio B and different people like that, who liked Studio B, but people who had a different sound, big string sections and everything, we did all those kinds of things in Studio A.

I worked for Chet for five years, and then, after that I went independent; also, I became a producer. In the list of the 500 greatest hit records that the music business has ever had, look who's got the number one—"Jim Malloy-#1-Sammy Smith," "Make it through the Night," written by Kris Kristofferson of course. Kris is a real good friend of mine. Well, he used to write for me. When I was a producer and a publisher, I produced and published both for a long time. All the big names are on that list, but I'm the first in Los Angeles. It really pissed them off.

During my time in Studio A was when I started seeing some more changes. I think the best thing they ever made was the UA limiter, and the LA2A and Pultec. That's it, the two best things they ever did for this business. I used both of them, and I needed them. I used it in the voice, that's all. I never used it on anything but the voice. Nothing. Just very light. And I used it as a limiter, not as a compressor.

For one thing, one of the reasons I used it as a limiter was because the needle was up like this, and when you limited, you could tell what you was doing. And when the needle's down here, where it was when you put it on the compression, you just never really knew where the hell it was at as far as I was concerned. In fact, when I built the big studio, the first big studio on the West Coast, we had a Pultec for every channel. We had a bank of Pultecs. Now I tell that to people, these kids nowadays, and they all say, "Jeeze, I'd love to have one of those things!" They get about 5,000 for them now. That's what they were getting. I hear that those old mics and stuff, how much they think it was all worth now, and it was just phenomenal.

I never used a compressor on anything but the voice. Never. Never used it on a vocal group or anything else. I did it all by remixing. They were all full too, and there was nobody doing it for you. I would use the compressor to set the voice, because we were using those VU meters, and of course, you could see how much everything was limiting. You didn't have to guess at it. And I always set the bass first. That was the very first thing I always set, and then, I went to the drums and the piano and the guitar, French horns, trumpets, and trombones. I did all kinds of stuff with about 50 pieces.

All this stuff just came while I was starting in Studio A, that's when this stuff started being made. It wasn't even made before that.

I did the very first stereo record done in the United States. It was mastered in Germany. I got a call from a guy named Sid Frye from New York and said he's got some little label. He said, "I understand the Germans have just done a stereo record. I want to be the first one to do one in the United States." So, he booked Radio Recorders because it was about the most technical you could get, we had a guy that did nothing but build consoles, the interior, not the console itself, but the woodwork and all that. It was amazing the amount of people we had; anyway, he called about that and he told me he wanted to do a stereo album.

So, he sent us six microphones that had two outs, he said they were from Germany, they were Sennheisers. I set them up in a room like this around in a circle. Then of course I wired it. We wired the console and everything because I knew how to do that stuff. Anyway, I rewired the console and I just made 2 tracks, and I didn't have a middle. I didn't have any phantom because I didn't know how to make a phantom at that point in time. So anyway, we did "Louis Armstrong plays King Oliver," that's the very first stereo album done in the United States. When we got done with it, we sent it over to Germany because we couldn't even master it. Then, six months later we got a lathe and what they call a 45/45 head, and we started mastering and making stereo albums. We redid all the consoles and everything.

I only ever used one compressor in my life and that was an LA2A. That's the only one I've ever used. All of the rest of them sounded like they were grabbing to me, and they just didn't sound right. Cowboy Jack Clement, one of my best friends, Jack got a studio. Well, he's a great guy, real good friend of mine. Jack's got a couple little compressors that are in one of the bays up there. I've turned all of those on, and I didn't like the sound at all—sounded like they were grabbing. You know how on television, a lot of times the announcer will say, "AND…this is so and so"… it's too late. That's the way these compressors that Jack had. So, the cowboy, the way he is, went out and bought a couple of LA2A's. I don't do any sessions anymore for anybody, but Eddie Arnold was always a pretty good friend of mine because I got a lot of hits for him. The last thing in the world I want to do, but anyway, Jack talked me into it and I talked Eddie into it and I'm damned glad I did. We talked him into doing one more album. He was 87 I think. It was alright, I mean it wasn't like the old Eddie Arnold.

Joe put it out for us, he even got it up to 35 on Billboard. Well, they just did it as a favor to him because everyone in the world knows who Eddie Arnold is. So they just did it as a favor. They did it in one week, Eddie Arnold, to 35.

So really, LA2A is the only compressor I liked. If I hear a grab or anything I couldn't stand that. The LA2A's were the smoothest one there is. They now make a new LA2A. It's brand new, and it's $1600. The old ones are about $5000. They were $250 new. A U64 from Germany was only about $160. I'll tell you that's the thing that started making a lot of differences is the various choices of microphones. That made more of a choice to me than anything else that they'd done. My favorite was the 77. I did Elvis Presley and everyone on a 77. A fabulous mic. When you put it on in the cardioid position, it was pretty quiet.

I did the LA Symphony for three years. I just did it in the summertime, something about the way they work. I did Wagner's Tannhäuser with 90 musicians and 65 singers. Did it on 3 tracks, all mixed live. We did all of Beethoven's symphonies with Bruno Walter. I did a lot of classical stuff. A lot of them played for the symphony and still did record dates all the time. Except for the Slatkins, Felix Slatkin was probably one of the best film players I've ever heard. He just was flawless, and his wife was a cello player. She was flawless. They were fabulous you know. The Jewish people were actually much better musicians than most of the other people. A lot of the Jewish people were some of my best friends. The reason is because they're made to learn to play an instrument at a small age and some of them stick to it like Benny Goodman. He didn't want to play the clarinet at all, but that's what his dad gave him. They were really poor back in that day and he gave him that and he gave each son something to learn to play music. Benny and I would step backstage, and he would tell me about all of that. I've had a great life.

What I had was a bunch of friends. Al Schmidt and all of those people. Went out of their way to be sure I was good. They were great. I've always admired people like Alan Emmick and Al Schmidt and all of those people I used to know and work with. I talked with Al recently. Everybody tells me that he doesn't look his age, and he's still doing dates. When he really put the finishing touches on me and made me what I'd say is a great engineer, I was considered for five years the best engineer in the world by people, they came here from everywhere. Al Schmidt is unbelievable.

I haven't seen Al since I did an album for him down here with a group that he had. I haven't seen him since. Like I said, I've talked to him a couple of times over the phone. He always works at Capital. He said Capital just kind of gave him this room and charged him so much, but they did everything for him that he wanted you know. He's doing real good.

Chapter 8

Geoff Emerick

Engineer and producer Geoff Emerick is a London native who began his career in 1962, when he joined the staff at EMI's Abbey Road Studios at the age of 15. Emerick's greatest claim to fame is his long collaboration with the Beatles, which got underway with "Revolver," continued through "Magical Mystery Tour" and "Sgt. Pepper's Lonely Heart's Club Band," and ended with "Abbey Road." In the decades since, he has worked with everybody from Judy Garland to Elvis Costello, Art Garfunkel, America, Supertramp, Cheap Trick, Nazareth, Split Enz, Mahavishnu Orchestra, Ultravox, and Jeff Beck. He has won four Grammys for his various feats of technical wizardry. In 2006, Emerick published his own version of his time with The Beatles at EMI and beyond in "Here, There and Everywhere: My Life Recording The Beatles." Geoff passed away in October, 2018

I'm Geoff Emerick, and I was born in the city of London and was brought up in North London. From the age of six or seven onwards, I had a toy gramophone, and my grandmother had a horde of gramophones in her cellar, and I actually fitted them on this toy gramophone I had. And I just used to be in awe of playing these 78s, some were classical, some were sort of dance bandish stuff, middle-of-the-road stuff I guess for those days. And I just fell in love with music, in fact I'm fascinated by the disc itself, that the music was on that disc. So, I was sort of in love with music from the age of seven, and that's all I really wanted to be involved with, I didn't necessarily want to be an engineer, I just wanted to be involved with creating the finished music. Because even at that young age, when I was listening to those records, I was hearing certain things I liked within the arrangement, where I thought, "Well, I liked that bit, but I wished it was louder." And so on. And that's where it all started, really.

I started professionally in audio in 1962. I was in school, and I kept insisting to the careers officer, who used to find employment for those of us leaving school, that I wanted to work in a recording studio. I'd actually written to EMI, Pye Records I guess it was then and Decca—there were only like three or four record companies in those days. I received a rejection letter, there were no vacancies, and I kept on insisting to him that that's what I wanted to do. I wanted to do it, and by chance, the careers officer in the facility of St. John's Wood, where EMI Studios were at the time, had a vacancy that had opened up, and he didn't have anyone who wanted that job. So, he contacted my careers

DOI: 10.4324/9781003519829-8

Figure 8.1 George Martin said, "No, we've got to find another engineer," well, I think he knew in his own mind who that engineer was going to be. So I was called up the manager's office, and George was up there, and the manager said, "George has got something to say to you," and it's this, George looks at me and says, "Would you like to record the Beatles?" I ended up saying yes. So that was that, and that was Revolver, and Tomorrow Never Knows, was the first song.

Figure 8.2 The equipment was still the same, but one of the things you could really change was your mic technique, which was a very important thing, because you knew what microphones sounded like and as I've said we had no selective equalization as such on the mixing console apart from this presence box which we used to use for vocals mainly, so you had to EQ the session mainly with your microphones.

officer and I got the interview at Abbey Road; it wasn't called Abbey Road, it was EMI Studios then. So that's how that came about, I kept on insisting to the careers officer that that's what I wanted to do. I got lucky of course, with that contact of his from St. John's Wood.

At EMI, we had what were called BTR-2s, BTR 1s, and 2s. Would be 1s were mono and 2s were stereo, and there was a Red 51 desk and a Red 37. Let's go back to the tape machines. As I said, we were basically doing straight stereo recordings. And the joke was, you didn't start in the library, or sweeping the floors, you went in as what they called a button pusher, which meant you were in charge of recording the information onto the

Figure 8.3 So it was really sounding as if someone had thrown knit curtains across the speakers on the Neve desk. So Rupert and I, over the course of I suppose about two years, we had discussions up in the studios. And he actually started to change his method of constructing those consoles, and we ended up with the remote mic amps and so forth. And it got where we got close to the sound, but an API is an API, you know… But I like Neve desks because they're musical desks, and there's lots of warmth. When Solid State Logic came about, to me they were nonmusical. Technically what they could do was far superior as regards the video work, which hadn't really come into its being then, but there was many more things you could do on a Solid State Logic desk, technically, that you couldn't do on Neve desks. But a Neve desk to me is a musical mixing console, and without being disrespectful to the Solid State Logic, it was not musical. I didn't like the equalization.

Figure 8.4 Although I believe in conjunction with a Pro Tools rig, that dreaded word for me, which you have to treat with respect, because Pro Tools of course is just absolutely superb for film work. Without Pro Tools, you couldn't do some of the incredible things that are being done with film now. I've been working on a couple of film soundtracks, the great thing about that Pro Tools situation is everything sounds so clean and clear, and there's no sort of dirt anywhere, and if you've got that sort of color in the studio musically it might sound good, that sort of that darkness in the sound which is part of the recording, but if it gets into the cinema it's just like mud floating around. So you don't get any of that with the Pro Tools stuff, everything is clean, and clear, and crisp. Pro Tools is absolutely superb for that… But as regards music, my problem is I've been brought up analog. In digital, I'm not hearing things I want to hear, put it that way.

Figure 8.5 I remember the Sony people coming up and the Neve people coming up, we had a playback, because I think we were mixing on a 1610 U-Matic, digital. And we used to A/B the 1/2 inch against the 1610. Well John and I, my assistant, we always used to have a smile on our faces, because every time we switched to the 1/2 inch, the Sony people are all nodding their heads and smiling, thinking it's their digital. So we kept going A/B, A/B, A/B and measuring the output gain, and every time we hit the half inch, they thought it was the digital, but it wasn't, it was the ½". It still sounded better than the digital. And the only reason I'm saying that is I was brought up analog, and I can hear the digits working if that sounds possible.

Figure 8.6 I do love talking about harmonics. Going back to the Rupert Neve thing, Rupert tells this story, when he was designing his modules, he used to come to the studios with modules that he would tell me had been modified, and modules that hadn't been modified to try and trick me. And I'd always hear the deficiency that I did hear. And Rupert tells this story, I've heard this derives from me, he says that what I was hearing was a harmonic derived from 56k. Of course, you can't hear 56k. You can feel it.

tape machines. Of course, the multi-track was just creeping into England, and we had two separate rooms down the corridor which had two Telefunken Machines. One was a T9U, and the other was a T10. Not all sessions were multi-track, they were straight stereo, and if you were on a multi-track session which was just 4-track 1 inch, it was remote, you were asked to start and stop by an intercom because the machines weren't in

Figure 8.7 ...if we get right down to it, I like to just capture the moment. When we did Band on the Run, we went to Lagos in Africa, we go into the studio, which is EMI's studio again, and it's just basically a little tight studio with a control room. And you say, "Well, what mics have you got?" And they thrust a cardboard box in front of your face, "Okay, you've got one of these, and two of those, all right, fine," And then, there's no acoustic screens, so we need some screens, we made some screens, even Paul started to saw some wood up to make the screens. So that's what we've got, we've got a box of mics, some we're familiar with some we're not, we've got an EMI desk and an 8-track machine, and you have to keep on switching the sync amps depending on what you're doing in the machine. But you've captured a moment. You sort of make the best of that situation. And despite all the limitations, you still managed to capture everything you needed. And it was one of his best albums ever. So what you're capturing is the spirit from him and the band.

the actual control rooms. The stereo machines obviously were. So it was quite an important job because especially if you were working on classical sessions you were running four stereo machines in case there were any disasters, and some machines didn't sound as good as the others. So, it was just to cover up, but you had to change tape, you had to figure out how long this next take's gonna be, if it was an opera, or whatever, and realize you were two minutes short of tape, so you had to rig up four reels of tape and then put four new reels on and write all the boxes up, because it's all mechanical clocks.

Basically, the only outboard gear we had, the mixing consoles were just treble and bass, I think it's about 5k peak in the top end. There was a thing called the "presence box" which had 2.7, 3.5, and 10k on it plus or minus 10 dB, and that was, when I started, the only outboard gear we had apart from Altec compressors. I think shortly after that they also had an EMI de-esser, which a guy called Peter Brown who used to record the Hollies used to use it as a proper limiter. And you'll find, if you know the sound of the Hollies records, that's where a lot of that sound came from. The Fairchilds crept in about a year after, maybe '63, and that was the only outboard gear we had plus the echo chambers. And tape echo.

Someone left, and there was going to be an opening. So, the next really up-market job from being a button pusher was what we used to call the playback lacquer guy. You were actually cutting three tracks in a session. So, Cliff Richard—no matter what band it was—say with Cliff in the morning and afternoon, that would be say six songs that they would cut in six hours. So they would then leave a requisition to be given to you the following morning to cut 6 of each song, which was 36 playback records, which was only one artist, so you could end up in a day having 18, 19 seven-inch playbacks to cut, because there were no cassettes in those days, so the artists wanted to hear what the work was. So that's what my next job was.

And that was good fun, people left you on your own of course. And the only time you got back on sessions doing that job was when there was overtime available and there was no other second or button pushers available to fill that position, so you were asked if you could work overtime. So that kept you sort of back in the studio a little bit.

And then, the next promotion from that, if you were really, really lucky—I've got to go way back now, cause when I walked through those doors, that first time, I was told you've got to be 35 to 40 years old before you can become a recording engineer.

So anyway, again, because someone had moved around, Malcolm Davis who was my friend, he was a mastering engineer, and I took over from Malcolm. So, I then became a mastering engineer. And I was doing that for 18 months. One of the jobs- we had to remaster the American records that came into England from Capitol Records, even though they were distributed by EMI, distributed by Tamla records. But we didn't actually cut from the master tape and who knows why they decided to do this, they used to send us a 7-inch American disc which someone else used to dub onto tape, clicks, and all, and we used to cut the bad clicks out with scissors and then recut that tape from the 7-inch disc onto a master record, and that's the way those records were issued in England.

So, I became a mastering engineer. I'm over the moon, because I never dreamt I'd be a mastering engineer at that very, very young age, around 18 or 19, yes 18, because I was 19 when I did Revolver. Everything was changing around fast, obviously because of this injection of youth, plus the fact the Beatles were there and all the bands from up north, so they were going against the protocol of the way studios were run.

So then at 19, I was back in the studio as a recording engineer, it was called balance engineer then, and only because there was Norman Smith, who I used to work with as his assistant, as a button pusher on lots of his sessions. So, we used to get on very well, and he used to do a lot of George Martin sessions, so I knew George well obviously. So then, Norman was going to leave to become a record producer, so there was an opening for a new recording engineer.

Peter Vince, who was previously the record playback lacquer guy, he went straight onto masters and then back on to be a recording engineer. Prior to being asked to do the Revolver session, obviously with some tremendous managerial discussions behind my back because of being so young. I believed it was Martin obviously who liked me and put a word in, "Maybe let's try someone young," but it wasn't up to George to say that because his offices were away from the studios, but I've got a feeling that he injected that into the thinking. So, eventually I was then promoted to recording engineer to take over from Norman Smith, or to fill his space, and one of the first bands I took over from him was Manfred Mann. I did Pretty Flamingo, which was a hit, it was the first thing I recorded.

And I was a bit of a maverick, and I was changing the way things were. Because of being a mastering engineer and hearing the sounds on the American records which I knew, some of it was musicianship as well as equipment, obviously, but we weren't getting those sounds out of the studios at EMI, so I was always striving to find new sounds. I was very naïve about how you could get those sounds, but I was always trying to experiment. Further on I started to change the way the studio layout was done, and switched things around and the rest of the engineers, the older engineers, who'd been established there hated the idea of me doing this, they kept saying, "You know, we've been doing it like this for ten years and had no problems, now why are you changing it?" Nevertheless, I had certain ideas. So that's the way that all manifested itself, and about six months after than, Norman Smith wanted to carry on recording the Beatles, but he was then going to be a producer also, so it was only years later I realized it would have meant if he'd have been engineering the Beatles there would have been two producers on the sessions.

George Martin said, "No, we've got to find another engineer," well, I think he knew in his own mind who that engineer was going to be. So, I was called up the manager's office, and George was up there, and the manager said, "George has got something to say to you," and it's this, George looks at me and says, "Would you like to record the Beatles?" I ended up saying yes. So that was that, and that was Revolver, and Tomorrow Never Knows, was the first song.

The equipment was still the same, but one of the things you could really change was your mic technique, which was a very important thing, because you knew what microphones sounded like and as I've said we had no selective equalization as such on the mixing console apart from this presence box which we used to use for vocals mainly, so you had to EQ the session mainly with your microphones.

There's the Cole's 4038, which used to give the most beautiful high top, we couldn't do that with the presence boxes because they had 13k on them. So that used to give you a rich, well-balanced drum sound with plenty of depth. If, for instance, we had like an acoustic guitar, you'd go for a 56 or 54 then, or an old 47 like I used to use on the Beatles' stuff. If you wanted a more sort of airy sound, I always think of these things as colors, so we could have richness with the 4038, with its depths and its golds and its browns, if you're talking about colors, to the sort of blues and greens say for the acoustic guitar with the 54s. And if you want that sort of yellow color across the top then, depending on what the instrument might be, you might use a C-12, to give a slightly more "breathy" sound. So, I used to build up the tracks like that.

To me, it always starts on the studio floor and not in the control room because I had nothing in those days, I had stuff, but it was in the way you had to use it. So, it had to start on the studio floor, you weren't going to make it in the control room because there was nothing to make it with.

You could record what was on the studio floor. So when they were running it down I'd spend at least ten minutes listening, because we used to work pretty fast then. Not with the Beatles, on the Beatles stuff I had the luxury of time because all those songs were constructed down in the studio. But basically I'd wander around the studio when they were running through the rehearsal and pick up on the dominant tone, or find something that I liked. That I felt, whether it was a clash of harmonics, or something was nice about something I was hearing, and I'd figure out what that was and I'd build around that. Then I started to mix the sounds together and the nice sound that I liked, whether it was going to be the lead sound or not, or the lead instrument or not, that was neither here nor there. So, I used to build up the sort of shades of color in my mind.

So really it was more about the microphones, about listening to things, and about which mics I chose and where I put them. Which was great, and all the software that you've got today is mainly based on the sounds we were getting on the Beatles' sessions, where we were using little bits of string, and rubber bands, and destroying the equipment in the process to get new sounds.

That never changed. Paul knows I always do that, I like to just listen to something first in the studio to just get the vibe of what's happening down in the studio, and I still do that to this day, I never stopped doing that.

We still didn't have more gear, believe it or not. That only started when I started to record the Abbey Road album. The only thing I could do prior to that, when we were in the mastering room, we had a thing they called a "curve bender." Which was a very elaborate time control, but they weren't allowed to be used in the studios. Because we were striving on Beatles' sessions for new sounds, I used to commandeer one and get one into the studio, but management hated the idea as you probably can well imagine. They had their theory, "Well, if we let Geoff do it, everyone else is going to want to do it, and we haven't enough curve benders." The closest you can get to that is the Massenberg equalizer, which was a very, very good equalizer, you could do anything with it, basically.

So the curve bender was really only to be used in the mastering room. But I brought one down into the control room, so that was about the only thing that happened. We were on four 4-track 1 inch up until the White Album. I started that off on 4-track, but Abbey Road was the first 8-track album.

The first big change within the confines of those studios was when they had the TG desk, which was the new transistorized desk. And on that desk, we had the luxury of selectable frequencies, every channel had its own limiter and compressor, which was just unbelievable of course. And I think the boffins who designed it with some technical guidance from Fairchild. But that was the most beautiful desk, which EMI made. Which is now well sought after. I mean, all this stuff's become so valuable.

You know Mark Knopfler has the Red desk we used for Pepper. So Mark has one of those original mixing consoles. It's in pristine condition, and he also has the TG desk I did Band on the Run on in Lagos. Which again, as I've said, is the most amazing sounding desk.

So, the only thing that happened there, because we were never consulted as engineers as to what we wanted on a desk, was no break-in point, whereby you couldn't break into the channel strips to put a Fairchild in. The way you have to do, you have to come out of one channel strip and go into a Fairchild over at the patch bay, then come out of that and go into another channel strip.

The other thing that happened when we went to this, the first transistorized console to enter EMI, because we'd been used to certain bass sounds and guitar sounds and snare sounds, in the Beatles' session where we started to record Abbey Road, we couldn't get the same impact on the snare, or the bass, or the bass drum that we had through the tube desk.

So we had long faces for about three days because we could not get those consoles back into the mixing studio. They'd since been long gone. So, we were going to have to accept that this desk was going to be the new sound. Which was a softer sound in a sense. But we just could not get the power from the bass drum or the snare or the guitars that we used to.

That was my first experience with transistors. Every time something new comes along, like going from 8 track to 16 track, being 8 track of course we had 2 inch, so we've still got out quarter-inch-wide track, but it was really when we started to go 16 track where there were really problems hearing the changes because of the track width.

So we went to the transistor desk without any outboard gear to make up for what you were losing, also because the original 1-inch 4-track machines, which were tube machines as well, and were now on a transistorized machine. Which I guess didn't help either.

The way we used to monitor at EMI was line in and line out, so you could monitor what was coming off tape, that was part of the problem, but part of the problem also was in general line in. It just didn't have the impact of what the tube desk had.

The crux of the Fairchilds is the fact that I know what a Fairchild sounds like, and you can get 16 new Fairchilds, but they will sound slightly different. And it's even down to where the ore for the metal in the transformers and things was mined. We're talking about miles of wire inside it. No way anyone can ever, ever, with a piece of software create that sound. It's impossible. It's even down to where the metal is made, there's so much in that. That's why the 660's different than the 670, they share a power supply but the 660 is the one that's got the sound, not the 670. It was for the mastering room, and we never used them in the mastering room at EMI- in fact, we never had 670s at EMI. It was designed for mastering engineers.

I went to Apple because I'd left during the White Album, and Apple said do you want to come down to Apple because I couldn't further myself within the confines of a company like EMI. I'd reached the top at a young age, and I just wanted to move on. There was a toss-up to going back to join George Martin's Air Studios or leaving and going to Apple, and George had some problems at the beginning with their studios as to when it was going to be completed. So I went to Apple, to rebuild the studios that Magic Alex had built. And of course engineered the Abbey Road album.

When I walked in it was that console that Magic Alex had made which was unusable, it wasn't practical, let's put it that way. I had to completely rip out the whole basement, and I think it took two years to build, and we worked as a commercial studio for two years after that, before it started to go wrong politically.

So I had a Helios desk, and we moved our mastering room, we had a great mastering room there at Apple, which Malcolm Davis, originally my friend from EMI, he was the mastering engineer, he was a superb mastering engineer. So we then moved the mastering lathe to Boston Place which was their workshop where Magic Alex used to work which was near Marylebone Station, so that's where the mastering room was moved while we rebuilt the studio. So I ended up with a Helios desk, which was not exactly by choice, we actually designed the most magnificent mixing console with Neumann, which was never built.

Politics again. And that was never built, although we did design it, and it was based on the TG desk, but it was Neumann's version of what the TG desk was. They added a limiter and compressor on every channel and equalization. But it was never built, and we ended up with a Helios mixing console. And I think we had an MCI or 3M's multi-track to start with, then we got Studers in.

For microphones, it was just the normal, C12s, U47s, you know, the normal. And we had Fairchilds. It's been a long time since I've really thought fully on this. No, we did not have Fairchilds, because you couldn't get them then. We bought two from Abbey Road, from what I remember. And those were the only two that we ever had. Because you just couldn't get them, they didn't make them, because most of them were sent to Russia. They were built for the Russians, Fairchild's connections with the Russians.

You couldn't get hold of Fairchilds. It's not like today, where they get $30,000. That was only later. "Oh, just using Fairchilds," but they used to get that magic Lennon vocal sound, and they were unbelievable for any vocal, and any guitar sound. I could never use them for bass, though. I think it had something to do with the attack time, it always used to distort. It didn't really do anything for the bass, to be honest with you.

Going back to around 1971, about when it started, the amount of Apple gear in England was still nothing like in America. I guess our focus still was on the studio. The attention really was not on all the Apple gear.

I made that Stealers Wheel album down at Apple, that equipment was not hideous stuff if you don't abuse it, because the headroom is not that great on it, it's a beautiful sounding nice sort of desk. But the focus still was on the studio, not really what the gear was in the control room. If you had a couple of limiters, fine, you wanted to compress the bass, fine.

Further on when I left Apple I went to a studio with George Martin. And then because of me being used to that Helios desk, and a certain sparkle in the top end, again getting back to American records with this sort of really nice high end, when I went to Air Studios I was sort of disappointed in the sound of the Neve desks.

Now whether that was due to the cable that they used in the studio back into the desk, or not I don't know. But shortly after when I joined Air Studios George and I went to America to do the band America albums, we started to work at the Record Plant. And that's when I first had the experience with using an API board. And I think there was an MCI desk prior to that I'd worked on with another project. I was aware that, Oh wow-"I can hear that American top!" And it was an API board. Which I think the Record Plant had, that was on Third St. then, in the old Record Plant. So then, I was getting back what I'd been looking for, which was missing from Air Studios. So Rupert Neve and I, Rupert used to come to the studio, I'd sit down and explain to him what I was getting from these recordings I'd done at the Record Plant in America, using API desks, but I wasn't getting it from the Neve desks.

So it was really sounding as if someone had thrown knit curtains across the speakers on the Neve desk. So Rupert and I, over the course of I suppose about two years, we had discussions up in the studios. And he actually started to change his method of constructing those consoles, and we ended up with the remote mic amps and so forth. And it got where we got close to the sound, but an API is an API, you know.

But I like Neve desks because they're musical desks, and there's lots of warmth. When Solid State Logic came about, to me they were nonmusical. Technically, what they could do was far superior as regards the video work, which hadn't really come into its being then, but there were many more things you could do on a Solid State Logic desk, technically that you couldn't do on Neve desks. But a Neve desk to me is a musical mixing console, and without being disrespectful to the Solid State Logic, it was not musical. I didn't like the equalization.

Then we had automation. The first automation I was ever used to was on a Neve console. And the faders were quite big, and they used to chug up and down the old Necam automation. So, that was obviously part of my desk for a while. And then, EMTs brought out a small gold foil echo plate, which I liked. And of course, there's noise gate stuff come into being and AMSs. I never, ever really liked digital reverb; I'll still take a good-tuned EMT plate or chambers or bathrooms if we could find one.

We never used to use them back at Abbey Road. Although we had EMT plates, they always sounded dreadful to me. But I've got a feeling that no one there knew how to actually set them up. So we only ever used them maybe for an effect on a Beatle thing. It certainly wouldn't have been used on other sessions because they sounded fair awful. So EMT plates didn't really exist for me, I never really use them a lot of the time at Abbey Road, probably just once or twice. Just to get me out of a hole.

So, we had EMT plates at Air Studios, and we had one echo chamber. But basically, that was it, we had Neve consoles, and that took us right through to 1983, noise gates came into being, I tell you what did start to happen, at that time I had started to record at 30 IPS. Because again I was still striving to get something new, different, and pristine. When I started at Abbey Road, a lot of the classical things were recorded at 30 IPS, believe it or not. All the pop stuff was obviously 15 IPS, no pop stuff was ever recorded at 30 IPS while I was there.

Looking back on it, even going back into the fifties, some of the classical stuff was recorded at 30 IPS. And obviously for good reason, I would think. But I was unaware of what that reason was. All I knew was that it was done at 30; I was never able to experience what 30 sounded like against 15.

So going back to Air Studios again, I think I was the first one there to start mixing to half inch. At 30, and that was because the Ampex machine was running at 30. So I'd started to remix to half inch, 30 IPS, and it was like a whole new experience, thinking I was mixing to quarter inch, 30 say, and doing an A/B on that, and it was a whole new world.

I think it was probably around the time of Paul's album Tug of War, because I still try to record analog if I can. So we're still recording analog, and some of the tracks on Tug of War were on four 24 tracks, so I had to mix from four 24 tracks locked together. And on a couple of tracks we had to bring in another mixing console. And of course, no automation.

So the first automated desk they had in their mixing room at Air Studiosthat was Necam, but that was never installed on the big mixing consoles, they were never automated. So it used to take a long time, obviously, to mix those tracks of Tug of War because you basically choreograph the mix, as I did when we were mixing the Beatles stuff, you have to choreograph yourself to pull this fader up, this fader, down, switch pan positions, change EQs, and so forth. So you gradually build up the mix by choreographing it. So it took a few days to mix some of those tracks. And then, my assistant used to help, obviously.

Then, the CDs came out. And we had the prototype. That was during the time of Tug of War, we had the prototypes of the Sony 24 track digital to play around with on Paul's sessions. And I know they were prototypes because their problem was that they couldn't get the power supply small enough to go into the machine, in fact, the power supply was bigger than the machine, it was kept in the corridor.

So anyway when the CD stuff and the digital came in, I remember the Sony people coming up and the Neve people coming up, we had a playback, because I think we were mixing on a 1610 U-matic, digital. And we used to A/B the 1/2 inch against the 1610. Well John and I, my assistant, we always used to have a smile on our faces, because every time we switched to the 1/2 inch, the Sony people are all nodding their heads and smiling, thinking it's their digital.

So, we kept going A/B, A/B, A/B and measuring the output gain, and every time we hit the half inch they thought it was the digital, but it wasn't, it was the 1/2 inch. It still sounded better than the digital. And the only reason I'm saying that is I was brought up analog, and I can hear the digits working if that sounds possible.

There's nothing digital that I favor. No, I'm not used to it. The only thing I know by hearsay really is that the Prism boxes are best. I still try and work on analog, and I guess everyone knows about the Prism and that they can be extremely expensive.

Although I believe in conjunction with a Pro Tools rig, that dreaded word for me, which you have to treat with respect, because Pro Tools of course is just absolutely superb for film work. Without Pro Tools, you couldn't do some of the incredible things that are being done with film now. I've been working on a couple of film soundtracks, the great thing about that Pro Tools situation is everything sounds so clean and clear, and there's no sort of dirt anywhere, and if you've got that sort of color in the studio musically it might sound good, that sort of that darkness in the sound which is part of the recording, but if it gets into the cinema it's just like mud floating around. So you don't get any of that with the Pro Tools stuff, everything is clean, and clear, and crisp. Pro Tools is absolutely superb for that.

But as regards music, my problem is I've been brought up analog. In digital, I'm not hearing things I want to hear, put it that way.

I often wonder about recording someone's expensive Stradivarius violin. You stand in front of it in the confines of the studio to listen to what it sounds like sonically live. And then, you've gone through all this digital stuff, and I'm quite sure it sounds nothing like the violin that you've heard in the studio. I guess we're talking about the realms of harmonics now.

I do love talking about harmonics. Going back to the Rupert Neve thing, Rupert tells this story, when he was designing his modules, he used to come to the studios with modules that he would tell me had been modified, and modules that hadn't been modified to try and trick me. And I'd always hear the deficiency that I did hear. And Rupert tells this story, I've heard this derives from me, he says that what I was hearing was a harmonic derived from 56k. Of course, you can't hear 56k. You can feel it. And you know, with me being so sensitive from the age of seven.

And the other great thing was when I was six, the headmistress of the school brought in a flute player and showed a film about the symphony orchestra of the BBC, and again, that was a great experience at that very young age to see that. And why you sort of like that, I don't know, but you do, you fall in love with it. You're listening to these sounds all your life, so you're very aware when something's not right.

The digital stuff is trying, obviously, but there's something missing still. But there's a new generation now and that's the template, that's what they're used to. If they hear what I like, than that sounds alien for them. Not that that's necessarily a good thing, because we need to get music and musical appreciation back in the schools and for people to be taught all this as part of our culture.

It's like there's nothing really controversial, because if we get right down to it, I like to just capture the moment. When we did Band on the Run, we went to Lagos in Africa, we go into the studio, which is EMI's studio again, and it's just basically a little tight studio with a control room. And you say, "Well, what mics have you got?" And they thrust a cardboard box in front of your face, "Okay, you've got one of these, and two of those, all right, fine." And then, there's no acoustic screens, so we need some screens, we made some screens, even Paul started to saw some wood up to make the screens. So that's what we've got, we've got a box of mics, some we're familiar with some we're not, we've got an EMI desk and an 8-track machine, and you have to keep on switching the sync amps depending on what your doing in the machine. But you've captured a moment. You sort of make the best of that situation. And despite all the limitations, you still managed to capture everything you needed. And it was one of his best albums ever. So what you're capturing is the spirit from him and the band.

When I did Imperial Bedroom with Elvis Costello, I didn't want it to sound hi-fi. It didn't suit the music. So, what I did there I went back to recording at 15 IPS on the multi-track and I mixed it at 1/4 inch, 15 IPS. Intentionally a little low-fi. And also to get a little bit of extra tape compression. But again, that was applying what I knew. It's like if you make a rock and roll album, you don't need 15 and 20k in it. It's rock and roll, it's hard, and it's a way of applying all this stuff, you know? And again, you select that by your mics down in the studio, for a little bit of rock and roll, 47s on guitars, something nice and hard and beefy, no C12s in sight, no 54s in sight, they're not rock and roll mics, you know?

Chapter 9

Don Puluse

After completing his education at Eastman School of Music, Newark College of Engineering, and Manhattan School of Music, Don Puluse served in the United States Marine Band, "The President's Own."

Don was a Studio Recording Engineer at Columbia Records in New York City for 20 years. He received a Grammy nomination for Best Engineered Classical Recording of 1971 for his recording of the Leonard Bernstein Mass. He has also earned 12 gold and platinum albums, including Chicago II, Chicago III, Chicago at Carnegie Hall, Bob Dylan: Self Portrait and New Morning, Sly Stone: Stand, Everyday People, and Dance to the Music, Janis Joplin in Concert, Ted Nugent: Double Live Gonzo, and Labelle: Night Birds and Lady Marmalade.

Don developed a major in Music Production and Engineering at Berklee College of Music. Two years later, in 1985, he was appointed Dean of the Music Technology Division. He retired from this position in 2001.

In 1998, Don became Chairman of the Education Committee of the International Audio Engineering Society and was elected to serve as governor. He is currently on the AES Foundation Committee, which awards graduate scholarships. He served two terms as Chairman of the Boston Section and is currently on the Executive Committee of the Boston Section of AES. Don is also a former governor of the Recording Academy.

Don served on the teaching staff and Advisory Group at the New England Institute of Art and consults and lectures on the Music Recording Industry. He is also on the board of Symphony by the Sea, a North Shore professional orchestra.

My name is Don Puluse, I was born in Patterson, NJ, a Jerseyite until I was 17 when I went off to college.

I started in the United States Marine Band in Washington, DC, playing clarinet, I mean that's really what I was interested in doing, and I started getting a little disillusioned, just wondering whether I could really make a living being a performing musician. And we had Ross Ritchie, who was a recording engineer in the band, and we used to do broadcasts. We'd do half hour broadcasts, and we could do three half-hour broadcasts in two hours.

DOI: 10.4324/9781003519829-9

Figure 9.1 Pretty much what I did was so many sessions, I mean so many sessions, I can't tell you what it was like working for CBS records. When you talk about the heyday, it was probably that period because every day you did 2–3 sessions, or you got involved with a big group and were just there all the time. And I never did anything the same way twice, you know.

Figure 9.2 I really feel that getting the most out of equipment was using your ears, I really believe that. I never worried about anyone stealing things from me or anything like that because they didn't have my ears. As long as I had my ears it was what competition. I'm going to hear things the way I hear them, so I never thought about that.

Once in a while, there'd be a mistake and he'd get upset and then we'd go back, and next time, there wouldn't be a mistake; I don't think we did any editing in this program.

I went upstairs and said, "Ross what are you doing? What are you doing exactly?" And we started talking about it. At that time, which was around 1959, he suggested that I join the Audio Engineering Society, so I've been a member for that long. I remember going to the early conventions; they were at the Waldorf in the ballroom, they were very small compared to what's going on now.

So, I started getting involved, and I figured well, I've always been good at math and science and I'm a musician, maybe that's not a bad idea for me. So that's how I started. I left the band and went back to Eastman, finished my basic music degree then went to New York, lived at home, and was working on an engineering degree at North College

Figure 9.3 At CBS we used the Pultecs so much that they put them in every channel. We had a rack of them and they were hardwired so all you had to do was go to number 23 throw the switch and you're in. That's kind of extreme—every room, every studio, and every editing room. We also had midrange equalizers as well.

Figure 9.4 You did stereo drums and bass on two tracks, period, you locked them in. That's it. You got the sound and you locked them in.

of Engineering, and a master's degree at Manhattan School of Music concurrently. After three years of doing that I said I can't do this anymore it's enough school, I finished the master's degree but not the engineering degree. I went into New York and just read the yellow pages, knocked on all the doors, probably 100 studios that were listed, saw everybody from Tommy Dowd at Atlantic Records to John Eargle, who was quality control at RCA. I took a short-term job at a studio where they paid me a dollar an hour to keep the books basically.

The studio was called A1 Studio, in the Belvedere Hotel. And I spent time there until I got a job at Hunter College which paid real money, like $100 a week. That job was in the educational television center. I was the audio person. We had this huge RCA videotape recorder that was the size of three bookshelves, and there was an audio component. When we did classrooms, when we did anything, I would set up the microphone. But I did learn to use a tape machine, and when a job at CBS opened up I went into the

Figure 9.5 There were CDs that were fairly reliable and could be transported easily, but especially at that point, you did miss what we called the warmth of analog, you did miss the wonderful covers with all the information you could read instead of unfolding this thing you got in CDs. There was a charm to thinking about that as something that you missed.

interview as a production trainee. The agency said to me "have you ever been to CBS records?" and I said "Yeah I've been everywhere" so they said "let me call over" and he called and said they had a possible job for me, but it was in the studio, not in the A&R department. So okay, I didn't know what that meant, I just knew I would be with music and make a few bucks. So, I took the job at CBS records and that's pretty much how I got into all this.

At that time, we had the rotary knob, hand-crafted consoles. They were either radio consoles or custom-built. The custom-built studio consoles…it was interesting because we did have rotary faders at one time, everything was very transparent. There was a great patch bay there, you could get in with these WE double plugs, so you can get in and out of everything. If you wanted to turn something around you'd go out of phase, it was that simple. You'd feel the grooves and stick your thumb in. And when I first got there we had 8 track tape recorders. They had been used to using 3 track and 4 track for everything, and they were very confused—some of the engineers actually got confused by 8 track. "How are we going to keep track of 8 things at one time?" I said I have ten fingers, I'm a musician I'm used to using all ten fingers, and I'm not going to have a problem here. Basically, we had an Ampex, one of the early Ampex 8-track machines, probably after Les Paul it was us. We had many, many 3-, 2-, and 4-track machines, they were all over the hallways. People used to laugh, you'd come through CBS, and it looked like an editing floor, just the studios were all on different floors and different buildings. But the editing floor had as many machines as you could think of just sitting in the hallways. People would come by and say we had more machines in the hallway than any studio I've ever seen. And that was the nature of the thing. The monitors were atrocious, we didn't know what we were doing monitor-wise. We had 604s, and L4s I think RCAs, I think they were L4As. 604 E monitors, Altecs. And we had Ampex 3-track 300s, 350s, 8 track, 16 track, 24 track, ultimately MCI, Scully, Ampex, and Studer, but that was later. And finally, we also got A7s, JBL monitors, and Auratones at the studios, so that's when all that started, about that period.

We certainly had good microphones, we had great microphones, the U49s 47s, we had some Sony mics, we had the RCA 44 and 77, which were probably the only ribbons available at that time. The Electro-Voice microphones the 15, 16, RE 20s. We had lots of good Neumanns, KM 54, KM56, we had Sennheiser 421s, dynamic. Also, 441s and Altec 637s which were long-tube mics. We had EMT plates of course which were not used until the late 50s, until we got into the 250 digital reverb much later.

The 140s were plates. And the plates at CBS records were all in one room. We used to laugh about it because you'd walk into the room and there might have been, I don't want to exaggerate, so I'm going to say 50 in one room, and you'd look in there, and it'd be like a morgue, it was very weird, very weird. And you know they didn't maintain them like you hear about Phil Ramone or any of those people maintaining these things, so you would plug into these and learn which ones were good for certain things. Then you'd select them and go downstairs and adjust them and that's pretty much what you did with those. We actually wound up with a prototype digital type 24 track Sony as well, while I was still happening.

I didn't really start my career until 65 at CBS. Big gobos, we were known for that, we had these huge things. Boy, equipment-wise of course we had Urei compressors, we had Fairchild, we had some good stuff then, and ultimately we moved away from the custom-made console, because it was just getting too complex. Too many things to consider, so we went to MCIs, the 400s, and Neves, the 42, and 43.

The Neve was an automated console, very high quality, very great, clean, very good. And we had usually Studer and Ampex tape machines.

We had people in those days who would come in and talk numbers, you know? "Oh yeah, I use a 43 10 inch" and they would talk about all the numbers of the gear. That stuff never meant much to me, I'd look at the microphones, I would practice with them. Pretty much what I did was so many sessions, I mean so many sessions, I can't tell you what it was like working for CBS records. When you talk about the heyday, it was probably that period because every day you did 2–3 sessions, or you got involved with a big group and were just there all the time. And I never did anything the same way twice, you know.

I may have found a problem getting the piano sound I wanted. Maybe I would come across a pair of Sony C 37s that worked, and I would stay with that. But then I would change the drum mics, I would experiment, people would come in with strange ideas, the weirdest ideas and I never presumed that anyone was an idiot or that I knew everything. So when someone came in and said "you know we put a board in front of the bass drum and the microphone next to the board." I'd say "really I've never done that before let's try it" and usually what they did at home would be a joke. They did it at home, it worked at home, but you try and do that in a professional studio there's a reason why you don't do that but nevertheless every once in a while someone would come up with something really weird and it would work.

I really feel that getting the most out of equipment was using your ears, I really believe that. I never worried about anyone stealing things from me or anything like that because they didn't have my ears. As long as I had my ears it was what competition. I'm going to hear things the way I hear them, so I never thought about that. I was welcomed at one point, and most people were very helpful and cooperative, especially Fred Catero Who made his fame in San Francisco at The Automatt, he was very helpful, also Stan Tonkel, they were wonderful engineers. When I got in the studio, I got promoted because Roy Hallee was leaving, Roy had two weeks to spend with me. And he was so busy because everybody wanted to finish their projects with Roy that I almost learned nothing except watching him work. And asking as many questions as I can.

The different pieces of gear were nice, and we had good consoles that generally didn't go down. Only one day in all those years I had a problem, one day I almost lost a session, and it was about 6 o'clock at night and the chief engineer Eric Porterfield who was the coolest guy you ever saw in your life. Eric used to smoke a pipe, and no matter what you ran into his office with, what tense moment you were facing in the studio, Eric would say "hey did you hear about" and he would change the subject, and I'd go "okay okay Eric, I know I'm being hyper but listen I got this problem." Okay so let's go look at it. So one day the Neve console went out, it was gone. And we looked at whatever we could do and I went and got Eric and said "should we call the session off?" and he said "you know we may have to" and he starts screwing around behind the patch bay, unplugs a pre-amp and it was shorting the entire console. Unplug something and the lights come on. "That's all it was, don't use position 1 or position 3," or whatever it was, and we went on. So the equipment was very well maintained, very substantial. I'd heard of independent studios where they were still wiring as the session began. We never had anything like that. It was unbelievable. I was very spoiled by that great staff and people there. As far as how we used the equipment differently, because we had EQ on every channel that was unique.

Did you know that at CBS we used the Pultecs so much that they put them in every channel. We had a rack of them, and they were hardwired so all you had to do was go to number 23 throw the switch and you're in. that's kind of extreme - every room, every studio, and every editing room. We also had midrange equalizers as well, MEPQ or MEQ or something like that probably. We did a lot with reverb, and we experimented a lot with reverb and compression. Where they are in the chain, whether you pre-delay, post-delay, what kind of effects you put on that.

A lot of the stuff we used in those days was to try to get a real sound, trying to get the live sound. Once in a while you'd have a producer who was going for an effect, going for something different. But generally speaking we were trying to get the sound that we heard in the studio, and that's what we prided ourselves on—being able to hear that, go for it, and bring it home. I don't think of many tricks, at that point we were miking the entire drum set, we were not using minimal miking techniques. We were going for the entire set; every item was miked especially once 24-track came in. But even with 8 track I remember doing the early Sly stuff, Dance to the Music was done 8 track. You did stereo drums and bass on 2 tracks, period, you locked them in. That's it. You got the sound and you locked them in.

If you mixed to the 8 track, you still had 6 tracks for overdubs and vocals and whatever else you had to do, and of course the rest of the rhythm section. You might have to combine instruments to get it down to four because you knew there would be more, and going eight to eight was not a solution. You could do that with 4 tracks. I remember when the signal-to-noise just wasn't good enough, running on that 1-inch tape for 8 tracks. I remember editing a Broadway show, when you edited a Broadway show you were in the room next to the main control room, and an assistant producer, who was generally with Goddard Lieberson being the main guy, the Assistant Producer would bring the tapes into the room where I was with my control room next to the control room, Goddard would get a take and the assistant would bring it into the room, and we would listen to it, and if there was an edit to be made, we would try the edit so he could tell Goddard yeah it works or no, it doesn't work, and if it doesn't work, then they'd do another take. I remember the first time they went 4 track, they were so used to doing 3 track with stereo spread, and the lead vocal on the center track and the rest of the stereo on the edges. When they gave Fred Plaut, who did all of these Broadway shows, when they gave him the fourth track, Fred had this German accent, "just put the bass on the 4th track." It was like this huge stereo orchestra and vocals, lead vocal on one track and bass on one track. It seemed so incongruous, but he was so used to working that way.

I chose what I chose for what I was going for. If it was a really strong vocalist, a screaming vocalist, you might hit them with an RE 20. I would use, sometimes, 44 ribbon mics, believe it or not, on the bass drum. You took your chances but sometimes the fatness of the sound was unbelievable. And of course you really did rely on the musicians to be professional and get the sounds, and you could do that at CBS records.

I really used 87s a lot. We had a huge starbird stand so you could put microphones anywhere you wanted to. So I would use 87s on the toms and guitar amps I'd use dynamic mics, Shures or Electrovoices, a lot of Electrovoices, 15, 16, 20s. It's not exciting. Sometimes there was so much going on that you didn't take the time, or you couldn't take the time to be creative, you really try to get the sounds down as they were recorded in the studio. There were things going on where I saw sessions where they were mixing in the control room and they would have 8 machines out in the studio running reverb tapes. There were all kinds of things. Roy Hallee once synched two 8 tracks together by using the common capstan. He would have one machine here and the tape threaded through to the other, and the things that were attempted were remarkable. He would sync machines together; he did a lot of that creative stuff, but he also worked on projects that lasted a long time. Simon and Garfunkel, they would be in the studio a year and a half. They wrote everything in the studio, but they made a lot of money, so no one cared.

My big records, my number one records were Sly Stone and LaBelle. Lady Marmalade, Everyday People, I Want To Take You Higher. That whole era of stuff with Sly. I did a couple of albums with LaBelle with stuff based on the Lady Marmalade. Then I branched into all kinds of music, I did four Chicago albums, I did Mahavishna's album, which is a different thing in itself. Jaco Pastoreus, Jaco's album was pretty remarkable. I had a lot going on in that album, I didn't do the entire album, but I did a lot of the mixing and I recorded the big stuff, the orchestra, those portions of the album. Herbie Hancock in the studio. As I mentioned, things were going so quickly, one month I recorded the three best trumpet players alive at that time, Freddie Hubbard, Woody Shaw, and Miles Davis, all in that one month. And a lot of that stuff was very memorable, lots of stories, lots of things I remember about those sessions.

One that I remember a lot is Sly Stone. He and I worked together, there was an A&R man who would show up occasionally but basically Sly didn't want anybody there so he produced and played, and I was alone in the control room. Generally, we did very well, but one night there was some friction and I was sort of annoyed that he was treating me that way. We finished the session, we worked a few more hours, and we were walking out, I was probably 20 paces behind him, and he turned around, he was with someone, and he stopped, and he turned around, and he came up to me and said "you know man? I'm getting a lot of pressure. I got the record company on my back, we're only talking about a little 45, I got agents on my back, I got my manager on my back," he says. "That's a lot of pressure, and sometimes I got to hand some of that over to you." That to me was like the coolest, it wasn't an apology really, but it was kind of easing a rough situation, a very mellow manner, which I know many people wouldn't give Sly the credit of doing.

The years we worked he was amazing. Those sessions, I mean if there were drugs I didn't see them. The sessions were amazing. They'd come into the control room and listen back, and they'd dance, and Sly would say okay; he would start giving instruction. Freddie do this, Cynthia do this. He'd scream out these instructions and then run back into the studio, I mean run, and they'd be back in the studio before the 24-track tape on that tune could be rewound. It was very dynamic, very quick moving, those were memorable sessions.

There were so many, all of the Chicago sessions were pretty exciting, pretty interesting. Jimmy Guercio came to me, he was their producer, and he was probably 21 years old. He had come through and cut his teeth, been involved with Blood Sweat & Tears, before that he was Chad and Jeremy, he played bass and was the music director. He came to me holding the tape and said

> I can't work in California anymore Don, they don't pay attention to me. They've seen me in the studios for 5 years hanging around like a kid, I can't get anything done there. This album is going to get you a gold record.

And I said "sure Jim." First of all, engineers didn't get gold records in those days, for Everyday People CBS actually made me a gold record, it wasn't an official gold record. I still have it, it's very different and unusual, it's probably a collectors piece of some sort these days. But Jim promised me a gold record for this one, and I said, yeah, right Jim. What are you gonna say great? And we mixed Chicago, and we mixed and did some recording on Chicago 2. They had done Chicago Transit Authority; we re-mixed some of that stuff for stereo because stereo was starting then, and when we did Chicago 2, and it took off, it did very well. I was kind of wedded to the group the next few albums.

Gear I found disappointing? We had things like analog reverb machines, an echoplex, that Teo Masero loved to use, and it got a certain effect but of course it was noisy. And when you had noise coming out of something then you had the problem with masking. What was more disappointing was when a guitarist couldn't get his chops together for a solo or when a horn section was playing out of tune. It was more human stuff than I can think of as far as the problem of the recording. Dolby was coming into place at that time, was Dolby perfectly wonderful at the time? It was known for screwing up certain frequency responses until SR came in, SR was a wonderful device. I would say noise reduction wasn't something I loved using and would try to avoid it for the most part. A lot of people were actually not using, and sometimes if you did, you would be selective about what tracks it was on, but CBS Studios again every channel every track had a Dolby unit assigned to it. You could bypass certain tracks, the drums for instance because you just didn't like what Dolby was doing to the drum track or the bass. It was a banded frequency compression. Which sometimes worked well and sometimes was bizarre.

In early digital, the F1s that was a system that never seemed to live up to what could be done in digital recording. The DAT machines turned out to be a failure because it just wasn't accepted and wasn't used. There were a lot of things that fell by the wayside in that regard. We had Scully machines, we had 3M machines, we had Ampex. So, you know there was a constant preference of one or the other of those, depending on what you were doing. I also had the great fortune of working at CBS because they did have such a great talented crew, but sometimes that works against you. If you wanted a 30 IPS machine, they thought nothing of taking 15 IPS and converting it. And you know you convert a couple of machines that way, do some edits, and then try to put it together and the pitch is different and things like this. They were not Studer machines; once they were fixed, they were doctored. Generally speaking, as I say I was very happy with the department and what they accomplished.

As far as what we have now that we wished we had then, would it be nice if we were able to do some of the things then like we do now when we were trying to sequence? We used to sequence albums like crazy, live albums, and when you're sequencing live albums you have to feather applause and make things match. How much easier that would be today with Pro Tools. But I'll tell you, I'll use a George Martin quote on that. George said that with some of the technology today the Beatles albums probably could have been recorded in less time, and they may have been easier to record. Would they have been better? There are certain imperfections, things that happen in the studio, even now without the playback, the instantaneous ready that just changes the pace of recording. And is that a healthy thing or does that actually bite you in the rear end?

Speakers were always one thing that could have been improved. That was always an issue. I remember the 604s, one of the guys called me and said you have to hear how I improved the 604s. He said you know there were speaker enclosures, I cut a hole in the back. I said you can't just do that, that's a tube speaker. He said listen to how much more bass I'm getting. So the fact that we were so disillusioned, in buying so much and we had different speakers in different rooms and people had their own favorites. So that was a disappointment. And about analog recording, for all the wonderful warmth you still had discs that warped, that scratched, that caused issues. Those were the disappointments.

The first big change we went through was having the digital delays and not dealing with the morgue. Once you do that and you make that transition, it's so much more convenient and so much quicker. Once you do it, you say there's something that I'm missing that I got from those plates and you go back and you use the plates, not for everything, but when you need them. That was the first transition, going to digital recording when they came by with the original 3348? No, before that, the Soundstream. The Umatic. Once that started happening we had tremendous changes in the way we worked, the way we heard things. I used the first Sony 3348. They brought it in, it was the first prototype and we were recording a sax player. I remember they brought the machine in, we said what's that? It's a digital recorder, let's see what it sounds like, and it sounds pretty good.

We recorded Arthur Blythe and started recording on the 3348. "Why don't we hear that back?" "Well it's just a prototype." "Let's listen to it." We listened back to it, and it sounded really good, "why don't we use that?" "Well, it's really a prototype." "It's here, if it's here why cant we use it?" "Well you can use it but you should really continue recording on analog as well." "We'll use analog for back up but we'll playback, and do everything else on the digital." It was almost like they didn't want to go that far that fast. But it was good sound, it got a different feel. Of course, once you went to CDs there was enormous change, positive and negative. There were CDs that were fairly reliable and could be transported easily, but especially at that point, you did miss what we called the warmth of analog, you did miss the wonderful covers with all the information you could read instead of unfolding this thing you got in CDs. There was a charm to thinking about that as something that you missed.

It's all really just hearing, just listening to the room. Usually, we avoided the control room glass because of the reflections off the glass, but some people loved that sound. For the most part, if that was where it was at you would do that, you would do certain things like... Miles Davis for instance didn't like headphones, would not use headphones, and there was a system that you could put up, two small speakers and put them out of phase equidistant from the microphone and work that way but not with Miles, Miles wanted a big fat speaker in front of him, and he wanted to hear, very difficult to work with. There were times when the musicians had their own sensibilities as to the way things should go, and technically, they did not help you out. Miles wanted the sitar and the tablas in the room with him, and I said, when you come in, especially with that monitor speaker you're gonna wipe them out. "no no I have to see them, I have to see their faces." No matter what you did, you tried all kinds of baffling, and no matter what you did when the sitar played, you're reading –20, and when Miles comes in, that particular track goes up to +4. What do you do to eliminate that? Those were some of the challenges.

They're used to working in studio B which is a pretty good size room, they have very good enclosures for drums and other instruments. That's not what the musician wanted so you compromise all of the technology that there is and try to work with it later.

Also, 30th street has its own story, that's got its own history. They found this old church, went in, and had so much success that they said that sound cannot be changed, don't even clean the floors. When I worked there I had to wear my junk clothes because just rolling cables would get you filthy. We had draperies that could be placed around but nothing was done to the structure at all.

I did Chicago, Color My World at 30th street. I did a lot of live stuff there, we used to do the King Biscuit Flour Hour. Also, at 30th street I did Laura Nero, I Am The Blues. It's a great studio and not easy to deal with, especially using contemporary techniques where you're multi-miking. It's okay to set up a string section, put up a couple of mics, and get a good sounding string section. But even at that, you had to turn off the HVAC when you were recording anything that was at all sensitive. I did some recording with Glen Gould in that studio, where you can hear his squeaky piano bench, the chair his father used I guess. You can hear in almost every recording an occasional squeak from that seat. And all the Broadway shows, I did a few of those there, it was a great space for that.

It would be nice if all the technology that has become so prevalent and enabled so much, such as the home professional studio, if it were brought up to date, if it were more transparent, and if people didn't have to work so hard. No matter what you get you have to worry about computers going down, you have to worry about programs that are difficult to learn, where manuals are written but they're useless and people have to write several books. We used to have Robin Cox-Yelton rewrite all of the manuals, so the students could understand them, because no one could understand them. And even being digital, Nick Negroponte who was the head of the MIT media labs about 15 years ago wrote a book *Being Digital*, he said technology is not accessible. He said if you come to my house you'll see the 12 blinking on my VCR, this won't mean much to young kids, but he said I refuse to take the time to learn how to change that. And that is what technology is. Sometimes you have to take the time away from your creativity, away from your musicianship, away from the things you're trying to accomplish, just to get through the technology, that's what I'd like to see change. I would hope by now that this stuff would be gone.

Current technology gets in the way of the process, even though you couldn't afford to have a major studio in your home the way you can today. We still have to look forward to a time when we will be able to sit down and function without destroying our lives.

Chapter 10

Gary Chester

Gary Chester has over 50 years of experience in the industry. He began his career as a mastering engineer for United Artists Studios, where he mastered albums for Bob Dylan, Donovan, and the New Seekers. In his early years as an engineer, he recorded and mixed albums for Nancy Wilson, Jay and the Americans, and The Belmonts. After opening New York's Counterpoint Studios and running it successfully for many years, he joined the National Group and opened The Edison Recording Studio in New York's famous Times Square. A studio that was designed to record and mix large orchestras, The Edison, (located in what was once the ballroom of the Edison Hotel) hosted such acts as the Duke Ellington Orchestra and the Count Basie Orchestra in the 1930s—both of which returned to The Edison in the 1990s to work with Gary.

Besides being one of New York's premiere film score engineers, Gary records and mixes sessions for television, albums, and advertising. Among his credits are feature films composed by Howard Shore, Tan Dun, Angelo Badalamenti, Rachael Portman, Carter Burwell, Dave Robins, and Stephen Endelman; the soundtrack albums for Delovely, Dead Man Walking, Silence Of The Lambs, Bronx Tales, Naked Lunch, and Sweet Charity (the Broadway revival); the television specials And The Band Played On..., Liza Minnelli: Triple Play, and The Laramie Project for HBO. Albums that Gary recorded and mixed include George Benson, Marianne Faithful, Barry Manilow, Sinead O'Connor, John Tropea, Vanessa Williams and Linda Eder, John Faddis, The Vanguard Jazz Orchestra, and the late Carl Perkins. Gary also recorded and mixed music for advertising campaigns for all of the large ad agencies in the USA.

My name is Gary Chester. I was born in The Bronx, New York on February 2, 1946. I started in audio in 1970. My father was a musician. I spent a lot of time in studios as a kid. I decided I hated musicians and hated anything to do with musicians and the whole studio thing. So I decided I wanted to do something totally different, and I went to get a job at NCR fixing some of the early computers. They had just gotten out of card-punch, and they had magnetic tape. They sent me to Ohio for school for six months, I learned

DOI: 10.4324/9781003519829-10

Figure 10.1 I did a Belmont album, an a cappella album with that, and they would want a punch in. In order to punch in without getting a click, you'd have to raise the gate. So what you do if you're going to punch in, you'd raise the gate, punch in, then drop the tape back in and you wouldn't get a click, but sometimes there was no time for that because it was too tight. So you'd punch in and get the click. And then what we did is make windows. You'd get the click on the head, mark the track, and cut the window out, so you'd cut the click out. So when the tape would go by, it would look a little like Swiss cheese, and you would see all of these holes, these windows where you cut out clicks. Yeah, it is a riot to think of where it's come from.

Figure 10.2 ...basically I listen to the room, which is a Decca tree with outriggers, so it's five, and ambient mics, and I listen to that. And of course, it's going to have a specific sound. It's not going to be what you want, but it's basically the body of the sound. Then I take them down, and I build a close mics mix so that they sound as if it was also good, but something's missing. Now in between the two, I get the sound I want, and I change that relationship according to the orchestration. If it's very percussive and very fast, then I'll be using more close mics because it doesn't wash out. The more legato, the more room I use. And the solos, you gotta grab the close mics because otherwise it sounds like a 1970s symphony, I think there's an oboe solo but I can't tell. So it's a whole turnaround from the days that we started in the studio, sticking microphones in people's faces.

Figure 10.3 Musicians, when I do a session with musicians that are all playing together they're thrilled. "Wow man, it's been so long since we ever got to see each other! I mean unless we're playing out at a club, there's no interaction." There is what lacks now as far as the kind of work that I'm doing. I'm sure it exists some place. With bands, they must record together somewhere. What I don't see now is the beauty of playing in a room and changing the original concept as it happens. In other words, they're all playing live and so it speeds up a little bit, it's fantastic. Now you can't speed up a little bit when you're doing it this way because everybody's separate. So unless it's going to speed up it better be in the click and then everybody's got to speed up, a little accelerando "click"?

Figure 10.4 I've always had to make do with whatever I had. Even at Edison, I couldn't rent stuff. I'm the studio owner. Why would I have to rent things to do my sessions. Other people come in and rent stuff, but I had to use what I had. I couldn't charge rentals for microphones that I wanted to use but I didn't own. So I always had to make do with what I had, and that went for the console, that goes for the outboard, and that goes for the microphones. And in a way, it teaches you, you might not get the best possible product, but it teaches you to get the best out of what you've got.

it, I came back, I was working for a company. I thought I was in good shape, everything was nice, but then I realized how much I really hated companies. I was subversive for a company, but I was mellow for recording.

Figure 10.5 When Bill Haley and the Comets came out, they told us that that was going to die. That wasn't music, that was noise. Okay, it was noise, and then when metal came out it was like, what the hell is Metallica, that's noise and that did okay. And then rap came out and they were, that's gotta go. It's done better than all, and who are we to judge what's good or bad, but what isn't there now I think is that nowhere and no way will anyone have as much fun as we had. Because when you're in a studio 12 hours a day everyday working with people that you really like and talented people that you love, even some you don't love, but their talent surpasses the whole idea of if you care about them anyway. Unfortunately, at the time, you never really embrace the wonderfulness of it. It's always a look-back situation.

My cousin worked at a studio, before it was Mayfair, it was owned by United Artists. And he said, "Why don't you fix audio equipment?" and I thought, audio equipment, why not? And he says, "Yeah, you know, you come over here, not only will you make more money, but you don't have to dress up. You don't have to wear a tie. It's mellow, it's laid back. I mean, just fix audio equipment." I said cool. I think I could do that. I just had a kid, my first daughter. So I went, interviewed, they liked me, they knew of my father, so I got the job, and I left the company, and they were sorry to see me go because I was kind of making some pretty good inroads, but I hated the company.

And, about two weeks go by, and they call me into the office and said something like, "Gary, you know we realize you're not really fixing anything." I said, "Yeah, I know, I can't seem to—it's all tubes. I don't know nothing about tubes. I wasn't like a little Johnny Heathkit. I wasn't building radios, I was building cars." I said, "I don't know much about tubes…I don't know much about this stuff." I said, "I work with transistors, dials, gates, you know, circuitry, which you don't seem to have on anything." They go, "Yeah, that's the problem." I said, "Yeah, good problem. I left a good job. What am I going to do?" They said, "Well, how about mastering. Do you want to be a mastering engineer?" and I said, "Yeah, yeah, what is it?" and they said, "Yeah, well you cut the first disk." So, long story short, they showed me how to do this, and I did it. And I was back there with the Scully lathe with a Fairchild head, and they really took pride in their mastering because they didn't have anything. They just had your basic lathe, and it was up to you to try to make the most of it. I was mastering for like nine months, constantly looking through a microscope and constantly riding the groove size, the depth and width. I pre-listened to the stuff and I'd ride everything so it could be as loud as possible.

When the lathe broke down once, and I brought it to another mastering house, and the guy puts the tape on, sits back, and reads the paper. I said, "What're you doing? Aren't you going to…" He goes, "Aw, we got a preview head." It goes to the preview head and the lathe adjusts it. Then he plays it. I go, "You play it? You can't play that." he goes, "What? How else you gonna check it." He said, "You look through a microscope? Take a lifetime." So I realized what I was doing was very professional. So, I built this thing up to the point where I did Mungo Jerry, and I was doing these records, I was making the loudest records in New York, and that was what people wanted at the time, they wanted loud 45s and loud LP's. And in order to do loud, you really gotta be conscientious you know. You've gotta really ride it. I mean sometimes I'd cut the same disk five times before I got something that I thought would work.

I was doing that, and at the time, Mayfair had this little studio that they weren't using, and I had some friends of mine who I had gotten to know, Steve Loeb and Billy Arnell through Anacrusis music. And they said, "Hey, you think we could do some recording in that old studio over there?" I go, "I don't know, let me ask if I could use the studio." They said, "Yeah, if you can get it to work, you can use it." So, we went in on a weekend, and we started to record some stuff and I told them like, right off the bat, I said, "You know, no punching in, I haven't figured that part out yet. All we can do is full takes." It was 8-track. Full takes, no punching in, and nothing else pretty much. Just recording. So we started to do that. We started to fix up the studio, and then we got a record deal, and that really helped out a lot. And then, United Artists was starting to send over the people they're sending over from mastering. They had some artists, and the word got around that maybe the studio was old and ugly and weird, it was funky.

So I started to get more and more of their artists, and I did The Belmonts and Jay and the Americans and War and Nitty Gritty Dirt Band, and I was starting to build up a little reputation. Things were looking good, but then the people that took over the studio were closely connected to an agency. I'm not going to say any names. They were closely connected to an agency, so we started to do a lot of agency work. And I've done albums for UA Latino. So we started to do a lot of advertising. And that was where I learned the speed. You have to be fast…you have to be flexible. In one day, you could do campaigns, so you'd do like an MOR version, an R&B version, a Pop version, a Country version, maybe an Opera version, and a Classical version. So you'd have the same tune, orchestrated or arranged in all of these different ways. And sometimes you'd be crazy enough to say, "Let's change the drummer because he's more of a Country drummer." You know, they had these hang-ups. Bernard Purdy would be on the R&B. And it was fun. I mean you spend a day doing that kind of stuff. You know Valerie Simpson, Nick and Val would come in there and be the R&B people. So, at the end of it you had to be able to catch and grab the genre of all of these different types of music as quick as possible.

And then, another thing came along, that was this Lincoln Mercury campaign, where they were copying. So, they would go and ask the Four Tops to do their thing, and maybe the Four Tops would do it. And they would go ask the Spinners to do it and the Spinners would do it. They had asked Bette Midler to do it, and she said no, so they decided that they would do it anyway. So we did Going to the Chapel. And I listened to it, and we copied it so perfectly, to the point where there was brass only on the fade, and we had this little brass section come in, and they didn't play through the whole thing—only on the fade—it was like four notes. Harold Wheeler did the chart because he had done the chart originally. Anyway, long story short, we did it so good that they got sued. And it's like this landmark decision. No, they learned that if you're going to copy someone's song note for note and have a singer copy her style, I mean what you did was re-record the whole thing exactly as she did, it sounded like her, that one of the things to do is not to ask her first.

Anyway, the point is that many times, you had to copy something somebody else did. The thing that's interesting about that is when you're creating a sound, it could take months or weeks or days, sometimes you go in, somebody would spend a day on a drum sound, but when you're copying a sound, it doesn't take as long because they've done all of the swimming, all you've got to do is get out of the water. So it's interesting. In most cases, unless it's something like Pink Floyd, in most cases it's not so difficult to copy a sound if you go back and forth, you A/B it back and forth, and whoever's orchestrating has orchestrated it the same. Minus the noise they had in those days, you can get it.

The cutting room had two modules that were very bad, they were the same as the modules that were in the studios. They were handmade modules, probably 4 inches wide. Big volume pot, no faders. They had EQ, and they actually had little compressors on them. So the modules were basically volume pot, EQ, three different bands, and a little compressor. There was a flip switch that went in and out, input, output, and that was pretty much it. It had tubes. It was hot. And the control room was pretty much the same. At that time it was 8-track, so we had eight modules, and they were going directly to an 8-track machine.

Everything was made by hand because this was all cutting-edge stuff. This all hadn't really come out yet. So we had a 2 track deck with an 8-track head stack. And I remember that when you went on the sync head, you would have to go on the bottom and take the eight switches and go all eight switches to the right, and the sync head was always dull. It never sounded like the repro head because the sync head for some reason just sounded bad. And then when you went back you'd never want to play it back on the sync head because it sounded so bad. So we would switch and everything would play back, and then switch again to go back. And then when you go back, it was very time-consuming—and it was 8-track.

And I did a Belmont album, a cappella album with that, and they would want a punch in. In order to punch in without getting a click, you'd have to raise the gate. So what you do if you're going to punch in, you'd raise the gate, punch in, then drop the tape back in, and you wouldn't get a click, but sometimes there was no time for that because it was too tight. So you'd punch in and get the click. And then what we did is make windows. You'd get the click on the head, mark the track, and cut the window out, so you'd cut the click out. So when the tape would go by, it would look a little like Swiss cheese, and you would see all of these holes, these windows where you cut out clicks. Yeah, it is a riot to think of where it's come from, and I guess 8-track is where they started to have things like that.

Before that, it was just 2 tracks, so they didn't have to worry about it, they just did another take. Because 8-track was advanced, to some degree it created advanced problems, like the punching in. But then 8 tracks obviously got to be a problem pretty soon because we would run out of tracks, and we had to put stuff together. So they put in a 16-track head, the same deal, same deck, 16-track on the old Ampex 300s. They would pull anything. So, we had that 16 track, and at the time we didn't even think we could use 16. It was like, "What are we going to put on all of these tracks?" But the board was only 8 tracks, so they took each module, and they put two mic pre's in it, and they had two outputs, and there was one little problem with that whole setup, that in record and mix you had to choose the instruments that you would want to pan in the same place, EQ the same way with the same amount of outboard echo. So obviously, the first one was bass and bass drum, and then at the left would be guitar and the tambourine. And something in the middle with echo would be snare drum and something else that you would want some echo on. And that's how it had to be so there was a lot of thinking involved to what two instruments can get the same EQ, same echo, and same pan. And we did many, many jobs that way until we finally got a bigger console when they eventually changed the room, which was a Quad Eight.

The only outboard gear we had was a chamber, we had a live chamber, no EMTs yet. We had a live chamber and at the beginning, because I was the lowest man on the totem pole, I always had to go down in the chamber when we were adjusting it. I also had to shellac the chamber because the walls have to be really hard, so that was a trip. I used to shellac these chambers down in there in that little room, and you're gone. Then, you had the amplifier and the microphone down there, and they would try to be quiet and say, "Okay Gary, move the microphone here." and then, I was supposed to get out, but more than likely, they would blast me. We had live chambers on both sides of the hall for the two studios. So we had live chambers. For phasing we used two 2-track machines when we started to do phasing. For delays we used a quarter-inch machine feeding back. We didn't have too much outboard there was a Pultec or two.

After they put in a better console, the next reverb was the AKG spring. That was the next thing, the BX-20, that was nice, it was really handy. We used a lot of dynamic microphones at the time because that's what they were using. They were using 421s on a lot of stuff. I didn't even know what other microphones existed. These days when you're a staff guy, you want to use what they have. We had 87s and 421s, that was pretty much it. We had RE16s for the brass, not even the bigger dynamics, they were always 421s. And I remember seeing the other engineer, he had 421s on almost everything, except strings he used the 87s, so there weren't a lot of microphones, there wasn't a lot of outboard, but it had a specific sound. It was a sound of the early, early 70s. At the time I used to use four microphones on the drums basically: bass drum, snare drum, and two overheads.

We started with mono. Then when records started to be stereo, stereo-phonic, yeah, that was cool. So we had the stereo thing going, but all advertising they wanted mono because they were afraid of it. So we came up with this thing called compatible stereo. We would mix it in stereo for FM stations, but he had to monitor in mono. So what basically what it meant was rolling in and keeping the echo in the center. And so that when you switch back and forth, it wasn't a tremendous amount of change in the bass—things didn't get lost. And that went on for a while, and that gave us the opportunity to do some stereo for advertising.

I was at Mayfair probably eight years. By the time I got out of Mayfair, we had limiters. There wasn't too much, something to do chorusing, some limiters, mostly Ureis, 1178s, LA3As. We never had a Fairchild.

After Mayfair, I think it was '78, I went to Counterpoint. By that time, we had an SSL at Mayfair, and we had outboard gear, but not a lot. Your basic stuff. We had something to do phasing, something to do flanging, delay units, one of those little PCM41s. There was some equipment then. Counterpoint was where we really started to get some good equipment.

With Counterpoint, Jerry Ragavoy came to me, he wanted to build a studio. He originally had the Hit Factory, left it, left the studio business, was just a writer. He came, and he wanted to rebuild get back in the studio business. He wanted me to be a partner, and I questioned why he wanted me to be a partner, and he said, "I love everything you do," and I asked him, "Name one," and he said, "Well, you know," and I said, "No, I don't know. Which one? What do you like that I did?" I said, "Basically it's because I do a lot of jingle work, and you want the business right?" He said, "Well that would help." I said, "Okay fine, that's not a problem. I understand that." I was working with Joey Levine and others, and I had a strong jingle business, a lot of clients. So, he built the studio. He built the studio with a console that was the size of a small coffee table. I think it was a Tascam, some tiny little console that was a joke that he thought would work good. So the first day I started I did this Volkswagen commercial with Tom Dawes, and it sounded good, we got it to sound good. And the room sounded pretty good with this little console, but we were charging exorbitant amounts of money and this console, some people at home had stereos bigger than this.

So I said we can't continue on with this console, this isn't going to work. I mean we're doing a business and everything. So we got rid of that console. And then we got the Quad Eight. The Quad Eight was really cool, but it had some drawbacks. A lot of times in this stage of life, you really have to compete with everybody else. If they have 24 you have to have 24, if they go dig you gotta go dig. We had a 24-track dig machine. Clinton got a 32-track Mitsubishi. It's like aw, well they got 32 tracks. So we got a second 24, and we had 48 tracks. Now you know, the dig machine came out as a 48-track. Unfortunately, those who had a Mitsubishi were out of luck. Twenty-four track guys could come up. So it was an event, but it was always constantly trying to have the same thing that everybody else had. So the Quad Eight, although it worked very well, we ended up going for the SSL. And then we could build a second room and have a second SSL.

So that's what it was basically. We had the Quad Eight, and then we had the SSL, and the outboard equipment that we had was still pretty basic. We didn't have a lot of stuff. We had a couple of racks. We didn't have any Drawmer gates. We didn't have many gates because the SSL had gates, so we used those gates. We had Valley People, Kepex. We also had an Atari sampler that we used to try to use, that was interesting. We had the Lang Program Equalizer too, but that was just a throw-away, and the Cooper Time Cube. And we had the Eventide Harmonizer. Also, PCM 42s and dbx limiters, LA2As, the 1176s.

I got the Pultecs later at the Edison, I never really was a Pultec guy because we never had them. I think Pultecs were designed to correct certain problems with analog signal. And once you got into a digital signal, I found the Pultecs to be too sublimitive. We also had Orbans, I used those to EQ echo feed to and return. And I also used them for snare drum and bass drum, and I used the Lang Program Equalizer for high hats.

If you're a staff engineer, then you get to the point where you don't want to have to start from scratch every day. So what you do is you get certain EQ on certain things, and you actually just plug them in all the time there. The bass drum goes in here and it EQ's there. Snare drum plugs in here and the thing is there. High hat plugs in here, and it's there. These are the things you know are going to be the same all of the time because if it's your studio, and you're the main guy, you're going to keep the drums in one place. People are going to use the drums. You make sure you get up a setup of drums that everybody wants to use. Of course every now and then, someone's going to say, "I want to use my drums," or "I want to be in the middle of the room." And that's fine, we just start all over again.

But for the day-to-day advertising grinding out. You have to be fast enough so that when the drummer comes five minutes late, you're ready to record. There's no, let's get a drum sound. I don't ever remember doing commercials where anybody ever said let's get a drum sound. It's more like, we start and there's no drummer. Drummer runs in, sees the music, says okay, let's go, here we go, take 1. But of course, how far away is it gonna be? You just did the session before, it's the same.

The whole thing with advertising is that there's not too much time. I used to do these animated things for Saatchi. I worked with Dean Myers. You know we'd have like a wall of percussion in the back you know. You'd have marimbas, you'd have xylophones, you'd have these chimes, you'd have a triangle, timpani, grand casa, snare drum, wood block, cowbell. You'd have all of these things. How the hell are you gonna know where they're going to be? You know, you try to get them before. Now in Prague, the answer to these things is you don't close mic. Miking orchestrally was a major change for a studio guy because studio guys, when we were working we were always very interested in trying to get separation because we never actually put them in a place or a situation where we could try to get a real sound. I don't know why we didn't because it would've been very, very easy. Even with us, when we did Mark Cohn, there was a rehearsal. They were all in the room. Marc's in the room. The Supreme Court was their name; the girls were in the room. Everybody's in the room. Drums are in the room, everything's in the room. That could've been worked out. If we weren't just at rehearsal, we could've got that sound.

We ran tape, and it came out good, but it could have came out even better if we were actually trying to do it. There were times where we'd walk out of the room and let it play, but it was fun. Anyway the point of it was, we didn't think that way because we put the instruments in such a way in boxes and in rooms and hid them and get them behind this and there was no way you could do a live thing, it had to be remixed. But later on in life, when I got to the point where I had to work with larger orchestras, big jazz orchestras, 16, 18 players, then small orchestras, 42 or so where it's just like pop type stuff like Vanessa Williams or Sinead O'Connor. The film scores, which can go as high as you want, 70, 80 pieces.

And now that I've been going to Prague doing symphony recording, you don't think that way anymore, you think totally different. Now you actually try to capture the dynamics of the orchestra and cover yourself. So it's a whole different philosophy, and it's not different as a creative, but it's different as an engineer. This is a different way of working. You listen to the hall. I mean, when someone walks in a studio and claps their hands, and then they shove a mic down the tube of an instrument, clapping hands was pretty much a waste of time unless you're just clapping because you like the design. The singers, okay I can get it. But in here you actually have to listen to the room to see what it's like, and that's what you want to capture. Some engineers actually go as far as trying to measure the rooms so that they can recreate close mics so that it sounds like them. I don't usually have to go through that.

I've done a lot of direct to 2 track because when you got 80 musicians, and it's for film, you've got to think of your 5.1, So you basically use big room mics for that. And then you also try to get a group of close mics: violin 1, violin 2, viola, celli, basses, oboes, clarinets, bassoons, flutes, and then one French horn track, trumpets, you have a mic there, but you never use it, try to grab that bass bone because you want a lot of that bottom. You got them there, but basically I listen to the room, which is a Decca tree with outriggers, so it's five, and ambient mics, and I listen to that. And of course, it's going to have a specific sound. It's not going to be what you want, but it's basically the body of the sound. Then I take them down, and I build a close mics mix so that they sound as if it was also good, but something's missing. Now in between the two, I get the sound I want, and I change that relationship according to the orchestration. If it's very percussive and very fast, then I'll be using more close mics because it doesn't wash out. The more legato, the more room I use. And the solos, you gotta grab the close mics because otherwise, it sounds like a 1970s symphony, I think there's an oboe solo, but I can't tell. So it's a whole turnaround from the days that we started in the studio, sticking microphones in people's faces.

We did a session with Phil Ramone, a tribute to the big bands with Barry Manilow. Phil or Barry decided they wanted to use nothing but vintage microphones, and I mean vintage, I'm talking about pre-me, and I'm pretty vintage. So he found some guy that had these microphones. So Phil says, "Okay, we're gonna use one microphone in the center that comes down with a little ball on it." It's a Neumann of some kind. Unbelievable. It's like a tube that comes down with a little ball, a space-looking thing. Unbelievable... I could hear the high hat on that microphone almost as loud as where it was. Then we had skunkbacks, they look a little bit like 44s, but they've got a black line across the back. We used two of them for woodwinds, two of them for brass. We put the brass up on the riser on the side, and setup all that with all of these old mics. And then Phil said, "But I want to have new mics too. I just don't want everybody to see them. And I don't want to hear them." I go, "Well, how am I gonna put them up there? Try not to see them and not hear them?" He said, "Well that's your problem." So we had all of these 87s tucked behind, we actually had those boards in front of the sections because they were separate bands. It was like this band would be the Count Basie band or the Duke Ellington band or the Glen Miller band, whoever did the song. And they would use their road bands, they're not the original guys, they're long gone. And we stick the mics and hide them in there, and watch the meters. We sent the whole thing to Al Schmidt, so I don't know what he did with it.

So I didn't have any real mentors in this business. There was one mentor, there was Ed Smith, who was the other engineer at Mayfair, but I never assisted him because there was no such thing as assistant. So basically, I went into this studio, and tried to figure out how to make it work, when I couldn't figure it out or when I had a question, I would go ask Ed. The thing about Ed, Ed started in Bell Sound, he was a veteran guy of the 50s and 60s. He was well known and people loved him, but he was an interesting character because by that time he pretty well said anything. How does it sound? Ah, it sounds great! Ed, please, come on, it sounds terrible! Well, the bass might be a little too much, well thanks, give me a hint. Just give me some help here. So I got nothing. But it didn't take long between what I was doing with the equipment I had and working with the people that I was working with. And now these were people of the time.

They were interested. They had a very good idea of what was going on at the time, the sounds that were going on. Steely Dan and this and this, they'd know this, but he was way back with Roy Orbison. So really, what were they going to get out of him? Not much, except how do I get out of this situation. But, my situation didn't really have much to do with his situation. So, originally he was the chief engineer, and I was the guy that took the jobs that nobody would do. And little by little, because of the fact that I was younger, and it was a young business, I started to get more and more work. And as far as the advertising goes, they wanted all of the advertising to be contemporary, and I was contemporary, so they'd come to me. And we would have fun. So it didn't take long before he would come to me, and he would say things like, "Well what did you do?" I mean they never put the mic in the bass drum, but then the bass drum is like just potluck when the bass drum is part of the room.

I mean I may not have been the first guy to put the mic in the bass drum, but I didn't know anybody else that did it. I took the heads off the bottom of the toms and stuck mics in there too, I miked inside the things. I also miked under the cymbal, then I eventually gave up the idea. It was a certain sound. I don't know if you remember seeing a snare drum with wrinkles on the head. They would listen to snare drums so much that there was no ring. My father was a drummer, and he would take the tight snare drum and put a wallet on it to deaden it. And then later in life at the studios, they started to tape it with a little napkin.

We always did that. Then it got to the point where they started using those oil heads that didn't have much ring, Evans heads, And then they'd loosen them up so that it actually was crinkled. And they'd hit it, and it'd just be like a "swat," it'd be like a "wock" sound. So that was the sound at the time. And you know the big room sound, that was the room sound, that went away when Electric Lady and everyone got so tight, so isolated. So, sometimes the sound of music changes. Now it's electronic, so it's a different sound altogether. It's hard to tell what's real and what's not real anymore.

The business is totally different. I think the business now is totally different 20 years ago than the 20 years ago prior to its 20 years. I mean it. Business does change, but nothing's as drastic as the change over the last 20 years because at that time it was minor changes. I mean these microphones that I'm using now we used 20–30 years ago, the microphones haven't changed. They come up with new microphones, I deal with the microphones that I kind of know. I like Schoeps, I like B&K, I like Sennheiser...incredible Sennheiser microphones that you don't see too much in New York. The microphones that I see in Europe a lot I see here, but not as much. I mean 87s a big microphone in America. It's an okay microphone...it's a very good microphone, but there are better microphones.

There's Neumanns in Europe, but there are a lot of kinds of Neumanns. And there are those microphones that also are good that we didn't think about. We saw 87, 47, 67, although 67 is my favorite microphone. Changes in the business? In every aspect of the business, there's been major changes. I mean, the studio itself, total changes, they're hardly necessary. In those days, to build a studio could cost you a million dollars. Now to build a studio could cost you $70,000 dollars. I mean talking about the control room. If you're an artist, and you're going to use it a lot, that's better than having it at your own house. This started a long time ago. Now with the internet, why bring the guy over? Why not just send him a file? Send him the file, he puts the drums on, and brings it back.

Musicians, when I do a session with musicians that are all playing together they're thrilled. "Wow man, it's been so long since we ever got to see each other! I mean unless we're playing out at a club, there's no interaction." There is what's lacking now as far as the kind of work that I'm doing. I'm sure it exists some place. With bands, they must record together somewhere. What I don't see now is the beauty of playing in a room and changing the original concept as it happens. In other words, they're all playing live and so it speeds up a little bit, it's fantastic. Now you can't speed up a little bit when you're doing it this way because everybody's separate. So unless it's going to speed up it better be in the click and then everybody's got to speed up, a little accelerando "click"? Because the whole thing is going to speed up. But basically, the guy played by himself, so what does he know, you know? I wouldn't be a bit surprised if the drummer lays down the drums, they put the rest of the stuff in, then go back in the drums and change it because now it's a whole song, and they didn't hear it.

So without hearing the whole thing, it's a little harder, and it's definitely not as much fun. Fortunately, I haven't had to do it like that because that's where the film score thing comes in handy. Very, very little overdubbing, it's mostly live. The record business itself? What can I tell you. The musicians are playing on the road more because there's so much less studio work. Advertising is going the way of leasing and licensing music, which is great for those people who did it. So what hasn't changed? Audio engineers that want to be audio engineers now, the schools I've visited? A lot of them look like they just want a clothing line. They are learning about recording. In the schools that I've seen, they are actually teaching these kids everything, even stuff that I never knew, electron flow, capacitors, crossovers.

They're going as recording engineers, I've seen that the courses are all fundamental physics of electronics. And then, they get into mics and amps. Most of these students don't plan on recording too much live stuff. They seem to not be thinking that way, and they don't plan on working with too many big consoles, and they probably won't.

There aren't that many big studios. There aren't that many big consoles. So music will be more like project stuff. They build it as it goes. It's like a Mr. Potato Head, where the artist builds this thing. Of course, there will always be some production, but it looks like it's less and less. And the bands, I don't see any new Queen or Pink Floyd or bands that are really using recording techniques. I see bands that are playing together and coming out with songs that have to do with their feelings of life and their political or civic feelings. But not production. You listen to some of those old albums man... I tell ya. You listen to The Wall and you go, "There's an engineer."

Even early Simon and Garfunkel, Bones Howe, there was nothing there and they created this. So, it's not happening now like that anymore because I guess the plug-ins make too many options. So the question is "When are options too many?" In other words, we need options, we can't live without options, but too many options can destroy us. I mean even as a country.

What do I have now that I wish you had back then? Knowledge. Equipment-wise, no. I've always had to make do with whatever I had. Even at Edison, I couldn't rent stuff. I'm the studio owner. Why would I have to rent things to do my sessions? Other people come in and rent stuff, but I had to use what I had. I couldn't charge rentals for microphones that I wanted to use, but I didn't own. So I always had to make do with what I had, and that went for the console, that goes for the outboard, and that goes for the microphones. And in a way, it teaches you, that you might not get the best possible product, but it teaches you to get the best out of what you've got. And then, when you do move along in life, and you do get some more options, all the better, then at least you know where to go with them, you know what they are.

Anything that I had then that I wish you had now? I wish I had live musicians. I wish I had live musicians that really wanted to play together.

It would be common of me to say the next generation is nowhere near as good, or maybe going in the wrong direction. But that's always been the case. When Bill Haley and the Comets came out, they told us that that was going to die. That wasn't music, that was noise. Okay, it was noise, and then when metal came out it was like, what the hell is Metallica, that's noise and that did okay. And then rap came out, and they were, that's gotta go. It's done better than all, and who are we to judge what's good or bad, but what isn't there now I think is that nowhere and no way will anyone have as much fun as we had. Because when you're in a studio 12 hours a day every day working with people that you really like and talented people that you love, even some you don't love, but their talent surpasses the whole idea of if you care about them anyway. Unfortunately, at the time, you never really embrace the wonderfulness of it. It's always a look-back situation. If you look back, and you go, "My god man, I worked at Green Street studio one time with Billy Arnell, Steve Loeb, we had to do this whole album in the middle of the night." We had Will Lee, and Chris Parker, they were all new. They were all on this job. Everybody was down there in Green Street. We did the whole album live in one night. I mean at the time I was like, "Gah, this is impossible." I was complaining. I look back at it, I listen to it, or I look back at it, and I was like, "Man, those were the best days in life." I mean Will was coming out, Chris Parker was coming out, Tommy Walker, T-bone was just starting playing, you know. I got to work with all of these great players when they started The Brecker Brothers, you know. Neal Jason as a bass player. Fantastic people, good players. Allen Schwarzberg, as a drummer. They were great players.

Steve Gadd is by far the best drummer ever, ever, ever, ever done, Lou Marini before he was Blue Lou, Al Rubin I mean we had all those guys. They were working guys that would come in every day and work. I did albums with George Young 20 years ago. Jon Faddis, we were very lucky to be able to work, it's like the Jazz guys that got to work in the 40s with all of those Jazz guys that came up from Harlem, I've done a couple of albums with them like I did the Jimmy Heath album. During the break, James would tell stories. And his stories, my mouth would be open, and I'd stop talking because of the talent that he worked with and the people that he worked with that went on to become icons.

It's like they worked with everybody but nobody was nobody. Everybody was still walking in the back, couldn't go through the front door. This was an interesting time. This is a time where those guys can say, "Okay we done our time. I mean yeah, what happened after us, you guys did something else, but we are not complaining because we had the best of it." And I'm saying for us, we had the best of it because we saw the players every day that we loved and players that went on that are still playing great. And it was hands-on, it was, to say the least, organic. You touched it. You touched tape. You touched microphones you know. You rode faders, yeah. When the tape delay would stop, the whole thing would become as big as a nickel. There's a piece of equipment that we had to get, those Tape Eliminators, very important. I did a session with Phil Ramone and his whole sound was based on that 4 track tape delay, and he was doing Burt Bacharach and Dionne Warwick and all those guys as I was sitting in the control room and my father was playing, and the thing would sound absolutely incredible. I mean, sounded as big as the room, and then all of a sudden "pshh"...tape ran out. Phil shut the monitor off and looked at this guy as if—you're a dead man. Phil was critical because that's how you create the sound, and Phil would create the sound.

It was 24 tracks, but they always ran a 2-track live. I always run 2 track lives too now, on all this film stuff I always run 2 track live because for some reason or another. The thing when you're doing piece by piece somebody would say you're gonna cut the track and EQ it, and then you overdub it, overdub things, and you EQ stuff, and then you mix it and you EQ stuff. People say, "What? How come you're EQ'ing it? I mean didn't you EQ when you recorded it?" Yeah, I did. "Why are you doing it again?" This is the first time I've actually gotten a chance to hear them altogether because EQ, in my mind, does not only refer to the instrument I'm EQ'ing, it refers to what it does to the rest of the instruments or what the other instruments do to it. So you're really putting together a picture, and if you listen to this by itself, it might sound terrible, but in the picture, it works. You're building it. But when you do everything live, the EQ you do is the EQ.

That's it, you're hearing it all. So you can go direct a 2 track, and that's fine, and you listen to that. Then, when you go back to mix it again, somehow you can never get it to sound the same. You get all the cues, you get all the things you missed, but the overall sound, there's always that little, tiny thing it's lacking.

I noticed that in working with symphonies, when they don't have to use headphones there's a marked improvement in the playing in most cases. And that is because the musicians now have to listen to each other, and they can hear themselves better. So all those headphone problems that you've always had before seem to go away. And what you do in a situation like that is you try dynamically to change the moves that you would make on the console, in the room dynamically. Once you get that together, then you're listening to what might be your mix because you created that mix, and nobody can mix it as good as it can get to play that way. Because that's it, that's what you're going for. But naturally, if you're overdubbing, that goes out the window.

Unless there's one person in the orchestra who can't hear someone else. That always happens. Always happens. But in a lot of cases, it's been really fun. And the going to Prague thing has really been quite an adventure. I really like it.

Chapter 11

Al Schmitt

Al Schmitt is a 20-time Grammy Award-winning recording engineer and record producer. Schmitt grew up in New York City. After serving in the US Navy, he began working at Apex Recording Studios at the age of 19. In the late 1950s, Schmitt moved to Los Angeles and became a staff engineer at Radio Recorders on Santa Monica Boulevard in Hollywood. In the early 1960s, he moved to RCA in Hollywood as a staff engineer. While at RCA he engineered albums for Henry Mancini, Cal Tjader, Al Hirt, Rosemary Clooney, The Liverpool Five, and The Astronauts, and he recorded Sam Cooke's "Bring It on Home to Me," "Cupid," and "Another Saturday Night" and Elvis Presley's "G.I. Blues" in 1961. He also did motion-picture scoring work for Alex North and Elmer Bernstein. In 1966, Schmitt left RCA and became an independent producer. He produced albums for Jefferson Airplane, Eddie Fisher, Glenn Yarbrough, Jackson Browne, and Neil Young. In the mid-1970s, he returned to engineering, recording, and mixing artists ranging from Willy DeVille and Dr. John to Barbra Streisand.

Other career highlights include engineering Frank Sinatra's Duets albums, Ray Charles' Genius Loves Company, and almost all of Diana Krall's albums. Much of his work in the last few years has been with legendary producer Tommy LiPuma. During his career, Al has recorded and mixed more than 150 gold and platinum albums, and he was inducted into the TEC Awards Hall of Fame in 1997. He received the Grammy Trustees Lifetime Achievement Award in 2006. As a member of The Recording Academy's Los Angeles Chapter, Al served several terms on The Recording Academy's National Board of Trustees.

The Schmitt-engineered song "Moon River" and its associated album won two Grammy awards in 1961, as well as an Academy Award for Best Song with its appearance in the film Breakfast at Tiffany's. Schmitt won his first Grammy in 1963, specifically for engineering the Hatari! Soundtrack by Henry Mancini.

Al Schmitt passed away in April of 2021 at the age of 91.

DOI: 10.4324/9781003519829-11

Figure 11.1 Art Tatum would come down to the studio, and he used to practice on the piano. He'd get me to sit next to him, and he would show me little boogie-woogie licks on the piano. And you know, I was a teeny kid—I was like 7 years old, and from then on it was all I ever wanted to do. It was so exciting.

Figure 11.2 [S]till, to this day, I don't use any EQ when I record. And 99 percent of the time, nothing when I mix. It's all about mic technique for me, and where I put the mic and how I get my sounds through where the mics are, and what mics I use. It was all about the placement back then.

My name is Al Schmitt, and I was born in Brooklyn, New York.

When I was 7 years old, I used to go to my uncle's studio, so if you want to consider that starting in audio, that was it. That was back in the war, and I used to go to my uncle's studio. They were recording on acetate, but with a glass base because the aluminum had gone to the war.

That was the Second World War, and I was a young kid. I used to get on the subway and travel from Brooklyn over to my uncle's studio. He was my father's brother, and he was my godfather also. And he changed his name because of the anti-German thing in New York at that time, so his name was Harry Smith, and he worked with Brunswick originally, recording all the major stars from Pavarotti on, and then started his own studio. It was the first independent studio in New York City; it was at 2 West 46th Street. So that was it. I used to go and clean patch chords, and I would empty the chit from the

Figure 11.3 [O]ne of the things I always try to tell people is that the most important thing about a record is the emotional thing about it. People buy a record because it touches them emotionally somewhere. I don't know anybody who buys a record because the snare drum sounds good. So you've got to put it in perspective.

Figure 11.4 Back then, a lot of the producers were guys who knew a good song maybe or that kind of thing, but the reason that I became a producer was that these guys would ask for me on sessions when I was at RCA, and then, they'd be on their phone talking to their bookie or trying to get a hooker or something. And leaving. Some of the biggest hits I've cut were when the producer left.

records. There was no suction at that time, so he had a mink brush on top that took the chit off, and it was no heated styli or anything. So I used to do that and set up chairs and watch them record.

Art Tatum would come down to the studio, and he used to practice on the piano. He'd get me to sit next to him, and he would show me little boogie-woogie licks on the piano. And you know, I was a teeny kid—I was like 7 years old, and from then on, it was all I ever wanted to do; it was so exciting. And one of the things my uncle taught me that always stuck in my mind; he said talking about the equipment and all because I was a little kid and kind of rambunctious, he said "you have to treat all of this like it's a Swiss watch, very delicate. If you take good care of this, it will take good care of you." And I live by that today.

Figure 11.5 I used to get very agitated when things weren't going right. That'd probably be, to put it mildly. And I probably wasn't the most pleasant guy to be around at that time. I didn't yell at my assistants, but people had to be on time; nobody got to sit back and read a magazine like you see sometimes. I think I mellowed out quite a bit, and I have so much more confidence in what I do now than what I did back then. Even though I was making some great records back then, it was always a fight. And I was always nervous about how it was going to come out, even though I had a lot of experience at that point. That finally left me at some point. I think when I stopped drinking, the nervousness left me, and now, I just have so much confidence in what I do. I just look forward to recording and just knocking people's socks off with what I get done.

When I started working on my own, my mentor at that time was Tommy Dowd. My uncle got me a job at Apex Recording Studios, and the first guy I met was Tommy Dowd. He took a liking to me almost like his kid brother, and I took a liking to him. I kind of jumped in his back pocket and just watched everything he did and took down notes on everything. And we had an 8-input console, so we could use eight microphones. A lot of them were things like a Western Electric 639, a Salt Shaker, a 44D X, an RCA 77. I think we finally got a Telefunken U 47, and that was pretty much it. We didn't have any equalizers or any compressors on the board.

We had one equalizer. It was a cinema equalizer, and if you put it in, you could only add highs or lows or take out highs or lows, but if you put it in, you equalized everything—you couldn't just equalize one track. And everything was mono and 2 -track back then. We were going to a Presto lathe with a Presto head, and everything was done 33 1/3, 16-inch transcription disc. And then, we got our first Ampex 300 tape machine, and that was like, "Holy moley!" Before that, Tommy and I would have Take 3 on one 16-inch disc and Take 6 on another, and we wanted to use the first part of Take 3 and the last part of Take 6. And we had two playback turntables at the studio with an attenuator on each one, and we'd cue them up. He'd cue the one up, and then, I'd hold mine, and I'd hold the disc and keep the volume down and then let that one go, and then, he would look at me, and I would slowly bring it in, and he would beam the other one in—and that's the way we did our editing between two takes. So when we finally got the tape machine in and were able to cut it and edit, oh my god, it was like, "Boy, this is the cat's pajamas!" We thought we were really high-tech. That was in 1951.

We were pretty limited on things like equalization. That's why still, to this day, I don't use any EQ when I record. And 99 percent of the time, nothing when I mix. It's all about mic technique for me, and where I put the mic and how I get my sounds through where the mics are, and what mics I use.

It was all about the placement back then. When you only had a few inputs, sometimes you would have the bass on a riser, the upright bass, and a piano, where you'd have the 44 in between them, and we had to get a balance of them facing each other. It was a pretty archaic way to record, but when you look back on it, it was modern technology back then.

Microphones have always been my favorite equipment. Those were always my favorite things to use, so yeah, I did develop into microphones. I've come to love the Telefunken 47s and Neumann 67s—big fan of those. And we always used the preamps that were in the board; we didn't have outside preamps. The board was a Western Electric or something.

AKG also came out with some microphones that were very nice. Back in those days, you would record something, and we could leave it on a 16-inch transcription disc, and then, we did our own mastering, and the engineer did everything. You set up everything—you see, we didn't have assistants, so you set up the session, you did everything, you recorded, you edited and whatever, and then, you transferred it to a lathe, you cut a 10-inch master at 78 rpm. And then we had to lift the head up—as it went in, we'd wind out, lift the cutting head up, and then, we'd take that over to another table where we put a concentric on. That's how the records would reject. It's bringing back a lot of memories.

I still use the 67s and 47s, also the M 49s. I was using ribbon mics, 77s and 44s, quite a bit, and now, I use mostly Royers—they're a lot quieter and a better-sounding microphone. Then preamps came in. Neve came in with those boards in the 60s, and the Neve preamps were really special. We started getting Neve boards at RCA, and those were some of my favorites.

I don't want to get into mentioning names, but some of the consoles were so much better than others back then. And the same with some of the tape machines—the MCI was just crap. Terrible, you know? And people were buying it and using it, making records, and the records were sounding terrible, and you had to wonder. Because it was all about how things sounded, and we wanted the best in quality. And we still do today, but it was really important back then. I loved all the Neve stuff; Neve boards are still my favorite boards. My 88R is my favorite board right now. And microphones… the microphones developed, and there are some great Royer microphones, and there are some great stereo mics that came out.

I don't use digital mics; at this point, they're all analog microphones. So pretty much everything I do is analog. The only thing I use that's not analog is Pro Tools. It's like my tape machine.

When it first came out, I never used the Fairchild limiter. I just didn't like the way it sounded for what I was doing. But now I love it; I use it all the time, so it's amazing how I've changed as far as that's concerned. Because, you know, the limiter hasn't changed, it's just the way I do things. So I use it on vocals a lot—when I use limiting, I tap a dB, maybe two. Not much. I use it more for the sound of the tubes and the compressor. So that and some of the UA stuff—the Universal Audio stuff that Bill Putnam came up with was terrific stuff.

Some of the things I didn't like were when they first came out with stereo, and they were coming up with this stereo action. That shit was flying back and forth between the speakers, and I called it mal de mer. I would start getting sick listening to it. But they were trying to do anything... like when quad came out, they were trying to get more people involved, sell more gear, and sell some more records in some way. And they rushed things along so much that it's kind of like 5.1 now. None of the record companies want it done anymore—they don't care about; they don't spend the money. That's sort of sad. I don't think there's anything better than listening to a really good 5.1 mix. Elliot Scheiner's stuff knocks your socks off, and you hear things that you never heard on a record before; it's just unbelievable. And I love mixing now. It's so much fun because you do get to hear anything, and you get to be a little more creative with what's going on. I really enjoy that; that's one of my favorite things. Unfortunately, with the fighting back and forth with us and CDs and whatever, you know, we blew that just like Beta and video. So I don't know, I think the record companies shoot themselves in the foot all the time.

Making a record back then was so much more exciting because you had 50 pieces in the studio—you had a rhythm section, you had a singer. All we had was some gobos, and maybe you get a little isolation with an iso booth. And what you heard come out of the speakers was what you got. That was it—that was the end product. And you would do three or four songs in three hours, and then, you would be done. You could do an album in three days at three hours or four hours a day. And that was really exciting, and you had to be on your toes, because you had to follow the score—you had to know what solos were coming and when the strings parts were, where flute parts were.... So it was a lot more exciting, a lot more tension. Today, you sit there—how many tracks, 60 tracks, 48 tracks—and you've got it all, and I still try to mix like it's going to be the final. And I ride gain, and I always ride vocals; I do hand-limiting with the vocal all the time. But if you miss it, it's there, and you can fix it. Back then you couldn't—if you missed it, it was gone. Pl never forget a record that Tommy Dowd did—it was a huge hit years ago called "If I Knew You Were Comin' I'd've Baked a Cake" by Eileen Barton. And if you listen to the record, they're clapping, and then, all of a sudden, the claps are supposed to stop, but there's one guy that just clapped? And the feel of the record was there. They didn't have time to redo another one, and it came out that way, and it didn't hurt it. And one of the things I always try to tell people is that the most important thing about a record is the emotional thing about it. People buy a record because it touches them emotionally somewhere. I don't know anybody who buys a record because the snare drum sounds good. So you've got to put it in perspective.

I still use some of the old things. My mic techniques are the same, and my microphones and placements and how I set up the room. I think it's all pretty much the same, you know. We just have better preamps now and quieter sounds.

There's one I've been using lately. It's not out on the market yet; it's an UpState Audio preamp, and it is unbelievably good, just clear. I love that. I have some old Neves; I really love the 1081s. And I have a Martech preamp that I use that I love. I have a couple of UAs. I have Studers—four Studer valve preamps they don't make anymore.

I have four of the Mastering Lab tube preamps that they don't make anymore. I think Doug Saxton said they're going to start manufacturing them again. And the Great River preamp—it's really good. That's pretty much it, you know. But I have quite a bit of their stuff. When I work at Capitol, I work on a Neve board. I'm not as crazy about the preamps in this Neve, this particular Neve model. So I use all my own preamps, and I have plenty of those.

So, changes... I hate the volume they put on records today. I mean, they just squash the hell out of stuff. And it just sounds terrible. I hate that. Something I love today is the fact that

I can spend time doing surround mixes, and 99 percent of the time no one's around, so I get to work on my own—certainly one of the things I love, and we didn't have that years ago.

I was never a solid-state guy; I always tried to stay away from that as much as I could. And digital...I never liked digital when it first came out. It was 48 tracks, and I couldn't understand how anybody could record like that. You would A/B it against the tape, and they weren't even close; tape was so much better. But as things have gotten better now, I do a lot of stuff at 192, so I'm pretty happy with that. Although I still do a lot of tape, I mix down a lot to 1/2-inch tape; almost all my projects get mixed down to 1/2-inch tape. And the way the mastering has evolved, it's so much better now. I use Doug Sax all the time, and I'm constantly amazed at how he doesn't do anything and just sounds unbelievable. It's great.

I think also that a lot of the producers around today know a lot more about music than they did back then. Back then, a lot of the producers were guys who knew a good song maybe or that kind of thing, but the reason that I became a producer was that these guys would ask for me on sessions when I was at RCA, and then, they'd be on their phone talking to their bookie or trying to get a hooker or something. And leaving. Some of the biggest hits I've cut were when the producer left. I did a record with Connie Francis called "My Happiness" and the producer was David Rose; he had recorded "The Stripper."

So the producer left. He went to the Beverly Hills Hotel; he had some hooker there, and he left. And we were there, and we recorded "My Happiness." And then, we decided that it would be nice if she would try to double it. And it was modern, so we had another tape machine in, and we played back, and she sang along and recorded on the other one, and it came out. And I'll never forget, she said to me, "Now, if this record goes to number one, you're going to see a new car outside your door." Well, it went to number one—it was number one for about ten weeks. And I would come out of work every day and look for that new car, and there was no new car; it never showed up.

I used to get very agitated when things weren't going right. That'd probably be, to put it mildly. And I probably wasn't the most pleasant guy to be around at that time. I didn't yell at my assistants, but people had to be on time; nobody got to sit back and read a magazine like you see sometimes. I think I mellowed out quite a bit, and I have so much more confidence in what I do now than what I did back then. Even though I was making some great records back then, it was always a fight. And I was always nervous about how it was going to come out, even though I had a lot of experience at that point. That finally left me at some point. I think when I stopped drinking, the nervousness left me, and now, I just have so much confidence in what I do. I just look forward to recording and just knocking people's socks off with what I get done.

A big part of it's my attitude. I can look at meters and know how things all work—I don't even have to hear it to know whether it's going down right or not.

I've been using Pro Tools, but I use it as a tape machine. I know enough to run it myself, but my assistants are so great with it. We'll fix things here and there, tune something here and there, but we don't do as much of that as most people. That's pretty much it; I still like recording on analog tape. We just did a record with Shelby Lynne where I recorded on 2-inch analog tape, 16 track, and then, we mixed it down to 1/2-inch two track, and it's just a superb-sounding record; I'm really excited about it. It came out, and they even put it out on vinyl.

And I like the fact that vinyl is coming back, and they sold over a million vinyl records last year. And I mean, that's everyone combined, but that's still a hell of a jump up there, and more and more people are getting back into it. I just think it's great.

[Elliot Scheiner pipes up.] Ask him about Ann Margret.

I dated Ann Margret way, way back. She was like 20 years old, and I was 28 or something. And I dated her for about nine months. And we were pretty good friends; I produced her records. First I engineered her records, and when I became a producer, I was producing her records at RCA. And we became pretty good friends. I was working late in the studio one night, and I left—I got in my car and drove off, and I got on Sunset, and I pulled up to a red light. And I heard all this laughing and everything, and I turned around and looked, and next to me was this Rolls-Royce, and in it were Ann Margret and Elvis Presley. And I knew that my time with Ann Margret was over.

Chapter 12

Glen Snoddy

Glen Snoddy began his career in radio, moving into television and then working with Nashville icon Owen Bradley, with artists such as Patsy Cline, Johnny Cash, and Marty Robbins. He went on to run the prestigious Woodlawn Sound Studios in Nashville for over 20 years. In 1960, longtime Nashville session picker Grady Martin was recording a guitar part for the Marty Robbins hit "Don't Worry." A faulty mixing board caused the bass to become fuzzy. Everyone involved in the session agreed to keep the fuzz. The song reached #1 on the country charts and #3 on the pop charts, and fuzz was suddenly popular.

Fuzz became in demand in the country music centers of both Bakersfield and Nashville. Acts like Merle Haggard, Buck Owens, Waylon Jennings, Wanda Jackson, and Kay Adams adopted fuzz.

Glen Snoddy, the session engineer, saved the malfunctioning channel on the mixing board and brought it out upon request. Snoddy and Grady used the effect on several other records including "The Fuzz" by Grady Martin and The Slew Foot Five. Snoddy saw the commercial potential for a device that would produce the fuzz tone effect on command and sold the idea to the Gibson Guitar Corporation, who marketed the Maestro Fuzz Tone in 1962, the first commercially available fuzz-type unit.

Fuzz might have just become a novelty of the country music scene in the 1960s if it was not for Keith Richards, who used it in "(I can't get no) Satisfaction." "Satisfaction" brought the fuzz effect into rock. Fuzz was quickly adopted by classic rock guitarists like Clapton, Hendrix, Page, Beck, Townsend, and Davies. Snoddy's forward-thinking during the Marty Robbins session changed the sound of a variety of genres.

Glenn Snoddy passed away in May of 2018 at the age of 96.

My name is Glen Snoddy. Born in Shelbyville, Tennessee, just down the road. On the fourth day of May 1922. I'm 87 years old now. I moved here from Nashville, Brentwood, about 11 years ago. During that time, I've had a stroke but I'm fine, my mind is good,

DOI: 10.4324/9781003519829-12

Figure 12.1 So I was working with Owen Bradley quite a bit on the side, moonlighting, and he finally asked me to come work for him, so that was the introduction to recording. And we worked with all his problems, and his fantasies and whatever else he came up with. But that was another area of fun working, really, because we did all the things with Patsy Cline and Johnny Cash and Marty Robbins, and all those people. That was fun, and it was something that kept me sharp as I could be, and always something new coming up.

Figure 12.2 And the one thing that still follows me around even today is the fuzz tone. We had a console that was a new console, it had been brought down from New York. And it developed some problems, with the transformers and preamps, and this one time that we were recording Marty Robbins, Grady Martin's guitar was going into a direct input to the console, and this awful sound started happening. And it was a buzzing sound that the guitar was making; eventually, we called it the "fuzz tone." That's the word that came out of all that, but Grady said "Why don't we just use that on this record?" So the record was Don't Worry that Marty Robbins did, and Grady Martin played the guitar through the fuzz.

and I have trouble talking. It's a speech impediment type thing, and if I get tangled up and can't think of words, whatever, that's the problem.

Otherwise, I'm in pretty good shape. I started out in radio, well, I started out before that in World War II, I thought it was an interesting way to get where you wanted to go. I was certainly subject to the draft, so I saw this radio school advertisement, so I called them up, and I went to a local high school in Nashville where I was living at the time,

Figure 12.3 And I don't know, as a friend of mine said, I had this gentleman who's in Atlanta, he owned electronic equipment, and he used to sell gear, he sold Ampex's and all kinds of stuff, and I got to be friends with him, he told me one time, he said, "You know, the older you get, the less you know." I'm thinking now he's right!

Figure 12.4 Like the compressors, the LA2As, the Fairchild's, you have to learn how to use those. You've got to have enough patience and enough time with an artist, with someone that was willing to help you learn how to use them. It don't happen by themselves. There were equalizers like the Pultecs, and the Langs, we had all those. You finally get to where an artist will prefer one or the other. You know, "That doesn't sound like what we had last time." So you go and get what they had last time, "Yeah, that's better!" So artists make that a lot of that—especially those that have been around a while. Young artists that have not had much experience with it, they depend on someone to show them what to do. That works out very nice. But they will finally wise up to you, and they will say "That don't sound exactly like what we had before," so then you start scrambling to see what they want. It's a cut-and-dry thing most of the time.

and entered radio school for the government. It was the enlisted Reserve Corps. And we studied radio, basic electricity, how to do things with soldering irons, and all that. And it was really an eight-hour day job, for about three months. Well, you learned a lot eight hours in three months on one subject. So then we went to Memphis and studied three more months, so that's where I started to learn something about electricity, but all the time that this was taking place, I was thinking recording.

Figure 12.5 Most of the people I worked with, I guess maybe they trusted my judgment to some degree and, whatever I would choose, generally, they would accept that. But I tell you, the producers that I was associated with were strictly at our mercy in the matter of equipment to use. Most producers knew what they wanted in a song or a phrase, and I wouldn't know that. But the producer would have a really good idea what he wanted to accomplish with that song. And so you always had two different realms of expertise, one is concentrated on lyrics or the music pattern, and you're concentrating of other things that regard to making the session work, but it's really a different realm. So you've got two things working, and I think when you can get both people working on the same things, generally speaking, it's a better session.

Figure 12.6 Hank Williams' legacy was enhanced recently by the finding of a lot of old recordings. I don't know if you were aware of this or not, but Time-Life Music has unearthed a lot of old recordings. I have the whole repertoire. And I made some of the recordings at WSM in those days. So that was something that came out of the blue. I had received five shows from somebody that was interested in me getting the shows because I was mentioned on one of the shows by Hank Williams. So I've got that show at home. That happened back at my days at WSM. They were interesting days because you never knew what was going to happen.

Now, why I don't know, but as a child, I'd sit in front of a radio at home, my ear up to it. I didn't want to miss anything. And that's how I grew up, listening to Orphan Annie, the Lone Ranger, and all those shows. And I always wondered how they did all that.

And teaching students in today's world, you got to get these students interested in something, before you can teach them something. And I don't know how they do it these days, with all the problems they have in learning in second- and third-grade schools and all, somebody's missing the boat.

Do you know what my hobby is now? Repairing old tube radios. Never gotten away from 'em! I just finished one you wouldn't believe. Those old tube radios were amazing pieces of equipment.

Now in the armed services, you do what you're told mostly, but we went to radio school, and from there, we went into the army, we did our basic training and so forth. So I applied to the Air Force, the Air Corps, and was accepted, and went to Miami Beach for induction, and wound up in the University of Vermont to make an officer and a gentleman out of me, see.

I enjoyed that. We were up there six months or so, and the next thing we knew they washed us all out because they knew the bomb was going to work. All of us—everybody—you never seen as many mad people in your life. We were leaving, and it's cold! We were leaving Miami and suntans, and we got up there, and we was freezing! So, we were shipped back into the signal corps over in Fort Monmouth. We go through radio school again, so I had lots of radio school. And then after that, of course, we were studying stuff that the army designed. And we shipped to the Philippines, and we were working MacArthur's communications network in the Philippines. All the while waiting to invade Japan in case that bomb didn't work. Thank goodness it worked!

Anyhow, coming back and getting discharged, and I wound up here, in Murfreesboro, because my parents were living here at the time. And, I applied to the local WGNS radio station and was accepted as a transmitter engineer. In those days, you had to have a license to operate an AM transmitter. You don't need that anymore, but that was where I first started, and I was always conscious of what was going on on the radio. I remember one day, we had a studio uptown, I was kind of out in the boondocks at the transmitter. And I called a fellow on duty up there, and I said if you could get that microphone a little bit closer to the piano, it would sound much better. He said, "That's going to be awful difficult, because it's on transcription!" So I was trying to tell people what to do back then!

I went from there to a recording studio in Nashville. And we did anything you could think of that kept a recording studio busy. We did, for example, 520 soap operas, and those were the most interesting things to do.

I learned a lot, I had a basic knowledge of stuff, but applying these things to a particular thing like a soap opera. I know one day, we'd produce these, and then tomorrow, we're gonna crawl down the telephone line. I said what? They said

> We're going to start out, we're going to have a telephone hookup, and you'll do the person whose going to sing live, and then all of a sudden it's going to go down the telephone line and you're going to hear a false kind of a sound.

I said, oh, that'd be interesting, I'd better figure out how to do that.

So we did Ted Drake, Guardian of the Big Top—it was a circus show. All kinds of things went on. The brother-in-law of the boss was the soundman in the studio. I'd built a big three-bay turntable with dual arms, for doing sound effects records. And you needed an arm on either turntable to keep it going continuously that way. And these shows were live; we fed Chicago—the Mutual Network. And came up time for the big boom to go off; a cannon was going to go off—the soundman missed the cannon. They had to dub it in, in Chicago. Those are the kind of things you don't forget, you know?

That was Brown Radio Productions. Charlie and Bill Brown owned them, and I was there probably a couple of years. About 1949–1950.

And then, WSM reared their ugly head, and I went to work for them because television was just coming in and most of the engineers from radio had already gone to television so they were shorthanded on engineers. So then I went to WSM and worked there for about five years, and then, I went to WSM television. So I had a progression of going from radio to TV, and at the same time doing a lot of recording, because the owners operated Castle recording studios where all the country music people recorded, and I would moonlight there. So my wife and children never saw me. All day long and, sometimes, there in the middle of the night.

I was working on some things for Owen Bradley at the time, and the work in television, is, to be honest with you, kind of boring. Television work for an audio man, at least to me, was boring. Might not have been for someone else. You didn't get a whole lot in the first place, there was no playback in those days, you didn't have videotape. You were beginning to get it.

So I was working with Owen Bradley quite a bit on the side, moonlighting, and he finally asked me to come work for him, so that was the introduction to recording. And we worked with all his problems, and his fantasies and whatever else he came up with. But that was another area of fun working, really, because we did all the things with Patsy Cline and Johnny Cash and Marty Robbins, and all those people. That was fun, and it was something that kept me sharp as I could be, and always something new coming up.

And the one thing that still follows me around even today is the fuzz tone. We had a console that was a new console, it had been brought down from New York. And it developed some problems, with the transformers and preamps, and this one time that we were recording Marty Robbins, Grady Martin's guitar was going into a direct input to the console, and this awful sound started happening. And it was a buzzing sound that the guitar was making, eventually, we called it the "fuzz tone." That's the word that came out of all that, but Grady said "Why don't we just use that on this record?" So the record was *Don't Worry* that Marty Robbins did, and Grady Martin played the guitar through the fuzz.

Well later, we had people that wanted to use that sound, and I remember Tommy Sands and Nancy Sinatra came in for a recording session, and they found out we couldn't supply that anymore because that preamp had died. What had happened was the primary of the preamp had opened up, and this thing was sitting there arcing—the primary was arcing. And the guitar was just playing along fine, and every time, he hit a note it just quit. Burned the arc out, I guess.

And then I told Hal Burgess well, we'll have to get some way to get that fixed because there's no way to fix that transformer. So I got some transistors and we rigged up a thing, and we eventually sold it to Gibson. Gibson came out, and then the hot record on this was "Satisfaction" that the Rolling Stones did. But that was a big, big record. Well, then Gibson started to sell those things, and they did a good job of selling. So, that's a little bit of some of the stuff.

The console was made for Decca in New York. The man that made those consoles produced three of those consoles. And two of them wound up down here. Later, going forward a little bit, Owen Bradley sold his holdings to Columbia and then later on got a second console and put it in his home studio out on the lake. But the equipment was Langevin equipment, mostly our amps were Langevin tube amps, and then, when CBS bought the studio, then that turned into a different animal. They started in to make bigger consoles, made in New York, brought down, and installed. I kind of lost some interest in what was going on at that point. I'd been approached by some people to open up a studio on Woodland Street, called Woodland Sound Studios. So I eventually wound up at Woodland Sound Studios as manager, president, or whatever. And I was there twenty years, until I retired.

And I don't know, as a friend of mine said, I had this gentleman who's in Atlanta, he owned electronic equipment, and he used to sell gear, he sold Ampex's and all kinds of stuff, and I got to be friends with him, he told me one time, he said, "You know, the older you get, the less you know." I'm thinking now he's right!

We had a disc recorder at Bradley's, and I had a disc recorder at Brown's, we used to make our own transcriptions there for the soap operas that we did, called *Second Spring,* we did 520 of those. That's something else, there's nothing easy when you're the only engineer, you do the run-through, you do the rehearsal, you do the recording, andnow that you have it, you do the splicing of that show, and then, you play it back. So that's about five times, and then when you send it, you make the disc, that's at least six times, and when you send it out to get it pressed, and when it comes back you have to listen to it again. Sometimes, seven, eight, nine times, you listen to the same program!

And no assistant either. It was all a one-man show. But the one-man show, you learned to do things. You have to. It's like that crawling down the telephone line; I had to figure out how to do that.

At Woodlawn, we started out with a console that we put together from parts supplied by Electrovoice, that was a console that had strips and amps installed. You had to build it; you had to build the framework and everything. Rotary faders in those early days. Later, we had linear faders. And then about the time we got that built, which incidentally, we had to build a second studio, because business got good, and we had to build a second studio. Then, we would move that console into the other room and get a new console. And the one we got this time was one that was built in Baltimore by Neil Muncy.

Neil built good consoles, and we ran with that for a couple of years. And eventually wound up with a Neve console in the main room. From then on, we were Neve addicts, and we would move one console out, and move the new Neve into the second studio, and so forth.

All of our consoles had some kind of equalization, even before the Neve. Each channel in Neil's had EQ. We had 16 mic channels in the first one he built. But they worked good, he built a good console.

The Neve consoles had a punch to it, a clarity to it, it wasn't that you didn't hear it, you *did* hear it, of course, combined with other things like microphones that make a difference, you could get what we thought was the sound we wanted, let's put it that way.

That was about that time that we started seeing some of the outboard signal processing. The LA2As and those things were making a lot of noise. A lot of West Coast people involved in some of those. And that was one thing that happened at Langevin. Langevin had moved to the West Coast, and when they did, they farmed out fifty-cent transformers for preamps. Farmed them out to another company. We got thirty of them went bad in that console.

So, that wasn't too good of a deal for them and wasn't too good for us either. But, there was a lot of that going on in gear. It got to the point where you could go to an audio engineering conference, and I went to a lot of them, West Coast, and New York, went to one in Europe; at a lot of them, you got to the point where you didn't really know whether what they were trying to sell worked or not. And I was guilty sometimes of buying something that when you got it back to the studio and you tried to do what they said it would do, it wouldn't do it!

It's difficult sometimes when you're not the principal engineer, and you're trying to talk an engineer into doing something, and he doesn't understand it or doesn't want to do it. And it doesn't work! I think some of it was resisting technology, but on the other hand, I've seen it work the other way, when they turned the knob or to do something, either that piece of gear was faulty, or it didn't work. But, that's to be expected I guess.

Of course, the echo chambers usually all worked. The EMT140s, the plates, we had several of those. I think we had four or five plates, and then, there got to be somebody who would claim they could stretch those plates much better if they had double clips on them, and I fell for that a couple of times! But sometimes those kinds of things worked.

Like the compressors, the LA2As, the Fairchild's, you have to learn how to use those. You've got to have enough patience and enough time with an artist, with someone that was willing to help you learn how to use them. It don't happen by themselves.

There were equalizers like the Pultecs and the Langs, we had all those. You finally get to where an artist will prefer one or the other. You know, "That doesn't sound like what we had last time." So you go and get what they had last time, "Yeah, that's better!" So artists make that a lot of that—especially those that have been around a while. Young artists that have not had much experience with it, they depend on someone to show them what to do. That works out very nice. But they will finally wise up to you, and they will say, "That don't sound exactly like what we had before," so then you start scrambling to see what they want. It's a cut-and-dry thing most of the time.

Most of the people I worked with, I guess maybe they trusted my judgment to some degree and, whatever I would choose, generally, they would accept that. But I tell you, the producers that I was associated with were strictly at our mercy in the matter of equipment to use. Most producers knew what they wanted in a song or a phrase, and I wouldn't know that. But the producer would have a really good idea what he wanted to accomplish with that song. And so you always had two different realms of expertise, one is concentrated on lyrics or the music pattern, and you're concentrating on other things that regard to making the session work, but it's really a different realm. So you've got two things working, and I think when you can get both people working on the same things, generally speaking, it's a better session.

Hank Williams' legacy was enhanced recently by the finding of a lot of old recordings. I don't know if you were aware of this or not, but Time-Life Music has unearthed a lot of old recordings. I have the whole repertoire. And I made some of the recordings at WSM in those days. So that was something that came out of the blue. I had received five shows from somebody that was interested in me getting the shows because I was mentioned on one of the shows by Hank Williams. So I've got that show at home. That happened back at my days at WSM. They were interesting days because you never knew what was going to happen.

Did you ever work at A&R in New York? Phil Ramone and I were good buddies. We did a show out of Felt Form in New York, and it was a Grammy show. And Phil and I were in charge of the sound. We walked in there, after this had been set up, both of us walked in there, and as soon as we walked in, we saw it—we both saw it at the same time. Whoever had put the speaker system in had put it behind the performers. We had to move that whole thing out! Get it out in front of the performers. What a mess it was. I don't know how that happened, but things happened in New York that don't happen anywhere else.

Chapter 13

Bob Katz

Bob Katz has recorded and mastered more than a thousand recordings, including three Grammy Award winners and several nominees. Located in Orlando, Fla., his compact disc (CD)-mastering house, Digital Domain, is versatile in all styles of music. Among Bob's specialties are Latin-jazz, salsa, merengue, reggaeton, and the like; Progressive Rock (with many works on the Laser's Edge and Sensory labels); some Metal (including well-known band Necrophagist on the Relapse label); and Classical and "audiophile," with over 100 audiophile jazz, rock, pop, and classical recordings on the Chesky label, of artists including Kenny Rankin, McCoy Tyner, Livingston Taylor, and Paquito D'Rivera.

Bob has designed several digital audio devices, including the VSP Digital Audio Control Center and Jitter Reducer (which was once a Stereophile Class A-listed item), and is the inventor of K-Stereo and K-Surround, patented processes that enhance the depth and spatiality of stereo recordings and convert stereo to 5.1, licensed to Weiss, Digital Domain, and Z-Systems and soon to be a plugin by Algorithmix.

Bob's written a popular book useful for producers, artists and repertoire (A&R), recording, mixing and mastering engineers, "Mastering Audio: The Art And the Science," published in English by Focal Press, now in its Second Edition, and in Spanish by Escuela de Cine y Video. He has written hundreds of tutorial articles and reviews published in professional audio magazines since 1971.

I'm Bob Katz and I was born in Hartford, Connecticut, sometime in the middle of the twentieth century. I started in audio around, '68–'69. But even before that I was taking apart tape recorders.

The first real recording system that I used was one that I built myself. I used to go out and record direct two tracks to a souped-up Revox high-speed 15 IPS) two-track recorder, and I built a recording console in a suitcase, literally a Samsonite suitcase, and that suitcase is long gone but I am getting the physical sensation right now of lifting that thing and carrying it. And you know the clothing rack where you could hang your ties in the middle of the Samsonite that would flip up? My patch bay was attached to that. It was really cool, and I got some great recordings of local folk, rock, and other

DOI: 10.4324/9781003519829-13

Figure 13.1 The first real recording system that I used was one that I built myself. I used to go out and record direct two-track to a souped-up Revox high-speed 15 IPS two-track recorder, and I built a recording console in a suitcase, literally a Samsonite suitcase, and that suitcase is long gone but I am getting the physical sensation right now of lifting that thing and carrying it. And you know the clothing rack where you could hang your ties in the middle of the Samsonite that would flip up? My patch bay was attached to that.

Figure 13.2 I have always been extremely progressive, when I went out to do my direct-to-two-track recordings, I treated it just the way you would in a professional studio or on any high-end remote truck and all my equipment was aligned. I brought the MRL alignment tape and test gear with me and set it all up before hitting "record."

groups. And I was probably the only local engineer who in 1971, when I was 22 years old, took an oscillator and aligned the recorder on location. So I was very serious about that.

I never went mainstream. The type of music that I specialized in was largely acoustically based music, and the recordings I did were mainly folk groups and jazz groups on location in performance, or we'd set up in a room that I thought had great acoustics and I would capture it, not the kind of minimalist miking that I specialized in when I, later on, went to do the audiophile recordings for Chesky, but very small numbers of multi-miking

Figure 13.3 You can push it and get more and more fuzz out of it. But, the kind of tube harmonic distortion that it produces is very consonant as opposed to the harsh distortions that were on the Willie Colon, and I made that recording sound vintage instead of ugly. It sounded nicely vintage, I would say. And, it really transformed it. And there is absolutely no emulator that can do that. The thing about plug-ins and digital processors today is they've come a long way but many of them cannot be abused as far as the analog gear that we still have.

Figure 13.4 There is a little light at the end of the tunnel, and it's called "loudness normalization." The demise of the CD and the introduction of downloads actually has a potential ray of hope and the proliferation of a single brand of reproduction equipment that begins with "a" and ends with "ipod" has permitted a feature that you can find in every iTunes and every iPod called "soundcheck" which is a primitive form of loudness normalization and compression available to the consumer which can be turned "on" when you're at the gym and turned "off" when you're on the Hi-Hi. When A&R directors and record producers learn that no matter how much they turn it up, the iPod will turn it back down I think there will be less hyper-compression practiced. And when major producers learn that all of their listeners are protesting, then maybe there will be less hyper-compression.

Figure 13.5 The best that any engineer looking at this whole set of issues that you are talking about today can do is to open up your eyes to the new power of digital processing, but use your ears to know when it sounds like crap. Take advantage of the more powerful tools and use the knowledge that it is really the manipulation of harmonic distortion that distinguishes a lot of the older analog gear.

Figure 13.6 I was using the LA2As mostly on vocals, but not in those live recordings. For the live recordings, I built a compressor out of a DBX noise reduction unit. I took out the equalization and used it as a delicate compressor on vocals. I was aware of all the outboard gear in the world, and when I worked one summer at a 24-track studio in Vermont, I did a group called Foghat. And, sure, we used all the outboard gear that was there and mixed with API automation and the VCA faders, and I was kind of turned off by the fidelity compared to the fidelity of the purist stuff that I had already built, but after all it was a living.

techniques, using them in such a way that I captured the ambience of the space as much as possible and recorded it direct to two tracks and then went back and edited those, mastering them or editing them from tape to tape. And multi-track when I went to New York. If a jazz group hired me, we would record in the large studios using whatever gear was there but I just preferred going to the two-track approach. It's a real challenge, and if you are good at it, you can really refine your mixing skills, when you then go to do a multi-track job you don't fool around as much.

Figure 13.7 My favorite analog gear at the time was the Massenburg equalizer, and I built my own mic preamps. They used Jensen Transformers and discrete analog transistor electronics, and that was what was in my suitcase. And Neve consoles, they were pretty cool, the LA2's were my favorite compressor, I used them on vocals.

In New York, I did more and more multitracking, but I never transitioned to it. I flirted with it. I recorded the Widespread Jazz Orchestra, formerly known as the Widespread Depression Orchestra, at Vanguard Studios onto 24 track and mixed it there using their MCI console, and it was easy enough to do, but by the mid 80s, I had such a reputation as a purist recording engineer that the number of multi-track recordings that I've done in my life... I could probably count as 25 to 50 to 75 as opposed to hundreds and hundreds and hundreds of direct to two-track recordings, and then, so when I went to do work for Chesky, that was the ultimate purist technique.

My favorite analog gear at the time was the Massenburg equalizer, and I built my own mic preamps. They used Jensen Transformers and discrete analog transistor electronics and that was what was in my suitcase. And Neve consoles, they were pretty cool, the LA2's were my favorite compressor, I used them on vocals.

When I recorded live, the only compressors I had were a pair of Allison Gain Brains. Remember I am working direct to two track, so I took the output of six channels and fed them into the Gain Brains and then fed the output of the Gain Brains into the echo return of the next mixer in line, and the instruments that needed a little bit of compression to be pushed above the level of the other instruments in the first six channels, and the instruments that didn't need any compression were in the other six channels. All I had was bass, midrange and treble, fixed frequency EQ. I would pick the microphones to get the tonality that I wanted. And I would often mix to a pair of Stax electrostatic headphones in a back room.

I have been mastering almost exclusively since 1990, and since 1990, I've probably done about four recordings, maybe five and they've all been jazz, and they've all been to multi-track, either Pro Tools or in one case analog tape, and using the studio's facilities.

I was using the LA2As mostly on vocals, but not in those live recordings. For the live recordings, I built a compressor out of a DBX noise reduction unit. I took out the equalization and used it as a delicate compressor on vocals. I was aware of all the outboard gear in the world, and when I worked one summer at a 24-track studio in Vermont, I did a group called Foghat. And, sure, we used all the outboard gear that was there and mixed with API automation and the VCA) faders, and I was kind of turned off by the fidelity compared to the fidelity of the purist stuff that I had already built, but after all it was a living.

Much of the analog gear at the time was disappointing, except for the Massenburg equalizer, which was built to George's standards, which certainly agree with my own. And, the discrete Neve was in another world as well, with the API consoles that I would occasionally operate. I was pretty disappointed with everything else. And, if you want to know the truth, I am not that turned on by anything made today in the console field except for modern-day API, which is of course a rebuild of what was back then. I'm totally turned on by that. I think you can make great recordings with those things.

They've got vintage drum machines now. I think they're fantastic. I mean, I think those eight-bit Linn drum sounds are the best in the world to tell you the truth. Get that right. I'm being sarcastic.

The fact is that there is every kind of vintage sound. There are vintage solid-state sounds; somebody's got a Germanium compressor now and I remember Germanium transistors sounding rather harsh. So, I don't know what that thing sounds like. The key word in vintage really is colored, because if you have a vintage piece of gear that is not colored, then why were people turned on by it? Okay, so I think it's fantastic because every piece of color that you can get through a piece of gear is going to help provide variety in sound and not have it sound quite so much the same which is what happens so much these days. So is there anything in particular in vintage gear that's nonsense? A broken Pultech isn't even nonsense if it provides a color or even the hum that gives you the feeling that you're looking for. People are often searching for feeling by plugging in a piece of vintage gear, and I would say 50% or more of that feeling is what comes from the warmth of your enjoying using it and turning on the musician to enjoy it.

I'll get recordings where the clients said "I just wanted to use these Neve modules and record to analog tape and (muffles voice) this is the sound I'm looking for, and so I think that he overdid it a little bit" ... so in any recording, you can have too much digital or you can have too much analog and perhaps a nice balance of them all. If you're recording in a dead multi-track studio, then the variety of colors you need to apply in order to get an artificial sense of depth is greater than if you record in a more open, acoustic environment. You'll get that depth automatically without having to resort to all those little color things. So, I think that a palette of use has to just simply be aware of the surroundings that are around us. These days, I resort to a number of artificial means to accomplish the things that we need from these dry, lifeless recordings. And, many times, they're not necessarily through vintage gear. I don't believe there's any such thing as magic, but I'm willing to plug in a piece of gear that I own, such as the Crane Song Tracker, and just pass the signal through it, and it sounds better on the output and say "wow, that's great." It acts just like a piece of vintage discrete API gear in its own way, but it has a little more "liquid color" than the API and a little bit less edge. I think that it's distortion characteristics, harmonic distortion characteristics that create that, and we can't do that very well right now in digital, so that's great. But if we know that in the future, we are going to be able to emulate that with formulas—when they get that right.

I wish I had more headroom in my console then. Nowadays, I can afford higher voltage components. So, anything that I work with today uses higher voltages, higher voltage rails. You know that Rupert Neve has a new console, 5088 I think is the number, and it has plus and minus 46-volt rails? I'm salivating already!

As far as what we had then, I'm dying for another C24. I think it's the most incredible microphone and I broke up with a partner—I got the Studer and he got the C24. I think I got the better of the deal but that was a gorgeous microphone.

As far as some of the changes in the business, I'm rather depressed by the last decade. If you want me to talk about the loudness race, you're going to run out of RAM. In the second edition of my book, I had a revelation, which is that the invention of digital recording has actually caused the extreme loudness race that we're in. And I do it with demonstrations in facts and figures. In Chapter 14 of my book, I demonstrate that digital recording is the cause of it, and if digital recording had not been invented, I think that "Californication" wouldn't have happened and the latest Metallica would not have happened.

The basic idea is that digital recording permits peak normalization which was never possible before. The RMS level goes up and up as the peak level kisses digital full scale. I mean people were saying, "Well, the meter's pinning, well that must be about plus 3 on the VU meter." What we're literally permitting to happen is VU meters that are constantly pinned that are running 12, 14, 16, 17 dB above their 0 VU range...that's what it has come to. Think about that. And, unfortunately, since loudness trumps anything and everything, it sets the bar for the competition, and since the loudness race has always existed, it's pretty hard to back off.

Now, if you're not asking the question, I'll answer the question that comes next, which is "Is there any way out of this?" And yes, there is a little light at the end of the tunnel and it's called "loudness normalization." The demise of the CD and the introduction of downloads actually have a potential ray of hope, and the proliferation of a single brand of reproduction equipment that begins with "a" and ends with "ipod" has permitted a feature that you can find in every iTunes and every iPod called "soundcheck" which is a primitive form of loudness normalization and compression available to the consumer, which can be turned "on" when you're at the gym and turned "off" when you're on the Hi-Fi. When A&R directors and record producers learn that no matter how much they turn it up, the iPod will turn it back down—I think there will be less hyper-compression practiced. And when major producers learn that all of their listeners are protesting, then maybe there will be less hyper-compression.

For mastering these days, my current two platforms are Sequoia and Sadie together. My book editor and colleague Eric James believes in what he calls "horses for courses" which is that there's no perfect DAW, and that you have to use one for this kind of application and one for that, and so on...whereas I really want my DAW to be the jack of all trades, and so whenever I switch from one to the other, I hammer on the next one and say, "You've got to have the features that we lost in the other one." And maybe it's a losing cause. Maybe I'll end up dropping both of those in a year and switching over to Pyramix, which would be another choice, but then again another unknown for me with its own potential compromises.

Among analog gear, I have a lot of Crane Song gear and I use the Pendulum OCL-2. It's a wonderful little tube compressor that's very transparent and yet has a very subtle liquid color. There was a Willie Colon all-digital recording that was made with a Mitsubishi—which a lot of people raved about, I don't know if it was misused or abused or whatever, but this recording was very harsh and very bright and very distorted, and it was made in the early 80s; and I got it transferred digitally to a.wav file before I mastered it; and it was almost unlistenable. It was just terrible. And Greg Gualtieri who was the designer of the Pendulum OCL-2—I have two of them now, one in studio A and one in studio B—I had him build in a saturation circuit that allows me to push the internal first gain stage of the OCL 2 much further than in its original design so it can be more than just a transparent compressor, or semi-transparent compressor. You can push it and get more and more fuzz out of it. But, the kind of tube harmonic distortion that it produces is very consonant as opposed to the harsh distortions that were on the Willie Colon, and I made that recording sound vintage instead of ugly. It sounded nicely vintage, I would say. And, it really transformed it. And there is absolutely no emulator that can do that. The thing about plug-ins and digital processors today is they've come a long way but many of them cannot be abused as far as the analog gear that we still have. You can use a number of compressor plug-ins which, if used on even primary instruments in a mix with either a half dB to one dB of gain reduction just pushed a little bit and not trying to get too much character out of it, sound quite good or more than acceptable. But when you need to be aggressive with it for some reason they don't seem to hold up as well. And that's where the outboard gear comes into use in my studio.

I am not a Luddite. As I have mentioned, I have always been extremely progressive, when I went out to do my direct-to-two-track recordings I treated it just the way you would in a professional studio or on any high-end remote truck, and all my equipment was aligned. I brought the MRL alignment tape and test gear with me and set it all up before hitting "record." Today, I'm not afraid to use either digital or analog gear in any combination. And, I've found ways of getting warm, vintage quality sounds out of all digital processing. So, I don't think that you have to use any vintage gear at all for the average recording session unless you run into those severe issues like the Willie Colon that I mentioned.

For example, I am taking incredible advantage of the TC electronic system 6000, which has one of the most powerful sets of digital processing tools available in a single box today. And, there are people that have no idea how to use those kinds of things who are still stuck in their analog domains and can't come close to the power and the clarity that I can get with some of the tools that are in the system 6000. The best that any engineer looking at this whole set of issues that you are talking about today can do is to open up your eyes to the new power of digital processing, but use your ears to know when it sounds like crap. Take advantage of the more powerful tools and use the knowledge that it is really the manipulation of harmonic distortion that distinguishes a lot of the older analog gear.

I have clients who would not imagine, would have no idea that their master just got passed through three or four pieces of digital gear in series, they would have no idea whatsoever because it can be warm and open and full of depth and give great, great, great results. I even invented an algorithm that takes advantage of techniques that we did not imagine back in the analog days to accomplish capturing or recapturing the depth in recording. And it's all digital and it sounds, pardon my bias, it sounds fantastic. Ask any mastering engineer who is familiar with it.

Chapter 14

Danny Leake

Guitarist Danny Leake was a Chicago recording studio mainstay in the 1960s and 1970s. An in-demand session player while still in his teens, Leake can be heard on numerous records that date from those times. Leake eventually expanded his talents by becoming a much sought-after live sound and studio recording engineer. Leake's exhaustive discography includes Chicago soul favorites Tyrone Davis, the Chi-Lites, and other acts produced by Carl Davis on Brunswick Records as well as vocal group Heaven and Earth. Now focused on engineering, Leake co-produced some exciting and interesting 1970s disco that still sounds fresh today. In the late 1970s, Leake formed a writing/producing partnership with English dance producer Ian Levine. Recording out of Chicago, the two recruited and developed local talent and, in the process, created some of the most crafted, infectious, and long-lived disco music released from that genre's heyday. Levine and Leake's productions included songs with strong melodies and emotionally layered lyrics, surrounded by the highly inventive arrangements of Fiachra Trench, full orchestras, top session musicians, and sophisticated sound engineering. Two acts that Levine/Leake produced remain perennial favorites of classic disco lovers and serious dance aficionados: James Wells and Barbara Pennington.

During the 1980s, Leake became more involved in the technical aspects of making a record. Under the tutelage of industry veteran Murray Allen at Universal Recording Studios in downtown Chicago, Leake developed into an adept engineer in the field of studio and live concert engineering. When Allen (the owner of Universal) moved to pursue other business interests, Universal was sold and dismantled, to the lament and sorrow of many musicians and engineers. Leake started his own audio engineering company, Urban Guerrilla Engineers, whose activities took him all over the world, recording both indoor and outdoor events. He also was a multi-term president of the Engineering and Recording Society (EARS) of Chicago.

Danny Leake passed away in April of 2020. He was 69 years old.

DOI: 10.4324/9781003519829-14

Figure 14.1 More than anything else I had a concept. I had what a lot of kids don't have, don't get the chance to have, I had a very good concept in my head of what a good sound was and what I wanted to get. Then, it just became a thing of "Okay, what gear do I have to have to make this happen for the sound that I have in my head that I want to hear?" I took that same thing in digital, when digital came out it was more of a thing of "Okay, now what can I do to do what I do on this?"...Being a musician had a lot to do with it, but it also had a lot to do with hanging out with guys who knew what they were doing, something a lot of cats don't have these days. I trained about 15–20 guys who are out making records and doing movies now. We got a chance like they got a chance to hang out with me, I got a chance to hang out with other guys. And these days I see you know, cats are buying big Pro Tools units. They sit in their bedrooms, and it's like incest because they're basically dealing with their own stuff as opposed to hanging out with somebody who knew what they were doing.

Figure 14.2 And for them, I did the first Budweiser rock n roll spots, rock spots with the orchestra and the rock and football players, and all the rest of that junk, and it won great awards and stuff and they pulled their entire, I think it was six million dollars of work from Streeterville for Universal. I sent the guy back a letter and said "Thanks for the clients, and maybe next time, a black person walks in here and asks for a job maybe you won't tell him the same thing you told me."

Figure 14.3 It was a jazz group and he'd come to the studio and he'd say, "You know, when we play live, there's a certain thing that happens. I'd like to play that way in the studio." And everybody was telling him he couldn't do it. No, no there'll be leakage, you can't do that, you have to do it separately and blah blah blah. And somebody told him to give me a call, and I said "Well the truth is that's how we used to do it back in the day." And what I did was I found him a studio that was big enough that we could have everybody in the room, the one concession I got them to make was, "Why don't you sit here in this booth in case you want to change anything that you don't want." But the eye contact is still there and it was a great recording. Guy got some critical reviews and we're doing another one next year, but I get a lot of stuff like that.

Figure 14.4 What I talk to a lot of kids about today is a 24-track machine is very much like a 35-millimeter camera. Okay so you say like 35-millimeter camera is not reality, but there was an artistic thing that was happening to it. With a 24-track machine, you could change the lens on it or you could change the focus, messing around with the bias. You could change all of that, you can change how sound came off the tape and what kind of tape affected it also. There were a lot of variables, I said, in order to make what was happening. I used BASF, I mean I used that stuff all the time because it had a certain thing that I liked. So with digital, I said "Well, what you put in is what you get out." And so now, you're in a position of having to do a lot of high work processing trying to get the certain things that tape used to just give you automatically.

Figure 14.5 A good friend of mine is an owner of API, named Larry Droppa... I asked him "Hey man, what about this Waves plug-in thing man, what does that sound like? Is that close or is that some bullshit?" He says "Well you know, it sounds pretty good, we didn't want it to sound too good because we're trying to sell the hardware units. I must admit this is very close." I picked it up and tried it out on some stuff and it feels very much like the old API hardware units that I remember. It definitely has a different sound than some of the plug-in stuff that was floating around. So I'm like, "Okay, can I make a track with this?" Well, see, ordinarily I would've jacked it out of the inserts into the analog thing and brought it back in trying to get that sound, and the sound was there. I keep telling people as the computers get more powerful and as the speed of processing gets up, then I get closer and closer and closer to the magic analog units that we talk about...The magic was the faults of it, the randomness of it, because it's not perfect and it wasn't a perfect thing and it had this art thing going for it.

Figure 14.6 I remember some kids sent me a bunch of beats and stuff, and I told them "You gotta understand man, there's nothing here that you've given me that I haven't heard before." They said "Well, what do you do when you program stuff? What do you do drums with?" When I need percussion? "I'll be truthful with you man, I make a call to Lenny Castro or whatever" I said "You know why? Because these are guys who beat things in rhythm for a living, they're going to approach it a lot differently than I am. I'm a guitar player. No matter what I think of, they're always gonna be better." Get cats that are specialized in that. Get musicians.

I'm Danny Leake from Sardis, Mississippi, a little hole-in-the-wall place that my mother ran away from as soon as possible. I don't remember anything about Mississippi; she ran up to Chicago and Chicago's all I ever really knew.

I started out as a guitar player, and I was always interested in playing guitar and I got really good at it to the point where I got a chance to start playing sessions and touring when I was still a teenager. I got a job with The Five Stair Steps when I was 17 years old, right out of high school. It was a funny thing, I was sort of in that position where they used to have the old chitlin circuit you know, the old theaters and stuff, and I had a chance to experience all that before it went away. I've always had a chance to experience old things before they went away. Like, I remember four and eight track. And I got into the studio, and all the little meters and tape machines sitting around sort of fascinated me. I said "Hey, how do you get into this? How do you learn this?" and he looked at me, laughed, and turned around and walked off, and I thought "Well, what's so damn funny?" Well, what was funny was that no blacks at the time in Chicago were doing any type of studio work or anything like that. There were some guys working out of their basements, but no major stuff.

So I started getting all the books that I could read; then, I got drafted into the army, and I won't even talk about the war service, but once I got transferred over to Germany, I ran into a situation where there was a bunch of us musicians trying to get their chops back up before they got out of the service. And we got together as a band, and we started making really good money because the Germans paid really good money for really authentic stuff, and I got the idea, "Hey, we could record some records and sell them on the gigs and stuff." This German studio and this guy just recorded nothing but oom-pah music, he had no idea what we were trying to do, so I sort of fired him, and I said "I can do this." And actually, I got it onto the tape some kind of way, I forged a pass, went to a festival in Cannes France, and told everybody I got flown there from Chicago, so they thought I was a player you know. And I actually managed to sell the group to Roy Featherstone at EMI records.

So we released an album as Pure Poison. I had gotten out of service, put another band together because half of the guys stayed in the service, and we toured England. But being EMI artists gave me access to Abbey Road Studios, so I used to just hang out there all the time, and I got to meet a lot of interesting people, cats that cut The Beatles and things like that, and I learned a lot of stuff from those guys and I thought, "You know, I really want to be an engineer." I came back to America and I said, "Okay, I'm going to get a job as a grunt in a studio, sweeping the floor just so I can learn." Found that nobody would hire me again because I was black, so I went back to playing the guitar, and again, I started making really, really good money, but I was still studying the stuff.

I took an accelerated course with the Institute of Audio Research that was out in LA. It was about one month. It was a real intense thing—we didn't even go to a studio, we just met in this hotel room in Al Grundy's, and just talked basic stuff. Then, I got back to Chicago, I'm playing guitar in sessions, and I used to hang out after the gigs and guys would think, "Oh yeah man, he's really into the music." But really, I was watching what the engineer was doing. And one day it hit me; I looked at the guy and it all came together. I said "I know exactly what he's trying to do, and I know why it's not going to work. I know what he's doing wrong." And I just watched him crash and burn.

So it was a cool thing to say I think I have a handle on this, and I had a chance to produce a guy, he wanted me to help him mix the tracks and I said, "Well we can't mix it at this studio. We need to find a place where he can possibly mix it." And we ended up at a place called Paul Sereno's, and Paul said, "Yeah, well I got a great engineer for you." I said, "I want to mix it myself." He said, "Well, of course you know if you screw it up you gotta pay for it." But I started wiring up all of this stuff that I had learned from the guys in England and I asked him "Tell me what you think of this. I'm playing this thing, he's looking at me, I've got the whole studio wired in." He offered me a job, wasn't for a lot of money, but I didn't care, I was making a lot of money playing guitar. What was more important, I had the keys to the studio.

I stayed there for about two-and-a-half years. I worked my way up to the head of the studio, and later on, we sort of fell out and I was going to move to LA, and I thought "Well, you know, if I'm as good as I say I am or I think I am, I should be able to work here in Chicago too." My kids were here, and I went to several studios, CRC was a major studio here, I knew the owner, and he wasn't there when this happened. I went to a place called Streeterville; the guy told me "Hey man, I've heard the stuff you've done, you've got really good skills man, but I can't hire you because none of my clients will use you because you're black." I said, "Okay, I appreciate you being honest."

And what happened was I stopped off at Universal Studios, which is the biggest studio in town, Murray Allen, you know, and I said "Look, I know you're not looking for anybody, but I just want to leave a resume in case you ever thinking about hiring somebody." He took the resume; he was like, "Hey, let me take you on a tour." He took me on a tour of the entire place. It was much bigger than I thought it was. He had film mixing suites and all kinds of stuff there, and he came back and he said, "Okay, what do you need to work here?" I hadn't even thought about that. He called the studio manager and they actually offered me more money than I'd even thought about, but he had heard a lot of work that I'd done, and I had actually stolen a lot of record business from the studio. I was a pretty good engineer at the time, and his thing was he didn't care about the race or anything like that, he just wanted the studio to sound the best it could, and he hired me and it's funny because for six months nobody ever spoke to me. I'd say hello to people they'd just walk by, and I thought I was there for affirmative action or something.

And it didn't change until all of a sudden everybody realized, "My god, he's got my clients because our clients started coming." I also went back to Streeterville. I had a major client there, Arthur Einstein, and I had a dinner meeting with this guy I was like, "You guys write some really great stuff man. It's a shame it doesn't sound any better on the air than it does." I said, "Give me a chance to do at least one of your things man. I guarantee you'll never go back there again." And he said, "Do you know anything about rock?" I said, "Yeah, I was hanging out with the guys in England and everything." And for them, I did the first Budweiser rock 'n' roll spots, rock spots with the orchestra, and the rock and football players, and all the rest of that junk, and it won great awards and stuff and they pulled their entire, I think it was six million dollars of work from Streeterville for Universal. I sent the guy back a letter and said "Thanks for the clients, and maybe next time a black person walks in here and asks for a job maybe you won't tell him the same thing you told me." I worked my way up to Chief of Music Engineering in Universal, yeah I stayed there about 11 years, and that was my first experience with digital.

When I started recording they had old Scully 8 tracks and things like that, and I thought that was a lot of tracks back then, you know? I saw it go from 4 to 8 to 16, 24. So I had a chance to experience all that stuff.

Paul had 24 tracks. That was in 1977. He had an API console in the main room, and actually what a lot of people didn't realize, he had an old Neve 8028, had 12 buses and junk, but it had eight 1073 modules, and that was in our B studio that nobody wanted to work in. That's one of the things that helped me get the gear over at Universal. I did one freelance gig at Universal, and a buddy of mine asked me to come in and record a bunch of stuff for him, and Murray had bought a new 8078 big Neve, which is actually a big version of the small one that we had over at Paul's.

So when I came over there, everybody was expecting that the assistant's going to do all the work because nobody knew how to operate the Neve, and I just grabbed a bunch of patch cords and started working, and because I knew the console I said, "Well, okay, the other one's 12 buses, this is 32 buses." Everybody looked pale, it was funny, when I was working there was a whole crowd of people back in the back, but I didn't realize what the big thing was. Everybody was surprised I knew anything about that console. We happened to have one at Paul Sereno's. Paul was interested in that, he was first on a lot of stuff. We had the first FET boxes that we had gotten from George Massenburg out in California because he'd been working out there doing demos of Paul's. They said "Hey man, we want these fat boxes" they called them, so we had a bunch of those.

We had the first automated mixing in Chicago, the Allison, bouncing from track to track. Tons of 1076 Kepexes we had some LA2s, a couple of Pultecs, standard stuff. What was cool was that the console was an API with the 550 equalizers, so right from the jump you're starting out with something good. So I had gotten used to really good-sounding stuff you know, and going to Universal was even better because he had the 1078 Neve and Universal had like six of everything, everything was in boxes and if you had a session you just brought the boxes in and connected them.

He also had Pultecs, and he had LA2s, LA3s, you name it. He had just about everything that you could possibly want in a studio back at that time and even more so. When something new came out people brought it out. When digital reverb came out, he had one of the first units. People were like, "Here, try this."

We had the PrimeTime reverbs, the PrimeTime delays, we had the Ursa Major stuff, the Lex 224, the first one, and the delay also, the PCM41's, 42's, things like that.

I had bought a Super PrimeTime because I liked that. I was one of the first cats to start buying his own gear because basically, I was the record guy, but did spots too, and I was trying to get my record sound on the spot stuff. So you want to be quick. I had a lot of stuff preset, but the cool thing about Murray's place, because he was such a giant in the industry, was that everybody always tossed stuff out at him, like when B&K started making studio microphones, 4006s, omni-mics, everybody was afraid to use them, but they sent them to Murray to check out. I read this book, Microphone Technique and Application, where he talked about cool things about omni-microphones so I tried it out and it was great, so I bought four of them. Those are nice mics, I like those. He had about six 47s, let's see, there were two C12s, another six 67s, he had a couple of M49s. Man, you name it, RCA 77s, 44s, all that stuff.

It was a fun place to work. I miss it a lot. It was designed by Bill Putnam, and it's funny, when you want that sound made you go out to LA to Cello Studios or Allen Sides' place, it's got the same sound because they were all designed by Bill.

It's funny, later on, everybody was like crazy about LA2s, and LA2 really wasn't that big of a deal to me. I had Aretha Franklin in the studio one time, I put an LA2 on her and she was so loud and so big and so fast that it just went past the LA2 before it could even grab it. I was like, "Okay, enough of that, let's hook up the 1176." because you need that kind of horsepower and that kind of speed. I like the Pultecs on vocals. I liked what it did on the top-end stuff, especially a lot of vocals that I was working with.

It's my vocal chain; at Universal, for instance, I always had a good C12 out there. I have the console 1078 EQ, but I also have a Pultec just to hit that top because it was just something nice that happened with the tubes up there. Later on, when John Hardy came out with his preamps, I used to bypass the preamps in the console and use the Hardy preamps because they just sounded cleaner to me. Some people wanted that sort of thick sound that the Neve's had, but when I wanted something that was exactly what was happening out there I went with the Hardy's.

Murray put an SSL in studio B. The first thing I did was cut a session and compared it to the stuff I had done on the Neve, and it was a very, very different sound. It wasn't the type of sound that I liked. I also didn't like the fact that you went through about 10–15 stages of electronics that you couldn't bypass, but you could bypass on the Neve.

More than anything else I had a concept. I had what a lot of kids don't have, don't get the chance to have, I had a very good concept in my head of what a good sound was and what I wanted to get. Then, it just became a thing of "Okay, what gear do I have to have to make this happen for the sound that I have in my head that I want to hear?" I took that same thing in digital, when digital came out it was more of a thing of "Okay, now what can I do to do what I do on this?"

Being a musician had a lot to do with it, but it also had a lot to do with hanging out with guys who knew what they were doing, something a lot of cats don't have these days. I trained about 15–20 guys who are out making records and doing movies now. We got a chance like they got a chance to hang out with me; I got a chance to hang out with other guys. And these days I see you know, cats are buying big Pro Tools units. They sit in their bedrooms and it's like incest because they're basically dealing with their own stuff as opposed to hanging out with somebody who knew what they were doing.

I had a guy who told me he thought the system was broken because of the quality of things that were coming out of the system, and he called me in to do something for him and when I did it for him, it came out the way he wanted. "Wow! Why can't I do this?" I mean, you can do that but this is not a part-time thing for me. I said, "I was a guitar player making a hell of a lot of money, and when I really got into sound, one day I looked up and said damn, I haven't played guitar in a year." If you get really serious about it, I taught my assistant it's not a part-time thing with me. And because of that I studied really hard, and I don't care what it is. If I'm recording on a Mackie with some toy stuff, it's going to sound a certain way because I'm off working on it until it does. Again, that comes from a concept of "Okay, I want to hear this, now how can I get what I do on this?"

I hung out with those guys sort of stealth. Like I said, I'd just hang out and observe, and I read everything I could get my hands on. I think I have every REP magazine from 1970—something all the way until the point they died in a box upstairs, and I read them all. That's sort of where a lot of my training came in. And then sitting around watching cats and getting an idea of what was cool and what wasn't. It's all about having a concept in sound and you can't have that unless you hang out with somebody who knows what they're doing.

After Universal went under, I went freelance. I ended up doing live stuff actually. I was working with Johnny Gill up in Flyte Tyme, with Jimmy Jam and Terry Lewis up in Minneapolis, and he said, "Look, I'm going to Japan next week and I don't have a front-of-house guy, can you do that for me?" I said, "Sure, how hard can it be?" The first gig was at a place called the Tokyo Dome, which holds about 65,000 people; it was a festival gig with Hall & Oates, the Doobie Brothers, some of the biggest acts of that time. And a bunch of guys that had been doing stuff for years and years and I had never done a live thing in my life. I was sort of faking it, but I'm a good faker. I'm a quick learner.

To give you an idea we had one guy doing live sound, he had a Neve out there, he was doing live sound with a portable Neve. And I brought some outboard, I brought a Harmonizer, a digital delay, an outboard EQ, so everybody thought "Oh he knows what he's doing." I didn't have a clue. I sort of made it up, but I thought the show sounded horrible and everybody told me it was the best thing they heard, and those guys are going "Damn, maybe I need to figure out what he did so I can reproduce it."

I told them "You ever go out again, I'd like to work with you again." And I toured with them for about a year. I hung out with a guy called David "Dansir" McCullough. He wanted to do studio work, I wanted to know more about live stuff. We did a trade... he showed me street engineering, I showed him street studio engineering, and that was cool. After that, I got the gig with Stevie Wonder because Stevie had been touring and he got the idea that he wanted to tour with just live guys. He says

> I want to get rid of the synthesizers. I just want this thing called the Natural Wonder, where there's going to be an orchestra, a 50 piece orchestra, my band and me. The only thing is I don't know how to make the orchestra live with a band that plays that loud.

Just off the top of my head, oh, I'd say just stick a microphone in front of everybody in the orchestra and call it a day.

It's funny, I joked around with a buddy, it's fine now that I got the gig, let's figure out how to do it. And what helped me out was I had worked with the CSO and Lyric opera, a lot of orchestras like that at Universal, so I knew what orchestras sounded like. So clipping microphones on the orchestra when I pull it together, I knew there were certain things you had to do to make it feel like an orchestra because strings aren't meant to be picked up by a little microphone. I scooped things out, I built a reverb thing just for them, and I got to the point where I could turn the orchestra up as loud as the band, and the band was playing 110 on the stage. So I got that gig.

Later on, I did the same thing for Dennis DeYoung when he decided he wanted a 50-piece orchestra with a rock band, and usually in a situation like that, either the rock band was wimped out for the orchestra or you couldn't hear the orchestra over the rock band. I got a situation where I could turn the strings up as loud as the rock guitarists and stuff and it was a great show. But I did a certain amount of that. I ended up freelance more than anything else, so I did a lot of work out in LA, bounced around different studios. I'd go through the AES (Audio Engineering Society) every year, so I met a lot of people, made a lot of connections.

Then, I was doing some Ramsey Louis records, and the first record I did for him, I'm very proud of this record, they were going to New York to master it, and I said, "Oh that's great." Cool, cool, they're going to Sterling, and I didn't think anything about that. I happened to be in New York that week; they said, "Hey man, we're mastering it, come on by." I said, "Hey, okay." So I came by and they were mastering with this guy who's name I'll just leave out, but I'm sitting there and things really sound strange to me. I wasn't there officially, because if I was there officially I would've said, "Let me play something so I can get used to the room." I said "hey maybe there's something strange here that I don't know about." I said, "I don't want to even make any comment until I hear it at home."

So I got a copy of the mastering and it was butt-ass awful. I was like, "Wow, whoa, what's wrong?" Well, turns out the guy who was mastering it had never mastered real instruments. He had done a lot of hip-hop, a lot of things, well he got Ramsey's piano, and he thought the piano was too bright so he rolled the top end off the piano. But then he thought "Aw gee, it's not exciting enough." So he put it through an Aural Exciter, there was all this high-end crunchy shit I was hearing, and he was mastering it on a set of KRK's, which was a little strange anyway. I mastered with Bob Ludwig, I knew what real mastering was, and I told him; I said, "Look man, this is broke," and he said "aw, you're just saying that cause you mixed it"' I said "No, no, no."

Well, I had borrowed a TCM 5000 I was thinking about buying for reverb, but it had a CD-mastering thing in it, which I didn't know how to operate, so I screwed around with it a little bit, and what I did was I took some of the safety DATs that I had of the mix and ran a few of the tunes through there and went to Ramsey's office, they're playing the mastering the guy did, I played this thing. He was saying "Damn man, that's gorgeous. When did you do that?" I said, "Look man, I did this in my bedroom at about 6 o'clock this morning, there's no way I should even come close to what this guy did." I said "I'm not saying that Sterling's a bad place." because I knew a lot of great guys there. "This guys isn't one of them. Take it to a real guy and please redo it."

And that's what they did. They took it to Greg Calbi, excellent, talented guy. Calbi did a wonderful job on the record. And that got me fascinated with the mastering trip. I said, "Boy, this guy totally negated everything that I had done." What exactly is mastering? Because usually I'd send stuff out and it'd come back, it would be wonderful. I was like, "What exactly is it?" and so I got interested in mastering, and it turned into a hole that I poured my money into. But it was a fascinating thing. I found that for real mastering, for me, is not so much remixing a guy's track, you're almost like a restorer of fine art. Just like if you were going to restore the Mona Lisa, you'd basically make it clear so people can see it better and really appreciate the art. You wouldn't repaint the painting, and you would use a light touch. That was my concept on it. I guess that comes from being a mixer myself, and what's really cool was that a lot of guys, my greatest fans, man, are mixing engineers. They say "Hey man, I got the mix back and it still sounds like my mix only it sounds great everywhere I play it."

I do a lot of that now. Always, when you get deep into something, things get crazy. First I had Genelecs and those went. And then at the AES, I met Brad Lunde and Trans Audio and the ATCs and I love these. What was funny about it was that we put something together, wire them out of phase, put pink noise out of them at 95 decibels for 3 days, burning the system in. Whoa, I was like, okay… so I set them out there where Jake is, went out of town for 3 days, came back you know, set it up. I said "Okay, now" put some stuff in here man, this is great. I spent basically a BMW I was going to buy for this. Then, I put the CD in and it was horrible. I was like, "God, that's awful!" I put another one in and it was awful. I'm putting in all of this stuff that I thought was cool and they were awful, and I thought "Aw man, I spent all of this money and they suck!" and I put this track in that was actually by a guy I helped train, Rich Breen, he was nominated for a Grammy for engineering, I put that track in there and it was gorgeous. It was like I could reach in and grab things and that was how great the recording was. Then I put another thing in and it sucked, then I put another thing in and it was good.

Then I realized "Whoa, what's happening here?" It was that this is exactly what's on the track. These things don't help you with anything, there is no hype there, I said. And what made them really great for mastering speakers is that I could hear instantly what was wrong really fast, and if it was right, there was nothing to do. I didn't have to search around trying to figure out what the speakers are trying to tell me. Hey, bang, it was there. And what they also told me is that the gear in my chain wasn't any good. I started replacing all of that stuff and got to the point where I'm happy now. So basically, I've been doing that.

A lot of my work these days comes from guys who want to do a lot of live stuff, want to do something concerning microphones, which is fun for me too. I got a call from a guy the other week, said he wanted to do what we had done here a year ago, it was a jazz group, and he'd come to the studio and he'd say "You know, when we play live, there's a certain thing that happens. I'd like to play that way in the studio." And everybody was telling him he couldn't do it. No, no there'll be leakage, you can't do that, you have to do it separately and blah blah blah. And somebody told him to give me a call, and I said "Well the truth is that's how we used to do it back in the day." And what I did was I found him a studio that was big enough that we could have everybody in the room, the one concession I got them to make was, "Why don't you sit here in this booth in case you want to change anything that you don't want." But the eye contact is still there and it was a great recording. Guy got some critical reviews and we're doing another one next year, but I get a lot of stuff like that. As far as using microphones is concerned. Also that's a reason why I was able to make the transition to live a lot easier than most guys. When I came up, a rhythm date was 10 or 15 guys in a room at once and you had a bunch of faders to deal with. It was never one fader at a time or with a trackball.

There are pluses and minuses to the trackball or the mouse. I thought that when I made the transition to working with Pro Tools and the whole mouse and editing thing I said "I'll probably get a controller and end up with faders and I'll figure out how to do my thing on this." And what was fascinating for me is, now I find I'm on the edit page, I'm not looking at the fader page at all. I like the idea of being able to move lines, and I got real quick and fast about it. However for me that is not the technology, it's not the end of the thing, it's always the music. I got a thing on my website I said "music should not be a slave to the technology." And at all times it's always about "What can I do to make the music better?" Well I found that being able to go in and dip this word or raise this word, I said "Gee, it's pretty much like what I used to do on the old Neecam with the flying faders," but I can see it now. So I was like, "Damn, I wouldn't have thought that I would find myself sitting on a page looking at wave forms." as much as I do.

Analog gear that was particularly disappointing? LA2s were disappointing for me at the time, but I found out later on more than anything else that old analog gear, especially tube gear, that they were just about hand-built pieces. They're like old vintage cars. Just because it's a 47 doesn't mean it's a great 47. They were all different you know. And it's the same thing with analog pieces. If you find a wonderful one, that's wonderful, but don't necessarily think that the one that you get in the next studio is going to sound the same way. I used to rent certain pieces and I would always say, "I want this piece # so on and so on and so on." So I knew what it sounded like. The LA2s at Universal were sort of a disappointment for me compared to some of the ones I worked on later on. So, the LA2s are something I didn't use a lot. 1176s I used a lot, the LA3s I liked on guitars. I thought I liked the LA3s more than I liked the LA2s.

Analog this analog that, it's just like I was over at Columbia College the other day and Pro Tools fell over, and they had to record on the 24 track machine, and that was a wild experience because these guys never knew if the thing was aligned or whatever, but it was an old Otari machine, and I gotta be truthful with you, I would never record anything on an Otari. My thing was, we had hotrodded MCIs and after that it was Studers for me. The Otari's always sounded funny, they didn't make it for me, but for these kids, it was their only experience in analog. So I said "Analog, but you haven't really heard enough analog to really make that call." Definitely, the machines were different, but what I talk to a lot of kids about today is a 24-track machine is very much like a 35-millimeter camera. Okay so you say like 35-millimeter camera is not reality, but there was an artistic thing that was happening to it. With a 24-track machine, you could change the lens on it or you could change the focus, messing around with the bias. You could change all of that, you can change how sound came off the tape and what kind of tape affected it also. There were a lot of variables, I said, in order to make what was happening. I used BASF, I mean I used that stuff all the time because it had a certain thing that I liked. So with digital, I said, "Well, what you put in is what you get out." And so now, you're in a position of having to do a lot of high work processing trying to get the certain things that tape used to just give you automatically.

Not as radically, but definitely, the DAs and ADs, that color the sound in a certain way. Like I said, when I got these speakers, all of a sudden nothing worked. The converter? Toss. A lot of gear, toss. So I ended up with the head units, and each one has a different color. Bob Ludwig has about ten different converters. One thing I got from Calbi, I mastered something with Calbi, and Calbi had several tape machines in there with different electronics and he said they're all different, and I'd get my 1/2-inch tape, "Well, we'll have to listen to this. Well, let's try it on this one, this electronics." And each thing colored it a different way. One colored them in a way, "Hey, I sort of like that." Then, it was different converters and stuff. It's like you're painting the picture with sound, and converters and microphones and things like that are different paints that you use to make the picture. And what I find really interesting, well, I want to check out, there was this unit it was an Adamod or something like that, this is an analog piece that mimics biasing on a tape machine for guys going to digital work stations. I said "I gotta check that out!"

My experiences with Pro Tools, when I started making that run in, I was still cutting it straight to analog because I wanted the ability to edit, I would take that, and I would toss that up on Pro Tools in 96, but only after the HD rigs came out. I couldn't even deal with the ones before the HD, the 888 units; I just heard the sound dying. Everybody else thought I was crazy, I may be crazy man, but I hear it.

Anything I have now that you wished I had then? Well I tell you, I produced a thing in 1989 for a guy named Darryl Tookes for SBK records, and we were moving things around and I had to re-edit stuff and ended up using converters. I would've killed to have had the head converters then.

If I had the ability to do things in 96 24 bit, I would've killed to have been able to do that, and at the time, we really didn't understand what was happening bit-wise or clockwise no one was even talking about clocks as far as sampling rate. But when I first started cutting digital… this is 1979 on the old 3M 32 track systems, I was still approaching it like it was analog tape, which was, you'd fill the track up as much as you can and back off a little bit and call it a day. It was digital, you didn't have to worry about levels anymore, you can cut them really low, big dynamic range and blah blah blah. Well, I still hurled my stuff up to the red then backed it off. I found out that it was a 16-bit system and I was using all 16 bits, and everybody else by cutting low was using less bits, and my stuff actually sounded better. I didn't know scientifically what I was doing, I just lucked out just from me using my old analog techniques, but I think now, with 24 bits, you don't have to paint the red.

You want to hear something funny man? The old guys were mixing the F1s, and I had a beta hi-fi machine. I used to bring my beta hi-fi machine from home and drop stuff on that because that, to me, sounded better than the F1.

Anything I had then that I wish I had now? I wish I had a Neve console or API console. I miss the concept of consoles period. I mean big gear. We can talk about microphones and things, but I had a DMX 1580 from AMS. Yeah, the delays on those suckers, these days you're like, "Oh, well, let's use a digital delay." You use a delay in Pro Tools, if you use the regular delay that they got in that, and I used to have a trick man, with the 1580, where I would take it off of the clock a little bit, maybe 14 milliseconds on one side, ten on another side, and I would put a guitar over here and put it over there, and it wouldn't exactly be two, but it would be like this thick guitar. And I tried to do that on some of these newer digital delays and it doesn't do the same thing.

And I didn't really think about it so much later until I went up to CRC to do a mix, and I had a 1580 there, so I did the trick with the 1580. I was like, "Damn! This is exactly what I've been trying to do on this other shit." Because I don't have a 1580. I wouldn't mind having one of those, and everybody told me, "Oh man, why aren't you over here mixing in the box man?" I said, "It aint the same. This unit probably worked because it wasn't perfect." This was a sort of a random thing, it just worked. I listen to old records man, I hear that shit all of the time. I say, "Yeah, I know he used a 1580 to do this."

Changes I've seen in the business? One of the major changes I've seen in the business is that the budgets have gone down like crazy. People don't want to give people enough time to what I call create art. The record company shot themselves in the foot by not demanding quality on a lot of stuff. I've seen situations where a record company gives an artist a budget to go buy gear rather than go to a studio, and they wonder why the quality of the record is gone. "Well what the hell, people don't care about it anymore, we just put anything on it," but what happens is they've cheapened the quality of the product to the point now where people don't want to pay for it, it should be free. It all sounds like shit anyway.

I used to get major hassles with record companies over things like tape bills for live recordings that were nominated for a Grammy. I had a record company call me up and say "Hey, we're going to supply the tape." And we're doing a live recording, four days, I don't know. "Why do you want to supply the tape?" They said "Think we can get a better deal on it." I said, "Now you understand we ain't talking about 24 track 2 inch tape, I mean, we're talking about DA78 tapes. They're about 5 bucks apiece." and they were saying, "Well we think…" I said, "Look, what's going to happen is you're going to send that shit too late for me to format all of the stuff, and we're going to end up with not enough stuff to do the first day recording." I said, "What you're going to do here is you're going to pay the man what he's charging you for the tape... okay?" He says "What're you..." I said "You're going to save maybe 100 bucks or something like that, take a chance on hurting the project."

I got into arguments like that, and I thought about, what was it, 76? I got hired to go out to California and play on a date, and I remember telling the guy, "Well you know, basically I've been playing out of Chicago, my guitars aren't set up to travel, I don't have cases." He says "Hey man, don't worry about it." I remember they sent me a first class ticket and a first class ticket for my guitar. I remember I got on the plane, they were saying, "Well you're going to have to check that." I said "No I don't baby, it's got a ticket. By the way, I'll have a scotch and coke and he'll have the same."

Back in those days you could talk about those guys all you wanted, but they spent money, and they spent money to develop new artists, they gave people tour support, the music was valuable, and the artists were valuable. And I don't see that now. I don't see that now. It's always about how cheap can you do it. It ain't a question of quality nine times out of ten. With most mastering-wise and most record companies, it's "how loud can you make it?" not if it sounds good. How loud can you make it? You heard about the Metallica thing? I mean, I actually had a chance to hear it man, I popped that thing in and those meters, that shit went all the way up and just hung there. I was like, "Damn there's no dynamics on this sucker at all!"

The metalheads are complaining it's too loud. I had a guy in Australia when we were on tour with Stevie, he had bought it and he was like, "You know something man? I got some pretty loud CDs here but this son of a bitch is like 3 times louder than the others, I can't even program this thing in." Of course what Lars said, "Well you know, the producer really wanted to come out and smack you in the face and you know, we know what's happening, you guys don't." I said "Yeah, but you're fans say it sucks." I'm glad it happened man.

The main thing is that there's no budgets, no real support. You got guys running record companies who used to sell cars and refrigerators who aren't really what I call music people, and that affects everything on down, and it's causing studios to go out of business. I know from the quality of some of the mixes I get in here to master that there was a time when these wouldn't even pass muster on a regular A&R thing. But these days nobody cares. They say "Well people don't care anyways, they're listening on ear buds." Yeah, but still, if you don't care, you just give them anything, then why should they pay for it? I've had people tell me that my kind of knowledge and my kind of expertise is not needed anymore. However, I said "I'm still here."

I'm still working because eventually cats come back. I know a bad thing where guys are trying to shave studio budgets and things like that. I just refuse to do it. I said "30 years of experience of doing the stuff and the type of gear I have should be worth something." And I find that for me, I have a small set of clients who always come back. People who have appreciation for the sound and for the expertise will come back, and once in a while man I get some young kids who come in that they want to touch up a tune and I get a chance to educate them, so that's a good thing. But the industry is very weird right now.

It's like the age-old arguments between digital and analog. They're two totally different systems of doing things, and each one is good in its own case. I know from cutting some of the first digital stuff, and my technique for recording period was always I would get how I wanted it, and then before the guys got the first take, I'd drop something down and play it back. I'd say "Okay, now what didn't come back?" And I would make adjustments on that.

But I'll always start off with what I wanted to hear, and in cutting digital I set it up the way I wanted to hear it and it came back exactly the same. Hey, that's a cool thing. But then, musician-wise, I discovered something, like the little latency that happens between the input and the output of the machine, which really didn't affect a lot of cats, but Steve Rodby, who was a great producer in his own right, a bass player, plays with Pat Metheny for years, that little bit of delay was enough to screw him up. He heard right away before we even knew, before any of us even knew what latency was, because I was listening to the machine the same way I did with most analog recordings. I had to set up a situation where I was listening to buses off the console rather than off the tape machine. That was a new experience for me. I was like "Oh, okay." You do what you have to do with it, that was a difference.

The converters weren't as good; bit rates weren't as good back then even on top of the 32 track. The three-head machines sounded better than all of the digital machines at the time. We ended up going with Mitsubishi machines only because 3M machines were so problematic, if a little dirt got in there it got so crunchy. We even got to the point where we had a little thing rigged up to rub the tape before it went through the heads. 3M eventually took that and put it on all their machines. It wasn't a wonderful thing. We ended up going Mitsubishi, which I didn't think sounded quite as good even though we had Apogee converters on them. I did a lot of digital recording. I used to be known as Digital Dan, and I ended up going back, I compared those digital recordings with the analog recordings I did. The analog recordings sounded more like music to me. I said "Okay, well," I really thought that digital stuff sounded good at the time but then I listened to it with these ears that I got now, I said "Okay I got bad converters," this and that and the other.

Digital can really sound good now, but unfortunately, we have a situation where a bunch of people who haven't been trained, some of them don't even really have a good concept of what's a good sound, and they're recording on digital and people tend to say, "Oh, well digital sucks." Well no, digital doesn't necessarily suck. Maybe the techniques that were used to record this particular record suck. Now, it's not necessarily the medium itself. I think the converters these days are way better than they were back then, they get better each day, but I told one cat, I said "What do you think of this converter, that converter, what do you think of converters in Pro Tools?" He said "Well, I don't think anything about them." I said "I got a Digi 002." I said that none of the converters have ever been used. I use it more than anything else for letting the computer know that it can run the software, but I take all of the digital outputs in it, I'm using all outboard converters and god knows what else, because I can't stand to listen to that stuff. I said "It depends on what you want to hear." If you go to a Prism converter, spend $5,600 go on one way and $5,600 to hear it back. You spend $11,000, you listen to it, yeah, there's a difference. But then you find other stuff. I belong to a mastering list and I remember Bob Katz came up and said "I found this little converter man. This is called a DAC1, Benchmark. This thing sounds just as good as my $5,000 Weiss." So I bought one, tried it out, I said "God, that is fucking awesome." So I bought another one too.

Nowadays I go to a studio, most of the time I'm dealing with digital stuff, I just take whatever I got, put it in a bag, and I just go up there and just disconnect all of their stuff and hook it up through that so I've got an automatic starting point. But there's so much.

I don't know, I'm not an anti-digital guy even though some guys think that because I talk about it's bad sometimes, but it's not the digital. There's bad digital; there's good digital. Good digital sounds really good. Bad microphone techniques with digital sounds bad, and good microphone technique on bad digital sounds better. It always comes down to the quality of sound and the work that's being done, and I think that training-wise, the cats who go through the schools they get a chance. Most of the guys out on the street they don't. They're sitting in their basements, and they're comparing this stuff to badly recorded records.

So they have no idea how good the sound can be. I read an article where the guy was talking about "Yeah, well, I got to get the drums really popping. I got my drums sounds up man, and then, I put them on the 2 buses, then I ran through a 5 band compressor." and he did this and that and the other, and then I listened to the record man, it sounded awful. But there's probably a million kids reading these magazine articles who are going to try to do that and think it's cool.

Compared the newer digital stuff that I'm doing to that old analog stuff, it's closer, but also I consider that I'm a better engineer now than I was then, and I got to factor that into it a little bit too. I'm using better techniques. It's like anything else, you do a lot of it, you get more experience, you get a little better at it, and I listen to stuff back then, I said "Ugh, I don't know what I was doing then." and then I listen to stuff now I say, "Yeah, I like this a lot better." So that factors into it too.

I'm happy with a lot of digital stuff. I know guys who say, "Well man, I would never mix in the box, oh no." and I've mixed some things in the box that have worked incredibly well for me, sounded really good, as good as anything that I had done back then. I mixed a Ramsey Louis record down here. I had rented an HD rig and it came out the HD rig, basically putting stems into a Manley 16 by 2 tube mixer, and they were running that to the head unit to a hard drive. Because of some hassles I had with them I never bothered to listen to the record, and I was putting a demo together last week, I got someone looking for some work for me in New York, and I happened to put this track up, I'm saying, "Damn, that really sounds good."

It sounded as good as, I have an album on Bob Katz CD hall of fame, it was a Ramsey and Nancy Wilson record, it's that record up there with Steely Dan and all the rest of that stuff, and this particular record sounded as good as that, but it was done here, just about and almost in the box. And I've done other stuff completely in the box that I've been impressed with.

A good friend of mine is an owner of API, named Larry Droppa. Droppa used to do the ear monitors for Stevie Wonder, which is how we hooked up. I asked him "Hey man, what about this Waves plug-in thing man, what does that sound like? Is that close or is that some bullshit?" he says "Well you know, it sounds pretty good, we didn't want it to sound too good because we're trying to sell the hardware units. I must admit this is very close." I picked it up and tried it out on some stuff and it feels very much like the old API hardware units that I remember. It definitely has a different sound than some of the plug-in stuff that was floating around. So I'm like, "Okay, can I make a track with this?" Well, see, ordinarily I would've jacked it out of the inserts into the analog thing and brought it back in trying to get that sound, and the sound was there. I keep telling people as the computers get more powerful and as the speed of processing gets up, then I get closer and closer and closer to the magic analog units that we talk about.

The magic was the faults of it, the randomness of it, because it's not perfect and it wasn't a perfect thing and it had this art thing going for it. Like at Universal man. I had Neve equalizers and stuff, but I also had this little lunch box thing with four B&B equalizers. I used to like the combination of the B&B equalizer and the Neve equalizer. That was my kick and my snare, and I just liked that combination. I like taking a little bit of a bunch of units as opposed to taking one unit and beating it to death, you know, and that worked for me a lot. And it's funny, those units sat in my closet there man for four years. I had stopped using them and I was cleaning out the closet. I was figuring I'd sell some stuff, buy some new gear, whatever. And I put the thing on eBay and I was like, "I don't know, it's worth 250, putting it for 250." They bid this sucker up to like 2,500 bucks. Finally, some guy from Australia picked it up. I mean it's crazy.

With all of this technology and everything else, I find a lot of young cats get involved in the technicalities, computer, cut and paste, and all the rest of that junk, and not really pay that much attention to the music anymore. But I tell cats

> If you want to learn, if you want to really get a great sound on someone, the first thing you got to do is get your ass out of this control room and go out in the studio and listen what the guy is doing because that's really what he wants to hear.

I see dudes they start fooling around with the computer and patching in plug-ins and doing this and that and whatever without ever going outside and listening to what the guy is trying to do. And this becomes the situation of the tail wagging the dog, and I think on a lot of tracks these days technology is wagging the dog as opposed to the dog wagging its tail. I think if people pay more attention to the music or have the technology servicing music, I think you'll end up with better music. Right now the music is sort of serving the technology so to speak. You got people in the studio who ten years ago wouldn't even be given a record contract let alone what's happening now and everybody's being Pro Tooled to death. I can go on about that.

I remember when it didn't have that stuff, but had a sequencer and I had a pitch bend control operating an H3000, and each correction I would put on a different track. I mean we found ways of doing stuff. But you say "Yeah, well, I just want to tweak this just a little bit, just so this thing, just a little bit." And nowadays, people can't sing without computer assistance, and that's one reason that ran me out on the road too. It's fun working on the road because you can't hide. A lot of them try, but you can't hide. You can't sing boy; it comes out right away.

The only thing I'm doing live right now is Stevie, it's fun working with him because what he does is he does what he does, but he hires a bunch of guys who are incredible players, and they play his stuff wonderfully and sometimes he'll go up on the stage and make up tunes that nobody knows how to play… and watching these guys scramble to make it happen is a great thing. And every night's a different night. So you work with a genius like that, then you work with cats that say, "Oh, oh, I'm a genius." Hey, you just did some drum beats dude. Somebody else may be impressed with that, I'm not.

I remember some kids sent me a bunch of beats and stuff, and I told them "You gotta understand man, there's nothing here that you've given me that I haven't heard before." They said "Well, what do you do when you program stuff? What do you do drums with?" When I need percussion? "I'll be truthful with you man, I make a call to Lenny Castro or whatever" I said

> You know why? Because these are guys who beat things in rhythm for a living, they're going to approach it a lot differently than I am. I'm a guitar player. No matter what I think of, they're always gonna be better.

Get cats that are specialized in that. Get musicians.

The other day an engineer took me aside and said "Damn man! You're 50 years old man, you ain't gonna get no work ever again man." Well I don't know about that. I do as much work as I ever did quite frankly.

Chapter 15

Leslie Mona-Mathus

Leslie Mona-Mathus is an award-winning New York-based audio engineer/producer. Her professional achievements include two Grammy nominations, a Gold Record, a Bafta, and multiple Clio and Promax awards.

Throughout her career from staff engineer at Automated Sound, to freelancer at major studios and music houses in NYC, to Howard Schwartz Recording, and now ABC, Leslie has recorded and mixed everything from records to jingles, spots, promos, and long-form for major film companies, adno agencies, broadcast, and cable networks.

Her ongoing career and artistic endeavors drive Leslie to seek out new projects whether they be musical, television, feature, or independent films to work on whenever possible. Her love of her craft and her commitment that hold her to the highest standards of recording continue to push her forward and keep her thriving in an ever-changing industry.

I'm Leslie Mona-Mathus. I was born in 1957 in Hoboken, New Jersey.

I started in audio at the age of 18, right out of high school, which was in 1975. Sheerly out of love of music and inspired by, believe it or not, the work of Eddie Kramer with Led Zeppelin. They were my favorite group at the time, and it always fascinated me the sound of the guitar work on their albums. Fully intending to go to college and fully intending to probably become an entertainment lawyer at the time, I was looking for classes to take at the New York New School pre-college to get a jumpstart on things, and I came across this audio engineering class, which I knew nothing about really other than loving music and wanting to be a part of the business, knowing I was not artist material. I fell into this class, which ended up not being at the New School, because it was already booked.

It was at Bell Sound Studios, it was called the Audio Institute of America, and it was a summer class, a ten-week course. My parents were very supportive and the minute I walked into a control room and saw a console I just thought, "Wow, this is what I want to do." This was in the summer before college, I already had my apartment rented and my course schedule laid out for Montclair and I asked my parents, if I could find a job can we just delay going to school? They kind of looked at me very strange and said okay. I came to New York with a friend of mine one morning and went to the Yellow Pages

DOI: 10.4324/9781003519829-15

Figure 15.1 And that was the thing too at Good Vibrations that I really learned was about busing and signal path and to tape and from tape so what goes into has to come out of and that sort of thing. Those were the days of learning and understanding signal path, and the difference between a bus and a channel and a tape return, where you send things at what points, is the compression before or after the EQ and before it goes to tape or are you going to do it once it goes to tape and you put it back and mixing. Those were the days of learning that kind of thing.

Figure 15.2 I had recorded it well and that was the whole key, I learned how to record well, I learned how to get it to tape right, and I learned to understand where to draw the line in terms of processing, to give myself the options once it went to tape. So I would have control during the mix. And that I think was with White Tiger, with this particular band, where I learned how to do that the best because it was totally mine—I wasn't standing behind other engineers watching them.

when there were still Yellow Pages and phone booths to be found and I ripped the recording studio pages out of the phonebook and proceeded to knock on doors and found a job.

I got the opportunity to work at a studio, Good Vibrations, which is at the top of the RKO Building, 1440 Broadway. They let me work there, or learn there, for $20 a week when they remembered to pay me, and the engineer was John Fausty who did all of the Fania Records work. I was 18 and that was my start. I kind of had ups and downs but I really learned a lot, met a lot of great people, Johnny Pacheco, Mongo Santamaria, Willie Colon. It was great, and from there, I kept moving along through the business and loved it.

Figure 15.3 I remember my first multi-track digital recording, and I can tell you I missed the air around the cello, I missed the noise. I did. But noise is human, noise is what we listen to around us every day, so there was a noise floor that I immediately missed when it went to digital. I've gotten used to it now, but I still miss it.

Figure 15.4 Certainly digital has given us the ability to manipulate and not lose performances. But I often miss tape. I miss tape compression. I miss, I don't want to say dirt, but dirt. I don't like digital distortion, I find the harmonic distortions I do get with digital hurt my ears. I'd rather good old-fashioned blatant distortion. I definitely, definitely miss the options to go outside the box. I think people have become so spoiled by getting that total recall, we used to just mark our little sketches that we have of the board where the knob used to be and hope it came back close to what we had, I'd rather have that. I still don't believe that these days it comes back fully perfect anyway, no matter what you tell me, it's like "this didn't sound like that."

And never really went back, went back to college but never full-time, but it worked out well. People tried to talk me out of it along the way unsuccessfully, but that was the beginning.

At RKO studios with the salsa bands, it was a lot of RCA 44 ribbon mics on the brass section, otherwise mostly dynamic mics. Not too many condensers, I mean there were some, the tube condensers they had were beautiful 47s and I think some 49s at the time, API console, and 16-track 2-inch tape. All analog obviously, at that stage, there was nothing digital.

That was 1975. I got the job before September in the summer. And they also had a film mix room there, which was all 35-mm mag dubbing machines. So I even had a little exposure to film mixing, which was great.

The studio owner had a wife, it was Bernie Fox and his wife Beverly, and she was probably more the reason I got in there. There was always the machismo, but I was still quite innocent so I never thought anything of it. There were definitely moments in time, that were things that were inappropriate that happened. I always made a vow, I don't know at what point, but I felt that to be taken seriously as a young woman, a very young woman, I mean looking back if I were to see my daughter doing this at 18 I'd probably would pull my hair out, of keeping my personal life separate from anything or getting involved with anybody in the business. I think that was very important to my survival, because I always felt that if I did use any part of my personal self to get further ahead, then it wouldn't be real, to put it politely. I just wanted to be taken seriously, I wasn't a "feminist," and I wasn't doing this to make any strides for womankind. I was doing it because I loved it. And from day one I made notes from any engineer I worked under and listened and watched. Where to put the microphone? Why did they put the microphone there? What microphone are they using on what instrument, how are they treating this and the levels to tape and so on and so forth. I applied myself, I almost had to report to my parents, I didn't have to, but I liked going home to tell them that I was actually learning, that I actually really felt responsibility, it wasn't just fun. I was learning and I took that really seriously.

I was a setup/breakdown person, so I learned. They had the big old booms, these mics required it, so I learned about the space and how to use the space and how to set up a percussion area, a brass area, learned about overdubbing and woodwinds and so on which was incredible. Look up John Fausty's work and listen to it; he was a master. And they were the finest and best musicians in their genre of their time. Actually, I ran into that a lot along the way in New York while I was working.

In terms of me getting my hands-on at that particular facility, I basically just did a little bit of editing, some mastering, assembling, and learning how to handle tape. I don't think I actually did any recording there. I was part of the film mix, and my job was to thread and run the dubbers, which I later found out was a union job and they had basically gotten away without paying, yeah, "Oops." But I didn't know it. I even watched, learning how to adjust by frames, watch the film editor adjust sound. Looking back I almost didn't know what I was watching in terms of the film aspect of it, but I don't think I got my hand on equipment till the next place I worked at, a place called Sound Exchange which Bernie Fox went to after Good Vibrations closed. And that was Richard Factors of Eventide, on 8th Avenue and 54. I actually was a solder slave for Richard Factor to earn some extra money and soldered boards and chips into his digital delay line. At that time, they had a Flickinger console with an Ampex 16-track 2-inch and lots of outboard API EQs, and of course Eventide processing.

They were just beginning. He had the Omnipresser and the digital delay, and I think he was working on the Harmonizer at the time.

Those were my first sessions I think I did at that studio. I had like these faders that had a little bend in them, they were like a space odyssey kind of a thing. I remember drums were a big thing for me and honing my ability to record them and have some control over them. I remember just doing sound demo sessions, we had a lot of demo bands come in and Bernie would turn over the reins to me, and experimenting with the EQ and tape level. I remember there being a four-track and thinking about the Beatles back then and how they possibly could have done what they did on a four-track. I bow to George Martin.

I remember doing a couple of 4-track sessions, there where people didn't pay for the 16 and bouncing back and forth. You had to bounce non-adjacent tracks. This is bringing back stuff I haven't dealt with in a long time. I guess those were my first sessions—I remember, before getting married, there was a little studio in New Jersey I had started to do some work for. I do remember the band was White Tiger and they were a very Led Zeppelin-y kind of band. Marshalls and lots of fun. But all analog. And the thing I remember about analog too, especially at Sound Exchange, being able to patch around, everything had to be patched through, and that really helped me with learning and understanding signal path. And that was the thing too at Good Vibrations that I really learned was about busing and signal path and to tape and from tape so what goes into has to come out of and that sort of thing. Those were the days of learning and understanding signal path, and the difference between a bus and a channel and a tape return, where you send things at what points, is the compression before or after the EQ and before it goes to tape or are you going to do it once it goes to tape and you put it back and mixing. Those were the days of learning that kind of thing.

At Sound Exchange, nothing was in the board, everything was outside the board. You didn't want to use what was in the board. Oh and some Fairchilds too, which I wish I had now.

As far as my favorite gear, I have to say I became a spoiled child when I went to Automated Sound and got to work with Neve and Studer. I found the difference there. API's equalizers always were beautiful to me, and this is a part about being a woman that I didn't really notice until I became a mixer. Listen to the difference between my mixes and a guy's mixes. Did my sensitivity to high ends come out, because I don't want to say my mixes were dull, but they were duller than a male counterpart. I had to find a way, and I still grapple with this to this day, of brightening up my mixes that goes a bit against my ear. Making them overly brighter in certain frequencies and certain areas. Also now I'm compensating for air and the one piece of analog that I still encounter today which is probably the worst thing is Beta SP audio, which all my mixes go to before they hit air.

The Neve equalizers and compressors became my favorites. That was in-house at Automated Sound. I was an assistant and eventually a mixer there. And LA2s and LA4s and LA2As. Also Pultecs. They didn't have any Fairchilds, but it was all Macintosh amplifiers on the big monitors. There was a big roundness and softness, and a wonderful thing to the sound at that point.

I think coming from lesser gear, an Ampex 16-track to a Studer and the Neve consoles, it made my life simpler. But, because I had to work so hard with the other equipment to make things sound good, I was able to apply it to what I thought was better equipment. I don't want to say it made it easier but it made me become better as a mixer because I understood how to work with bad stuff so the good stuff was like wow. Even bad patches that would happen, dirty knobs that would happen, knowing and having had to struggle with equipment to get the sound the way you wanted, the ability to work with the better equipment, I hate to say, some things are not better, different, more up to date. And an inline EQ where you don't have to patch it just gives you the freedom to explore and become more creative in other ways because you're not dealing with the technical craziness of certain things.

So it became more transparent to me and it let me think about other things, let me listen to a different part of the spectrum. Maybe concentrate more on my panning and depth, front to back left to right as opposed to thinking about where that crunching sound is coming from, the aesthetic of it. Less the technical of "what's going on here" and listening to more of the aesthetic. It put me more in it and in the creative process. As opposed to being totally overwhelmed with the technical what could go wrong and cleaning. A lot of people I'm sure remember the days of the Ampex, the bad batches of tapes, you know it's like "what is all that stuff on the head?"

I really felt that change starting with the band I mentioned in the studio in New Jersey, White Tiger. Much to the chagrin of the studio owner I took their tapes and mixed them on the Neve and Studer in New York. Only because I felt I could not do it in the little place that we were at. At that point, I would say I became a spoiled brat in terms of being a mixer. Once you have your hands on something good, it's hard to go back. I could talk about that in terms of digital too. Once you have certain tools and you get used to applying them, so I actually brought the band into the city and mixed at Automated. I can go back and still listen to those mixes, I actually have one, I was 18 and 19 years old, and it helped pay for my wedding. I was probably a little older than that, about 20. I had recorded it well and that was the whole key, I learned how to record well, I learned how to get it to tape right, I learned to understand where to draw the line in terms of processing, to give myself the options once it went to tape. So I would have control during the mix. And that I think was with White Tiger, with this particular band, where I learned how to do that the best because it was totally mine, I wasn't standing behind other engineers watching them. Although that happened, always taking notes from those I was working with, there were those who did process a lot more going to tape, those who say they'll fix it in the mix, those that got it to tape the right way, so clean, crisp, clear, so that they could work with it.

And mic placement is the beginning. I think it was mic placement and being out in the studio, going to Good Vibrations and even being second at Automated, the little Sound Exchange I was like a free spirit I could do whatever I wanted to do. There wasn't enough going on at that particular studio that I was able to learn from somebody, or being put in a position where I had to do something a certain way because this is the way you did it. When I got to Automated Sound the two main engineers there, one came from A&R, the other from Associated, and I was basically now becoming second, third generation Phil Ramone school of recording. And now we're not working with RCA 44s anymore, now we're working mostly with Neumanns and 414s and Sennheisers on the drum kits. I don't think we even had a tube mic, I'm sure we had one stashed someplace. But learning how to listen to the instrument, and really listen to it all begins there, it's where the sound comes out and how you want to capture the sound, putting that mic in the right place and obviously putting the musicians in the right place in the room, it all starts there. And getting that to tape and clean. That's the key.

I ran into Quad Eights after leaving automated and being freelance, and it was one step forward two steps back. And when I ran into MCI boards I crossed my eyes, and MCI machines and Quad Eights and so on, I would say if a studio had outboard Neve EQs, A&R always had a rack, I always used them. I always used LA2s and LA4s and 1176s. And even with working with Suzanne Ciani on Trident boards, what'd she have, an Amek and a Trident, they were very harsh. Amek boards were the closest sounding to Neve boards. But I always loved the 1176s, they were always one of my favorite pieces of gear. So yes, I always did go in terms of outboard gear, if I had an API EQ that I could access and bypass some MCIs, always went to Neves or APIs and Ureis, Pultecs. If they were available to me I would turn to them. I still do in a digital world, but it's the digital replications. They're not the same.

I really didn't like MCI boards. Let's begin with the preamp, there's a memory I have of coming out of working in the preamps. There was a singer Kasey Cisyk who was just an amazing voice. I had the opportunity to work with her many times and I'll never forget, after Automated I went to a facility that had MCI, Howard Schwartz, but he doesn't have MCI anymore. But of course at that time it was big with Criteria in Miami having that there was also a place uptown on 54th, Sigma, they also had MCI. This was a little before SSL. But I remember opening up the microphone, and it did not sound like her. It just didn't. And I couldn't understand it, I had a very difficult time with it, I couldn't make that board sing. It was right at the preamps and I didn't have any options, I didn't have any preamps that I could go to besides the ones in the board. That was very disturbing because it truly felt like it wasn't the same singer at all and I had no way of getting around it and it peeved me a great deal. So are there things that I miss? Or that I would still use? I would love to still use some of the Neve preamps. The grace has become the preamp of choice at this stage in the game. I would still use a U47, there are things I'd love to use to this day, U49s, U47s, some of those old preamps and definitely some older EQ.

Is there anything I have now I wish I'd had then? I think back to Suzanne. In terms of record production, I wish I had the ability then to manipulate takes of certain performances and intercut. Digital editing, the ability to save a solo and not actually punch in and lose it forever or run out of tracks. Be able to save and go to and bring in something from three days ago that wow, that was really good, let's take part of that bridge and put it in here. Not knowing that would ever exist I didn't miss it back then, the things I miss now.

It's funny, less equipment-wise, but I do miss people's regard for the art of audio in what I'm doing now. Mixing now mostly for television, sometimes radio, I used to have an edict that I would have one music project a year, to keep me there. I kept true to that for a good period of time. Most notably doing solo piano recordings, which were great. So now I miss rooms, I miss good rooms. I miss beautiful pianos and just working with 2 to 4 microphones and the challenge of getting a piano recorded just so. Couple of nice matching pair of C12s. The root of it all, I do miss good microphones, I miss that.

I was just reading some articles about what are we mixing for at this point in time? Are we mixing for MP3s now, or mixing for iPods, or are we mixing for the richness and the beautiful big sound that we used to have? So yeah I miss the warmth of some of the old equalizers, the warmth of Neve, the transparency of a good preamp with a great mic, and a great board and great EQ. I miss being able to listen on a great set of speakers, starting out listening for me then being able to mix for the consumer and wondering how much I need to compress it before the mastering engineer gets a hold of it. Or am I really the master engineer before it goes to mastering? Working with Suzanne a couple years ago I could not believe what was done in mastering to my mixes and how much damage can be done. I mean I was aware of it but I hadn't had it happen.

So I miss, I guess it's the grassroots of where I started. I miss all the stuff, I remember my first multi-track digital recording and I can tell you I missed the air around the cello, I missed the noise. I did. But noise is human, noise is what we listen to around us every day, so there was a noise floor that I immediately missed when it went to digital. I've gotten used to it now, but I still miss it.

I kind of saw the writing on the wall for me personally, and this might address women in audio issues as well, I transitioned into post-production in 1991 after the birth of my second child. Basically because I felt I could just see the business itself was shrinking. The formula used to be record work, which was my weekend work, working on projects with Suzanne. Somehow I wound up doing new-age music. Put it this way, being a little rocker girl and starting out on the heels of Eddie Kramer and wanting to be a Jersey rock and roll girl, but somehow I ended up doing New Age. Sort of weird. I was on that borderline of sort of making it, breaking it. And working with Elliot (Scheiner), right after he mixed Aja and listening to the Aja masters hot off the press because he was doing a monitor check and I was told to be his assistant and I better not let anything bad happen. Those were the words that my bosses gave me, do whatever you have to do but make it work. However, I never really got into working on a genre of music with the type of artist that I was hoping to starting out.

But there were those artists who liked my work and the type of music they happened to do was new-age stuff and it kept me in business. But to supplement that I was doing commercial work and jingles. So what started happening is synthesizers became more prevalent, thankfully with Suzanne I was on the cutting edge of that because she had every piece of equipment delivered to her house by both Yamaha and Roland so I was one of the first on the Synclavier and next to the Synclav was a Buchla. Really working for her was a blessing to me because it made me have to keep current. And so I then was on a Macintosh when sequences and stuff started coming out and all the new programs started coming out. So then, all these folks started doing their stuff on a Synclav and handing you a DAT.

The formula used to be, a 30-second spot was about a 4-hour gig. So that meant from recording the rhythm section to overdubbing and mixing and out the door. The formula was then you would go in for two hours and overdub some vocals over a prerecorded track someone had done on their Synclav. So it became a necessity for me to continue to make a living to transition, and the transition to post-production happened in 91. And that required me to go to Howard Schwartz, when I went to Howie at that time, he looked at me and said, "you're a music engineer." And I said "Howie, come on" but he goes "no, post-production is a different ball game" but I was doing sound design before the term was even coined with Suzanne. We were sampling tennis balls in a bathtub in her house and using them for whatever on one of the first, so I was sort of ahead of the curve. And we were using sound design in musical composition right from the get-go with her.

So I had to take this sort of circuitous route where I went, okay I took an in-house job at an ad agency and that's when I got on my first real digital workstation, which was Sonic Solutions. And that was at McCann Erikson, and from there working in-house, a lot of the people there, producers knew me, and the edict was we can't do final mixes out of this room. Because then we'd have to give that to all of our clients, and then, they couldn't bill the money they were billing for going out of house. I got in a couple, but it was a hard thing not for me not to have my stuff go to air. There was a little bit of an ego thing.

It was tough. But that gave me the time to work at becoming a good digital editor. And learn Sonic Solutions. Which was a pretty deep editing system, and obviously one of the best-sounding editing stations. I still have it. I could overlap three sound files with their fade window. It was created as a mastering station. So in sort of the way I related coming from Neve and Studer and having to work on an MCI, I can say I started out on a Sonic

Solutions station and had to learn how to work with Pro Tools. I had 30 undos, and I don't want to skip too far ahead but it became necessary that I had to go to Pro Tools. Well, Pro Tools was at least starting to sound good by then.

I stayed on Sonic Solutions and came out to ABC Sound because they were looking for Sonic Solutions editors. And I stayed with that and then I went back out and ended up finally back at Howie's as a post-production engineer, having gotten a couple clients under my belt. It was there that people were either on audiophile which I worked on a little bit but never got too deep with, but was a good sounding, George Meyer loved that, he's a good editor. They had so many kinds of workstations there but they did get me my own Sonic Solutions Station. That was part of me going there—I had to have that. But there came a day that I had to make that switch and I actually had both workstations up and running next to each other, and when they told me I only had one undo on Pro Tools, I looked at them and said what? Because I had 30 on Sonic, so you get spoiled, and you get spoiled with crossfades.

The preference between digital and analog? Is there a preference? I said I missed it. Certainly digital has given us the ability to manipulate and not lose performances. But I often miss tape. I miss tape compression. I miss, I don't want to say dirt, but dirt. I don't like digital distortion, I find the harmonic distortions I do get with digital hurt my ears. I'd rather good old-fashioned blatant distortion. I definitely, definitely miss the options to go outside the box. I think people have become so spoiled by getting that total recall, we used to just mark our little sketches that we have of the board where the knob used to be and hope it came back close to what we had, I'd rather have that. I still don't believe that these days it comes back fully perfect anyway, no matter what you tell me, it's like "this didn't sound like that." So I still don't have all the faith. And I like the tactile element to the studio, being able to reach across and tweak something. ProControl, I don't know. I love grabbing a fader, I think that the rubber banding in the box is just crazy.

Chapter 16

Steven Epstein

Steven Epstein has earned 17 Grammy Awards and 35 Nominations, including three for Classical Producer of the Year in a 45-plus-year career that has brought him into professional contact with many of the greatest musicians of his time, including Isaac Stern, the Juilliard Quartet, Yo-Yo Ma, Rudolf Serkin, Chick Corea, Wynton Marsalis, Placido Domingo, Isaac Stern, Itzhak Perlman, Bobby McFerrin, Midori, and many others.

The longtime Sony/BMG/Masterworks producer is maintaining his relationship with that label while pursuing a variety of independent projects. He's also staying in touch with his early love of technology and broadening his skill set to include digital editing at his home project studio. Epstein is also adjunct professor of Classical Music Recording at McGill University in Montreal and is currently the Senior Executive Producer for Sony Classical.

My name is Steven Epstein. I was born April 9th, 1951 in Manhattan, spent most of my growing up years in Queens village, New York, and moved back to Manhattan in 1976, working ever since.

I actually became interested in audio when I was about ten or eleven. I knew I wanted to be a producer/engineer maybe when I was 13. And I'm very lucky that I followed through on my interests and I lucked out, timing was right and everything when I graduated college eventually. There was a job opening at Columbia Masterworks which I applied to, for a music editor. September 4th, 1973, was my first day. I don't want this to sound like, "it all started at a 500 radio station," do you remember that? "In Fresno, California."

So 1973 September 4th, I worked as a music editor for Tom Frost, Tom Sheperd, Andrew Kazdin, and what I would do is, either I would be handed a musical score that was marked up by the producer who didn't have to work with an engineer and was on to another project, I would work with an engineer and cue that engineer where to cut based on those edit points in the score. Or, if I was entrusted enough, which I was and which is part of the job, I would choose the takes for that producer, go to an engineer in the post-production studio, do a rough edit or maybe better than rough edit, and present it unmixed to the producer, and then, he would make comments and I'd go back in the studio, choose other takes, whatever. So that's pretty much how I started professionally.

DOI: 10.4324/9781003519829-16

Figure 16.1 It's interesting because when I first started recording orchestras with thirty-forty microphones, we always figured we had to EQ something. That was always part of the mix. Of course add reverb. I've been doing it for about 35 years, maybe in the late 70's early 80's I started moving away from multi-miking, seeing what Telarc was doing with their minimal miking. What Bob Fine did with Living Presence, which actually influenced Jack Renner for his Telarc recordings of minimal miking. Anyway, I started gravitating away from that, using a tree and outriggers. Then less and less processing, and that's the point. To the point now where I basically use DPA 4006-TL's as main mics for doing a classical album, being so familiar with the characteristics, virtually never EQing anything, certainly not the main mics.

It started with my first record at the age of two, and from that point on, I was bit by the classical music bug, it predominated my life.

The one record that started it all for me was Wellington's Victory by Beethoven. It was a Mercury recording, one of the Living Presence series I think it was, and I remember my neighbor had a Magnavox stereo console and I had a dinky mono Admiral television set which had a phonograph in it. I brought the record over to his place. It was a mono recording. And I couldn't believe I was actually hearing all sorts of sounds, triangles that you couldn't even hear on my other system, all sorts of details, and I was maybe about ten or eleven. And then I remember going back to my house and just cranking up the volume and listening to the speaker, trying to hear the same things. And at that point, I became sort of an audiophile, the early stages of an audiophilia.

Then I just became interested in looking at the backs of record albums and seeing "produced by Andy Kazdin," seeing his name, for some reason, it was mostly the Columbia Records producers I was very interested in. My neighbor turned out to be, just an amazing coincidence, he was a lawyer for CBS Records, and he ended up being the president of CBS Records, Walter Yetnikoff. So it was great cause I'd get free records, and I asked him upon going into college I said, "Can you help me out when I graduate?" He said, "Give me a call." He had actually moved to Greatneck, Long Island, by the time I graduated.

So when I graduated, I called him up and he sent my resume to Tom Sheperd. Tom Sheperd called me up, I had an interview, and then, I eventually got the job as a music editor. I went to see Tom Frost when I was in high school, my first year of high school, just to see what do I have to do to prepare. He was very nice, and it was wonderful poetic justice in that after graduating college I went right back to him and there was a job opening at the time. It was very lucky.

Figure 16.2 Eventually, Buddy and I went to do a recording in Vienna, Mahler's Fourth Symphony, the Vienna Philharmonic. And we wanted to go with a tree. We'd never used a tree before, but we decided let's use it. We used the Schoeps for that first recording, Schoeps MP2 capsules and outriggers, and we started balancing, the first time we worked there, and it was sounding terrible. So we moved the mics, with a tree it's up or down basically, we moved them up and down, and it still wasn't sounding good. I said "we're screwed. We're not getting the sound and this is the last time we're going to be here most likely." So, we're trying to figure out what to do, and as we're thinking the orchestra's playing and warming up and I'm thinking "Oh, that doesn't sound that bad." And at that point, I realized not to jump to any decisions until you hear an orchestra or performing ensemble that has warmed up for at least eight or ten minutes. Sometimes you don't have that luxury. Most of the time you have to get balanced as the orchestra is warming up. But the thing is, even if an orchestra or an ensemble plays in one venue for their whole lives, there's still time that it takes for the sound to become burnished, and then, we maybe make one modification and we got a great sound and we're all pretty happy with that. And what I'm using now is either tree configuration, depending on the acoustics of the hall, or only two microphones or a curtain of three mics, or omni-directionals. There are spots, always spots, but we try as a challenge not to ever resort, or rarely resort to the spots in the mix. The only way we can do this, the union rules now allow us to balance at rehearsals and if the rehearsal is going to be in the same venue as the recording session, as long as you don't roll tape, you can hone and refine with your microphones to get the optimum sound.

Columbia basically had remote kits, and they consisted mostly of the AKG C12's. I think we had 30 or 40 of them, we had virgin capsules that were never used. It was unbelievable. By the way when Columbia, in the late 80's, sold their remote kit, they put their mics on sale, and two people I know got most of the mics. You know how much they sold each of those C12s for? $25. When I tell people this, they're amazed, yeah I could retire on that. So anyway, they had the C12s and we were using 67's and 87's for microphones. But at that time, in 1973–4–5, the recording console was homebrewed, built on the eighth floor of 49 East 52nd Street, and prior to that, 799 7th Avenue. So, the consoles had rotary pots.

30th Street Studio where I did a lot of recordings back in the 70's, The Church, that was a sacred territory as far as I'm concerned. Then, some jerk at CBS decided to sell and make a quick buck. It was incredible real estate, let alone anything else, but they tore it down. A tragedy. Nevertheless, the main console in that room until the very end when

Figure 16.3 From that point on things got better and better, and I was very impressed by the technology at that point. I knew somebody at Voice of America, and they'd ask me to counteract an argument by Ed Rothstein, he's a critic, he's a music professor, and he's got great ears, and he hated digital. We're talking about the beginning of digital, and I had heard a couple of really good digital recordings, so they asked me to counteract his argument, and I did. And I did say that if you have one great recording that really sounds great in digital that exonerates the whole system. Maybe all of the other recordings are poorly miked or who knows what? But I subsequently changed my tune, seeing the improvements in digital recording, quantization noise and all of that stuff back then, it really was not terrific.

Figure 16.4 I still use the DPA mics, they're my favorite mics. They are virtually B&K microphones, started off as the 4000's. The sales guy for B&K came to our studio, I was working with Buddy, and he said "B&K just came out with studio mics as opposed to their lab mics, measurement mics, would you like to try them?" We said "yeah, sure, why not?" These are 4003's, and so we try them. Then I remember shortly thereafter that one of the design engineers from B&K had come to my office sometime earlier, we were using different mics, he said, "We designed these microphones to be used as a two way pickup for orchestras so you can pick up an orchestra with only two mics," and I said "Hey look," I said "No way, that's impossible, with all due respect." To make a long story short, years later, a good portion of my recordings have been made literally with just those two microphones.'

Figure 16.5 **30th Street Studio where I did a lot of recordings back in the 70's, The Church, that was a sacred territory as far as I'm concerned. Then, some jerk at CBS decided to sell and make a quick buck. It was incredible real estate, let alone anything else, but they tore it down. A tragedy.**

they got an MCI board, but until the very end, it was a home-built rotary pot console from Columbia Records. Eric Porterfield, he was the guy, he was the brains behind that. Frank Laico did a bunch of recordings there, pop stuff mostly.

We had an Ampex 8 track there, dinosaurs, clunky machines. 16 track MM1000, 2" tape, and of course the quarter-inch machines. Mostly Ampex 440's. Prior to that they had the 300 series. So that's the production end of things. Post-production, we had Pultecs all over the place. We also had Tube-Techs. Pultecs had this wonderful, tube sound, a broad pattern. We were using some Fairchild equipment. I was introduced to the early parametric equalizers. There was a company called SAE, which made a parametric. There was a company called Orban, which was the next one. We were using all of that stuff, and then, George Massenburg came out with his parametric, and so we were using that a lot. And the EMT plates, we had like 20 EMT plates in this room. Could you imagine those gigantic plates? Some of them were kept up, some of them weren't. They had to be tuned but they weren't always. There were remotes, the plates were kept in this room downstairs, and there were remotes for some of them, a remote to adjust the decay with a little meter. This is bringing back memories.

When I started, all the post-production was done at 49 East 52nd Street on the fourth floor. All of the editing and mixdown rooms were there. The speakers we used were KLH 6's, believe it or not. We were blowing tweeters every other day. And they were atop the old Altec Lansing H7's, which were the most piercing, horrible-sounding speakers, which we never used for classical, but they were these big pieces of furniture that we'd put the KLH 6 on. So we used the KLH 6's, which was actually pretty good for me because I was using AR3a's at home. I was an AR3a person.

We were using the Urei Little Dipper. I remember Andy Kasden taught me this trick how to use the Little Dipper. He said if you have a 2track and the timpani is too loud what he does is he tunes it to the fundamental of what the timp is playing and sets an incredibly narrow Q, which is what the Little Dipper did. And it's amazing, you could really diminish the presence or prominence of that timpani if it was too much. Obviously it was good for whistles and all sorts of other things too. So we used the Little Dipper, we had Pultec compressors, Urei, Fairchild.

It's interesting because when I first started recording orchestras with 34 microphones, we always figured we had to EQ something. That was always part of the mix. Of course add reverb. I've been doing it for about 35 years, maybe in the late 70's early 80's I started moving away from multi-miking, seeing what Telarc was doing with their minimal miking. What Bob Fine did with Living Presence, which actually influenced Jack Renner for his Telarc recordings of minimal miking. Anyway, I started gravitating away from that, using a tree and outriggers. Then less and less processing, and that's the point. To the point now where I basically use DPA 4006-TL's as main mics for doing a classical album, being so familiar with the characteristics, virtually never EQing anything, certainly not the main mics.

I remember Buddy Graham, he was one of the greatest engineers of all time. He started off as a mail boy in 1945. Does Fred Plaut ring a bell? He was the de facto engineer back then, the classical guy, Broadway shows and everything, but he was a great photographer as well. He was spending more and more time taking pictures at the sessions, and George Szell, who was a tough conductor, started getting a little bit annoyed with Fred focusing more on his picture-taking than his engineering. This was the Cleveland orchestra, and Fred was a great engineer. So, Buddy was Fred's assistant, running the tapes at that time, and George Szell asked Buddy if he would engineer, and Buddy did. Everything worked out fine, there was no antipathy between everyone, but Buddy's first recording was Beethoven's 9th with the Cleveland Orchestra, a gigantic piece like that, 3-track is probably what they did.

So when I started working, Buddy had been working since something like 1960 as an actual recording engineer, and I worked with him when I started in 1973 all the way through his retirement in about 91. He subsequently passed away, but I remember two crucial moments in my career as a producer.

We always used the multi-C12 pickup for a live orchestra, we couldn't use C12's on 30 Street Studio because of the RF, it's near the Empire State Building, so we ended up using 87's or 67's there. Anyway, so we're doing an orchestra and we went from the old C12's to three 414's. So we went from all of the C12's, each microphone being its own entity in the sound picture and ambience to using the 414s, a curtain of three 414's and 84's for the string spots and for other spots as well. Maybe 87s/67s for the brass horns, and then it just wasn't making it, the sound wasn't working out. So we said "Should we dare put the 414's in omni?" We never would think of doing that. So we ended up doing it and it actually sounded a lot better. I was doing it not so long ago and it still doesn't sound that good frankly, but nevertheless it was an improvement, and that was breaking a big tradition that was going on at Columbia Recordings back then, using omnis instead of cardioids.

Eventually, Buddy and I went to do a recording in Vienna, Mahler's Fourth Symphony, the Vienna Philharmonic. and we wanted to go with a tree. We'd never used a tree before, but we decided let's use it. We used the Schoeps for that first recording, Schoeps MP2 capsules and outriggers, and we started balancing, the first time we worked there, and it was sounding terrible. So we moved the mics, with a tree it's up or down basically, we moved them up and down, and it still wasn't sounding good. I said "we're screwed. We're not getting the sound and this is the last time we're going to be here most likely." So, we're trying to figure out what to do, and as we're thinking the orchestra's playing and warming up and I'm thinking "Oh, that doesn't sound that bad." And at that point, I realized not to jump to any decisions until you hear an orchestra or performing ensemble that has warmed up for at least eight or ten minutes. Sometimes you don't have that luxury. Most of the time you have to get balanced as the orchestra is warming up. But the thing is, even if an orchestra or an ensemble plays in one venue for their whole lives, there's still time that it takes for the sound to become burnished, and then we maybe make one modification and we got a great sound and we're all pretty happy with that. And what I'm using now is either tree configuration, depending on the acoustics of the hall, or only two microphones or a curtain of three mics, or omni-directionals. There are spots, always spots, but we try as a challenge not to ever resort, or rarely resort to the spots in the mix. The only way we can do this, the union rules now allow us to balance at rehearsals and if the rehearsal is going to be in the same venue as the recording session, as long as you don't roll tape, you can hone and refine with your microphones to get the optimum sound.

A big turning point I remember is when I was mixing an album on an MM1000 multi-track 16 track, which had an abundance of hiss. I would say I wasn't that enthused with the recording, an orchestral recording, and these two Japanese engineers came downstairs from the eighth floor, which was where they built the equipment and they had their labs. And they said, "We're working on something, would you like to come up and hear it? It's called digital." This is like 1980, maybe 1979, I said "sure." So I go upstairs and I see these two U-Matic machines, it was PCM, I don't even think it had the 1600 yet, I think it was some other video.

So I went upstairs, and they said "We can edit on this. Here's a recording we did with whatever orchestra, I want you to cue the engineer, we're going to make an edit from one machine to the other," which was machine to machine editing. So I cued it to the cymbal crash, then I cued the next cymbal crash, and they put it together then ch-chsss. Okay that didn't quite work, but it was amazing seeing these two video machines edit audio like this. Then Eric Porterfield came downstairs again with these guys and they brought their equipment downstairs, and they said, "I want you to see something. Here's a 1 kHz tone on analog tape on the VU meter." He put it through that VU meter and it's going like this, wavering. "Now, look at this 1 kHz tone recorded digitally." It's rock-solid. Of course he didn't say what else was missing from the signal back in the early days, what would happen at 18 KC.

But it was impressive, wow. From that point on, things got better and better, and I was very impressed by the technology at that point. I knew somebody at Voice of America, and they'd ask me to counteract an argument by Ed Rothstein, he's a critic, he's a music professor, and he's got great ears, and he hated digital. We're talking about the beginning of digital, and I had heard a couple of really good digital recordings, so they asked me to counteract his argument, and I did. And I did say that if you have one great recording that really sounds great in digital that exonerates the whole system. Maybe all of the other recordings are poorly miked or who knows what? But I subsequently changed my tune, seeing the improvements in digital recording, quantization noise and all of that stuff back then, it really was not terrific.

I won't say who my colleague was, but my colleague was told to do a recording session, he was working with a particular artist, a pianist, and the New York Philharmonic. It was a concerto, and he was asked to do it digitally. Back then, they only had 2track digital, there wasn't multi-track digital, and this producer was very much into multi-track, he did it very well. Well, he refused to do it, and got fired. He had another job actually so he didn't care, but the point is he called it correctly, that he had a feeling he was going to get canned.

Then, a couple of weeks later I was in a situation with digital recording in Chicago. The pianist was Lazar Berman, the Chicago Symphony, Erich Leinsdorf conducting. It was not Orchestra Hall, but a Medinah Temple, a really nice room for big orchestra stuff. And I was told I have to do it 2 track, and I said, "Well, can I do a back up on multi-track?" because I had Soundstream. That was before Sony, and Tom Stockham wouldn't let me do it, I had to do a 2track recording. I did a multi-track analog backup, but I had to do a concerto in 2 tracks with a limited amount of recording time, very scary. So, we just bit the bullet, the engineer Buddy and myself, we balance the orchestra, got what we thought was a correct piano-orchestra balance, and we turned out just fine. I lucked out in many ways, but the point is that was a fully digital recording.

I still use the DPA mics, they're my favorite mics. They are virtually B&K microphones, started off as the 4000's. The sales guy for B&K came to our studio, I was working with Buddy, and he said "B&K just came out with studio mics as opposed to their lab mics, measurement mics, would you like to try them?" We said "yeah, sure, why not?" These are 4003's, and so we try them. Then I remember shortly thereafter that one of the design engineers from B&K had come to my office sometime earlier, we were using different mics, he said "We designed these microphones to be used as a two-way pickup for orchestras so you can pick up an orchestra with only two mics," and I said "Hey look," I said "No way, that's impossible, with all due respect." To make a long story short, years later, a good portion of my recordings have been made literally with just those two microphones. They're in there, once that evolved from those microphones.

In fact, the late John Eargle, I'll never forget, there was an article in Electronic Musician Magazine, three recording engineers and producers of classical discuss miking techniques. I was reading his, and he mentioned, "forgive me, I know I'm going to be chastised on this and criticized, but it is impossible to make a commercially successful album of an orchestra with only two microphones." Well, I respect John Eargle very much of course, but prior to that I'd made most of the Sibelius Symphony cycle with two microphones in Pittsburg with Lorin Maazel and other recordings. I said I've got to write a letter to the editor of the Electronic Musician. So I typed it on my computer and it turned out to be a really long letter, and lo and behold it was printed, the whole thing was printed like two issues later or the next issue. I wasn't expecting that. And I mentioned what recordings I had done that were successful and got very nice write-ups. So those microphones in fact, were able to do that. And you could do it with other microphones too depending on the judicious placement of your mics and the characteristics of the mics involved, but for me, those microphones were just the most natural-sounding mics for instruments.

So, there were 4003's, then they made a matched pair of 4003's they called 4009's, and so we were using 4009's. Then the 4009's and the 4003's disappeared. During those two models the 4006's came out because they were phantom-powered as opposed to the others, and they were less susceptible, the 4006's, to RF. So we started using the 4006's even though they called the 4003's and the 9's their Mercedes Benz. The 4006's were very good. I think they may have had a higher noise level. Then, they came out with the 4006 TLs, which are superior to all of the other microphones, and that's what I'm using now. I own three of those and the studio is using those, that's what we use, the smoothest, most beautiful sounding mics for concert-type recording.

But as far as other microphones and other equipment, the Schoep's series, MK2's, MK4 cardioids, MP2S's, MP2H, their tube version that you could use those same capsules on. Beautiful sounding microphones. The km series, km84's and km140's, 130's, the km184's. And the TLM 170's, large diaphragm, they are very robust, wonderful for sax pickup, wonderful for brass. But I'm trying to think what vintage, quote-unquote, that we still use. Otherwise, I like to keep as little in the chain as possible. Even if we do resort to EQ on anything it will always be either in the box, on the computer. We use Pyramix. I use Sequoia on my own home equipment. I love Sequoia, it's so user-friendly.

As far as preamps, back in the old days we never really used anything other than what was there. Then it started off with Hardys and Jensens, they were the same. They were wonderful preamps back then, very solid sound, projected image. Then there was a Swiss one which was very fast, but it was a little bright sounding. Then we went to Millennia, which we still use occasionally, which I like, it was my favorite. I primarily use Grace these days, which is newer. What I thought wasreally wonderful was Doug Sax's Mastering Lab tube preamps, I used them on several recordings. Wonderful for strings, main mic pickup type of thing.

Mark Levinson came out with a line, which is wonderful, his Cello line. One thing was called the Audio Palette. At home I'm using the Palette, it was a great EQ device, very warm and rich sounding, again very broad like Pultecs. I shouldn't blame that particular device, specifically because when things became more exposed in the digital realm, recording not to analog tape but to digital, anything in the circuitry became that much more amplified as far as any of the defects of the equipment. I wanted to use that, we actually rented it, you plug that analog device into the circuit, and immediately, it's out of the circuit in the sense it's out, but still plugged in. And I heard a degradation of sound. I heard an effect of sound. So I decided I didn't want to use that and I started going more with digitally based EQ, either at a console or Weiss, again, very easy to EQ, just to clean things up a little bit. Or if we're doing solo with concerto, take out some bottom of the fiddle, just little, dirty leakage. So with the digital evolution, I much much less, if at all, ever use analog components.

I love the vintage C12, but as far as vintage, to be honest with you, I don't have enough experience with vintage components. I had friends that were using compression, but for me it would be in my Broadway or Jazz recordings. I'll either use the Weiss box, it has a wonderful compressor in its system, or the TC6000. It has a compression algorithm which is extremely clean, and I only compress up to a point until I hear pumping. Soon as I hear any artifact, it goes down. So if I could squeeze 3 or 4 dB without having an effect, great. That's what we're doing in Broadway and Jazz. I never ever ever do classical compression because I want to keep the dynamics.

Anything I have now that I wish I had then? I wish I had changed my miking technique earlier on, went with less mics earlier on. Again, the limiting nature of the analog medium, with all of the anomalies, with tape hiss, with even Dolby, which was great, but it just wasn't as sensitive, the playback equipment wasn't as sensitive back then. So you could get away with components or recording gear that wouldn't necessarily be as pristine and as highly resolved as you have nowadays, because you have no choice. Back then microphones, which may have been noisier would not manifest themselves as noisy mics, they would just be part and parcel of the analog era. So if I were to say, Gee, I wish I had the DPA microphones to use back then, I'm not sure. One of the things with the digital medium is when you're adjusting your miking technique now, the room that you're recording in becomes even more of part of an instrument so to speak, because it's much greater resolution in the sound, coloring it in a good way, not if it's a bad room. The trick is getting the ratio of presence to distance, obviously, and rather than doing that with ambient mics and throwing another set of mics into the mix and having it decorrelate, I like getting that ratio with two or three microphones and just moving them until I think its right, with the safety of having other microphones available. But you have to tailor your microphone setup to the given situation. I know some people who were using Schoep's omnis back then and they sounded damn good, and I was from the school where we never used omni's, or rarely, back in the early mid-70's and the later 70's.

What I had then? Virgin microphones and virgin capsules. If there's anything I would have to say that if the EMT plates could be made to have much less noise inherent in the system. Those plates are wonderful, but they're emulated so well in other software. I can't say if the software emulations are as good, that's a tough question because I would say they're very close, maybe so close it's imperceptible. We're talking about stratospheric differences, it's subtle.

Another thing is it's just so much easier to edit these days than it was back then. To cut analog tape, Columbia record's engineer would be standing behind me on his Ampex 440 tape machine with several layers of masking tape, and then on top of that masking tape, which was fairly shiny on the top, was quarter-inch or half-inch splicing tape, and what he would do is when you cued him into place and he cut the recording tape, he would take his razor blade and cut the splicing tape, which was on top of this masking tape so it could go right through the masking tape and peel right off. It was great. It was really clever. So you could do it just like that, it just goes right down the line, put it on his Editall splicing block and make the splice. But how many times does the splice not work? Okay, can you clip a little more off? Oh great, we clipped too much off, can you put some back, and now we hear it, okay, go to the B reels. Can't make that splice, forget it. So that was scary, and I will never forget my scores, which god knows where they are now, there are pieces of tape, the spliced tape, put into place in case we ever needed to use it.

So the editing was a bit different back then, and that's a major change. I love editing on my Sequoia system, which is very similar to Pyramix and certainly Pro Tools and all of that. It's very convenient, and it's just incredible what you can do. But other things that have changed, well, miking techniques, with regard to the fact that you have a much lower noise floor than you used to, that you can move your mics back. In fact, in the early days of digital, among other problems, was this rather grating sound, and I think part of that had to do with the people still using the techniques in analog, which was a much more forgiving medium than digital was...maybe still is.

Chapter 17

Lou Bradley

A native of Pensacola, Florida, Lou Bradley began engineering there in the late 1950s and early 1960s and followed this with a four-year stint at Bob Richardson and Bill Lowery's MasterSound Studio in Atlanta, where he tracked the likes of Joe South, the Classics Four, and the Tams and Billy Joe Royal before relocating to Nashville in 1969. In Nashville, he worked as an in-house engineer at the Columbia Records facility that had previously been owned by legendary country producer Owen Bradley (not related to Lou) and his brother Harold: an army surplus Quonset Hut where the famed "Nashville Sound" was crafted by Colombia along with the efforts of Chet Atkins, Bob Ferguson, and Bill Porter over at RCA.

Still producing and engineering today for the likes of Merle Haggard, George Jones, and Willie Nelson, Lou Bradley enjoyed his time at Columbia, when he engineered sessions produced by another Nashville legend, Billy Sherrill, featuring artists such as Johnny Paycheck, George Jones, Tammy Wynette, and Charlie Rich.

My real name is Louis Marshall Bradley, Lou Bradley, and I was born in Pensacola, Florida. I started in radio, and I started recording and played music in Pensacola. I wound up in Atlanta in 1965 after the army. I had a little studio in Pensacola, I had a Gates Yard board. It was in the radio station but at night they were off and allowed me to use it for whatever I wanted to do. And I would, I rigged up a secondary mixer that we used on remotes to make reverb independent in each channel, which nobody else could do down there. And I converted a Zenith T.V. spring reverb, people were starting to use those in amps. And I had a live room I could use then. I recorded to mono-tape and made records for people. And I went to work in '65 at MasterSound recording studios, which was owned by Bob Richardson and Bill Lowery, Lowery Music. And they partnered up and upgraded the studio and changed the name of it from whatever they called it before, it became MasterSound.

They hired me in '65, I was there and working in radio and getting some electronic schooling. But I knew that was starting, and that was why I went to Atlanta, found a job on an outlying station and started working part-time there and they hired me full-time after about two months. We were doing 3-track recording and overdubbing to another 3-track. And we'd go down six generations, with the Sel-Sync and that was a chore. You

DOI: 10.4324/9781003519829-17

Figure 17.1 I like to say there's two prayers a mixer prays, a good prayer and a bad prayer. And you hope you pray the good prayer that there's a session going on or you've got a tape to mix and you bring it up and it's happening, and you know it's there, you know it's on the tape or it's happening out there. And you pray Lord let me get it to tape and not mess it up. And a bad prayer is that you know it's not happening, just give me a clue what to do. I think experience teaches you what prayer to pray.

Figure 17.2 So that's when he started to build recorders, and he had already started building consoles, and he was building components for consoles. He built some transistorized equalizers for our console. We had three positions that didn't have EQ and they didn't have a mic pre, so he built us a transistor EQ, it had more range than the console EQ, the console had Fairchild equalizers which were two knobs, kind of like the Langivens that we had over at Columbia, even though the Langivens were a little different. You had a little more selection than you did on the Fairchild, and you could select two frequencies on the bottom end and three on the top. And he was building a console for Mack Emerman and for King Records so he started an assembly line deal. And I remember asking him what's your biggest problem, and he said finding good bearings and good transistors, we have to do our own quality control. We buy a box and somebody sits and checks every transistor that goes in the kit, because they won't all be the same.

Figure 17.3 Before I came to Columbia, I always would put a delay tape in front of the chamber. You know, pre-delay. Used to put the tape in there, you can still put a good amount of reverb on the singer and that gives you a little more presence on them but pushes the reverb away from the singer. At Columbia, we had two 4 tracks holding the return behind the chamber. Most people don't put a delay behind it. It was just hardwired into a panel, each chamber came back to a panel in the console that could be assigned where you want to assign it. And you could hear the pure chamber, and you could hear the slap separate.

had to start off brighter than you really wanted it, because you really couldn't brighten it later on. You'd bring up the noise. But we made records, I did records while working there but, the Classics IV cut their hits there, Spooky, Stormy, and Traces, Billy Joe Royal had a hit called Cherry Hill Park. With the Tams, they were real big on the, on the Carolina coast, man they're still the king. And there's still two of them left, and both of them have a Tams out. And we recorded Roy Orbison and other people down there, Joe South.

Roy Orbison did all of his recording in Nashville. And so he came down there and we did one album on MGM with him. His heart really wasn't in it for some reason, he was just kind of in a dull mood. And we made a couple of good records that were on the charts, but we didn't get a monster with him. But the boy was great, you know, just a big voice and a nice guy.

And, we did some others, James Brown cut there one time, and Major Lance put out several things on sax there. Then Columbia Records hired me out of Atlanta to come up here and I settled into the Quonset Hut, I was in hog heaven.

That was a great studio. They're bringing it back now as part of that Belmont-Curb program. Because of the music deal. The Quonset was Columbia B, and it was a great studio. I probably cut 101 records there over the years. But just great studio. Charlie Rich, Tanya Tucker, Tammy Wynette, George Jones, Merle Haggard, Johnny Duncan, John Anderson, Johnny Paycheck. I don't know how many people. We did an album with Andy Williams. And then Bob Luman.

I went to work in the Quonset Hut in June of '69, and me and the console I worked on for 13 years arrived the same day. And it was a 16-track Columbia console that Eric Porterfield and his crew in New York built. He was a neat guy. He was head of their engineering development staff. He had a real unique personality. He was just the most laidback New Yorker I was ever around. He knew his business and we hit it off immediately because I went to work and the first day on the job, I was behind the patch bay

Figure 17.4 One time Andy Williams came in to record, Billy Sherrill and I did most of Ben Cheryl's records for about 13 years. We worked together a lot, and I was doing Andy and Dick Glasser, he was Billy's producer and he came into the control room and he said "I'm just here along for the trip" he said "I'm not here to be involved at all but can you answer me one question: how did you get the cymbal sound on the Most Beautiful Girl in the World?" There was a little barrier wall to keep people off the producer, so I got him a high stool and I said "sit right there, I'll show you" because I knew what he was hearing. They started working on the song. I said I'm going to get my mix up then take my hands off the control and show you. It was live recording and it was a neutral-sounding room. It had wooden walls but then dead, it was old acoustical tile and so on, and so forth all around so it was neutral and it just sounded good. You could talk in the room, music played in the room sounded good, so you had to use the room. And so they started, but in a situation where they've got leakage, until they get together it sounds awful. See that's what spooks a lot of people, when you've got to deal in a situation like that is when they first start. If everybody's not locked in, it sounds bad. So I'm just kind of watching him out of the corner of my eye and I get to my mix pretty quick. And about the third time through they locked in and I looked around and he had this big grin on his face. He said "I'd have never got it it's the leakage." I said that's right. Here's how we recorded, we had say the drums, there was a little divider, the bass, and then the pianist sat in front of that. And then the singer's standing right there, right there in the middle of it all, with all them guitars around. I mean those things could sing, everything was right there. So you've got to deal with it. And it was the leakage.

wiring in microphones and he said, "I've never seen a mixer want to do that." And that's how we became real good friends.

He designed it, it was a 24 input console with 16 out because it was when the 16 tracks arrived too, going from 8 to 16. Not like Atlanta where we went from three and four, we didn't do much four-track recording even though we had one. We went from three-track to eight-track. We had a 4four-track, if somebody was on a budget, we might go to four-track and have that one track to overdub on. But most of the time we'd bounce down, go down three, four, five, and six generations overdubbing on the three-track. And that was not uncommon, we didn't have big orchestras. And we'd do it all at once.

So, it was 16-track, but it was strange, some of my first sessions at Columbia were four track. Then they would bump it up to 8 and then to 16. And so one day I said to Billy Sherrill, I started doing his work, "why don't we just cut an 8 track? And then we'd transfer that to 16." And "why don't we just cut on the 16 track to start with?" and he says "that makes sense to me." And that's how we started just cutting on the 16 track.

Figure 17.5 Anyway, those things came along and you just have to use them. I've kind of always been about equipment and about musicians. Whoever's there and whatever's there is what I'm going to make the record with that day. Because if you've been working with a lot of great musicians and having success, then you come in there with somebody that you don't think is as good, then you've got a mental block right there, there's no way we could have prevented that. Well whoever showed up that day was who I was going to make the record with and not grieve over it when we didn't have so and so on drums or guitar or on piano or the backup, whoever's there is what you're going to work with, that's your horse to ride that day. And sometimes you're greatly surprised.

Figure 17.6 Here's another pearl from Tom Dowd, and I use it every time I work. From the time the sound's made in front of the microphone until it goes to the record room, have a reason to do anything you do to the sound. Just common sense. How many times have you seen people just plug in and switch in, make adjustments before they ever hear it? He was a minimalist, and I don't know if they're ever around anymore, but he was a minimalist as far as EQ and everything. He would move the mic before he'd turn the EQ knob. He was a real neat guy. And I learned from him.

I was one of the first ones to use Dolby's in Nashville. We had the original big gray ones. Columbia made their own switching which just switched the console from the fader to the tape machine to the console, in front or behind the machine, which is what Dolby does anyway, But we had 16 of those big ones. And I started on eight-track with it, I remember I did a Bobby Vinton session on an eight-track with Dolby. We'd gotten the Dolby and nobody used it. So I rolled the rack in the mixing room, I wanted to find out about Dolby for myself. The Dolby itself had real good amplifiers. The problem was the signal path with the Dolbys, and one thing I learned was to give it headroom. What I learned was that Dolby worked better in a zero-in, zero-out. And I'm not talking about elevated, where you reduce the playback setting 3dB back in, on elevation. On higher energy takes, you take the playback down 3 and then you can raise the record 3, so you're recording 3 dB hotter than standard level, but it made sense to me that that was fooling the Dolby by 3 dB.

It worked on what you sent and it undid what it did and gave it back to you. And so, a lot of people said it makes it sound duller. And every time I worked around or was around somebody doing that, it's true, I'd listen to it going down in the playback and I think it fooled it a little bit. So I always worked standard level but the Dolby itself could stand it, so if you got hot and the tape could take it, you didn't have to worry about peaks as much. But still, cutting Billy Sherrill records it got real quiet, real loud, and I enjoyed the dynamic range cutting Tammy Wynette, Charlie Rich, those guys.

Of the Porterfield boards, there were two kinds of boards. There was the standard CBS, I called it, and they had some unequalizers, they didn't do much EQ. And if you ever saw something like those New York sessions you'd see banks of Pultecs patched in because the equalizer didn't do that much if you really needed to do something. It was a four knob equalizer.

The original console in Columbia B, the Quonset Hut, was a Langevin console, it had Langevin faders, five wire faders, and Langevin EQs. So when Eric built that board they built it with Langevin EQs and Langevin faders, which was their only Langevin board. And it had Melcor, the amplifiers were Melcor transistor amplifiers. And I remember, I went from tubes to transistors in my period there when I was real active. And I remember this about the first transistor amplifiers, you almost had to work them where there was noise, they didn't like a lot of signal. And they'd clip real easy so you would have to almost work on the low end toward the noise floor to get a real good clean signal through them. And then of course that changed over time, they really got better.

The console I worked on in Atlanta was built by Jeep Harned of MCI, and it was the first console he built. There were rotary fader knobs, rotary little knobs with constant rotary faders. He built it, it was a three track tube, had 12 inputs and three outputs. I was there for five years and he would come every year or every other year. And he'd think about them, one time he came he said, "we're going to change." It was transformers in, transformers out. Make it a cathode follower circuit coming out, so he said "this is" it was one of the cleanest tube consoles I ever heard.

And, he was building tape recorders. He was in Fort Lauderdale, and he got started in recording doing maintenance for Mack Emerman. He would keep radios, he had a hifi sound company down there, put in sound systems and sold hi-fi gear. He was just a brilliant electronics guy, and a real nice guy, I really liked Jeep. And he was building recorders for people on 300 decks, just picking up telemetering decks out of Cape Canaveral, they were just all over down there. In fact Bob Richardson went down to his partner to find enough to build a master five-slave duplicator. And Jeep built it, when he came up to install it I was working with him, checking it out, getting it lined up. And he told me "I just built a 16 track for Westlake on a 300 deck." And we had an 8 track one inch on a 300 deck, and it just wouldn't handle it, you would always have to keep your hand on whatever reel was feeding, because the resistor that set the tension was always too tense, and so it was, you'd fast forward and you'd do this and the other way you'd do that, it was that routine. And I said, "well how did it handle the tape?" And his exact words were "it didn't, that's why I'm going to build my own machine."

So that's when he started to build recorders, and he had already started building consoles, and he was building components for consoles. He built some transistorized equalizers for our console. We had three positions that didn't have EQ and they didn't have a mic pre, so he built us a transistor EQ, it had more range than the console EQ, the console had Fairchild equalizers which were 2 knob, kind of like the Langevins that we had over at Columbia, even though the Langevins were a little different. You had a little more selection than you did on the Fairchild, and you could select two frequencies on the bottom end and three on the top. And he was building a console for Mack Emerman, and for King Records, so he started an assembly line deal. And I remember asking him what's your biggest problem, and he said finding good bearings and good transistors, we have to do our own quality control. We buy a box and somebody sits and checks every transistor that goes in the kit, because they won't all be the same.

He was really an innovative guy. He was kind of the Henry Ford of recording equipment. And he was really focused on the quality of it too. There's a thing that AES did where Al Schmitt and Tom Dowd hosted it and they had a lot of pioneer guys, they had Jack Mullin who did the first recordings of the Crosby show and Ampex guys and Scully guys, and they interviewed Jeep on the phone, he was in bad health, and he and Studer experimented with a 3inch analog tape, I can't remember if it was 32 track or something, and he said "we were working together on it but we canned it because the average person couldn't handle the tape." It's heavy, think about it, 2inch tape is heavy enough, but I found that interesting.

In the Quonset Hut we had a couple of Pultecs and also a couple of the midrange Pultecs. We had the one that I called it 'had more' midrange in it. This one had midrange you could get 500 cycles and 400, whereas with the other, one you couldn't. We had a couple each of those, and we could always bring extra ones in. And we had a couple of LA2A Teltronics, and we had the predecessor to the 1176, they were tube compressors from universal audio. They were real finicky. If the tubes got out of balance it didn't work right, so you had to constantly monitor the tubes in them. But they were good to track. I'd just use that on Tanya Tucker to soften her vibrato. I wasn't trying to eliminate it, but she had this real quick vibrato. It would track that vibrato and soften it a DB or so.

And something else of interest thinking about her, there were several artists I recorded with dynamic mics as opposed to a U67 or 87 when they came along. It's just like a voice print that the voice, an individual voice makes. Some mics fit that print, it's like a footprint. It just eliminates some things you don't want to hear. But it makes it warm, I recorded her and Dennis Yost, all his hits, his Classics IV with it. I recorded Tanya on a SM56, the predecessor to the SM57 because we didn't have 57s yet.

That's what I recorded her hits with, and I recorded Dennis Yost. John Anderson, I recorded all of his hits on the Shure. He had a lot of air that moved, and Dennis had a lot of rasps. Charlie Rich I recorded on a 49. Seems like we had some there at Columbia. It had a smoother spike, whereas the 47 was higher than the 67, the little spike they put on the top of them. And the 49 was a little smoother, and Charlie made a lot of lip sounds, and that just made his voice sound better to me.

The 87s were just coming out and most likely that's going to work on most singers. I record Haggard on one, when I still do him now and I record him on an 87. In fact he's got two or three U87s out there that are really good U87s. Most 87s one to the other sound the same. 67s and 47s are a different deal. The big old tube ones.

Of course with eight tracks you still run out of tracks, and we didn't have another eight track to mix to. We just had one eight track. And I would ping it off the sync heads, but all they did was give you something to reference to. You might ping guitars and insignificant background parts and things like that together and really EQ the heck out of them. But, say you're going to try to combine some vocals, boy, they didn't sound good. So, I would ping off the playhead, fill up seven tracks and say ping the bass and drums down off the playhead. But that put the bass and drums together. But everything else on there was out of sync, but it didn't, ping some other things to the bass and drums track and work my way through, and wound up with three or four tracks depending upon how I combined it. And then we could overdub more and it sounded good, so that was something I used to do.

And you had to think about stereo. First we were making mono records, and with three-track things were left or right and the vocal was in the center and occasionally a solo instrument.

In the Quonset Hut we pretty much used what we had in the rack and the console. When I first went to work there, you've got to bear in mind the mindset of all the people involved in the process. They'd been cutting three tracks and printing reverb, they might mix the three track again. So when they designed the console we had seven EMTs or we could make one of them a live room, we had live rooms too there, two live rooms, since I always kept six EMTs and a live room, and we could print that on seven of the tracks.

And, we were printing it, then when we went to eight track we'd monitor reverb and not print it down in Atlanta. So that was a little strange and most everybody I think was conservative when we were printing the reverb. Because in the mix you could add more, and you couldn't take it off. Until gates come along. But anyway, the reverb, we had seven EMTs, I think they had a total of 14 EMTs in the building. Each studio could have seven or six and a live room.

I'd use the live rooms a lot of times on drums, especially if it's a song where they're doing a rim shot, going from a snare back to the side stick deal, which they do a lot in Country. I'd use that room, that live room on that. Then, I started just monitoring. That was something I kind of started doing. It was monitoring, and we weren't printing it, and then add it later?

We did a lot of things, and before I came to Columbia, I always would put a delay tape in front of the chamber. You know, pre-delay. Used to put the tape in there, you can still put a good amount of reverb on the singer and that gives you a little more presence on them but pushes the reverb away from the singer. At Columbia, we had two four tracks holding the return behind the chamber. Most people don't put a delay behind it. It was just hardwired into a panel, each chamber came back to a panel in the console that could be assigned where you want to assign it. And you could hear the pure chamber, and you could hear the slap separate. And a lot of times, and we would take the EQ of the delay and had some old Ampex four tracks where you could select the recording cue, and you could dull it up, and that would be good sometimes to fatten the voice, because you didn't get that sizzle, and get a little, nice little warm bump after it.

And then, other times, I'd go for loud brightness in that. If you listen to some of the old Ray Connif records they did in New York, a lot of that sound, they were using a live room, whatever they used it was real bright. But you can hear that slap behind it. And I still do that. I'll take whatever my reverb is and run it through a digital delay, behind the chamber. And, and you get some good effects that way. You've got a space there, and you can get a nice bloom under it. You can hear that on some of those Tammy Wynette and George Jones, some of those records.

And if I was really going to make something out of it, I used to put an oscillator on that machine, adjust the speed of it. To put it in tempo, and you could do it 15 or 7 and a half, and get some slap. But, that's something that you might say was away from the norm instead of just plugging in the EMT or the room and don't do anything to it. And they had some EQ, or filtration built into them.

I got to go in Capital reverb down in the rooms, those echo chambers down in the basement at the Capital tower and I was totally surprised. I went to overdub on a record. I had some time to kill before I went back to the airport, and someone asked "you want to see those?" He says we used number four today, which was everybody's favorite. Al Schmitt mixes there just to use number four, and it really sounded good. And, the second time I went he was there and I couldn't get 4, but I was just overdubbing so it didn't matter and the other one we had sounded good. But that first time, we climbed down a rebar wall or a ladder, down this concrete wall, and everybody kept telling me "oh they got these big chambers in the basement." They're not big, you know. They're on the narrow side, and the trapezoid shape of course, and the only thing that's plumb is the floor. And just, just plywood painted and they've got 2 JBL speakers and 2 Shure SM81s, and that's it. And they've got some EQ operation just normalled in there. He showed me that it's just a live room. And the ones we had at Columbia, the first ones were just rectangular rooms. And then, we lost those to a mastering room and so they built an L-shaped deal and it's still there behind the Quonset Hut up above the storage rooms. If you get behind the Quonset Hut and look up and you'll see a door, two live rooms in there.

I like to say there's two prayers a mixer prays, a good prayer and a bad prayer. And you hope you pray the good prayer that there's a session going on or you've got a tape to mix and you bring it up and it's happening, and you know it's there, you know it's on the tape or it's happening out there. And you pray Lord let me get it to tape and not mess it up. And a bad prayer is that you know it's not happening, just give me a clue what to do. I think experience teaches you what prayer to pray. But say there's something off. So say a singer is not quite in tempo, you know, with his phrasing or something, and then, you wonder what can I do with that? And that's where you can do some things with slapbacks and echos at that given point that can hide that. It's not as objectionable, those little things. I've always done things like that through the years.

If you worked with really good EMTs, it was really hard to hear a digital that compared. If you had a bad EMT, and the secret to the EMT plates was the setup. You know you had to get the plate taut, the way it was best described to me about adjusting them, you adjust it until just before the spring breaks. And that was it, you had to get just the right tight.

Anyway, those things came along and you just have to use them. I've kind of always been about equipment and about musicians. Whoever's there and whatever's there is what I'm going to make the record with that day. Because if you've been working with a lot of great musicians and having success, then you come in there with somebody that you don't think is as good, then you've got a mental block right there, there's no way we could have prevented that. Well whoever showed up that day was who I was going to make the record with and not grieve over it when we didn't have so and so on drums or guitar or on piano or the backup, whoever's there is what you're going to work with, that's your horse to ride that day. And sometimes you're greatly surprised.

And the same with equipment, I've seen guys that if they couldn't get their certain mics, certain pieces of gear it's like boy, it's the end of the world. Mike Clark in Atlanta wound up owning and running the studio, it was Southern Tracks. He passed away last year but it was MasterSound, then Bill and Bob split, and it became Southern Tracks, a world-class studio. Then some hot shot, I don't know if he was a New York or LA producer come in there and he said, I don't know here in Atlanta, he thought he was out in the sticks you know, he said "I wonder if we, any way we could get a so-and-so mic in here?" And Mike said "I've got three of them." He had an unbelievable collection of microphones. This guy's attitude certainly changed, all of a sudden he knew he wasn't in some dumpy town in a dumpy studio.

I just try to work with what's there, and sometimes, you find things that way. You're forced to use a mic you might not otherwise. I never was a big fan of AKG mics until I started working on some bigger consoles. On Neve consoles AKG mics sound entirely different than on the other consoles. On the other consoles, they sound abrasive. The AKG 414s and 421s? And I've worked on several Neves the last few years and they really sound great to me. And that's just something I've stumbled on, you got to keep an open mind. Just think about a drum set, how many possible places you can put a mic on drums.

Here's one, Tom Dowd taught me this. He came to Atlanta with Jerry Wexler, Joe South enticed him to come down and record with his group. And he had a young singer from Macon, a good little kid, RB Hutton. A&M wound up taking the record from Lowery. First of all he made the drummer really tune his drums right, Tom did. If the drummer doesn't do that, you can't manufacture it. And it was the best that this drummer's drums ever sounded. But he put the mic looking across the snare, using a U67 for the snare drum, looking across the drum at the high hat. Bear in mind this was before you had consoles with a gazillion inputs, and it gives you a perfect balance on the hat and the snare. And somewhere back in time he figured that out. Moved it around to the other side. The trouble is you almost need a starbird boom to get that mic down in there where you want it. And if you happen to have a couple of starbird booms then you can do that. That was something I picked up from him.

Here's another pearl from Tom Dowd, and I use it every time I work. From the time the sound's made in front of the microphone until it goes to the record room, have a reason to do anything you do to the sound. Just common sense. How many times have you seen people just plug in and switch in, make adjustments before they ever hear it? He was a minimalist, and I don't know if they're ever around anymore, but he was a minimalist as far as EQ and everything. He would move the mic before he'd turn the EQ knob. He was a real neat guy. And I learned from him, that's two things I learned from him. Looking at the hat across the snare. And the other is to have a reason to do anything.

Here's something, say you've got an uneven kick drum. Of course I realize we're in the era of heavy digital hard disk recording, but say you need to put a limiter on it. Very seldom I use gates. Say you feel like you need to limit the kick drum, but if you do, you'll pick up more snare. Of course you could gate but, if you've got a compressor that you can use a slow attack with slow release, it won't compress on the snare leakage but it'll catch on the kick.

And I've found just that little adjustment, on the attack, release, if you've got a limiter that can do that. I worked every day in a live situation, there was leakage all over, and if you use gates, people want to use a gate to take it completely out. You would have more success with it if you'll just do a reduction of 5 or 6 dB. For instance say you want to gate the toms, or you get drum leakage. And if you limit, make the gate work in the four, five, and six thing instead of going for total isolation. Unless you're going for an effect now, that's a different ball game. But you can help yourself that little amount and gain the presence of whatever's leaking into that mic, and it works a whole lot better. And it's not noticeable.

One time, Andy Williams came into record, Billy Sherrill and I did most of Ben Cheryl's records for about 13 years. We worked together a lot, and I was doing Andy and Dick Glasser, he was Billy's producer and he came into the control room, and he said "I'm just here along for the trip" he said "I'm not here to be involved at all but can you answer me one question: how did you get the cymbal sound on the Most Beautiful Girl in the World?" There was a little barrier wall to keep people off the producer, so I got him a high stool and I said "sit right there, I'll show you" because I knew what he was hearing. They started working on the song. I said I'm going to get my mix up then take my hands off the control and show you. It was live recording and it was a neutral sounding room. It had wooden walls but then dead, it was old acoustical tile and so on, and so forth all around so it was neutral and it just sounded good. You could talk in the room, music played in the room sounded good, so you had to use the room. And so they started, but in a situation where they've got leakage, until they get together it sounds awful. See that's what spooks a lot of people, when you've got to deal in a situation like that is when they first start. If everybody's not locked in, it sounds bad. So I'm just kind of watching him out of the corner of my eye and I get to my mix pretty quick. And about the third time through they locked in and I looked around and he had this big grin on his face. He said "I'd have never got it, it's the leakage." I said that's right. Here's how we recorded, we had say the drums, there was a little divider, the bass, and then the pianist sat in front of that. And then the singer's standing right there, right there in the middle of it all, with all them guitars around. I mean those things could sing, everything was right there. So you've got to deal with it. And it was the leakage.

If I could make the switch, I'd run like some sound out on the studio speakers and turn on the mic when I switched to overdub vocals. Most, a lot of times I'd you know wouldn't have to do that but it would happen. And, and I still do that. We cut Haggard, I just finished an album with him and he cut sitting right in front of the drums, he was about as far from the drums as that table right there.

I've got a live sound. Yeah, but then you've got to do some overdubs, you allow for that. But he said it's the live recording in it. I said that's right, and I knew that's what it was. Doing that every day, you get used to it.

Chapter 18

Jim Reeves

Jim Reeves has been engineering and producing recording projects for more than 50 years, for Columbia, Atlantic, Paramount, Epic, Date, Okeh, RCA, United Artists, and many other labels. He has been the resident chief engineer for jingle houses such as Clef 10, Producer's Recording, and Terry Fryer Music in Illinois. He has been Front Of House sound engineer in concert halls and convention centers all over the world.

A singer and musician from age six, still plays out and arranges while engineering and producing, and his technical background includes design and installation of recording studios and sound systems in nightclubs in New York City, Westchester, New Jersey, Connecticut, Barbados, and Puerto Rico.

While working for David Sarser, who built Les Paul and Mary Ford's home studio in the 1940s, Reeves moved up from fetching coffee, mopping the floors, and cleaning the toilets, to doing mic setups, editing dialogue and music cues, and cutting acetates on Neumann, Scully, and Fairchild lathes, while moonlighting recording sessions of his own Doo Wop group for auditions for gigs with WMCA and disk jockey Cousin Brucie. He would eventually get thrown into a session here with the Supremes, and there with Johnny Ray and Benny Goodman, and Ruby and the Romantics.

I'm Jim Reeves, born in Tarrytown, New York in 1943. My interest in audio started at home really, hanging out behind the television repairman who used to come to the house. I had some Music Minus One records, I bought a Wollensak tape recorder, and I had that hooked up from the bedroom out into the television speaker. I would grab my Shure 55S microphone when my relatives and their friends came over, I'd pull out my Music Minus One records and I'd go out in the living room and I'd sing to it.

And I had a singing group throughout my teenage life. We argued about arrangements and who was flat and who was sharp and we'd get into, you know, emotional disputes about things, and I decided if I had another tape recorder I could do all the parts myself and show them the arrangements that way and then we wouldn't be distracted by the political issues between us. And that led to hums and buzzes and problems with wiring and me building my own console eventually. So I started probably when I was 13 or 14,

DOI: 10.4324/9781003519829-18

Figure 18.1 One of the things I think that happened in all of these recordings, because you were going to tape them and because you were dealing with the signal-to-noise ratio, the hiss and/or the distortion limitations, saturations of the tape, you had to compress beforehand, and what always happened with a compressor? You'd get a reasonable setting with it and the band would run it down five or six times, and then, they would do the take and now the adrenaline kicks in and they're singing their brains out or playing their brains out, and now the compressor is compressing 15 db, 20 db, and what are you going to do about it? You're recording now, you can't change it because you'd have to adjust everything every time that change came up in the mix. So you would live with it and just curse and get mad at the musicians. Why couldn't they do that while I was running it down with them? It's ruined. It didn't ruin it, it just became what it became. Also people used to ask me about bouncing down tracks, we were limited with tracks so you had to bounce tracks down so you could open up a track to add a new part. "And did you feel that the quality was ruined by bouncing it down?" I said "Well, I never look at it that way. I look at it like we won't get that new part unless we do this. Then this sound becomes this new sound. Now when we bounce it down to the other track, it becomes something else." It's just another process, which is again what made those old records sound the way they did. It was because that's what you had to do to make it work.

and I have actual recordings of things that I did live at our Lenox Hill neighborhood house on East 70th Street in Manhattan.

Then I built my own console. I started out with a couple of light switches. I went down to the five and dime store, Woolworths, and got a bunch of regular light switches and I taped them down to a little wrought iron table that held my record albums, and just cut the wires and spliced them into the switches so I could go from one machine to the other. And Wollensak had a little extra-special jack on it, a TRS type jack, but nobody even called it that then, the long tip was line level. When you used the shorter Wollensak plug it only hit the first connector and that was mic level.

So I took advantage of that when I built my first little mixer and used the mic input because it had more gain, and I took three pots and I tied them together and I just started developing things over time. At first with the light switches, I just switched things hard-wired from one machine to the other machine and somehow, I don't remember exactly how, I got my mic involved in that. I would take the one Wollensak and I'd put it on the highboy, which was this dresser that was about five-and-a-half-feet high so it was about my height, and it sat next to me while I stuck the Shure microphone in front of it and me,

Figure 18.2 The monitor was almost off. But I was just sitting there scrubbing tape, because I can edit with my hands tied behind my back. And while I'm talking, I'm scrubbing the tape, I do the splicing and all that. And Roy goes, "OK, it's getting late, do the edit, we have to go." And I said, "No, I did the edit already." And he actually sat there and he says "No, don't fool around, we have to go." And he got angry with me. And I said, "I'm not fooling around." And I said here, and I rewound the tape, I went over and I grabbed the volume control, I turned them up, I hit the play button, and it played flawlessly through the splice. He comes- jumps up out of his seat, runs over to the machine, rewinds the machine, plays it again, looks at the splice, turns it upside down, puts it back down on the machine, and he says "Come with me," grabs me by my arm, firmly by my arm, he says "Come with me!" And he drags me out of the room, brings me upstairs, and he says "What do you want to get paid?" And I didn't want the job. I didn't want to work there. I had never gotten more than a 100 bucks a week at that point. Which was a big coup with Herb Abramson, I was making $50 at Studio 3, and Herb said "What do you want?" And I said $100, risking everything, biting my fingernails at the time. And he said "No problem." Which made me feel like I should have asked for $200! But I don't think $100 was easy for Herb either to do, in the end, when I talked to Barbara about some of that. And, so I said, "I don't know- a thousand." Well, with that he stuck his finger on his tongue and moistened it as he went through the union scale book, and paged through everything, and said "Well, I can give you top scale, and then I can give you 10% night differential if you want to work at nights and blah blah blah..." So I ended up with about $800 something a week.

and I would play back my first harmony part and sing the second harmony part to the second Wollensak, and then I would take that tape and do the same thing. Now I'd have two parts and I'd add the third part.

At that point I realized, it's awfully hollow sounding by copying this played-back first version through the mic with my live addition to it, and I know it has a line input on it, why can't I directly transfer the first generation to the second machine electronically and then sing, overdub the second part acoustically to that, and that would keep the quality of the generations better.

So I developed JRSL. That was Jim Reeves Sound Laboratories, and I would make an announcement before every recording saying "dedicated to new-and-improved sound quality recordings of my music," and I wish I had that tape, but unfortunately it's gone. But I did lots of doo-wop things and the Mills Brothers' Across the Alley from the Alamo and the Lennon Sisters' things, everybody who harmonized, Les Paul and Mary Ford things. I would've had a harmony to Mary's parts. So those were the roots of it. And

Figure 18.3 I loved working in The Church on 30th Street. One of the stories with the Church was we recorded Bobby Vinton at Studio B, on 52nd Street. But somehow we ended up at The Church to overdub the vocals, on this one song, Just A Little Loving Early In The Morning, a Barry Mann-Cynthia Weil song, a beautiful song. And I'd been out to Bobby's house several times, he was really gracious and he would stop parties with Alan Klein and Cousin Brucie and people like that and say "This is my engineer! He's more of a producer than my producer!" It was really great, he had a beautiful jukebox in the basement and he had lots of babies, he had a lot of children, he was very Catholic and his wife was very lovely. So here we are at the church, to do vocals for this thing. And he started singing Just A Little Loving Early In The Morning, and he just did not sound like he was interested in any loving at all! He was kind of mumbling, and I said "Bob," I said "Do you drink?" And he said "Well, a little bit," I says "How about...," and he says "Well, I got a little Dubonnet in my trunk in my car." So we went outside, and we climbed over all these cars packed into this parking lot and got out the bottle of Dubonnet, and we started walking back and I says "Wait a minute- go ahead, I'll meet you back at the studio." And I ran off to the newsstand at the corner and I bought a Playboy magazine. Came back to the studio, had a couple of drinks of Dubonnet, I took the centerfold and I taped it to the back of the Neumann. And that's how we did the lead vocal to "Just A Little Loving Early In The Morning." And I have to say it was a better performance than we were getting before.

then I got the American Concertone machine, which had three heads and it was a tube recorder.

I even edited it on my Wollensak, which was a bitch because you had no gate for the heads, you had to stick a pencil in or something to hold it up against the heads and gauge it somehow to turn the mute off so that you could scrub the tape, and splice at 3 3/4, and I still have a project based on that that my lead singer in my singing group, and I did years ago based on the Buchanan and Goodman records, which were the Flying Saucer records, where they would interview the space creature and splice in his reply by using an excerpt of a record, like "Creature would you come with me if I asked you to?" And then it cuts to Elvis Presley saying "put a chain around my neck and lead me anywhere." It was a novelty record. So we made one like that.

When I was in high school, I asked my science teachers to help me with electronics, but they didn't know audio. They knew basic electronics and magnetism, coils, and tube things, but they didn't really know much about audio recording or the electronics of it, but they let me bring my Wollensak. I had one Wollensak that had always had a problem

Figure 18.4 I didn't finish the story about the Supremes standing there, they're on these three stools. And they're smoking! And they go puff, "Stop!" puff "In the name of love!" puff-puff "Before you break my heart." They were sort of bored as hell, and yet I'm looking around the room, saying, "Did we buy new equipment? Was there something changed in the studio? Why does it sound so great?" And you start to realize that some people play my piano, and I go, "Oh man, I got to get work done on it." And the next person will come in and you're going, "Oh god, my piano sounds awesome!" Same thing with my drums. You know I had this band in, the kid's playing and he's sort of just dropping his stick on the snare. And I said, "You know the snare isn't gonna play itself- you need to hit that snare to make it sound like something."

Figure 18.5 I had a lot of experience with live bouncing from the Wollensak days, also I discovered that Ampex had a series of consumer machines that were as crappy as anybody else's, they were awful. So there was the professional world and then there were the okay, consumer things. But the one thing about consumer things is that you are creative with it, you know what your obstacles are and you have to overcome those to get your ideas down, and they're less complicated so it doesn't dissuade you or distract you from your musical ideas. That's the important thing and that's the important thing I think with all of this recording process is that you don't let the technology, the equipment, or the gear get in the way of the music. It's supposed to help you.

and it had a motorboating thing, it would just go prlrlrlrlrlr, would do that once in a while, and I used to bang it a few times, and it would stop. I tried to repair that and I kept running into problems with taking the unit apart. I had sent it to Wollensak, Wollensak charged me $9 and sent it back and it still had the problem. Then, I took it locally to another guy and he charged me $6 and it still had the problem. I said "Well if they can't fix it and it's mine and I own it, I'm going to go in. I'm going to gamble and see if I can't do it."

I attempted to take it apart and there was this one part that would not let me take the chassis off, and my teacher Mr. Rowan, looked at it and he just pulled it up, and it never occurred to me that you would pull it up, and that's the last time I ever let anybody repair anything. I've been repairing my own stuff ever since, and with the thought that God what's going to happen, if I can't fix it, why do I think that anybody else could, because I'm pretty thorough about it.

So in Catholic high school I was a failure, but in public high school I became an honor student within three months. There's the whole different attitude, and there they embraced what I had to say and do, and I loved it there. They had an empty machine shop that wasn't being used, that was my last year of high school, and they gave it to me. They said, "We don't care, as long as you're learning something, here's your shop." And I had the key, and I could go in and I had lathes and I had bending machines and I had drill presses and I had the whole nine yards with that.

So I built my first little console for the two Wollensaks. Bring the thing home and I plug all the plugs into the two machines and every time I turn the machine up, the volume's up past three, I get one of them to three, I get the other one up to three, they were going "Ewwwwoooop" "Ewwwwoooop," I was like, "What the heck?" So I studied it for weeks trying to figure it out, and I finally gave up on it. I just started taking parts off the console, one by one I was dropping them off of the chassis to eliminate what it could be, and I got the last jack off the chassis and it went away. I only had one jack left on the chassis of the panel. It stopped, and as soon as I touched any one back on again, the same thing would happen, it would get this squeal to it.

I went to the plumber's store and I bought rubber washers, and I put the jacks back on the console with the rubber washers so that they wouldn't touch the chassis but they would still be physically in place, and then finally started moving on with my recordings with it. Then I met Skitch Henderson's partner, Dave Sarser at Studio 3, which was the guy who was the violinist who played a Stradivarius with Toscanini in the NBC Symphony Orchestra and was Les Paul's buddy and had put together his first 8track, The Octopus, he helped him design that. They got past the stacked head issue where the erase head, the radiation of the magnetic field, would pass into the next channel because they were so close together. So they ended up doing two 4channel erase heads, one an inch ahead of the other, they staggered the heads and that's how they originally got around that.

Then some guy came up with that, although Dave Sarser said that Les said he invented the sel-sync overdubbing switch selector that changes the record head to playback and so on. And there was actually this other guy who invented it, but Dave would say that Les would say that he invented everything. So I started working there and he had an awesome console. It was only nine rotary pots, nine channels.

That was Studio 3. It was called Studio 3 because it was Skitch Henderson, Dave Sarser, and Ruth Henderson, Skitch's second wife. They put the money in and started this little jingle studio in the Peter Stuyvesant Townhouse across the street from Hammaker Schlemmer in Manhattan, 57th Street and Lexington Avenue, which was a half a block away from my uncle's drug store, which was in the Capitol Records building.

Started working there, mopping floors, cleaning toilets, getting the coffee, and eventually some editing. We did a show called, "Show and Tell" for Pickwick International, and it was children's stories, but there was a record player on top and a slide projector in a simulated TV cabinet, and you would put a slide into the top, there was a turntable on the top, you'd put the needle down, turn the thing on, and as the record would play within the first 12 seconds a slide would go in and play the first slide and then everything else was by stopwatch timing, each scene in the slide was correlated to the music and dialogue of the actors on the record to make a visual experience of Peter Pan, Cinderella, or the Elephant Boy, things I've never even heard of before.

But they did a series of hundreds of those things, and we'd have a cast of actors in the booth and then we'd have a little combo Jazz, bass, drums, guitar, and piano ensemble in the other room live, and just run these shows, and I had to time every one of those. I had to edit them down so that they were 14.2 seconds per scene because that's when the slide would change on the machine. So it was interesting that when we did it again in Spanish or Italian or German or something that it didn't fit, you really had to edit the heck out of it to make it fit because the music track would stay the same and it would just change the language on it.

So I had lots of experience with editing with that, and again, lots at home. We also did all of the Steinway piano commercials there. We had an Ampex 300, full track quarter inch machine. Then Dave had another Ampex 2 track machine, which was a quarter inch half-track, both 7.5/15IPS machines. And then, a third machine which had a full-track erase head, a full-track record head, but a half-track stereo playback head. So you could take a two-track tape, put it on there and play it back, and copy it again to the two-track machine. Or you could take a full-track tape from the one machine and record it to the full-track head of the other machine even though it had a two-track playback, you wouldn't care. So that way you could copy anything to anything with those three machines. And then the Ampex 300 deck that was a two-track also had a half-inch three-track head assembly and a quarter-inch three-track head assembly. So I didn't use that very often because I didn't, at that point, get involved with pulling the heads off. It was his domain at that point.

Then in the back, where the vocalists performed, the little booth off to the left of the control room, in the back end of that was a Fairchild turntable and cutter with a Grampian head on it, a cutting lathe to cut the records because that's where we made all of these little Show and Tell records. The labels had to be put on just the right way so that when you put the needle down, the timing worked out for the slideshow.

Eventually I got assigned more things, and of course I had the keys to the place so I would bring my singing group in, or friends that sang, and we would do little sessions at night or on the weekends, and then I'd pull all of the plugs out of the patch bay, label them, grease mark the console volume settings so that I could just go about my session, and then restore it for Dave in the morning, who didn't know what was going on. Although one day he said "The next time you use the studio for a session, don't plug the preamp output into the output of the power amplifier on the patch bay". I guess I missed it by a row or something.

So I started bringing my band in there, and I still have some evidence of that on a CD now of all of those things. I call it "Bridges to my Heart" with reference to, in the doo-wop songs, it was always the bridge which was the most fun part of the record, the climax, or at least the transition that took you into the climax. So I have a lot of recordings there that I did doing just monotrack to two track in the machine and back to the mono. Record one thing in mono full track and then I'd record it on one side of the two track while recording the next part on the right side of the two track. Then, I could mix those back to the other two track again and add more as I went to that and so on, and I could get multiple tracks out of it.

It was way before any of the multi-track things. I even have a recording I did on my American Concertone here where I just sat one day and I played Blackbird. I can't play guitar, but I learned the harmony lines to the guitar part, and so I'd learn the first one, I played and recorded that, and then, I played the harmony part to it and I overdubbed that to the second track, and then I played those two parts back to the first track again, added the vocal then I transferred it back. You know, sound on sound, and I remember I always had an attitude about machines that had sound on sound on it because it just wasn't professional, it was so amateurish. I did it much more professionally.

I had a lot of experience with live bouncing from the Wollensak days, also I discovered that Ampex had a series of consumer machines that were as crappy as anybody else's, they were awful. So there was the professional world and then there were the okay, consumer things. But the one thing about consumer things is that you are creative with it, you know what your obstacles are and you have to overcome those to get your ideas down, and they're less complicated so it doesn't dissuade you or distract you from your musical ideas. That's the important thing and that's the important thing I think with all of this recording process is that you don't let the technology, the equipment, or the gear get in the way of the music. It's supposed to help you.

I don't think it occurred to me for years that I should know where my vocal level is on a preamp, it should be at 11 o'clock or 11:30 would be an average vocal thing or if it was a snare it might be back at 8 o'clock or you might have to stick a pad in it and put it up to 1 o'clock or whatever the setting would be on the dial, and you should know those things so that if somebody's ready to record, you can make an intelligent assessment of capturing that recording without blowing it by having it too low and getting too much tape hiss or by having it too loud and overloading. That's always been a dilemma.

In the meantime, I started working at Atlantic Records for Herb Abramson. That was over on the west side. It was 1964, I was still working at Studio 3, as an assistant or the porter, I was the porter. I was doing more things at that point, but Dave was still doing the sessions and I was doing my side sessions unbeknownst. I went around town to Muzak, and Muzak said they would hire me if I took a course at RCA, which was going to cost almost as much as what they were going to pay me, and RCA's courses were six months of soldering. I had already been building things. One of the first things Dave taught me was how to solder an RCA phono plug. The day I walked into his studio he was working on an Ampex 600 machine and his joke was "Well it has .02 percent flutter, but you can count on it." and he chuckled.

He was showing me the Ampex 600 and then he started teaching me how to solder things and techniques about soldering and what pitfalls there were and about the shield and the shielded wire, what its purpose is, and hotwire and the balanced circuits and unbalanced circuits and what they all mean and why they happen, and certain cable that was better at losing less capacitance and less loss in the lines, the Belden 8421 I think was a very cool wire to use for high impedance stuff because you could run along the lines and it didn't lose as much highs from that.

Well, at that point I had sorted out my problems with my equipment and I had learned something about alignments of tapes and heads, the significance of heads. In the one Wollensak I put in a two-track head assembly for playback, so I modified it to a stereo playback, and incidentally, I cleaned up both of those machines and sold them for more than I paid for them. I love cleaning equipment. I love shining it up and making it look brand new and, keeping everything in good working order and looking good too. I like aesthetics. Although there's something to be said about the funky things. When I went over to Incredible Sound Studios, Chris Huston was producing. Chris produced The Rascals, produced It's a Man's Man's Man's World, Van Morrison albums, Led Zeppelin.

Well, he was the guitar player in a group called "The Undertakers" that opened for The Beatles at the Palladium. I saw the poster, it says The Undertakers opening. At his place his first thing was he insisted on turning the crossover for the 604E Altec speaker in the utility cabinet, the crossovers were sort of dangling out the front of the cabinet, it was painted black, disappeared a little bit into the funky control room, and he insisted that the crossover had to be turned up full so that you could hear the crossover, the transition, better between the lows and the highs. Whatever, but he made great records, he was a very creative guy.

He'd do things like put his finger on the tape machine and slow it down while they were performing, the bridge might be coming up, he would dare to just throw his finger on the tape, slow it down to a stop, and then let it go so it would come back, so what would happen is they were playing da da da-da da... blablablablableep... BAAAAA! It would come back into the next beat you know. He would just create. He was crazy with ideas. He actually once invited me over to his house, well, several times, but this one time, he was into remotes and he would jingle his keys and his lights would go on, and then he would hold one key and he would jingle his keys again and the stereo would turn on.

And then he would play you a whole album and then he would laugh after it was over because he played it at 45 rpm and you didn't notice. You just didn't have any idea that the guy was singing that much higher, you might've thought it was a girl, but you just didn't notice that it was at high speed, at least the things that he played. So he was always very creative. He was also a proponent of, if you're playing a record and it sounds too bassy, you go over to stereo and you turn the bass down and you keep it balanced all of the time. It's up to you to determine that. If it's wrong, change it. If you don't just accept what it is, do something about it.

When he would come and visit me at the studio and I'd be at my Pultec and I would look at the knob and I would be turning it as I was looking at it, and he took his hand and he threw it in front of my eyes and I grabbed my face over my eyes and he said "Don't look at it! Listen! Just listen." only he had an English accent when he said that.

I got little tips from a bunch of different people like Joe Venneri from The Tokens was my client for a while and we'd be doing sessions at Studio 3 and I was always changing the volumes. You know how in the movies, when you see the guy at the steering wheel and he's moving it crazily, you know that in real life when you drive a car you just hold it there and it goes. You don't need to go up and down with the steering wheel, and I would be mixing like that, the guitar would disappear so I'd bring it up, then it'd get too loud and I would bring it down, so what happened to the drums, what happened to this guy, where has the vocal gone, why is it this, and I'd keep changing it all of the time. Joe kept looking over at me and I would see him looking at me and I'd wonder, "Why does he keep looking at me?" Then finally he said to me "You know, what you need to do is you need to get the general balance. You have to average out the mix and let the band do the rest," but that added to what Herb Abramson said to me at A1 Sound when he was interviewing me.

He was always late, the beauty of Herb, my biggest gift was Herb was always late, so he said "Well you know what to do. Get started, I'll be there, I'll be there." So I was always thrown into a lot of sessions that I wouldn't have gotten into. He worked the night shift. I ran all of the sessions in the daytime by myself, and he would come in late and then ask me to stay and send me back in the cutting room and teach me how to cut records on the Neumann cutting lathe, and you know, in those days you didn't have a cassette to take home to reference, you cut it on a record and took it home. In the interview, which he was two hours late for, and by that time I knew everything there was to know about the studio so I was easily able to impress him and he hired me right away, but he said "Well you know about how to ride the vocal." He went over and he actually had a vertical fader console then, which was this converted lighting board, like a dimmer board that did audio, and he'd say

> You know if they're going to sing a loud note, you'd grab the pot and you bring it down, and if they were going to go to a real low pitched note, they gotta sing softer, so you're going to ride that thing up right? You know about that.

So I guess you could say that was early digital mixing because you used your finger. So you rode gain. People don't do that anymore, they don't ride gain. They just sit there. They set a level and they let it go, then they smash the hell out of it with a limiter or something. That doesn't make them a bad person, but there are sometimes that gives you too much limiting, even though it satisfies the dynamic it just ruins the sound in the performance. So you use less limiting and a little bit of riding it with your finger, and maintain the lyric in the mix without hurting the sound of the singer, keeping the energy there.

One of the things I think that happened in all of these recordings, because you were going to tape them and because you were dealing with the signal-to-noise ratio, the hiss and/or the distortion limitations, saturations of the tape, you had to compress beforehand, and what always happened with a compressor? You'd get a reasonable setting with it and the band would run it down five or six times, and then they would do the take and now the adrenaline kicks in and they're singing their brains out or playing their brains out, and now the compressor is compressing 15 db, 20 db and what are you going to do about it? You're recording now, you can't change it because you'd have to adjust everything every time that change came up in the mix. So you would live with it and just curse and get mad at the musicians. Why couldn't they do that while I was running it down with them? It's ruined. It didn't ruin it, it just became what it became. Also people used to ask me about bouncing down tracks, we were limited with tracks so you had to bounce tracks down so you could open up a track to add a new part. "And did you feel that the quality was ruined by bouncing it down?" I said

> Well, I never look at it that way. I look at it like we won't get that new part unless we do this. Then this sound becomes this new sound. Now when we bounce it down to the other track, it becomes something else.

It's just another process, which is again what made those old records sound the way they did. It was because that's what you had to do to make it work.

It helped the creative process in that you gave it up, you just said

> That's what it took and that's what it became, and there's nothing much I could do about that, at this point we can just move on with the next idea and keep going until it becomes something that we like.

So you were making the record in the process. Each improvement or advantage as it was put, you know, we loved to play with the toys. So, oh, well they gave us more tracks, now we can record guys on separate tracks, let them go home, and we can fix it later.

All more about satisfying our own angst to play with electronics, but when I think about it, when I listen to the making of Pet Sounds with the Beach Boys and you hear a take start out in one perspective, and then it's take 15, and then it's take 22, and now, it's developing and people are playing something different, a mistake happened, I mean at one point Brian Wilson says "Hey, I liked it, what was that?" He says "Aw, I played it wrong." He says "Yeah, do that again, that was great! That's better than what you were doing." And the whole balance and everybody's performance starts to whittle into the final record that we ended up loving and buying, and a lot of times the performances aren't that great, but they made air time anyway and we started loving it. And if you changed one thing about it, you'd get shot.

Don't change that, it's great, I love it. So anyway, back to A1 Sound. I started working there and Herb would show up late, so I was called in for a midnight session at A1 when Sam Cooke was murdered. Berry Gordy of Motown Records wanted to do a memorial album with the Supremes in honor of Sam Cooke. So there was this Sunday night midnight session in the pouring rain, I was with my first wife at the time, and I took her album with me, she wanted me to get an autograph of the Supremes. I said "Well I can't do this" but I had to do it. So I brought it with me, and the Supremes came in and everybody was all wet and they put their umbrellas down and everybody set up the studio, and I put them in front of the glass on three barstools and the band was way behind them, and one of the things they did, which was a medley of "Stop in the Name of Love," "Where did Our Love Go?" and "Baby Love." Herb was supposed to be doing the session, not me, but he was late. He said, "You know what to do, go ahead you know, I'll be in, I'll be in."

And Herb, I gotta tell you something about Herb, Herb founded Atlantic Records with Ahmet Ertegun. He made artists that he had produced and released their records, it was all him, and here I was working with the guy and had no clue of it at the time. I didn't learn it until the 90's when I opened up a Billboard magazine and it said "Inductee to the Hall of Fame, Founders of Atlantic Records, Herb Abramson and Ahmet Ertugen inducted." And I said "I knew it! I knew it!" I knew he had to be more than a former dentist that owned this studio, and I always wondered at the time, "I wonder if A1 could mean Atlantic 1." Turned out I was right. Tom Dowd preceded me, I was the next guy in.

On a nice note I spoke to Barbara, his widow about six months ago, I was trying out something on the PC with the auto-dialer and it accidentally called her number in Arizona, which I tried several times because somebody gave me a lead of where she was and there was never an answer so I thought she moved, and she just walked in the door and I said "Do you remember me?" I said, "It's Jim Reeves." She said, "Oh my god!" I haven't seen her in 40 years, "Black, wavy hair, you were Herb's favorite engineer. He never let anybody have as much control over the studio as you," and I was like, "Man!" that was music to my ears. It was an amazing thing to hear. She was about 15 years younger than him. She was a young girl, and her hair was down to her ankles like Crystal Gayle. Always very friendly and nice to me in the studio and helpful, she was in the office pretty much in the daytime while I was there running sessions.

We had a great 40 minute discussion on the phone that day. I don't even think she got her groceries into the refrigerator, and she told me the story of how Herb saved Miles Davis's life outside of this club one day. The cops used to walk around and check all of the doors of storefronts to see if everything was secure and nobody had broken in, and Miles came out of this club, the Metropol or something like that, to have a cigarette, of course he was black and this was like some Irish cop or something and he said "Hey, what are you doing here?" and he said "I work here." and the guy started getting on his case and had an altercation, and the cop hits him over the head with the club and knocked him down, and Herb saw it from inside, came flying down the stairs, ran outside, and threw his body in front of him as the cop was ready to come down and hit him again and said, "He works here, he's a musician here." And they called an ambulance and had him taken away.

Barbara said that she can't believe she didn't kill herself running down the stairs in her high heels and her tight skirt, and said that if that cop hit him another time it probably would've killed him because he was bleeding profusely from the head and they got him to the hospital in time and Herb just went back inside because he stepped out of it at that point.

Now, when I worked with people like Don Covay, J. J. Jackson, and Titus Turner, the guy who did High Heel Sneakers, things like that. What a great place to work at, but when Skitch called me up one day and he said "I heard you're engineering over there. Why aren't you engineering here? "Well, I said, "You only need me as a porter over there." He said, "Well, Dave doesn't want to work full time as much now and he wants more time to develop these other electronics things." He got into cassette design and duplication and things like that, and he was getting older, and I said "Yeah, I'll come over!" because I loved the intimacy and just the whole thing about Studio 3. Career-wise it probably wasn't the best move because here I was in the midst of all of this R&B action and I went back. I was working with Benny Goodman and Johnny Ray and Sarah Vaughn and people like that. It was a whole different type of recording genre.

At A1 Sound there was Mike Edl, the maintenance guy, who was this kind of annoying, little curmudgeon. I wired in a Gotham Audio universal limiter, and I did it in a hurry, I wanted to get it in the patch bay, and in the middle of the session when I'm with the client, he comes in and he goes to the back, he goes "Who wired this atrocity in here?" and really got on my case for the sloppy wiring. He was right, but I had no time, I was trying to get it working for the session, and Mike was a funny guy because back in the 60's, had wired a doorbell to his reverse on his car so if he backed up a doorbell went off. I think he beat General Motors to that idea. And he had a telephone dialing system that when you came in the house, you dialed this rotary dial and it would turn on the lights, much like Chris Huston, but Chris did it all wirelessly. Mike had his stereo system setup where you could dial in a number and stuff would happen from the telephone system.

So he was a crazy person, but there was a three-track, Herb had bought two Neumann lathes at an auction in a basket of parts and assembled them into one working Neumann lathe, which I learned a lot of cutting skills on through his teaching, and we had a 3 track Presto half-inch tape machine which we did all of these recordings on, and he got finally a 4 track head and we found some other electronics, I don't know whether it was a Scully or an Ampex or something, and wired that up and we became four-track with that system. So every time you went to the fourth track you had to pull out a plug and move something over to get the fourth track going. I forgot this, my friend Glen Kolotkin reminded me this because Glen, there was a guy right after me when I left to go over to Skitch's, Mark Fields, and then Glen started working there. And I met him because I came over and visited one day and was telling him how excited I was to be back at Studio 3, and then we re-met years later at Columbia Records and became partners and produced records together and are still friends to this day, and he recently got his Grammy for Supernatural. So he's had a great career and is still making records down in Florida.

Anyway, so I went back to Studio 3, then I talked Skitch into giving me ten grand, I got my first Scully four-track machine, I got four Altec speakers that had two 15-inch woofers and a multi-cell horn in front. I put four Gotham faders on the monitors just so I could have control over those easily. I just wanted to get into sliding faders because I still had rotaries on the console, and so now I was four tracks and did lots of four-track recordings, and you know, the whole thing with tape always was calibration, aligning them, setting the bias, setting your azimuth, constantly doing all of that stuff, which was very interesting, but it's bound to be a pain in the neck because if you didn't have all of that stuff done up front, chances are your recording wasn't as console-like. It didn't mirror the console as much.

Yet I remember Dave had attenuators on the meters. He had half dB stepped attenuators on the VU meters, and I didn't get it. If your meter was telling you what your tape was doing, why would you turn your meter down? He wasn't easy to get answers out of, but eventually what he pointed out was that if he got a good mix and the meters were buried and he was using up the headroom in the console and it was really sounding great, he wasn't going to change the mix on nine faders or turn the master down, it sounded good the way it was. So he would turn the attenuators down to get zero level, he would put tone in the console or he would simply go over to the tape machine and turn the tape machine down to match the meters. That's the key I didn't know. I didn't know he turned the machine down because the idea is you put zero level on the console and then you take that same meter reference and you turn the meter up on the tape machine to match it. Now you know what's on the console is on the tape. That's the simple process of it. But, then there's the creative process where you get silly and you say "Oh this sounds great!" And now you're overdriving everything, but it still sounds great.

I had a session with Roy Cicala at the Record Plant once, and I got this great reverb sound on this record, and he loved it. He says "Great! What did you do?" I said "Well, I'm overdriving the EMT chamber plate," and he goes "Oh, I don't want any distortion on my record. Take it off." I was like, "But it sounds great! What are you talking about?" "No, I can't have distortion on my record." He was funny. He loved to mult the tom-tom mics. He wasn't interested in having each mic come up on the board. He would mult all three tom-toms and put it into one preamp and then compress the hell out of it. He loved it.

At Studio 3 there were two Pultec EQP1As, and then I guess it was an MEQ5, and another later version of the EQP that had one more notch on the high end, it went up to 16 instead of 12 or something like that, and instead of it going to maybe 2k or 3k it went down to 1.5 or 1. There were one or two extra notches down toward the midrange and then one more notch up on the top. The bottom stuff was all the same, but it was slightly different. So there were two Pultecs, the MEQ, and then the high and low filters, and then there were four Altec compressors that weren't in the chassis. He put the meters up on a panel so that it only took one panel space, a 2U rack space, we didn't even call it U rack spaces then, just a bigger rack space or a smaller rack space, and we called it echo then, we didn't call it reverb. Put some echo on it. Otherwise you would use slapback, or tape echo would be the other effect.

I remember discovering phasing. I cut a reference disc from tape and I wanted to compare the sound quality of the record to the tape machine. We had a Thorens TD 124 turntable with variable speed on it, and I started the tape and in the first measure I stopped it on the downbeat. Then, I played the record, brought it up on the console, and as soon as it got to that downbeat I hit the Ampex and then the tape started playing with it, so I could A/B one or the other, and then what I did was in order to get them exactly at the same point, I would slow down or speed up the turntable to get it to sync up with the tape. As I did that it started this "wwsheeeeeeoooowwshooooo," and I was like "Wow!" I said, "That's how they do phasing!"

Well, I almost invented it myself by discovering it this way, and then I said "Well. You can do that with tape machines if I line them all up and I hold my finger on one then the other."And then at some point Dave taught me how to do that, how to vari-speed a machine by taking a 100 volt output transformer, I'd need an amplifier of at least 100 watts, and a 100 volt transformer on it. I knew about a 70 volt line because you used that for distributing it on PA systems if you wanted to do several speakers and didn't have a lot of power, you used the 70-volt transformer on the output of the amplifier, and then, each speaker had a 70 volt transformer on it with 4 ohms or 8 ohms or 16 ohm taps that went to that speaker to adjust the level at that area of the room for multi-speaker rooms. They made them with 70 volts and 100 volts, and you took the 100 volt output, you pulled out the dummy plug that hooked into the hysteresis synchronous motor, between Con Ed and the motor. When you used the vari-speed you put an oscillator in the front of it and you set it to 60 cycles or 59 and you just rotate that to vary the speed of the machine.

Anyway, so there was a lot of alignment going on. You had to adjust your bias. First, you demagnetized your heads. You adjusted the azimuth, and Dave's technique, without an oscilloscope, was that you multed the two outputs of the Ampex together and you then adjusted the playback head azimuth until it peaked at its highest at 10,000 or whatever, it would always be a little different at 15,000 then it'd be at 10,000 but whatever. Get that azimuth up so that the head was aligned with the tape as good as it could be, at least from that angle, and then you put your test tape on first to magnetize the head, set your 1k levels of playback and your 10k EQ, then you'd record tape and you'd adjust your bias and then you do your high frequency equalization and then you adjusted the low frequency of the playback, which never made sense to me that you couldn't adjust the low frequency of the recording because that meant that every place it went to, you had to adjust the playback of the bottom and if you didn't, it was whatever it was.

So there was always that hassle, and then of course the more tracks you had, the more you multiplied that. So you had to have at least an hour with 16 track ahead of time, and then it got worse if you had to change from 16 track to 24 track heads on the same machine.

Then you had to put it back, so there's hours of setup, and then you get anal about it, "Oh, everything has to be perfect, oh it's not quite there." You become a fanatic at it. Dan Hartman, who I recorded Free Ride with, he had a studio in Connecticut, and he loved to overbias to get some distortion on it. He hated it just being a clean recording. He'd just take it over the top to get that sound out of the machine.

At Incredible the mixers were Ampex, they made these stainless or satin finish two rack space, four or five channel mixers with an A/Both/B selector and one master, which is five pots and a master pot, five channels of gain and two outputs, an A and a B or both, and he had four of those hooked up and four Pultecs, one on each output, and that went to an Ampex 4 track machine and eventually an 8track machine. The process for 4 track then was you recorded the whole rhythm section on one track, and Chris would get the balance and then he would whittle the EQ, between balancing and bass and treble EQ of the Pultec, and there was only the one Universal Limiter there, which he used to like to put on the guitar.

When I first started there, of course I watched them a few times, before that I would come and visit. I didn't even work there at the beginning. I was still working over at Studio 3, and he'd come over there to Studio 3 and I'd go over there and hang out at sessions, it was called Talent Masters then, this was before it was Incredible. At A1 one thing that Herb loved as an equalizer, he had a stereo Marantz, the stainless steel hi-fi consumer preamplifier, and he used that for EQ. He would just crank the hell out of the top end. He would boost the bottom end. Yeah, that was one of the equalizers there. We had a Pultec or two. I can still see the room. I can see through the glass, and I can see the long room and where the drums way in the back. We had the limiter I put in, which was Teletronics, I guess it was a Teletronics. This was like the one at Incredible Sound, there was a detented input and output and a meter. That was the whole thing, and I didn't see that for years and years after that anywhere. It was like I made it up just like the Telefunken. We had a Telefunken at Studio 3, and then, I never saw another Telefunken again. Maybe there were some at Columbia Records, but I started to think I made it up because years went by and I said "Wasn't there a Telefunken?" Then, I found out that the Telefunken was simply a Neumann that was distributed by Telefunken, and they took Neumann's logo off and they put their logo on. That's all it is, it's a Neumann.

In New York, I also worked at Moogy Klingman's a 12 track studio called Juggy Murray's. One of the sessions there where everybody was live, we had the singers there, we had the horn players there, and they count off the thing and nothing happens. The drummer is supposed to kick in first but nothing happens. So we go, "Alright, what's going on? What's happening? Let's go, we're rolling and nothing." So I walk back through everybody, like the gauntlet of musicians and singers and lead singer, everything, and I get all the way to the back by the drummer and the drummer is passed out at the drums and there's an empty jug of Gallo wine. Or Ripple, it might have been Ripple. He was three sheets to the wind and that was it. So I started the tape machine and played time on the drums for the session. I was solid enough to just keep time on it. I couldn't play anything fancy, didn't want to even try, and that's how we got the tracks laid down, and then, he eventually redid the drums on it.

I have no idea who the band was. There were a lot of things to think about at a session, and who and what was going on, it was like, "Do I know? Do I get a chance to find that out?" You're busy getting the ashtrays out for everybody and somebody wanted some water and the music stand was not high enough or it was falling down.

I also worked at Simon Andrew's place, the original Right Track when it was down on 24th Street. He had some Allison automation, which was kind of weird switching between tracks 23 and 24, you had to send the data back and forth on that, and he started out at 15 bucks an hour at this place, and I said Simon, you're crazy. I helped him a little bit with that. He was a waiter at the club I ran. He came right over from England, and he was a waiter and he refused to pool tips with the other waiters and waitresses. He said "Screw you. I worked on that table. I'm keeping the money." Saved up about 20,000 bucks, got this little loft down there and I said "15 bucks an hour, are you crazy? Everyone was charging about 35 then." But he was a business guy. It was like $5 for the box. There was you know, whatever tape you used you charged by the foot. You used the organ it would cost you money and if it was after 5:30 it was another five bucks an hour. If it was after midnight, and he had interns that he didn't pay. They worked around the clock, and six months later he was 24-track and he had a Steinway. He's a great marketing guy.

When I came up to the new place on 48th Street he greeted me at the front of the place and tears came out of his eyes. He was so excited to show me where he had gone from where he was. Which moved me a lot that I excited him enough to bring tears to his eyes, but I walked in the control room and I walked past the speakers and I heard this vortex in the hiss, and I said "You know, your speakers are out of phase." He said "No, that's not possible, the guy just left and it's not possible. It can't be." He climbed back behind the rack and he saw the Western Electric plug in the back of the amplifier was reversed. He says "Goddamnit JR you're right!"

I have a lot of stories about anomalies that nobody ever caught before I walked in the door and I would catch immediately. Even Glen's speakers, his woofers were out of phase all his life in his Voice Of The Theatre speakers. It drove me crazy because he lived in an apartment on the top floor when we were at Columbia Records, and I lived down in the garden apartment, and I helped him set up his A1s when he brought them in from his apartment on 64th Street and I said "Hey, they sound out of phase. Let's reverse it." So we reversed the phase and put them back and they never sounded right to me. You gotta understand, Roy Halle, Don Puluse, all of these people are coming to Glen's house to listen to their records on Glen's speakers. About two years ago I went down to Florida where he's living now, I'm playing something, but I said "Glen, you know what I think? I think your woofers are out of phase with each other." His friend Pete, Glen's longtime friend said "Oh yeah, crap. Are you kidding? This guy's got a Grammy sitting out there in the hallway, and you're going to tell this guy with these fantastic ears..." And then Glen says "No!" he said, "I respect Jim." So he took the back cover off one of the things, reversed the subwoofer, and he's been calling me ever since. He says "For years I would come home, I got A7s because I wanted the same thing that Columbia Records had to listen at home to playbacks." He said "I was never happy. I'd always go back and remix it. It was never right," and he says "Now everything for the first time in my life, sounds right."

Then I found out why! He assembled the speakers. They didn't come from Altec built. And we never talked about that, until then I said "It's pretty amazing Altec would..." and he says "No, I wired them." He said they came as a kit!

I worked at Columbia Records. Well, that was different because at Columbia you were in the union, immediately. I was interviewed at Columbia, and you know I was babbling a lot. I'd lost my studio, you know these gangsters come in and they took the studio over, and I still had a couple of groups I was producing, that was Skitch's studio. Skitch came to me one day and said "I'm gonna write the studio off for taxes, and sell it." I said "Well, don't do it. Let me buy it from you." So I started paying him off in notes. I got a partner, and the partner was connected beyond what he realized.

And the next minute I walked in one night and it was all a bunch of them there. They wanted it for an after-hours club. I had no idea what their motives were, what was going on. I was just a dumb kid and I was being slapped around and they made me sign papers, and I ran away with my tail between my legs, happy to be alive. I didn't think I was going to get out of there that night.

I hung out with Johnny Nash down in Jamaica, I bumped into him in Kingston. It was the cheapest place to go. And I didn't know they had no beaches there! Anyway there's Johnny, we had worked at A1 Sound together and he embraced me and I hung out at his house every day, I had this hotel room, but I stayed there and ran around to West Indies studios and Jamaica Recording, Federal Studios, and places like that. Just hung out and did sessions down there for about three months.

And then I came back to the city, started reengaging with the groups I was working with, I still had a deal with Epic Records with this one group and I went and started producing there. I wasn't allowed to touch anything because it was union, and my engineer in the mix room Don Meehan said "Well, you do this stuff. Why don't you get a job here?" Because I was broke. And I said, "I don't want to work here, it's like a hospital in this place. It's very bureaucratic, and it has no vibe to it or anything." But I went for an interview and while I was interviewing Russ Payne, one of the mastering engineers, had prepared some tape for me to edit. And into my interview with Roy Friedman the studio manager I was babbling away, "Oh and I did this- blah blah blah... but you know I've recorded this, and I know about this, I know about that, and when I was doing this, this happened..." and while I'm doing it, I'm looking around the control room and I saying, "Well, OK, what are those two geared knobs- that must be the monitor volume control." Interesting little gear mechanism so you can change the balance and push the gear in and then they both worked together.

The monitor was almost off. But I was just sitting there scrubbing tape, because I can edit with my hands tied behind my back. And while I'm talking, I'm scrubbing the tape, I do the splicing and all that. And Roy goes, "OK, it's getting late, do the edit, we have to go." And I said "No, I did the edit already." And he actually sat there and he says "No, don't fool around, we have to go." And he got angry with me. And I said, "I'm not fooling around." And I said here, and I rewound the tape, I went over and I grabbed the volume control, I turned them up, I hit the play button, and it played flawlessly through the splice. He comes- jumps up out of his seat, runs over to the machine, rewinds the machine, plays it again, looks at the splice, turns it upside down, puts it back down on the machine, and he says "Come with me," grabs me by my arm, *firmly* by my arm, he says "Come with me!" And he drags me out of the room, brings me upstairs, and he says "What do you want to get paid?" And I didn't want the job. I didn't want to work there.

I had never gotten more than a 100 bucks a week at that point. Which was a big coup with Herb Abramson, I was making $50 at Studio 3, and Herb said "What do you want?" And I said $100, risking everything, biting my fingernails at the time. And he said "No problem." Which made me feel like I should have asked for $200! But I don't think $100 was easy for Herb either to do, in the end, when I talked to Barbara about some of that. And, so I said, "I don't know- a thousand." Well, with that he stuck his finger on his tongue and moistened it as he went through the union scale book, and paged through everything, and said "Well, I can give you top scale, and then I can give you 10% night differential if you want to work at nights and blah blah blah..." So I ended up with about $800 something a week.

Oh, one thing to add to my splicing thing at Columbia Records, my audition, was that I was so used to splicing at 3 3/4 inch that at 15 IPS I could practically throw the razor blade at the machine from across the room and still make the edit. That's what occurred to me that day, are you kidding? Wsshtt! Easy, right? Like a samurai sword.

I spoke to Glen recently, and he and Don Everett was only getting 200–300 bucks a week there. I had no idea. I never had any idea of that part. All I know is I didn't want to work there, and even when I think about it today, I still didn't get my thousand, did I? They still ripped me off! That was '69.

But the thing I didn't like about Columbia—well, among other things, the thing I didn't like about it was I was always in touch with my machines, it was a part of the whole recording process. I would rewind quickly, I knew where I was on tape, I knew what tracks I was on, and I could get back to a place really fast so I could punch in. And at Columbia, there was a guy in another room, who ran the machines. And there was another guy who set up the mics. I could tweak the mics, and finalize the positions of them, but he handled the earphones. So I just came in, sat down at the board like a prima donna and up is louder, down is softer, get your patch bay in order.

When I first came in there I sat for three weeks and I studied patch bays with Harold Turalski, the maintenance guy. And you could patch everything. It went from the tie line in the studio to the patch bay, normalled into the preamp input, the preamp output went to the booster amp in the console, came back from the booster amp in the console back to the patch bay. Into the fader, also, into the echo pot, there was an extra patch point you could go to. Every sub master, there were several groupings of things, like left-right, and left-center, and right master. There were nine sub channels. There was left-one, center-one, right-one, left-two, center-two, right-two—so for these big three-track and four-track recordings you could group three busses of the singers. And three busses of the band, the orchestra, and maybe the strings and horns, you could put them all up on these subgrouped masters.

And again, with the gears, where you could pull the gears up and change the relationship between the three masters and then just grab one and they'd all rotate together. Amazing! Amazing console, but they had groups into groups into groups into groups, and all went to the patch bay first! Nothing went from point A to point B. It went to the patch bay, so you had this wall that was 10 feet long, with double-ended jacks, not the single ring-tipped sleeve, the double ended, so you could reverse the phase on anything by flipping it over.

All quarter-inch, tip sleeve, dual tipped sleeve, tandem plugs, including the speakers! There was a time the speakers, the talk-back relays—everything was in the patch bay. The producer said, "Can you turn off the mics I want to go and talk to this guy." I turn off the mic, and I want to know what they're saying, so I took one of the speakers out in the studio playback and I plugged it into a preamp, equalize the hell out of it and brought it up on the console so I can hear what they were talking about.

At Columbia, I worked with Johnny Winter and Edgar Winter, I worked with Bobby Vinton who was great to work with. My first forty or so piece orchestra thing. Jimmy "The Wiz" Wisner, really, I don't know how much of a producer he was, but he was a composer, arranger kind of guy, and he did all the arrangements with the orchestration. I was there for three years. I got to work with Joey Dee and the Starliters, I worked with Dave Clark of the Dave Clark Five.

I loved working in The Church on 30th Street. One of the stories with the Church was we recorded Bobby Vinton at Studio B, on 52nd Street. But somehow we ended up at The Church to overdub the vocals, on this one song, *Just A Little Loving Early In The Morning*, a Barry Mann-Cynthia Weil song, a beautiful song. And I'd been out to Bobby's house several times, he was really gracious and he would stop parties with Alan Klein and Cousin Brucie and people like that and say "This is my engineer! He's more of a producer than my producer!" It was really great, he had a beautiful jukebox in the basement and he had lots of babies, he had a lot of children, he was very Catholic and his wife was very lovely. So here we are at the church, to do vocals for this thing. And he started singing *Just A Little Loving Early In The Morning*, and he just did not sound like he was interested in any loving at all! He was kind of mumbling, and I said "Bob," I said "Do you drink?" And he said, "Well, a little bit," I says "How about..." and he says "Well, I got a little Dubonnet in my trunk in my car." So we went outside, and we climbed over all these cars packed into this parking lot, and got out the bottle of Dubonnet, and we started walking back and I says "Wait a minute- go ahead, I'll meet you back at the studio." And I ran off to the newsstand at the corner and I bought a *Playboy* magazine. Came back to the studio, had a couple of drinks of Dubonnet, I took the centerfold and I taped it to the back of the Neumann. And that's how we did the lead vocal to "Just A Little Loving Early In The Morning." And I have to say it was a better performance than we were getting before.

So, that was one thing, I worked with New York Rock & Roll Ensemble, I did Georgie Fame live with a full orchestra, strings, horns, rhythm section. Herbert Lovelle, Chuck Rainey, and Eric Gale on guitars. I did Otis Blackwell at the church—I still have those recordings, I have outtakes of those recordings, and with Sissy Houston and her singers singing background stuff, Otis Blackwell's "Don't Be Cruel," and "The Shadow Of Your Smile."

Also John Cale from the Velvet Underground, I did a Moog synthesizer album with him called "Vintage Violence" in a little vestibule. I did Tom Rush's vocals in Studio D, which was a little sacristy studio in the same building at the church. Nobody seems to have that name right, it was Studio D. It was C and D. That was pretty much Frank Laico's room in the daytime. Don't tell anybody that the speaker fell on him one time because he doesn't want his wife to know.

He said it fell off the damn chain, crashed on his shoulder. I just saw him in New York a couple of years ago for that AES convention panel. He's such a great guy, and so humble. He's like, "Well, yeah, I did record *New York, New York,* and then they took the tapes, and then they did, I don't know what they did with it," I said "Frank! You recorded *New York, New York!* That's it!" What do you say?

Really nice guy, and he used to kill me because I'd walk in there for my session- waiting for my session- and he'd be doing a session with some rock and roll band which bored the hell out of him. But he could get those drum sounds up in five minutes! It used to take us forever to get that stuff together. "What do you- how do you- what do you use?" I used to come in, it's like, "Look at that!" He's used to doing these whole orchestras, what's the big deal about a set of drums- you just go like this, and this, and this, there's your drum sound.

And of course, I'm like that now too. I had Steve Holley from Wings ask me once, he said JR, "Can we come in on a Sunday and spend the day getting drum sounds," so I said, "Yeah, sure, it usually takes me about fifteen minutes, but let's do it!" And what was incredible was that we were producing an album together, and the drummer that we were using, we got the sound check with him, and Steve says "That's great, mate, you want me to come in? I'll go out there and play it, come in so you can hear what they sound like." And Steve goes out and plays the drums, and you cannot believe how incredibly better they sounded when Steve played them. And I was the only one who knew! The drummer said "Oh, my drums sound great!" And Steve says "Yeah, how's that?" I didn't record the difference, we just observed the difference. I told Steve this, I didn't tell the drummer about it, but I told Steve about it. And that makes such a difference; you learn that over time, that some musicians just have the technique to get sounds out of their instruments. Russ Kunkle was an amazing person for that.

The Supremes, I didn't finish the story about the Supremes standing there, they're on these three stools. And they're smoking! And they go puff, "Stop!" puff "In the name of love!" puff-puff "Before you break my heart." They were sort of bored as hell, and yet I'm looking around the room, saying, "Did we buy new equipment? Was there something changed in the studio? Why does it sound so great?" And you start to realize that some people play my piano, and I go, "Oh man, I got to get work done on it." And the next person will come in and you're going, "Oh god, my piano sounds awesome!" Same thing with my drums. You know I had this band in, the kid's playing and he's sort of just dropping his stick on the snare. And I said "You know the snare isn't gonna play itself- you need to hit that snare to make it sound like something." And actually, at a live show we were doing in a small club I had to try telling him to play softer and he wouldn't. He'd gone and completely absorbed that idea of hitting the hell out of the drums.

I think you might grab a piece of gear because the guy doesn't have the sound in the first place, and it's more of a compensatory value. I made that word up, didn't I? To compensate for the lack of what's going on. Sometimes there's almost *nothing* you can do to get what you're after. I'll recap that a little bit because it's probably if you can keep in mind what you *want* to happen, and you have enough gear to make it happen, you probably can get what you want out of it. Maybe if there's too much noise, you have trouble with it, you EQ it enough to go after what you want. That's why I like condenser mics because they're hot and they're less noisy and if you want to go extreme with some EQ for an effect, you don't have to worry about the anomalies getting in your way.

So after three years at Columbia, I was doing a session with this band that I was told went through six engineers, and I really didn't pay much attention to that, I just thought, well, whatever, I didn't know why. But I remember working with them the one night and everybody's getting high, and I walked out to the bathroom, and I came back to go back to work. I finished the mix, and I didn't go back in the room. I guess I was too stoned, and I got very inhibited, and I walked and I got in the elevator, and I walked out and I never came back.

I was kind of bugged with the bureaucracy at Columbia Records and the abuse. They would just book me night and day. I remember I finished a Frankie Valli session at six in the morning and they had me booked at eleven, and they, you know, it just didn't matter to them who I was and I became sensitive to it. And I wanted to reevaluate, and I knew I had union rights to take a leave of absence, although they pressured me- "Are you coming back? Are you coming back?" And I finally said fine, because I didn't want to feel so irresponsible, I said fine, I'll quit then.

So I went to Florida for a few months, came back, I was producing quadraphonic for John McClure who was president of Masterworks at Columbia, and he was going to get me a staff producer's job there, I had been doing quadraphonic while I was an engineer now I was producing it, and then he left with Lenny Bernstein, and I said what the hell am I staying here for? So, I left there.

Roy Cicala from the Record Plant kept bugging me. I'd done sessions at the Record Plant with Gary Puckett and some Lou Reed stuff, and he kept bugging me to come to work at the Record Plant, I said no, I'm not going to work with these idiot producers, I'm sick and tired of these guys, every guy in a band that had a hit record, they give him a budget to become a producer, and they don't know what they're doing. And I just didn't want to do it. So he convinced me to work on the truck, the Record Plant truck. And I said I will, but only as an assistant. He said "Are you crazy?" and I said no, I'd make a great assistant, who'd know better than me about where to put the mics and things like that. So I worked with Frank Hubach for several months and then Frank got sucked into Nimbus Nine productions by Bob Ezrin who went up to Canada and so I took over the truck. At that point I was more comfortable about it. We had a great time doing it, we were a great team and started doing that, King Crimson, and Manassas here in Chicago, and I did ZZ Top's album in New Orleans, and lots of stuff. The Watkin's Glen concert.

And that was still 16 track, we were still 16 track! I'm still bugged. I don't understand, I worked at world-class studios all my life, I'm making some hit records, great people, great musicians, and I'm still doing 16 track while these other guys are doing 24 track.

I didn't even talk about the Dolby stuff. At Columbia Records I did the first Dolby'd album ever released, as it turns out. The producer told me when it was released, he says "Hey, guess what—we're the first ones out there with a Dolby album—just found out from research at Columbia."

So the Record Plant truck was great, and then I did a lot of sessions at the Record Plant, and also did some things with John Lennon there, and I won't go so far as to say I did sessions, but I did do an awesome splice that nobody could do. While in a huddle with John and Harry Nilsson, when we were talking about backgrounds on the record, four engineers were scrubbing the tape and I knew, while I'm having this conversation, that they weren't in the right place. So I finally said, "Can I try it?" And he said, "Yeah, sure." So I excused myself from Harry and John, went over and marked it—boom, boom, marked it—rewound it about a minute and sat down and continued our conversation. Splice went by like this and John winks at me, nods to me, "Cool." Which was perfect, the exact effect I was going for. That was a great moment for me.

Chicago! Well, I'd got married, I was doing jingles. Edd Kalehoff in New York, really great composer, talented guy, I loved working with talented people that had access to lots of music and musicians. We worked with *Saturday Night Live* guys as the horn section, Dream Girls was the rhythm section, and I never really got to find out who their string players were, but anyway we had Wynton Marsalis before anyone ever heard of him, Alan Rubin, Lou Marini, Tom Malone, Lew Soloff occasionally, Eric Weissberg on banjos. And it was awesome. We did lots of jingles, I made a lot of money, so I got married!

That was at Edd Kalehoff's studio. Anyway, and I made a lot of money in residuals there because I refused to not go on contract, I said "Why is the guitar played who makes fifteen mistakes and gets one right, and gets cheered for it, and I can't make any mistakes and I don't get residuals? I don't get it." So I made some nice money from that and I said "Hey, I guess I can get married." I married my girlfriend, we bought a house in Westchester, stopped getting along and she mentioned the "D" word, and said, "I'm going to Chicago with the kids, you can come if you want to."

So I moved out here, couldn't get arrested for a year. Everyone wanted to hear my rock and roll stories, that's when I found out I actually had rock and roll stories, because I was with all my peers, and we *all* had stories, I mean we talked to each other about stuff, but we never thought for a minute that anybody cared about anything we had to say about our experiences. And so I went for interviews with everybody before I got here, and after I got here, and lots of, you know, empty promises. And nothing happened for a year. And boom, I got the building here, and I also started working for Terry Fryer, who is like my Edd Kalehoff in New York, he's a great jingle producer here, and worked with him for a few years, got the studio developed here, and finally said it's OK, I'll just do the studio thing here. So I started doing that and I've done about 20–30 CDs here since then.

And I'm not using too much tape anymore. Only because we used to complain about it all the time, the signal came out of the console, comes off the tape, and the transient response wasn't as good. You'd lose the top end on your snare, you'd get this big bump on your kick drum on the bottom, that everybody loves now! That's what they want to have! And we were the big purists, we wanted what we were doing to come off that tape. And all the alignment issues, and the anomalies about it, and speed, if there were hysteresis synchronous motors and ConEdison was a little slow that day, so was our tape speed.

I have a recording and suddenly we were overdubbing the horns, and the tape was too near the end of the reel, and all the horns are sharp, everything else sounds flat. So that's why they make NAB hubs, so you don't slow down too much.

But that didn't work really. With Wynton Marsalis, I had a 3M machine, the closed loop machine, I'm saying, "Wynton, you're a little sharp, could you trim down a little bit?" And he's pulling it out, and I'm looking at Edd and I'm saying, "He's still sharp." And he's, "Yeah, you're right." And, "Hey Wynton, you want to pull it out a little more, you're still sharp," and Wynton's with his sullen look looking at his trumpet, saying, "What the hell's wrong with this guy." He is pulling out, he's pulling out, and he finally pulled out the whole valve, it just came right out of the trumpet. I said "Oh. What is going on here?" It's very hot in the control room, and it turned out that for the first time in two years that I'm using the machine, it gunked up, and it started slowing down. I cleaned it up, and put this thing back together, and it worked. We were doing the *Walking Tall* TV series. That got me out to Hollywood, got me lunch with—Morgan Fairchild for her birthday. That was a good lunch, "So Jim, what brings you to Hollywood?"

I gotta say that now I'm getting back to, it would be fun to just do an analog session, up is louder, down is softer, spend the time on aligning the machine, just get everybody in and playing live. If they'll play live, and just play it until it turns into a record, I'd like to see that again. A little tired of software failures and upgrades, and it's always going to be the next version. You used to put a tape on, and you hit the button, and you were recording. And it was there, it didn't crash, all the data didn't get lost. Today if you hit an undo button at the wrong time you can lose an entire 30 tracks of recording. It's an amazing thing.

But on the other hand you can go home at night, and you cannot have to stay up until 4 o'clock in the morning to finish the mix because somebody else is coming in in the morning and everything you've patched in will be lost or sit there for an hour writing down the settings and hoping you can recapture it again. Now you can save the session and come back whenever you feel like it. So there's a lot of things to be said about that.

There's also a lot of things about doing the remix starting from scratch, because you've discovered something new. Maybe you didn't get back what you had but you may actually have created something better as a result of it. It's been good! I liked it—I'm still liking it. As long as they're out there wanting to record, I'll be here.

Chapter 19

Dave Moulton

Dave Moulton is an audio engineer and producer, author, composer, educator, and acoustician. With degrees in music from Bard College and the Juilliard School of Music (major studies with John Becker, Jacob Druckman, Emil Hauser, and Vincent Persichetti), Moulton began working in audio in the late 1960s, founding Dondisound Studios in Red Hook, NY. In 1980, Moulton joined the faculty of the State University of New York, College at Fredonia, chairing the Sound Recording Technology Program there. In 1987, he became Chair of Music Production and Engineering at the Berklee College of Music in Boston. He resigned from Berklee in 1993 to devote full time to recording, composing, research, and writing.

Moulton received a joint Grammy nomination with engineer Curt Wittig for their work on a CRI compact disc (in Circle Surround) of music by George Crumb that was nominated in the category "Best Engineered Album, Classical" as announced by the National Academy of Recording Arts & Sciences. As a recording engineer, Moulton has also worked with the Concord String Quartet, jazz saxophonist Sonny Rollins, folk singer Jonathan Edwards, pianist Robert Jordan, soprano Kyoko Saito, and the Handel & Haydn Society, among many others. He is the author of Golden Ears, an audio ear-training course; Total Recording, a comprehensive text about recording; and Ten Essential Audio Lectures, a series of audio education CDs.

Since 1982, Moulton has been working on wide-dispersion loudspeakers and is a founder and Vice President of Sausalito Audio LLC, a firm specializing in such designs for the audio industry. This effort led to a collaboration with Bang & Olufsen (which licensed, then bought patents from SA) for the design of the technologically groundbreaking BeoLab 5 loudspeaker, a similarly advanced B&O audio system for Audi, Aston Martin, and Mercedes AMG as well as the remarkable BeoLab 3. Moulton has also been involved, with his son Dr. Mark Moulton, in the subjective measurement of audio systems and devices for companies such as Lucent Technologies.

DOI: 10.4324/9781003519829-19

Moulton is a monthly columnist for TV Technology Magazine and has regularly written for Recording Magazine since 1992. He also teaches privately and at the Parsons Center for Audio Studies in Wellesley, MA. At present, he is devoting all of his efforts to the development of high-performance architectural loudspeakers for domestic home theatres and is also the Director of Groton Hills Music.

Figure 19.1 ...that led me to having stuff in my house that other people wanted to use so I found myself in the studio business entirely by accident.

Figure 19.2 It was a really nice microphone and between that and the Crown, they kept me out of a lot of trouble, because those pieces of gear were so well built and had such headroom and such good noise performance as well that you could be really stupid, which I was, and get away a lot.

My name is Dave Moulton. I was born in South Bend Indiana in 1942.

I got interested in audio in about 1967. I got interested in synthesizers, the advent of the Moog synthesizer, and then actually got involved in a more professional way around 1969, and I've been here ever since.

Figure 19.3 I knew absolutely nothing and I had no teachers, so experience was my teacher.

Figure 19.4 They would take the LP masters which we'd worked really hard to get right, take the CD directly from that, which from my standpoint is unthinkable. Of course they sounded bad!

In 1969 I was teaching general music and chorus in a junior high school in upstate New York, in the illustrious town of Saugerties, which is next-door neighbor to Woodstock. I had been a starving composer, my background is as a musician. I went to Juilliard, majored in music composition, went out and was a starving composer, and began to teach simply to feed my composing habit. Then I discovered the Moog synthesizer and decided I needed a synthesizer in the worst way. So, I started saving up for synthesizers, I bought one and then discovered I needed a multi-track tape recorder, so I had to somehow get one of those, and I did. And that led me to having stuff in my house that other people wanted to use so I found myself in the studio business entirely by accident.

My first multi-track machine was a Crown CX844, which at that time was considered a really excellent tape recorder. It was a professional recorder, but it was not in normal use in studios. I bought it used from the Crown factory, and it was my understanding it had been in the White House and was used to record Nixon and Ladybird Johnson. And I don't know what else occurred as well. It was a four-track, and with it I bought the cheapest professional two-track ever made, from a company called Cape Sonic. They were made in Midtown Manhattan in a loft and I think they cost something like 500 bucks, it was a poor man's Ampex 350.

I had my synthesizer, it was kind of a knockoff of a Moog synthesizer, which I couldn't afford, by a company called Electronic Music Labs, EML. And so it had some mixers and it had some filters and so on, and that's what I used when I started out. I was really coming at this from an experimental basis. Everything I did was home-grown for the first six or seven years.

I think my first adventure was to build a patch bay, and once I got the patch bay working, my second adventure was to figure out how to make it all work and then to actually accept the occasional client who wanted to be recorded and figure out how to do that. Remember I'm living in a farmhouse in upstate New York. This is this perfect hippy sort of dropout life. Like shades of Big Pink, only those guys had money, I had no money. I was doing this on a junior high teacher's salary. And then I discovered I needed more money, and the only way I would get anywhere was actually go into the business.

I became a synthesizer dealer for EML to try to make enough money so I could afford to buy more synths and just begin to get into that acquisition and sales side of the business. So I bought everything and I helped them do R&D, and I served as an ad hoc musical consultant for them. They were all aerospace engineers who were out of a job, so it was a friendly relationship, and for a while, it was easy to sell them in fair volume, and I did.

Then it became obvious that I really needed a studio and at about that time, Teac and there's a funny story here, Teac formed Tascam. Now you go two years earlier I was looking for a multi-track tape recorder and there was quad around. I noticed that Teac had a four-track with a quad tape deck, and I wrote them and asked if they had one with Selsync. And they said no, they had looked into that market and had absolutely no intention of ever entering, thank you very much, and good luck with your career. And about two years later, Tascam arrived on the scene and I bought one of the first Tascam Model 10 consoles ever, serial number 00007 or something like that. Peter Yarrow of Peter, Paul, and Mary had actually bought it out of curiosity and decided they didn't like it and returned it and so it was sitting at the Harrisville studio and they were trying to figure out what to do with it, so I bought it from them. That was how I came into it.

I'd lucked into a Schoeps tube microphone that I really liked a lot. I can't even remember the number, I think it was CM56. It had tube capsules, and it had a pad on it as well. It was a really nice microphone and between that and the Crown, they kept me out of a lot of trouble, because those pieces of gear were so well built and had such headroom and such good noise performance as well that you could be really stupid, which I was, and get away a lot. It really forgave me, and I didn't realize how much it was forgiving me until I bought the Tascam, and all of a sudden had no headroom and discovered all the things that the Crown and the Schoeps, and other microphones like that, allowed me to do.

Some of my other mics? I had an old EV664, I had an EV635A omni. Then we bought some Shures, we bought a couple early Sennheisers, and I actually had a B&O Ribbon microphone that we got somewhere at an auction or something. We used that until a vocalist took out the ribbons. So it was that kind of catch as catch can, always get what's on sale and put it together. I had to figure out the difference between a balanced and unbalanced line. I had absolutely no technical preparation at all, so I bought the Audio Encyclopedia to teach me what I needed to know. There were no books.

I had a really good liberal arts education before Juilliard, and then I had Juilliard, which was a political education. Most stories are horror stories of just learning about things. For instance, learning about the fragility of magnetic tape on location early on. One of my first misadventures, and this is just part of the education process, was going on location with the Crown and a batch of microphones and recording. I should mention also the Crown came with an array of high-impedance inputs and mixing capabilities, and the preamp made it a pretty useful mixer all by itself. It was a four-track and it had eight mic inputs and eight line inputs and some rudimentary patching and distribution stuff and high pass and low pass filters. So by itself it wasn't too shabby and you could begin to do things, it was more than just the tape deck. Anyway so there I was on location and set a nice ten-and-a-half-inch reel of tape on the power supply and got back and had to call the client and explain that he had a nice sort of recording that dropped in and out every revolution and that we would have to do it again. Those sorts of things, those were my kinds of misadventures. We would just be very careful about tape and kept it far away from all the other equipment. Once I set a tape on the roof of my car and forgot it was there and drove off, got about a 100 yards and saw it playing out off of the roof.

I knew absolutely nothing and I had no teachers, so experience was my teacher. I had to learn fast, and then when I bought the Tascam, at that point, that was a very useful learning experience because it was so limited what it would do sonically. It was so easily audible that it was very weak in many regards, that after the Crown, where I could do anything and it didn't matter, I was able to start doing things like measure frequency response, and it had never occurred to me that there was such a thing as frequency response. And just seeing the difference between a really well-made piece of gear and a piece of gear made very much for the price point and cut way back.

I really wanted to make better synthesizers and I didn't get into any kind of real R&D other than consulting on synthesizers and what would be a better voltage control filter and what we really needed in an onboard generator until much later when I got into loudspeakers. Loudspeakers are an entirely separate story about ten years later.

I don't know if I got great sounds. I got some good ones on occasion but I just had to learn for instance how to cascade tracks when bands would come and hire me, and how do you do sub-mixes and how you focus multiple generations as they build up and how you think ahead about that. How you might do a drum and bass sub-mix and pull that to the end to add guitars and leave the vocals open then add the vocals while you're mixing down and actually get eight channels out of four. It's not a standard sort of thing.

We were all figuring it out for ourselves, and I had a better tape deck than most and that helped. I learned to work around the console, and I got a set of quad reverbs built for me, so I had 4 channels of quite good reverbs using the springs out of an organ. They did a nice job on that so it sounded pretty good. And early on I adopted the DBX noise reduction when it came out and bought a whole stack of DBX standards, the 117s, and that began to teach me about dynamics. Because it would both compress and expand, it didn't care, and was infinitely variable and I began to figure out what that did. That was also a really useful invention. Then I bought a batch of Sound Craftsman, actually the first EQ I bought was made by Advent of all people, if I recall, and it was a ten band graphic EQ stereo. It was for home use, for hobbyists. So I learned that and then I got some used Sound Craftsman EQs to go with it, then the DBX 117 compressors.

It was really the basic original semi-pro kind of approach, and I had no plans. I had some local bands who discovered I had a farmhouse with some recording gear and they could pay me very little money and I would work with them and build up tracks and turn out demos with them. Then I did school bands and stuff and local choirs, anybody that would come in the door, and I kept that up for about six years before the landlord wanted his farmhouse back. At that point, I had to build a real studio, and moved into a real studio and it got a lot more professional.

There is nothing from those days that I still use. I never sell anything, so the Crown and the Soundcraft are still stored in my attic. I was using a power amp, the predecessor that Crown made for the D60 series, called the D40, and before that were the amplifiers called the SA 3030 which was a pair of 30-watt solid state amplifiers and I still have one of those, and the D45 and the D60 in my attic. They're all in my audio museum of junk.

For me what happened was I started teaching more and more then I gave up my studio and became a faculty member. Then became an administrator and went back to having a studio in my house 15 years later, and started over, and I started over in the digital realm. It was a clean transition, but we need to talk about that. I was sort of there at the beginning of digital, and while I was teaching in western New York at SUNY Fredonia, after my studio days, I was doing recording there and having fun with that, and began making the transition into digital there, with location recording in 1985.

I didn't start with the F1, I started with the next generation after that, the 701s. I got the Sony 701 and I got a really good consumer recorder. Let me go back and give you a little better sense of my particular history, and it'll make other things easier to talk about. After I moved out of the farmhouse I actually bought a big commercial building that had a big machine shop and well-driller's garage in it and an apartment overhead. I made the machine shop and the well-driller garage into the acoustic room, and the control room and offices, and then separate offices in the apartment upstairs. I made it into a real studio, so I was able to actually do much more full-service work and again, staying with Tascam, expanded into eight tracks, and I was at the point where I had weekly clients doing commercials and typically billing 20 to 25 hours a week studio time, which was pretty good. We actually had employees and had weekly meetings with the bank, you know the standard business sort of thing.

That operation went on for about five years until 1980, when the State University of New York at Fredonia hired me to run their so-called Tonnmeister program because I had the Juilliard degree and the academic credentials they needed, and I had a background in education and enough technical confidence to impress them. So I sold the studio, it's now a barber shop, but before it was a barber shop some of my students took it over and did pretty well. They are still in the business and have a much better studio now. So I moved to Fredonia and took over the Sound Recording Technology Program there, which had an MCI console and tape deck.

I had an MCI 416, then later we updated to the Otari MX 24 track, the big one, I've forgotten its number. And there, they actually had a rack of traditional gear, so we had a rack of Ureis, and we had all the standard studio pieces there, because when the hardware listings were originally specified, that was the stuff to get, so we had a batch of Ampex two-tracks, we had an AKG BX20, reverb with the concentric springs. And so that was an interesting studio, and a lot of that was working really hard because I had 100 students in that program. so we ran that thing 24 hours a day, 7 days a week.

That was 1980, and we were one of the first. We were behind Miami and Berklee had just started, Miami was underway, and McGill was underway at that point too. But we were the only one to bill Tonnmeister. We stole from the original Detmold Tonnmeister curriculum and said everybody's got to have 20 hours of physics and electronics and math, they've got to have 40 hours of music, and they've got to have a standard liberal arts curriculum too. That was an interesting place, an interesting program, and I was really fortunate to have really good students and they've really gone on to some fame and fortune, some really nice names to have as a result of that. I was there for seven years, and while there National Public Radio began to re-train their engineers to put forth this new digital audio, and they started this series of summer courses called Music Recording Workshops. They did some in Denver, but they eventually adopted us as a home campus in the summer.

So I came to work for NPR every summer doing these really well-developed workshops with Skip Pesey and Neil Muncie and Paul Blakeworth, those guys were on the faculty. Then I managed to insinuate myself onto the faculty and that was really my introduction to digital because they were struggling with that, and we were trying to make sense of how well it worked and didn't work, and being confused about when it could be used in the broadcast context and when not. And after that, Berkeley hired me to chair their music production and engineering program. So I moved to Boston and I've been here ever since, and I stayed at Berkeley for six years, then went out on my own for a variety of reasons, I wasn't that happy at Berkeley. I taught freelance around, but also I got into loudspeakers seriously, and that's where I really am now, I'm working full time trying to start a new loudspeaker company.

Well, we'd moved to Fredonia, and I was talking about the studio there. And it's interesting, probably the pieces there that moved me the most were not the analog pieces but the digital pieces. And most specifically the Lexicon Prime Time was, for me, a huge breakthrough. It just showed me some things about psychoacoustics that I had no idea about— it filled in a lot. And we managed to win in a contest something called an Ursa Major Spacestation, which was a little eight-tap digital delay unit. And I got the most from those, and the old 1176s that we had, I used those and they were fine. I had no trouble with them, I was perfectly comfortable, but I never thought "Wow, now I can do a vocal!" It was there, a very useful tool, very easy and comfortable one to use. But I have to confess this, I don't think I was very skilled in the ways of the best engineers, and the use of compression or in the use of EQ, and it's only in the past five years that I feel that I've picked up a lot of the tricks. This is from a guy that I've worked with locally named Tom Bates, he's one of the old-line engineers from New York, and he's taught me an immense amount I sort of wish I'd known back then and put together. Be that as it may, some of his techniques with compressors, for instance, work well with the old compressor limiters. And it's exactly why they're favored, what they're valued for, vis a vis the kinds of working techniques he suggests for making something go really well with the vocal or with the strings.

Anyway, going back, I got hired away from Fredonia and went to Berkeley where I was an administrator. And at that point, I had an array of six rooms under my control and absolutely no time to work in any of them.

Our curriculum was focused on music production and engineering. We devised a curriculum to teach people how to be producers. Oh, by the way, also how to engineer in a record label context, and build that craft. Where Fredonia said you need to know music, audio, and science, Berkeley said you need to know music, audio, and business. That was kind of a real difference, that it was business oriented, and because there were so many players there, when you started to set up to do a production project, part of it was to round up the players, do the arrangements, and have them play on the session the way you would in a normal way. It was a wonderful laboratory, the sort of skill-building sensibility. Everybody's there and you can pop out a demo in the next half hour. If you need a pianist you go out in the hall and find a pianist, go out and tell him you need him for 20 minutes to play on a track, and he'd come in and do it. And that usually just doesn't happen anywhere. It's an intense musical world.

I was there for six years and then I went home and worked on loudspeakers, but also set up a post-production room in my house. And I actually built an analog room using a Mackie 32 input 8 bus and an array of analog and some digital recorders with very early Pro Tools stuff, which I was very dissatisfied with. I found that they weren't ready for primetime and I had a real sort of love–hate relationship with them. But it's evolved over the years, and about eight years ago I bought a Yamaha O2R to replace the Mackie, and I began to abandon little by little the analog pieces in my rack. The analog pieces were an array of delay lines—I was just seduced by delay lines. I have a whole rack of really beautiful Yamaha, I think they're called the DP5000 delay line, they would do 5000 milliseconds by two channels. I got six of them to do surround stuff. All of that stuff is mostly in retirement and with Pro Tools upgraded I got onto the whole what you might call most favored nation trading status with DigiDesign. I got a good OS9 system back in early 2001, early 2001. Then upgraded again last year so I have the latest greatest very fine system right now, an HD system. And I upgraded to a fresh O2R 96, so I have a completely digital system that will run at 96k from the input to the Pro Tools all the way out through the loudspeakers, without a single intervention. And that's pretty nice. So, that sort of brings up the gain.

As far as gear that I can't believe they're calling vintage now because it was substandard then, there's the EchoPlex and the EchoRec—either one of those. Any tape delay, tape-based delay unit. They're all horrific.

As far as what I have now I wish I had then there's Pro Tools. It just does everything—it's ready for primetime and it does everything. It was made for composers, and there's stuff I learned to do with a chamber music performance in college in 1959 that I can now do in Pro Tools and it makes for far better mixes. For me the meaning of the mix cycle is after you get levels set, and all your balances and all your returns, then you go to work and start being musical. Pro Tools allows it. Before, you had to have some really elaborate home theatre automation protocols that never allowed you to get there. You couldn't automate levels, you couldn't automate reverb sends, you couldn't automate very gentle EQ changes or riding gain to bring up the brilliance of a note, to shade the timbre of a note. Now it's all there.

I'm not very active recording right now. If I was recording and the cost was no option, I would love to have an array of Neumann U67s. I would probably accept a substitute of some of the U49s, that whole family. There are wonderful early large-diaphragm condenser microphones that simply do things that no modern microphone does. It may be useful here to talk about why I think that is. In any case, that's a place where the nature of the industry has changed, in changing microphone technology in a not altogether good way. That would be that after the Second World War, as we moved into more modern tube technology and the large-diaphragm microphone, the goal was to record very complex audio signals with a single microphone. And they were very much worried about diffused field capture and capture of low-level signals as well as high-level signals. They weren't concerned about extremely high levels—the highest level those microphones probably went to was 130 dB spl. And that's how Neumann and Shoeps, the other microphone manufacturers designed their microphones. And the result over the nine years was a low-level resolution that isn't there in modern mics. And you hear it particularly with any complex sources, like a symphony orchestra, when they play detail it's not there now. In our effort to make microphones deal with higher levels, we had to make diaphragms under greater tension, we had to change the nature of the diaphragm, and change the nature of the electronics, and I think we lost some low-level value. That's one of the reasons that those microphones are so desirable.

More than the limiter and the EQ, the microphone will make the difference. I find that the most important devices in the question of audio quality are the transducers. That's where the losses occur, and the big losses occur in the microphone. Some of them are inherent, and we won't even discuss those because you can't solve them—right now there is no way to solve them. But they lose a lot. They change the sound quality—irretrievable—and it's not a question of frequency response or phase response or directionality, but a question of ability to extract separate sources from the whole.

You're taking a very complex acoustical signal that came from 100 sources and changing it into a two-dimensional signal and we know there are losses, similarly, we know there are losses in loudspeakers. The losses in loudspeakers are huge and I say, "Boy do we have a long way to go."

One of the things I discovered from the Audiocyclopedia of all places, the testing measurements chapter, there's a whole section on square waves testing, and it shows the output per wave of various processing anomalies. The first time I put a square wave on a tape deck and looked at the output on an oscilloscope, I realized the whole recording process was impossible, it couldn't possibly work. You cannot record a square wave and have it reproduced and go its happy way.

From my standpoint, digital held a lot of promise with allowing us to think about things in ways we couldn't. I remember in the mid-70s I was out in California visiting my parents, and I managed to get an appointment at Stanford to go visit John Towney at CCRMA and talk to him about what they were doing. They were, at that point, sharing a computer with the math department, so they had certain hours they had the time, they wouldn't slow down so they could do things in the real-time, to do things like filter coefficients. And the promise that they could record things in a file and you could have them instantly there for you and non-destructive editing, non-destructive signal form, that anything you could do in the analog realm could be simulated in the digital realm. And it came almost for free once you paid for it. So I was fortunate I think to get an early look at that, that was around 1975, and they were moving right along but things hadn't happened yet. Towney had not yet written his paper with Yamaha, for synthesis. That had not come out yet when I visited Stanford. I think he did his papers that fall and it just exploded, and it was some of the best synthesis I'd heard.

When I got to Fredonia and I started working with NPR and they were very concerned because they saw digital audio coming to broadcast. It was coming. The point is that everybody who was going out to record, our affiliates, were switching over to F1s, 701s, whatever; and all of a sudden, this is what stimulated that, was the arrival of CE meant that their listeners would be listening to digital programs which would be much, much better than anything they could do in-house, and they had to deal with that. So we began studying it in our classes. I remember one summer, we actually set up an orchestra in a concert hall and made recordings, two-track stereo recordings, onto as many different media as we could manage. And as we were making the recordings, listening to them so we could hear mic to loudspeakers, mic to F1 to loudspeaker, mic through analog tape deck, quarter inch 7 and a half IPS, monitoring off the playback head, 15 IPS, 30 IPS, Sony F1 not for playback but just through the system. One of the dash decks, I think we had a dash deck. We had somebody's digital recorders. And see at the time that it happens you can hear that array of signals and their cleanness. And then they were recorded so we could sit down later and play them back and now we no longer have the original performances, but we have all the decks, even cassettes. See, we could evaluate the recovery of the captured sound quality of all the media. It was absolutely fascinating to notice that of all of them, digital was a huge step forward, so much better, just in terms of noise, and freedom from flutter and wow. Dynamic range was irrelevant—the noise floor was fine, the tape hiss was gone.

When you were there at the moment, the feel was there more. You were closer to what was coming in off the line. Much, much closer. So what loss there was in the mic signal was the analog loss. The tape storage killed it by comparison. And then about six months later I remember going to an AES-sponsored demo at a studio in Toronto where they compared the output in stereo pair recordings simultaneously to a 15 IPS half-inch recorder with Dolby SR versus the Sony Dash recorder. They toggled back and forth between them. And they were so close it was almost inaudible. So my take was, from those two experiences, that at its best, analog storage is just about as good as digital storage, and at its worst it's not nearly as good. And of the two, digital works considerably better. With that said, I'm fast-forwarding a little bit, after realizing that digital is just a subset of analog, we have no digital that wasn't analog first and won't be analog later, so it can never be better than analog. It can be less bad than analog.

The only place it really loses is in storage. Analog storage falls down enough that it falls behind digital storage. And if the digital isn't too lossy, then it ends up winning. And the final comment in this rant would be that at the time the first CDs were coming out, which they all were and they sounded bad, the record companies were unwilling to budget the time to re-master the mastered tapes to CDs. They would take the LP masters which we'd worked really hard to get right, take the CD directly from that, which from my standpoint is unthinkable. Of course they sounded bad!

Chapter 20

Ben Wisch

Ben Wisch moved to Manhattan in the early 1980s after spending his teenage years playing in bands, attending Berklee College of Music in Boston, and working with local talent as an engineer, keyboard player, and all-around good guy who helped out musicians and bands in any way he could.

In 1991, Ben served as co-producer, engineer, keyboard player, and mixer for Marc Cohn's self-titled debut album, which won a Grammy award for Best New Artist. This was the first in a continuing series of well-crafted albums that Ben has worked on over the past three decades.

In addition to taking on the role of producer, engineer, and/or mixer, Ben plays keyboards, percussion, harmonica, and sings background vocals on the tracks that he is working with. As a producer, he fits comfortably into his role of keeping the project on course, within budget, and never losing sight of the big picture. Reassurance, nurturing, and speaking openly and honestly about challenging issues are all areas where Ben continues to find his extensive studio and life experience incredibly helpful. This is a role he finds to be equally important to that of overseer of the musical flow, and he continues to refine his skills as he embraces more diverse projects, different personalities, and a variety of musical genres.

I am Ben Wisch, and I was born in Philadelphia, Pennsylvania December 21, 1956. I used to sit in my living room with two reel-to-reel tape recorders with my friends, and we'd record to one and then play that back and record to the other one while we overdubbed, and that's when I started in audio. I started learning about the magic, I was probably 15.

I was doing live bouncing on whatever could record, a cassette machine, a reel-to-reel. And then I got to Berklee College of Music, and my second semester there I found a studio where there was an eight-track Scully, an analog machine, and I remember the first time I saw them use a razorblade on a tape and I was amazed. I was like wow, that just opened up this whole world of possibilities for me. And that's also where I was told by a friend that being a record producer was actually a job, that you could make a living just directing people in the studio, and hiring musicians. It was at that point at Berklee, where I never graduated from, that I learned about the studio, learned about the career,

DOI: 10.4324/9781003519829-20

Figure 20.1 I made a key to the recording studio at Berklee, which was basically closed from 6 o'clock at night, and I would go in with my friends and record all night long and make it up as I went, try to twiddle the knobs and leave at the crack of dawn in the morning, and that was how I learned how to record.

Figure 20.2 I would look at what other engineers were doing, like the guy that was teaching me snare drum, bass drum, I'd get some basic ideas and then I'd try to copy that and play around with it. I learned at that point that there are no rules, that you have to go with your own intuition about what sounds good and do it.

and I went from there to finding singer/songwriters and helping them in the studio, and then came to New York.

I was working professionally at Berklee. I wasn't getting paid very much, but I was being seen as a professional. I drew mostly from the talent within Berklee at first, then people would hear that I was doing it and I would bring them in. My famous story is that when I found the studio I made a key to the recording studio at Berklee, which was basically closed from 6 o'clock at night, and I would go in with my friends and record all night long and make it up as I went, try to twiddle the knobs and leave at the crack of dawn in the morning, and that was how I learned how to record.

Along with that eight-track Scully, they had an MCI analog board, which was beautiful. It was black with red knobs. And that was back when they had one studio. Now they

Figure 20.3 It's subtle, each of those things is subtle, the difference between analog compression, digital compression, the difference between analog EQ, between going into an old vintage board versus not. Is it a huge difference? No, but they add up to a huge difference.

Figure 20.4 On Mark's record I was maxing out the EQs, the compressors. Everything was heavily processed even though you may not hear that on the record, but I realized then that you can heavily process with analog gear and still keep this charming, organic sound. I think that's when I really start to come into my own in terms of being able to hear and combine.

have a huge program with digital everything. But yeah, that was all they had, along with a big room. We used to bring little ensembles in, the brass ensemble or the rhythm section. Kids writing for strings and you'd hook up, audio would hook up with the writing department, and it's all good.

There was EQ in the board, and it was beautiful, that series of MCI was really nice. There was an 1176 in there. Not much really, it was basically an 87, an RE20, a 57, couple of EVs. They told you which mics to use on the trombones, which mics to use on the trumpets. There wasn't a huge selection, but really that period of time wasn't so much about the technical aspect. For me it was ultimately about learning how to create some space in the studio and deal with people and personalities while you're doing the technical thing.

Figure 20.5 You have to stay connected to what your gift is and then there's an opportunity for you out there. That's just the way the world works. That's what I believe.

I spent as much time as I could there. That's when I learned. I couldn't do much in a classroom or a group of people, but when I was recording my own thing, eventually I'd bring an artist in and get some players, hire a rhythm section, and just start jamming and playing around with the EQ. I would look at what other engineers were doing, like the guy who was teaching me snare drum and bass drum, I'd get some basic ideas and then I'd try to copy that and play around with it. I learned at that point that there are no rules and that you have to go with your own intuition about what sounds good and do it.

I always carried my little Sonic speakers around with me. I still have them, I managed not to blow them. Any favorite gear? I always loved Neve boards, so I was always attracted to studios that had old vintage Neves. And then when SSL came out, I loved them. I love the ease of operation on that thing, you know the master compressor and automation when that came out. Yeah, I enjoyed those beautiful analog compressors. At the time that's all there was, it's not like you were looking back then at these beautiful vintage compressors. Now with all the digital stuff, you look back and go, "Wow, what a beautiful sound. What would help to expand it?" So, I loved 1176s, LA2As, all that stuff, Pultecs. But it's actually now that you see how deep it goes.

To me, you still don't get the same sound out of a digital compressor. They work great and in some cases maybe even better for certain applications. But my work is predominantly based around vocals, singer/songwriters, so that sound, using tube compression and analog EQ and compression, and those components make the difference for me between really good and awesome. It's subtle, each of those things is subtle, the difference between analog compression, digital compression, the difference between analog EQ, between going into an old vintage board versus not. Is it a huge difference? No, but they add up to a huge difference. And when I did an A/D test, when people said, "You know you have this beautiful API board you should really break out your channels and use the board as the thing that processes all the sounds together, rather than use the digital." So let me do a test, so I did a whole mix in the box, printed it, and then I broke it out, and did a whole mix through the API, and printed it. And just even looking at the waveform you could see it was a massive difference. It was beyond, you couldn't argue with it. The analog one had these huge dynamics and the digital was much smaller. So from that point on I decided I'm going to take advantage of it. The problem is it's not automated, it's heavy and clunky, so I basically set everything to 0 and then do all my processing and everything. Once it's analog I process analog, but before I get there, all my rides and everything are programmed. I've got a tech now, when he comes to work on my board he's so happy because he never sees these, he says "I never get to work on this much metal." Because it's heavy, this thing weighs hundreds of pounds, and each bolt is solid.

I never stopped using the DBX 160s. You know the TubeTech is essentially like an LA2A, I wish I had a few of those, I still love LA2As. All this stuff is pretty old now, the Anthony DiMaria has got to be ten years old. This board is from the 70s and even that doesn't sound that old to me, but it's vintage. Really what I use is all the same, the new stuff is digital, the new stuff is in the computer. And microphones. But when I'm looking for gear, plug-ins, I avoid it. Most of the stuff I do is pretty organic, pretty natural. Most of the sounds come from the instruments.

When I came to New York I had a pretty good sense of what sounds these components made. I used to work at Quad Recording and they had an SSL board, I'm thinking of Mark Cohn's first record, which really is the record that established me in the record world, and they had a rack of eight API EQs in a rack; they had 1176 compressors, LA 2s, and I kind of knew the sounds they made, the grainy quality that each of these things would bring out. On Mark's record I was maxing out the EQs and the compressors. Everything was heavily processed even though you may not hear that on the record, but I realized then that you can heavily process with analog gear and still keep this charming, organic sound. I think that's when I really started to come into my own in terms of being able to hear and combine. I remember his record was jam-packed, using all this stuff, and then through the SSL board which was great. But then I came up with a sound for the piano and came up with a sound for the vocal and reused each of those things, 1176s, LA 2s, API EQs. A U67 microphone was used on that one too.

The only difference now is that I'm recording with Pro Tools. Even when some of that digital gear started coming in like the Rev 7, everything sort of had one sound that could really do well, even some of the digital stuff. You had to find that sound and that's what you'd use it for. It wasn't like you could take a compressor and put it on anything and it's probably going to make it sound better. I always found something. A lot of it was cheesy and not very good quality, like the Primetime. Remember the Primetime digital delay, one of the first, but even that you could get a sound out of.

The things I see that are remakes of the classic things, LA2s, Teletronics, and Universal Audio, the microphones they're re-making, they're taking designs from the tube mics and re-making them in better ways. That's what I see.

The only thing I have now that I wish I had then that I think of is the experience.

Everything else is always changing. Life back then was different, I look at my life now, my setup now, and it works great for my life. Back then it was a different world, back then there were all these major studios and some smaller studios and you had the assistant and the intern and the wannabe intern and the three guys out the door waiting at 9 o'clock in the morning with their resumes from Berklee College of Music. It was a whole different energy, the record business was booming, everyone was making money, there was no home recording equipment or anything so everything was in this mysterious sort of magic place, the recording studio. Back then it was big boards, racks and racks of gear, coffee, and muffins. Those places are still there, but I've been in this situation for so many years, first in a dusty back room somewhere and then eventually in a nice space of my own in Manhattan with this vintage gear, the tube stuff. The truth is, for better or worse, I'm not a gearhead, you know? I don't have a ton of stuff. I think I've invested my money more in personal growth, so I have what I need and trust that it's enough because next week it's going to be different. As far as gear from back then, I wish I had a couple of those Fairchild compressors. You can get them, you have to spend a fortune though.

I've got Pro Tools HD3, I've got Apogee converters, which I've always liked. That's basically it. I don't use Logic. I don't do a lot of sequencing and MIDI work. I can do anything I need to do in Pro tools. I use the API, it's a 1604. That's my input, and everything goes in and out of that. I use the Anthony DiMaria on my mix, I use the DBX, and I love the TubeTech and the LA4s. The API is really the meat and potatoes.

The latest thing I bought is a red microphone, a tube microphone modeled after, depending on the capsule, C12, 47, and a 251. I got the 47, I wanted the darkest one. I'd like to get the others too, I had bright microphones and I wanted a dark one so I got that.

I've always kind of been in the underground, I'm not in the mainstream so I'm not as affected by pop culture and record business culture. I've always worked with independent artists, and the changes in the business are so many. Starting with the fact that when we were young, getting a new album, opening it up, and listening to it with your friends was like that was getting high, even if you weren't getting high. It was happening. So, it wasn't just musical, it was cultural, it was social, it was very different, and it's very different now for kids. I'm not saying better or worse, that's a whole other book. Now, it's different, music plays a very important role but it's along with many other things that technology has offered, such a broader spectrum of opportunities to do things, play games, watch movies, rent DVDs. Music is a component of all those things but it's not THE thing, so it's a different business. It's not like the days when there was a set way to get into the business, you follow that path. Now everybody can have a studio, and ultimately, I think there's nothing wrong with that, even if you don't know what you're doing. There's more opportunity. You have to be good at what you do, even if you work in your basement and learn. What's different is the business now. Music's always changing. Couple hundred years ago Mozart was top 40, then it was big bands, and jazz, and then rock n roll and then it was sounds of the Seventies, California, and now it's hip-hop, and next week it's gonna be something else. That's the nature of life. You have to stay flexible and open if you want to kick around this business for a long time. I'm moving on to, what do you tell kids … find what you're good at. You have to stay connected to what your gift is and then there's an opportunity out there for you. That's just the way the world works. That's what I believe. That's what 51 years will get you. You're surrounded by it all the time, you see it and you go, "Oh, so that's the difference. I have this oversight I can see, they get hung up on all the little things." What is real happiness, what is real peace and love, where does that come from?

Chapter 21

Paul Stubblebine

Paul Stubblebine began his mastering career in San Francisco in 1973. For 11 years he worked at a recording and mastering facility on Folsom Street which, originally owned by CBS, was later bought by David Rubinson and became known as The Automatt.

During the CBS period, in addition to the CBS catalog, the studio also brought in outside work from the Record Plant and Wally Heider's including records by The Grateful Dead, The New Riders of the Purple Sage, Sly Stone, Santana, Joan Baez, Bill Evans, Tony Bennett, and Jane Fonda's phenomenally successful workout record engineered by Leslie Ann Jones.

This is also where the mastering was done for the U.S. releases of Rough Trade and Factory Records including Joy Division and New Order. During this period, records mastered at The Automatt were on the charts continuously.

Paul then went on to become chief engineer at Rocket Lab, also in San Francisco, where he worked until starting his own company, Paul Stubblebine Mastering, in 1997, and The Tape Project in 2005.

I'm Paul Stubblebine, I was born in Portland, Oregon in 1948.

I started in audio in 1969 I guess. I started in live sound for a rock and roll band. I had determined that I really wanted to be involved in recording but I landed a gig with an old friend who was doing live sound for a band called the Sons of Champlin, which was also one of my favorite bands on the planet at the time, so I jumped on that. He was actually as much interested in recording as live sound, but we built them a PA, we traveled with them doing their PA and in between gigs we took the equipment to our friends' rehearsal halls, which were often at their houses, you know, the band commune kind of thing, and we made recordings. And we recorded the Sons live a lot when we were doing the PA gigs. So we were, you know, a couple of young naïve hippies having as much fun as it was possible to have.

Then the band broke up and we, my partner Bruce Walford and I, looked at each other and said, "Well what do we want to concentrate on?" and clearly it was recording. And so we didn't look for another band to do live sound, we started looking at what we were going to do about recording. And just at that time we bumped into somebody Bruce

DOI: 10.4324/9781003519829-21

Figure 21.1 What's happening is: get an okay performance, think that if you fix a few things it'll be a good performance. It isn't, it's an okay performance with fixes. And we are making more crappy records and less great records. Great records happen when the artist surpasses themselves. Someone has to be pushing them to surpass themselves. When the artist says, "I'm just going to phone it in and let the engineer fix it" that's not how you get great records. And that in my opinion is what is happening today··· I mean that's a fundamental job of a producer to get a better performance out of the artist. The producers could simply stop approaching it the way they're approaching it and say, "Oh no, we're using this, to get the best out of you and make the best of it, but you still have to give me something, more than you think you even have in you."

Figure 21.2 The earlier console had a custom CBS passive EQ with no nomenclature, it had four knobs with click steps and no nomenclature. In fact, that entire console had no labeling whatsoever. It had started as a four-track console, it was used to cut Bob Dylan's Like a Rolling Stone, then it had been shipped to San Francisco and was used at Studio B there for several years. The last hit cut on it before it was decommissioned was Dr. Hook doing The Cover of The Rolling Stone. So, bookends there··· And those EQs were very, very nice sounding. Very well chosen, musically chosen curves. And you know, you'd set your top one which would be a treble, and you'd click it one stop and it would be a little bit of boost at this frequency. Well, the next stop would be more boost obviously, but it would also shift the frequency a little bit. So they were literally chosen by the guys in New York primarily, the recording engineers working with the console department, and they were very nice.

Figure 21.3 And when he would put up even a rough mix, even the mix that you'd listen to while you're checking to see if the vocalist is in tune, his mix sounded like music every single time. And I realized that that's really important and it's the engineer's job to make it sound that way for everybody in the room, and in the headphones. That it's not enough to say, "Well you know I, I don't need it in balance because I'm listening for certain things." There's other people in the room and it should sound like music every time you hit play, and with Fred it did.

Figure 21.4 I was doing some stuff with a producer named Sandy Perlman, I started doing mastering for him, then he moved to San Francisco and he built a studio and I did some stuff in it. And he was a fabulous collector of outboard gear, he had one of the best selections I've ever seen, and he had Fairchilds. But you can't talk about Fairchilds in general, you can only talk about the individual one, because they don't sound the same, one to the next. The way they age, they just don't··· I found many of the Fairchilds to be very, very dark on top.

knew who had a building that he'd always been interested in, and he'd always said to her if she was ever going to leave that he'd like to be the first to know. Ran into her on the street, she was getting ready to leave. So we took over this building in San Anselmo and with volunteer labor and trades for studio time and all the ways that you can do something without any money we built it into a recording studio.

It was a former church in San Anselmo and we built it into a recording studio. It was pretty primitive the way we started, primitive not only in the way it was built but our

Figure 21.5 And then the beginnings of the V series even were pretty crappy sounding, and I own one I'm trying to offload to some poor sucker. But they're pretty crummy sounding, and yet I fully expect someone is going to rack up V series modules and start selling them for a $1,000 a piece. I've got 60 to sell them when it happens.

Figure 21.6 And that part was not on either one of these tapes, because in the middle of the night under the influence of extreme pharmaceuticals, he had had a great idea and wanted to put it down and he had wiped the good part off the tape and put some garbage over it. So, yeah you know, if you want to take an ideological stance of course you support artistic freedom. I'm just saying it doesn't always work out the best for the artist either.

recording technology, because we just had 2 track recorders and mixers left over from the PA, a lot of PA mics, and a few decent recording mics. But we got started. And then, the Sons got back together and broke up again more than once after that, but we had already made our choice and we were going in this direction. And we did a couple of records for the Sons there eventually, and the fact that we were still connected with them helped us as well, because we got to borrow equipment through the Quicksilver Messenger Service.

The management was tied together plus they were both signed to the same label, same executive producers, a lot of ties there. And at one point we're getting ready to do a Sons album and instead of doing it two to two, which we'd been doing up to that point, they

Figure 21.7 I'm noticing an unhealthy gear fixation in our business. We have a very popular website called gearslutz where all people do there is talk about their obsession. It's what they made the site for. And it's easy to focus too much on that, and I say that as someone who has spent a lot of time sifting out and picking the best gear, and I feel I'm capable of doing the work I'm doing because of the gear I've picked. So. I'm not really the best person to say this, but I just have to observe that I think that there's a whole unhealthy obsession with gear. People think that the process of making records is about giving them a chance to use this piece of gear that they're so enthralled with to get this weird sound. A lot of people approach recording now not as trying to get something that was happening in the room to come across to a person, and they really think that's a starting point and what you're supposed to do is turn everything upside down. Okay fine, if it's artistically interesting I'm all for it. But it isn't the whole point to give you a chance to use this fuzz tone that you bought that Jimmy Page used to use in 1976. That is not the point of the exercise.

wanted to do it eight-track. So this was, you know, 1970, maybe 71, eight-track was state-of-the-art.

Some well-funded studios were going to 16 but 8 was still sort of one of the standards. And Capitol had given Quicksilver an eight-track machine and a bunch of recording gear so they could do some recording. And they loaned it to us and we did this Sons album on one-inch eight-track. And then eventually we got our own machine and then eventually 2 inch over the years, built it up.

But it's interesting to note the way we did it initially, two to two. We had two two-track recorders and we would record the entire band mixed live to a two-track tape, then we would do overdubs by playing that tape through a mixer, feeding it to the headphones, and the guy would overdub his vocals, maybe we would do a solo in the middle as well, record the output of the mixer, the live mics plus the music bed from the first two-track, onto the second two-track, and that's the way we made records. So it was live mixed to stereo twice.

One of those machines was a Viking, one of them was a Sony, and we had a mono Ampex 350 that we sometimes mixed to, if we were making a mono mix. The first stuff I ever did that actually came out on record came out on mono 45 from that Ampex 350. And having done that, I can say I understand absolutely why musicians wanted more flexibility, and so did the engineers and producers.

At the same time, I can say there's value in having limitations and working within them. That it tends sometimes to focus things. In our case, that meant the band had to actually play. And I found it very interesting, maybe ten years ago, I observed that I had gravitated, after all my experience on multi-track, punching in and editing and so forth, to the two places in the business where you actually make decisions and they stick. One is mastering and the other, I was doing a lot of live stereo recording. Acoustic music, mostly classical but also some bluegrass and jazz and this and that. And I was just drawn to that, the fact that the musicians are performing, the engineer is performing, and hopefully the equipment is performing. And you get something and what you get is it—it's a recording. I like it. I'm not saying it's the only way to make recordings or that I am not glad for many records that have been made that couldn't have been made without multi-track. I'm just saying that I found it a very interesting observation about myself personally that I had drifted into those two areas where you're not postponing the decision and saying, "We'll fix it later" and "Well, we'll spread this mayonnaise on everything and then we'll decide later which ones we're going to use." I had put myself in the position where we were making decisions that stick.

Initially, we'd be overdubbing vocals and occasionally a guitar solo, but often times the guitar solo would be played live too. So that was actually the tricky part, making sure you mix the solo where you would want it, when you had a vocal before and after that wasn't there while you're actually doing the recording. And you know, I learned by making mistakes. You know, you balance the band and that guitar sounds just right. But then when you do the next pass and you've got a vocal there and you get to the solo and all of a sudden, the guitar isn't jumping like the vocal was. Well, that's a serious mistake. So that's how I learned, by screwing up. And we could edit, so if a guy said, "Alright, you know, I got the first two verses and the chorus but coming back after the solo I really screwed up." Say, "Okay, well we'll back it up, we'll do it from there again and I'll splice the mix version together." And we did that for, well, not an awful lot but we did some of that. But doing that also taught me how to hear a balance of the band when the vocals weren't there but when the vocals would be there, and I really learned I had to balance the band a little differently. My partner Bruce Walford was a very good recording engineer, sadly no longer living but I had a great partnership with him, and we talked about what we were doing. We would analyze our mixes and keep trying to get better. We would talk about how the kick drum, the snare, and the bass create a sort of an anchor for the mix. Not saying they're more important than anything else, but saying that where you place them in the mix creates a certain anchor for everything else, and then noticing how if you load up the center with a lot of instruments, nothing but vocals fighting, but if you spread some of the other stuff out, it creates a pocket for the vocals.

Again we learned by doing, we learned by screwing up and trying again and talking about what we were getting and what we wanted to get. For me, I thought it was a tremendously valuable thing to do for a while. And even when I got to the point where I was doing most of my mixes from multi-track after all the parts were on it, the lessons I had learned there were really useful to me. For when you get all the stuff laid down on your 16 or 24 track and you get it in the mix and all the guys from the band are there and all the guys in the band are saying "Why don't you turn this up? Why don't you turn this up?" nobody in the band ever says "why don't you turn this down?" which leads to the old joke: what's the perfect mix, it's when everything's louder than everything else. But then my early work taught me that if you want something to really speak in the mix you have to make sure there's room for it in the mix. And if you just try and shove everything up to the max they're just fighting each other and you, all you get is note salad.

That fact that I could sit down and get the stuff up and sort of feel what was fighting other things and find ways to separate them so they weren't fighting, either with stereo placement, with EQ, or with echo treatments. Took me a long time but a friend of mine named Bob Olson, a great engineer, one time made this offhand comment that, in terms of the problem of mixes sounding different when you play them on different speakers and so forth, said

> if you differentiate your instruments with EQ it'll change everywhere you listen to it. If you differentiate your instruments with reverb and some will differ on different speakers but the basic way the instruments work together in the mix will still hold together.

And I found that to be a tremendously useful perspective to bring when it came to mixing. It took me a long time to become friendly with reverb and understand it as a tool.

The tools that we use, like EQ, seem totally obvious, we all have a seven-band graphic in the car we know what it does. It turns out it's more subtle than that but it's close to obvious. But compression and reverb are considerably more subtle. It took a while to understand the kind of things that you can do to do what Bob was talking about, differentiate the elements of the mix with reverb, for instance. Turns out the amount of delay before the reverb is really a key factor. I was lucky to learn this coming up. After our first studio, I went to work for Columbia records. They had a studio here in San Francisco back just a few blocks from where we're sitting. And one or two of the studios had chambers, all the studios had EMT plates.

And they had extra four-track machines that were only used for delay. You could do a four-track mix if you needed to, but they were parked in the studio, every single studio, because they were used for delay. They were used for delay in concert with the EMT plates. This was such standard operating procedure at the Columbia studios around the country that they built their own consoles at their division in New York City that did this. Each console had for each plate a special section that mixed the delay: you could mix it before the chamber, after the chamber, whatever variation you wanted, that was literally built right into the console. And the guys I was learning from had been doing this for years and they understood what this was about, I was going "I don't get it" you know, but over time I got it. And I understood what you could do with that, and how you could make an EMT plate ten times more usable in a mix by having that capability of delaying, usually before the chamber. The only other thing I want to add is that, for me, one of the most used controls on a digital reverb is the pre-delay.

The very first digital processors came in at the time that I was working there. The Eventide and the Delta T. I don't think I saw a spring reverb in use there at that time. Springs were just the Hammond springs, there, you know with the Fender Twin Reverb. It wasn't until later that AKG came out with springs that you might actually think of using on a whole music mix.

As far as EQ, those consoles that I mentioned were built by CBS, and they had a couple of different ones of different vintages there. The newest one and then the one that came in later were both filled with API 550s. The earlier console had a custom CBS passive EQ with no nomenclature. It had four knobs with click steps and no nomenclature. In fact that entire console had no labeling whatsoever. It had started as a four-track console and was used to cut Bob Dylan's Like a Rolling Stone, then it had been shipped to San Francisco and was used at Studio B for several years. The last hit cut on it before it was decommissioned was Dr. Hook doing The Cover of The Rolling Stone. So bookends there. They had converted it to eight-track and then 16-track. It actually had some rotary faders that were geared together. So you'd turn one and gears would turn the other three.

But you know they expanded as far as they could and then they replaced it. And those EQs were very, very nice sounding. Very well-chosen, musically chosen curves. And you know, you'd set your top one which would be a treble, and you'd click it one stop and it would be a little bit of boost at this frequency. Well the next stop would be more boost obviously, but it would also shift the frequency a little bit. So they were literally chosen by the guys in New York primarily, the recording engineers working with the console department, and they were very nice. Additionally, we always had quite a few EQs in the outboard rack, and those consoles had the most extensive patch space anyone had ever seen. You could literally do anything your mind could think of if you had enough patch chords. And in the rack, there were always Langs and Pultecs, a variety of limiters too, the UA stuff, and the RCA BA6As in every studio. That was a pretty standard complement of things. That's what we would see at the studios. Pretty much that.

Basically the whole tool kit was there, you used what you wanted. The most important thing I did there was learn from guys who knew more than I did. I started my first studio and my partner and I, as I described, really worked at it. We were serious about trying to get good results, but I eventually got frustrated that I was trying to teach myself what I didn't know. And I could only go so far. So eventually I moved to CBS, my partner moved to Fantasy, and I got to work with a number of really great engineers and I just watched and absorbed as much as I possibly could. The head of the studio was Roy Halee, one of the best engineers there's ever been, even til today.

I was just a grunt in the beginning. I helped with setup, and then eventually I got to the point where I did second for him on a couple of projects. But I would even volunteer to help with his setups just to watch what he was doing. There were several other good engineers there on staff, Roy Segal, Glen Kolotkin, and a guy that had been one of the mainstays at the Hollywood studios for a long time named Pete Romano, who really could do the legit stuff, better than anybody in town, he was great. If you had a big string date or something, Pete was the guy you wanted. So I just learned from these guys and they would put me in on a demo session or this or that and I would get a chance to use all this stuff, and I could never get the results that the other guys were getting. So, I would ask them and they would show me stuff. It was hard to learn from Glen Kolotkin because he was so fast, I'd never seen a guy so fast. He would just go zip zip zip zip zip and the sound would be there in the speakers, it was just amazing. But, still, I could look around, see where he had placed the microphones and I could look at what he had done with settings, but it had to be after the fact because in real time I literally couldn't follow him. This guy was so fast. Other people would spend days.

Roy Halee would spend a minimum of two days, usually three days at the beginning of a mix just creating his echo effects. Just really getting the chamber singing and moving mics around in the chamber, moving speakers around, retuning the EMTs, fine-tuning the delays. I mean literally, he would not rest until he had reverbs that were just brilliant. Part of the reason his stuff sounded so good. And at that time Fred Katero was not on staff there, he was an independent, he'd been on staff in New York and had come west as an independent. And he already had a huge track record of hits with Barbara Streisand

and Simon and Garfunkel, and Chicago and Moby Grape and all this other stuff. He came west to work with David Rubinson, the producer who came west at the same time. Fred would come in sometimes on projects and then when it became an independent studio owned by David Rubinson four years later Fred was the chief engineer, and I would finagle myself on any session I could with Fred just to watch what he did. And Fred was the guy who just absolutely got the meat and potatoes right. He would always have a kick drum sound that was just right there. There was nothing flabby about it, there was nothing boomy, I don't know how he did it. Put an SM 7 in front of the kick drum and made the drummer tune it until it sounded right, but it was just always right and every one of the drums would sound and be in proportion, which of course you get automatically with a great drummer, but if you've got a good drummer and you have to get a little help from the engineer, he never failed to get it all right.

And when he would put up even a rough mix, even the mix that you'd listen to while you're checking to see if the vocalist is in tune, his mix sounded like music every single time. And I realized that that's really important and it's the engineer's job to make it sound that way for everybody in the room and in the headphones. That it's not enough to say, "Well you know I, I don't need it in balance because I'm listening for certain things." There are other people in the room and it should sound like music every time you hit play, and with Fred it did. He just had a natural balance and the way he liked to use the multi-track, he actually mixed as he went to it. And you could put up the monitor faders in a straight line and have a mix. Some people think, well, you just pan as much level as you can on each track, and their monitor faders wind up all over the place. Fred didn't, and you know both could be valid but the way he did it, he could get a monitor mix very quickly, because he had started that way and he had mixed it that way as it went to tape. And he would just put it right there. So, I got to work with those guys and, I must say I feel extremely fortunate. I'm not sure that sort of apprenticeship really happens anymore for very many people, but I got one. And that meant quite a few years that I was not the star, that I was not upfront working this space shuttle-style console. But it did mean that I learned my craft more thoroughly.

Also they started me on mastering fairly soon. I was on the cusp of the change in approach to mastering. For instance when Fred started, that was an entry-level job, but you weren't expected to change the sound of it. You got a tape from the editing cubicles that was supposed to be finished and your job was to hear what that sounded like and hear what your disk sounded like and do whatever you had to do to make sure your disk sounded like that tape. It was ear training. And by the time I started, we were moving over into the era of the mastering engineer making creative contributions.

So it was, we had the first of several independent mastering labs. The mastering lab in Hollywood was probably the first. And Bernie Grundman, even though he was working within a label at A&M at the time was essentially functioning as an independent mastering lab for other people as well. And a few places in New York were doing the same and down in Florida, and I'm sure some folks in Nashville. But it was the beginning of that, the mastering wasn't just a faceless guy in the label hierarchy that they send the stuff to, but it was someone you would go to because you trusted what he would do with suggestions and so forth. And we at CBS in San Francisco wanted to be that for the Bay Area. Because we were the only place at that time cutting stereo. This is LP, obviously. And there was one other guy that had a mono lathe, then eventually he upgraded to stereo so there were two places.

But essentially, we were the place and we wanted to be the place. So we functioned as an independent mastering lab. And we would do EQ and rundown sessions and work with the client and get it all locked in and then they'd go home. We'd cut parts and cut refs and send them out and then cut parts when they ordered them and stuff. So I got in right at the point when that was shifting from a kind of an entry-level learning position to an actual creative part of the process and stuff. And I got a little of both really. I got trained on stuff really just working with one of the guys that was cutting it. I started spiraling records—they were cutting Bob Dylan's Blood on the Tracks and Herbie Hancock's Headhunter. So those were the records that happened to be in the chain at the time that we were doing the cutting when I was learning to operate the lathe. So then for the four years I kept working at CBS I was doing both, I was doing all three things. Sometimes second, I'd sometimes be the first engineer, and a lot of times I was mastering.

In fact the way it worked there, anybody might be a second engineer except Roy Halle who was never a second. But even Roy Segal, who was really functioning as a manager and a great engineer in his own right, would occasionally wind up being a second. And most of the seconds there actually had been firsts and they just decided they wanted a lower-stress gig. They got paid the same, they had so much seniority, but they just didn't want to be on the firing line. And then there were a couple of young cats coming up of which I was one, and then as I say CBS closed down, transferred it all to David Rubinson, he reopened it as The Automatt, and I came back to work for him as a mastering engineer. But by that time actually I had started a studio of my own so I was still doing recording, mixing, and mastering all simultaneously for several years.

I had bought into a studio in Sonoma County called Sonoma Recorders—the studio in the chicken coop actually. It was a nice studio, with a nice small Neve console and a two-inch 16-track machine, and we cut some nice sounding stuff there. Then we moved it down to Sausalito, re-named it Harbor Sound and we kept that going for several years, then I closed it. I was still working at The Automatt and was doing mastering there at that time, so it was somewhere in that stretch of 78 to 84.

When I was cutting at CBS and The Automatt, our EQs in the cutting chamber were Pultecs. So I had Pultec filters and a set of Pultec EQP1As, and when I felt like I didn't have quite enough flexibility we got a pair of MEQ-5s as well. And I just learned to get what I was looking for out of that combination. I essentially use the same thing now although I use the EAR updated versions, which to my ear sounds as good as a Pultec and more so.

They're close enough to a Pultec. You could put a Pultec, a really good shape working Pultec, and an EAR one on the left and one on the right and dial the EQs, and the whole thing would still hold together, close enough. But the EARs, you could go just slightly farther with them. If you go to the max they go a little further. And they sound a little more clear and a little faster transients to me, so I use those still. That's kind of my main rig. Their version of the EQP1 and their version of the MEQ-5. And those are. I would have to say, absolute favorites of mine. The EAR limiter/compressor is one of my absolute favorites too, the 660 which is based fairly closely on the Fairchild.

I wouldn't say it's a slavish reproduction of the Fairchild but it's based very much on the Fairchild. And to my ear it sounds much better than any Fairchild I've ever heard. I didn't use Fairchilds very much then, but in the middle of that whole period when I was doing some stuff with a producer named Sandy Perlman, I started doing mastering for him, then he moved to San Francisco and he built a studio and I did some stuff in it. He was a fabulous collector of outboard gear, he had one of the best selections I've ever seen, and he had Fairchilds. But you can't talk about Fairchilds in general, you can only talk about the individual one, because they don't sound the same, one to the next. The way they age, they just don't. So I would say that these are based very much on that design, but they're wide open. I found many of the Fairchilds to be very, very dark on top, and these are wide open, totally transparent pieces. And yet you can get them to do marvelous things. I don't ever hit them real hard, because I'm just not into the sound of squash, the way I use them is kind of gentle but still doing something. They do something very nice that I like very much, so I use those, those are favorites also.

The compressor I use, in a way that does one thing, and sometimes I use it in a way that does something else. One thing I'm always looking for with that is it just tends to bring the low-level stuff a little more present. And low level does not mean just the quiet instruments in the mix or when the music gets quiet but even when the whole thing is rocking you know there are very low-level things that contribute a lot to the sense of space and the sense of tone color. And I like these compressors just barely tickling the meters moving maybe at half a dB, but still, just have a way of bringing that forward so that it sort of makes the mix hold together and clarifies it at the same time. Funny, funny thing but I love it. And that means that all that low-level stuff is just up where it won't get lost in the next steps. It won't fall off the table when you go to 16-bit, for instance. And the other way I use them sometimes is by getting them to pump just a little bit. I can actually take stuff that's been kind of flatlined and get it to thump a little, sugulate a little bit. So I don't always need that, but when I do I turn to that piece. But very often, I'd say the majority of the time, I'm looking for the first thing out of it, where it sort of just brings the whole thing forward slightly. And has this effect of making everything talk to each other in the mix and yet clarify the mix at the same time. It's a subtle but wonderful thing.

And then with the EQs, it's totally dependent on the program. I listen to the music and it tells me what it wants. And the way I work I know it's different from many other people. I don't go out of A/Bing as I work. I listen all the way through the stuff untouched before I get into it all so I've got a good sense of what's there. But I am only really concerned with where I want to take it, not with how far I'm moving the ball downfield. That is of no interest to me at all. I have an image in my mind of what this could be and I want to get it there. So, I don't bother listening to how far I'm coming from, I'm only listening to where I am until I get there. So I listen to the music, it tells me what it wants, and what I'm looking for is a full body thing top to bottom. The music, if it's music that moves the body I want it to move the body. You know not everything I work on is dance music but if it's rock and roll if it's jazz, even bluegrass is dance music you know. So, if it's made to move the body I want it to be having that. I want it to be easy to listen to.

Ideally I don't want anyone to listen to the record and say, "Hey man that's a good engineer." I just want them to say, "Hey, I like that song." You know? I think most people don't pay attention to it consciously, but there are differences in recordings between one you have to work to listen to and one that invites you in. And if you have to work to listen to it, that's mental energy that's not available for enjoying it. And if I can make it so that it just presents itself nicely, it envelopes you, it draws you in and communicates with you then all of that mental energy is available for enjoying the music. So that's kind of how I view my job.

There will never be a Grammy for mastering engineer, because no one ever wants to hear the comparison between the way it started and the way you got it. Including me.

I don't want the customer to hear the original source if the treated one is better, I want them to hear that. Because that's what it's about, it's not about showing off what I can do, it's about making the music the most accessible to the listeners, and the most enjoyable to the listener.

If I can do a little nip and tuck, a little nudge here and there to make it come across better and reach the pleasure centers inside the listener then I feel I've contributed something and I'm happy to leave it at that. Not to say, "Ooh cool, man, that mastering engineer's got more 10K than anyone in town." Not of any interest to me at all.

I've come to be disappointed with the sound of a lot of the early analog tape machines, even though I'm a huge fan of analog tape as you know, even selling analog tapes for high prices to audiophiles at this point. But I have come to feel that those Ampex AG-440s that we used lots and lots of at CBS were kind of soft sounding. Although if I had to choose between that soft and the kind of hard of the MCIs that we used afterward, I would still probably pick the 440. But I'd rather not make that choice. I'd rather have a modern ATR with improved electronics or a Studer A80 with great electronics. And there are plenty of good Ampex's too—I'm not slamming a brand. The Ampex ATR-124 is fabulous sounding and has other issues but fabulous sounding. And I have the Studer 827, the two-inch machine in the back that's mine. And both 24- and 16-track head stacks for it. So plenty of great-sounding analog machines and of course if you ever worked with a Stevens. That was an ear-opening experience, working with Stevens machines.

But yeah, I have begun to hear the differences over time of the machines and I would say that the Ampex 440s were kind of soft and the MCIs were kind of low res and a little crunchy. And I'll tell you, just on that topic I am reminded that when I had the studio in Sausalito we had an MCI two-inch machine that we had gone through and audiophile parts upgrades done in it. The entire machine, all the electrolytics in the signal path were replaced with film caps, all the resistors were replaced with metal films, and the chips were all upgraded to faster and better chips and stuff. It sounded vastly different from the stock MCI but still didn't sound as good as the MM1000, for instance. It still didn't and I said "How can this be? How can this be?" I eventually came to understand that in a tape machine, the machine is tremendously important, that the mechanism, in fact, starts with moving tapes past the heads and the way that's done makes a difference, a huge difference in the sound of the recorder. So, the MM1000, which used the same electronics as the 440 and the heads were built to the same specs and in the same head lab and everything else, that was a great-sounding machine. It's certainly not bright on the top end but just punches for days, whereas the 440s didn't quite achieve the same thing with the same electronics.

As far as what people are calling vintage now that I can't believe? The CBS Volumax, that really has to go right to the top of the list. This as you know was a piece that was made for broadcast when, particularly for AM broadcast where there were real repercussions if you over-modulated. So they made a brick wall limiter, and there was nothing subtle about the way it squashed. And the fundamental sound in the electronics was probably not too good either, because it sounded bad whether you were hitting it hard or not. And yet now people are selling that as vintage. I mean sure it's a tone color, I won't say it's transparent, but to suggest that it's good is a stretch as far as I'm concerned.

There's nothing else at that level, but I would say the early Neve, the first couple of generations of IC consoles were a big disappointment after their discrete consoles. I had a couple of their discrete consoles and I was spoiled. and then the 8108, the first generation they did of IC consoles, no one remembers because it went away so fast. It had terrible problems with the membrane switches too. It was their first try, instead of having controls all over the place you'll have one set of controls and you'll assign it to whatever channel you want to use, which was an unworkable way to do things, and the membrane switches were totally unreliable so people got rid of those for two good reasons in addition to the sound which was a third good reason. And then the beginnings of the V series even were pretty crappy sounding, and I own one I'm trying to offload to some poor sucker. But they're pretty crummy sounding, and yet I fully expect someone is going to rack up V series modules and start selling them for $1,000 a piece. I've got 60 to sell them when it happens.

Digital has brought us some real improvements in the way of working. I do a lot of my editing in the workstation, although much of what I work on does not require heavy editing. But I do some classical, in particular, I will do 200, 300, 400 edits in a full album's worth of stuff. And the ability to do that in the workstation is really good. And now, finally, I would say that we're rivaling, in terms of sound quality, that we're rivaling the best of analog. I didn't say we'd surpassed it or equaled it, I said we're rivaling it. By which I mean we are equaling it and surpassing it in certain departments, but not others. And digital certainly has the promise of being the same from one day to the next. That promise is also not fulfilled on a daily basis but there's the promise of it. And it copies without generational loss, which is also not as easy as it seems, but that promise is certainly there. So I really like those aspects that digital has brought us, particularly the really, really powerful editing capabilities.

As far as what I had then that I wish I still had? Well I wish I had a couple of BA6A limiters, and I wish I had that console from Studio A at CBS on Folsom Street. It had API faders, API EQ, and it was built in a certain way, they believed in headroom. There was headroom at every stage, and every single point in the console appeared on the patch bay twice. You had the output and a multi out from every single thing on there. And of course one input. And if you said, "Well for this sound I'm thinking of, I would like to string these things together in this order," you could just do it. And it all sounded good, the whole console sounded good. I forget what the microphone pre-amps were, I think UA and the booster amps I think UA because it was like passive controls and booster amps kind of thing. The EQs obviously were active but they were just unity gain black boxes. And I came to realize only over time when I worked on consoles that didn't sound like that. I mean if you had a great player who knew how to get a sound out of his instrument, you put a mic out there and you just opened up the faders and said, "Okay, we're going to town here." And you do that with Harrison, MCI, you wouldn't have that, you would say, "Alright we can get started, what knob will I turn?" And it could be the same player or the same instrument or the same mic, but those consoles just didn't have that quality. And I would include the first couple of generations of SSL and the early Neve IC-based consoles that I've already mentioned. I keep saying the early ones because they got much much better, the last couple of generations of Neve consoles were pretty good. The SSLs got better too, but. I feel sorry for the generation of engineers who came up without ever having the experience of just opening the faders on all this shit. There's a whole generation of engineers who don't even think in those terms, that you open up that fader and it's like. "Now what do I have to do to it to make it sound good?" and you know the result, the result is that we have records that have no sense of space around anything., If your console sounds good, you have a good mic, a good sounding room and musicians who know what they're doing, you can do it, practically all of it, with microphone choice and microphone placement. Getting the things in balance, and there's usually very little else that you want to do. And then you get a recording where everything has its own space in the recording and there's space around stuff and they play off each other, the parts play off each other and, and you don't have to manufacture it, the engineer doesn't have to manufacture that.

So you know I started when there was one release format, LP. And very shortly after I started, the cassette was introduced as an actual release format. So, I've been through several format changes and I've certainly been through the change from recording being something the record labels owned to the spread to the independent studio then the home studio. And I've been through the change from when there were budgets to do records until there were no budgets to do records. And to me, it seems like whenever anything changes, it changes for the better and the worse at the same time. So, I see how all these changes are positive and negative things. The democratization of the recording process is now the fact that every musician has or can have a home studio and be in complete control of their music. From a creative standpoint, you have to say that's great, except when it isn't.

And it has devalued engineering. I really don't even need to explain what that means because it's just so obvious. But it has also sometimes been good and sometimes not been good for the creative process as well. Sometimes an artist works best against resistance, and that can mean limitations of budget , of the recording process, and it can mean limitations where the record label says no we're not going to let you do it all by yourself we're putting you in with a producer. You have to fight with the producer, the producer will not let you do everything you want. So how can I be arguing against artistic freedom? All I'm saying is, I don't approach it ideologically. I just have observed that oftentimes creativity works best when there's something the artist is pushing against, whatever it may be. And that there are many artists who are not their own best producers. And they haven't done their very best work when they've been given total freedom. And I can go beyond that and say many artists have done extremely horrible work when they've been given unlimited freedom to do it. And you can point to artists who are in perfect control of their career in every respect and doing their very best work on their own and I say, "Fine." Again, I'm not ideologically here. I'm just saying for many artists it's not the best thing to go in without a producer and to have the thing in your spare room so that whenever you get an inspiration you go in. Actually, I think every artist should have that as a notebook, certainly, in some fashion, you know, a four-track cassette.

When I was working with CBS we started doing some work with Sly Stone. This was after he had broken up the band and was Sly Stone. And he was in what I would have to say is one of his worst periods. He was doing as many things bad for himself as he could cram into a day. And he wound up at the CBS studio because Epic, which was a CBS label, said, "We're not going to keep putting out the money because you're spending it all, you're not getting anywhere." He had been working at a studio across the bay, a perfectly good studio, it's not their fault. But somehow CBS had parked a 16-track machine in his house so that he could do just this, put down parts when he was inspired. And so there were two reels for every song, right? And by the time it had gotten to this point, they pulled the plug and said you must work in a CBS-owned facility and we were working with him, which he wasn't happy about. Again and again he would say, "Okay we'll put up this song" and we'd say, "alright well which version of it?" and he'd say, "We'll put up the song, the version of the song that has this part in it" and he'd play a cassette that had this really cool bass part on it. So we'd put up the song, take a guess which reel, put it up, listen to all 16 tracks, nope, that part's not there. Okay, put up the other reel and listen to all 16 tracks, not there either.

And this was before sync, so these two 16-tracks were never synced together. We had the first sync stuff there and we were running 16 tracks in sync, but they hadn't put SMPTE on the tape so they were never together. And that part was not on either one of these tapes, because in the middle of the night under the influence of extreme pharmaceuticals, he had had a great idea and wanted to put it down and he had wiped the good part off the tape and put some garbage over it. So, yeah you know, if you want to take an ideological stance of course you support artistic freedom. I'm just saying it doesn't always work out the best for the artist either.

This is what I find the most counterproductive about today's technology. I have come up through evolution of technology all of which has given us the capability of progressively improving the performance—which is a good thing. Certainly editing and punching in, which is a form of selective editing on different tracks, has been developed in order to give us that ability to selectively improve the performance and keep improving until we have something marvelous. And I am not against that, I've seen it used poorly too, I've seen it used to squash the life out of a performance and make some pretty crappy records. But I understand that it gives us a lot of power for good and it's been used to make a lot of great, great recordings. So we took it one step further in the workstation, not only in Pro tools, but Pro tools is the de facto standard for the industry. Giving us tremendous power to edit within stuff, take that chorus and simply slide it up to the first chorus and quantize and auto tune—all these things. So is it making better records? I'm sure there are a few really talented people who are making better records because of that, but on the ground what I observe is people keep working until they have an okay performance and then they say, "Alright I'm going home. You, the engineer, stay here till four in the morning fixing this, this, this, this, and this. And we'll come back tomorrow and we'll move on from there." And what you get is okay performances that are fixed.

Prior to the shift to the workstation when we only had punching in on 24 tracks to be able to progressively improve the performance, the artist had to give a better performance, and it kept the focus on that. The producer and the engineer and the artist were all in this together to get a better performance out of the artist and get it on tape. Now, you could use Pro tools the same way plus use the extra goodies, but in reality ,that's not what's happening. What's happening is get an okay performance, think that if you fix a few things, it'll be a good performance. It isn't, it's an okay performance with fixes. And we are making more crappy records and less great records. Great records happen when the artist surpasses themselves. Someone has to be pushing them to surpass themselves. When the artist says, "I'm just going to phone it in and let the engineer fix it" that's not how you get great records. And that in my opinion is what is happening today. It's up to the producers to say, "No that's not the way we're using the technology now, sorry." It's the producer's job to push the artist. And I mean that's a fundamental job of a producer to get a better performance out of the artist. And the producers could simply stop approaching it the way they're approaching it and say, "Oh no, we're using this, to get the best out of you and make the best of it, but you still have to give me something, more than you think you even have in you."

I'm a big fan of, a big appreciator of good sounding gear. I love it, I love to be able to make records that sound good. At the same time, I'm noticing an unhealthy gear fixation in our business. We have a very popular website called gearslutz where all people do there is talk about their obsession. It's what they made the site for. It's easy to focus too much on that, and I say that as someone who has spent a lot of time sifting out and picking the best gear, and I feel I'm capable of doing the work I'm doing because of the gear I've picked. So, I'm not really the best person to say this, but I just have to observe that I think that there's a whole unhealthy obsession with gear. People think that the process of making records is about giving them a chance to use this piece of gear that they're so enthralled with to get this weird sound. A lot of people approach recording now not as trying to get something that was happening in the room to come across to a person, and they really think that's a starting point and what you're supposed to do is turn everything upside down. Okay fine, if it's artistically interesting I'm all for it. But it isn't the whole point of giving you a chance to use this fuzz tone that you bought that Jimmy Page used to use in 1976. That is not the point of the exercise. But there are a lot of folks that seem to be confused on that point.

Chapter 22

Cowboy Jack Clement

Jack Clement scored major success as a songwriter, producer, recording studio pioneer, publisher, artist, and executive. He was born April 5, 1931, in Whitehaven, Tenn., near Memphis, and enlisted in the Marines as a teenager.

After four years of service, he toured in a bluegrass band, then returned to Memphis in 1954. He found work at Sun Records and worked as an engineer for sessions with Roy Orbison, Carl Perkins, Johnny Cash, Charlie Rich, and Jerry Lee Lewis. Another Sun artist, Elvis Presley, opened for Clement at the Memphis club, The Eagle's Nest. Clement wrote two of Cash's most enduring songs, "Ballad of a Teenage Queen" and "Guess Things Happen That Way."

After parting ways with Sam Phillips at Sun, he moved to Nashville to work for Chet Atkins at RCA, then relocated to Beaumont, Texas, where he met George Jones and convinced him to cut the song, "She Thinks I Still Care." In 1965, Clement returned to Nashville and financed a demo by then-unknown Charley Pride and persuaded Atkins to sign him to RCA. Clement also wrote Pride's first two hits, "Just Between You and Me" and "I Know One," and produced Pride's first 13 albums for the label.

Clement launched the solo career of Don Williams through his JMI record label, a project that also introduced Allen Reynolds as a record producer. Reynolds later produced Garth Brooks, Crystal Gayle, Emmylou Harris, Bobby Bare, and Kathy Mattea. In addition, Clement was Townes Van Zandt's first publisher, and Bob McDill also wrote for Clement's publishing company. Clement released his own album All I Want to Do in Life in 1978.

Prior to his death, his projects included producing sessions for Eddy Arnold, soundtrack work with T Bone Burnett for the Johnny Cash biopic, *Walk the Line,* debuting the Robert Gordon-led film documenting his life, hosting a weekly Sirius satellite show, and keeping up a semi-grueling series of public appearances.

He was inducted into the Rockabilly Hall of Fame, the Memphis Music Hall of Fame, and the Music City Walk of Fame. On June 25, 2011, a fire destroyed his home and studio on Belmont Boulevard in Nashville. Clement was unhurt, but many priceless recordings and memorabilia were lost. On April 10, 2013, it was announced he would be inducted into the Country Music Hall of Fame. Cowboy Jack Clement passed away in August of 2013, at the age of 82.

DOI: 10.4324/9781003519829-22

Figure 22.1 What's the most fun for me now is probably playing guitar. Ukulele I play, Yeah, I put that on all the records. You know, something that don't stick out in your face but it's a very easy thing to record, and you got all them overtones and stuff. You can have as much of it or as little of it as you want.

Figure 22.2 I started recording in about 1955. A buddy of mine and I bought an old Magnacorder ... I told him about this Magnacorder we could buy for about $450, and he'd buy it and in my spare time I built a little studio in his garage; I was pretty good with building stuff... So he bought the thing and we made us a little studio and started recording.

I'm Jack Henderson Clement, born in Memphis, Tennessee April 5th, 1931, that'd be on Easter Sunday. That makes me an Aries, about as Aries as you get, but I'm not really into astrology.

I started recording in about 1955. A buddy of mine and I bought an old Magnacorder from a disc jockey named Sleepy-eyed John in Memphis. I was going to college at the time and playing in this band. This guy had a band, they had a nightclub over in Prairie View, Arkansas, and every Friday and Saturday night we'd go over there and play. And then, I told him about this Magnacorder we could buy for about $450, and he'd buy it and in my spare time I built a little studio in his garage; I was pretty good with building stuff. Used to watch carpenters all the time when I was a kid. So he bought the thing and we made us a little studio and started recording.

Figure 22.3 I did that Million Dollar Quartet thing. We were doing the Carl Perkin session, Sam was running the board that day… we had Jerry Lee Lewis playing piano with him. Jerry Lee Lewis was new in town, his record was out and he hadn't taken off yet… That was a one-take thing, too… Carl was there, and he had invited Johnny Cash, his buddy, to drop by the session, that's the reason he was there. And then the session was about over and Elvis walked in with two or three girls, a small entourage. And everything just kind of stopped… Those guys are out there talking, jamming, whatever. And I turned it up and listened, I remember I stood up and said, "I think I'd be remiss if I didn't record this." So, I start rolling tape 7 ½, small reel, turned it on, walked into the studio and moved a couple of mics around in position and recorded about an hour and a half of that stuff. You know, just let it roll.

Figure 22.4 At that time they were just coming in and mastering it right in the control room, Bill Porter would come in and master. It was a pretty straightforward studio. They had four-track, well not when I first started working there, just two-track. I liked working on four-track there. We used three-tracks. We'd put the voice on one track, music split to two other tracks. And that gives us an open track to overdub to, vocals mostly, not much else. We were still doing most stuff live, we'd have everybody in the studio at once.

Figure 22.5 I worked in Studio B until I built my own studio. After studio B, I built Sound Emporium. It wasn't long before I needed a second studio, so we built studio B, legendary Studio B. It looked like a whorehouse. It was beautiful though, you know. It had a gazebo for a drum and everything. And then I had built two studios down there, and then added a record label and everything. Allen Reynolds was producing a lot of stuff. He needed another as he was using it so much. I built a third studio, a place called Jack's Tracks, which is still there, that's where Garth Brooks cut all his records, every one of 'em, except that Chris Gaines thing.

Figure 22.6 I had the first 16-track in town. It was an Ampex, and I had a Quad 8 console, it was one of the very first ones. It was a real modern studio for the day, along with the first 16-track in town.

Had a little, old low-impedance board to go with it, it didn't sound all that good, but we got started, and one of the producers came in with Billy Lee Riley. So, we worked it up in that little studio there and went down and rented a radio station; WMPS in Memphis and cut these two sides and we were going to press 'em up on our little label, called Fernwood; named after the street his house was on. And, took it to Sam Philips to have it mastered, and he liked it. He wanted to put it out and sign and offered us a penny a record. And I said, "Well, I'll have to talk to my partner about it." Then he asked me what I was doing. I said, "I've been working out at this building supply place." And I said, "I don't like it very much." He said, "Maybe you ought to come work for me."

And I said, "Maybe I should." Two weeks later June 15th, 1956 I went to work there. And I was in hog heaven. He had echo and tape echo. That's all he had. Mono, had a couple of tape machines.

We had an old RCA radio board, with six rotary pots, so it was real easy to operate. I never considered myself an engineer; I was an operator. I was one of the few musician types that started mixing I guess. Usually it was people with technical backgrounds. But I took to it immediately and started really enjoying it. I was out in the end to get into the production side of things. I started off wanting to be an artist, but I decided along the way I don't want to do that.

I worked at Sun almost three years. I worked with Jerry Lee Lewis there, I cut his first records. And I did "A Whole Lot of Shakin' Goin' On" in one take. We were working on a song I'd written called, "It'll Be Me", and I'm in the control room and I'm getting tired of it, so I went out there and said, "Why don't get off of this, we'll come back to it later, Jerry. Let's cut something else." And, his bass player, JW Brown, who was also his first cousin, later was his father-in-law, he said, "Hey Jerry Lee, do that song we've been doing on the road that everybody likes so much." We carried on, hit 'play' and 'record' on that Ampex, sat here at the board, got the mix all set up for the other song, and we did "Whole Lotta Shakin' Goin' On," no dry run, nothing, just did it. I did a lot of stuff with Johnny Cash at Sun too. I wrote a lot of stuff for him, played guitar on it, played that guitar on Ballad of a Teenage Queen, Guess Things Happen That Way, "Big River," I played guitar and bass drum at the same time on "Big River."

And I did kind of a lot of stuff. I did Charlie Rich's Sun Records during that period. Did a lot of stuff with Bill Justice, Raunchy. Remember that one? Whatever came out of there in '56 to '59, I did most of it. Sam did a few things but once I started, he was burned out on the board.

I did most of the operating, 'course I was a musician, so I was basically musical director on a lot of the stuff, hanging around in the control room. I did that Million Dollar Quartet thing. We were doing the Carl Perkins session, Sam was running the board that day. I hadn't been there very long. And he was still doing Carl Perkins. And, we had Jerry Lee Lewis playing piano with him. Jerry Lee Lewis was new in town, his record was out, and he hadn't taken off yet—I'm sure it was released 'cause we cut Crazy Arms one day, and had it out and in stores the next week. Edited it one Thursday and had it in stores the next Thursday. Had it on the radio the next Monday. That was a one-take thing, too. I had thumbtacks in the piano. Anyway, Sam and I were in the control room and Jerry Lee's playing the piano. Carl was there, and he had invited Johnny Cash, his buddy, to drop by the session, that's the reason he was there. And then the session was about over and Elvis walked in with two or three girls, a small entourage. And everything just kind of stopped. Sam went, and I'm sitting in the control room. Those guys are out there talking, jamming, whatever. And I turned it up and listened, I remember I stood up and said, "I think I'd be remiss if I didn't record this." So, I start rolling tape 7 1/2, small reel, turned it on, walked into the studio and moved a couple of mics around in position, and recorded about an hour and a half of that stuff. You know, just let it roll. That's the only time I ever actually did anything with Elvis in the studio. But, I knew him pretty well, he used to drop by there a lot. Homing instinct.

That's where he was based before he started working in Nashville and I had played a gig with him. He had been going about a month and he was playing a gig at a place called the Eagle's Nest, a nightclub outside of Memphis. And I was the leader of an eight-piece band, I was the leader and emcee of that band and he was the floorshow. He'd always break a string on his guitar and I'd let him borrow mine. Used to be some scratches on there. I used to point to it and say, "Elvis did that." But I had it refinished about 20 years ago. I played that guitar on a whole lot of records; my pride and joy, there. Bought it when I was 20, in 1951.

After Sun I kind of started a little label which didn't make it. Did that for about a year. I had some money coming in because I'd written songs, Teenage Queen, Guess Things Happen That Way. The back of A Whole Lotta Shakin' Goin' On, It'll Be Me, and some other stuff, so I had money coming in. And I pissed it away trying to start a record label.

And that wasn't happening so I went to work for Chet Atkins here in Nashville as his assistant. I did that for about a year, and I decided I'm tired of all this stuff; I'm tired of Memphis, I'm tired of Nashville. I want to go someplace where I can make reasonable music. So I loaded up all my stuff down to Texas and built a studio there. And within six months or so we had a million-seller, a thing called Patches by Lee Dickie, and stayed there. Went there in '60, '61, lived there until '65. I was there about three and a half years. It was a good time.

That was Gulf Coast Recording Studios. It was a nice studio. It was mono, you know. I had a three-track, but we never did hook it up. Didn't have the board to go with it. But we did some good-sounding stuff there. Bunch of Cajun music and all that, a lot of them around there. Beaumont's only 26 miles from Louisiana. There were a lot of Cajuns around Beaumont.

We had another radio board there, a Gage radio board. It still had rotary pots, but it had an echo chamber in back, and it was good. It was a room with plaster walls and, you know, angled and stuff. It sounded good.

I built the studio; I was the carpenter. I had a couple of guitar players help me with it. It was a beautiful-looking studio, really. We did a little trading for work, and my partner, Bill Hall, he had a brother, and I got him free.

After Beaumont I moved to Nashville for the first time. When I was working with Chet I didn't live here, I commuted. But I'd come over here most every week, for two, three days. That was Studio B, that's where I worked. I did all the Charlie Pride records there. Everything, about everything I did, I did in studio B.

Bill Porter was there and then he left; went to Las Vegas. Jim Malloy was my main guy. He and I came down about the same time, '65. He came from California and I came here from Beaumont, Texas. And he was a hotshot around there. Everybody said, "There's another engineer Chet's moved here." So we got to be buddies. Chet told us we ought to get together, we did. And, he became my main engineer. He was great.

We had EQ on the board, but it was really more like tone control. It had a low end and a high end. Then they would master it and do some EQ. That was part of the procedure back in those days. And they did the masters right there in the control room, but then they changed that.

At that time they were just coming in and mastering it right in the control room, Bill Porter would come in and master. It was a pretty straightforward studio. They had four-track, well not when I first started working there, just two-track.

I liked working on four-track there. We used three-tracks. We'd put the voice on one track, music split to two other tracks. And that gives us an open track to overdub to, vocals mostly, not much else. We were still doing most stuff live, we'd have everybody in the studio at once.

I did a whole lot of Charley Pride stuff there, I did his first album. I paid for it. Got him on RCA, then I wound up doing 20 albums. We argued a lot, but the outcome was good. Those records still get a lot of play. The first thing I did with him was "Snakes crawl at night", remember that one?

That's the one I paid for myself. Got him on RCA. I had an office up in the RCA building, which I rented from Chet Atkins and Owen Bradley. They owned the building. The big building, where studio A is. So I had an office, a little two-room office up on the third floor. And Chet was right down under me on the first floor. So, I had him pretty handy.

When I was going to do Charley Pride, I told him I would let him have the first crack at it. We were still good friends and everything. He was always good to me. When I got back from Beaumont, he would cut my songs and all that. And so I told him I'd let him have first crack at it, which I did. And he liked it a lot. And a couple weeks later he said he just didn't know what to do with it, how to handle a black country singer. And so I set about to try to get it on another label and didn't have much luck. So, I was right on the verge of pressing it up myself, you know, put it out, press up a few hundred copies. I had buddies in Texas and Memphis who would play it. Like, they played it when he did come out on RCA before he got started.

And then, about a month later, I was right on the verge of pressing it up ran into him down by the coke machine on the main floor by the big studio. And he said, "What did you ever do with that colored boy?" I said, "Well, I haven't done anything yet. I'm thinking about pressing it up myself." He said, "Well, I've been thinking about that. We might be passing up another Elvis Presley." He told me if I get him another acetate he'd take it out to an A&R meeting out in California the next week. And I did, and he did. And he came back and said, "We've got a deal." That was the first one. I did two sides with him. Got a deal. I'm pretty lucky, the first record I ever produced, I got it on a record label. The thing with Billy Lee Riley?

Actually, I started off with Sam Philips—me and him couldn't master a record, you know. So I didn't come in there as an engineer, I came in there as a producer. I produced every record that he put out. Like I said, the equipment is so simple that the first thing I'd want to know is how'd you get that echo. Well, you had to use two mics to do it, you know. You could only use it on whatever you had two mics on. And you needed to use one of the pots on the board and we only had six of 'em. It wasn't long before I talked Sam into getting a mic splitter. A little thing with five or six on the side, little rotary pots so you could have echo and everything.

I worked in studio B until I built my own studio. After studio B I built Sound Emporium. Wasn't long before I needed the second studio, so we built studio B, legendary studio B. It looked like a whorehouse. It was beautiful though, you know. It had a gazebo for a drum and everything.

And then I had built two studios down there, and then added a record label and everything, and Allen Reynolds was producing a lot of stuff. He needed another - was using it so much. I built a third studio, a place called Jack's Tracks, which is still there, that's where Garth Brooks cut all his records, every one of 'em, except that Chris Gaines thing.

I tell you what, even when I had them three studios, I still wanted one upstairs. Now I got the one upstairs and I don't have to fool with them.

I had the first 16-track in town. It was an Ampex, and I had a Quad 8 console, it was one of the very first ones. It was a real modern studio for the day, along with the first 16-track in town.

So I had a Quad 8 board and a big 16-track and another same-size thing that we used for an eight-track that could be converted to 16. People still had a lot of eight-track stuff floating around. I had two great big machines. They were beautiful studios, but they've changed it somewhat. Built some echo chambers there and they were wonderful. T-Bone Burnett, everything he does in Nashville he does it there.

We built that in '69. When I first built that studio, the board didn't have a monitor system on it. They had to have a special monitor system made for it that sat over here and the board is over here. It had a true sidecar because it was all separate consoles.

Outboard gear? Well they started when they came out with Dolbys. That's when I decided I wanted to get out of the commercial studio business, rental studio business. And I'd had a record label and I was sitting there in one of the studios, runnin' the studio. So, I sold it. I sold it and moved, well, I married Jesse Colture's sister, Tracy Sharon, and she talked me into moving to Texas, Round Rock, Texas outside of Austin. I only did that for a year, then I came back. I had this house though at that time, and I came back here and started putting a studio here. That was around '73.

We've got some outboard John Hardy preamps. They're real good. I started out with something I bought, I think it was Jim Malloy's. It's got a small board but it sounds good. I had that in here. It was only about this wide, sounded real good. And then I wasn't using it for a while. I think I loaned it to somebody and it got stolen. Then Roger Cook, a songwriter friend of mine, he bought the second Quad 8 that I had in the studio down the street; the big studio. We went from a small Quad 8, which was originally a four-track, and then we had some outboard preamps so we could do 16-track. And then, when I built Jack's Tracks, I moved that one in there for a while. And then I replaced it with a bigger Quad 8 board, full 24-track. And then that one, they replaced it and Roger couldn't buy it and we moved it in up here. I made a deal with him if he could use the studio every Monday I'd furnish the rest of it and he'd furnish the board. That was great; we did that for a couple of years. We got a lot of good demos up there. He was mostly in the publishing business. And then, that was years ago, then I bought a little Sound Workshop, and I wore it out. It was good sounding and everything, did a lot of records with it. And then I got this one about a year or so ago. And we've got all Pro Tools now. I had a small rig, a Pro Tools rig before, just for when I run out of tracks, or I want to process something. But now, we've gone full HD Pro tools. It sounds fine to me. People have said they hear the difference, I think they're full of shit. Sounds okay to me. If it sounds the same coming back as it did going in, what else do you want?

It took a bit of learning time to engineer. I have an engineer now who started out as a carpenter. But he's come along, he's been here a number of years. But that digital stuff is a little tricky for him. He's getting it now. I've got another couple engineers. My son works here and he used to be my full-time engineer. He's back working here but he's real good with computers and stuff. I got him working in video editing.

We're doing pretty well, been shown on a lot of PBS stations. Been on here twice at the local PBS station. Some of the old films we have here, it's got a bunch of funny stuff in it. A lot of cheap Johnny Cash stuff. Home movie cameras, most of them were digital, small digital cameras. Some had eight in them.

As far as Pro tools, yeah, what I do is pretty much the same. Sometimes I spend more time mixing on something. I don't do as much on-hand mixing as I used to, but I can still do it. I have somebody set me up and I can do it. I used to mix all my stuff.

I didn't do the live mixing but I did all the remixing. Usually if I'm producing a record, I'm usually playing guitar on it, a lot of the time. I can plug in eight mics and I can listen to everybody and talk to everybody. If they're shooting video I can watch it on my screen there. I got another little thing I can plug in where I can talk to camera guys, and a green screen. I've been wiring this place for 25 or 30 years.

What's the most fun for me now is probably playing guitar. Ukulele I play, Yeah, I put that on all the records. You know, something that don't stick out in your face but it's a very easy thing to record, and you got all them overtones and stuff. You can have as much of it or as little of it as you want.

Chapter 23

Elliot Scheiner

Elliot Scheiner is a record producer and record engineer. Scheiner has received 25 Grammy Award nominations, eight of which he won, and he has been awarded two Emmy nominations, one of which he won, and three TEC Awards nominations.

He started as Phil Ramone's assistant at A&R Recording in New York City and quickly advanced to an engineer. By 1973 he began to freelance as an engineer and producer, becoming the first person in New York to work as a freelance engineer for other artists. Scheiner is considered to be among the best and most successful sound engineers in the world. He is also considered to be one of the most successful producers.

Scheiner has produced and engineered a range of artists, including Foo Fighters, Beck, Faith Hill, Steely Dan, Toto, Ricky Martin, Sting, Bruce Hornsby, Eagles, B.B. King, Van Morrison, Fleetwood Mac, and Aerosmith.

Scheiner was nominated in 2005 for an Emmy Award for Outstanding Sound Mixing for a Variety or Music Series or Special or Animation, for his mixing for Eric Clapton in: "Great Performances: Eric Clapton Crossroads Guitar Festival" (1972), along with Mick Guzauski, Ed Cherney, and Neil Dorfsman.

He mixed the IMAX film All Access in surround sound. The film footage includes Dave Matthews, Sheryl Crow, Macy Gray, Kid Rock, Moby George Clinton, Mary J. Blige, Al Green, and Rob Thomas. Scheiner and Bob Ludwig did the 5.1 surround sound mix of Roy Orbison's Black & White Night concert DVD.

Scheiner also collaborated with Panasonic to create the ELS Surround premium audio system for Acura's TL, TSX, RDX, and MDX. The audio system has received rave reviews from the automotive press, audiophiles, and musicians.

My name is Elliot Scheiner, I was born in Brooklyn. I started in audio in 1967. It was all analog. I was working for Phil Ramone. He owned A&R studios, he gave me my first job. Like Al, the main console we had was an old three-track broadcast console with big rotary faders. I don't even remember the name of it. And I remember because all the machines were three-track, most of the records were mono and two-track, and they'd gotten a three-track in and that became a big deal. But then four-track came in and they

DOI: 10.4324/9781003519829-23

Figure 23.1 I'd like to talk about the MP3 issues and trying to bring back quality and the organization that I'm with, META, and how we're trying to make people and young engineers more aware of quality recording and higher resolution formats that are available. We're trying to get educators and teachers that are teaching courses and training these younger engineers to hold with us on all these issues. So I always want to keep that at the forefront. We're also working with manufacturers who we feel put out high-quality products that are not selling out.

Figure 23.2 Went from three-track to limitless tracks, analog machines to digital hard drives. record companies to no record companies, and from vinyl to CD to MP3. I think I've seen everything, pretty much. I wish there was never MP3, ever. It's just the most horrible sounding codec, and it's ruined the industry. Not only in terms of how we hear music. I mean I understand the portability of it. But people have forgotten about quality music and quality recordings. I wish that had never existed.

didn't know what they could do with a fourth track and how they would even get the signal there. And I remember what we ended up doing was getting a little four-channel Altec mixer and I put it alongside, down below the console, and that was dedicated to that fourth channel.

At A&R we had a lot of tube microphones, they had a lot of 251s, C12s, C60s, C37s, Sony Altec salt shakers. And then at some point the U87 came out, the Neumann 87 came out. The managers of the studio felt it would be a better idea if we replaced the

Figure 23.3 What do I have now that I wish I'd had then? The GML EQ. Having something like that would have been really snazzy, considering how we made records then and how we make records now. Yeah, I would have loved to have had that. A 33609. I mean there's a zillion things, a Neve console would have been great. One more thing I wish I'd had, I wish I'd known Al back then. Really. I mean, you learn from engineers, the engineers around you. And I had the benefit of Phil, but I wish I was able to learn from Al at that point too.

Figure 23.4 I still use analog whenever I can. When I can, I use 24-track two-inch. If I'm working with a young jazz act or something, it's my thing, I'll do it because I know I'll get everything on one machine and it's not going to require that much tape. I'll try and do jazz stuff analog. If I had my way, I'd do everything analog. But I do use that, and I use Steinberg, the Nuendo system.

251s and the C12s with 87s because with the other mics, there was too much upkeep, too much maintenance, and they pretty much took them out of service. We didn't know that they were still in the facility, but everybody started using them, they became an all-purpose mic. And most of the guys pretty much hated it.

My favorite kind of gear back then, at that time, Fairchild was my favorite. I loved the Fairchild compressor, and I loved the Pultec EQPs. None of the consoles had any inline EQ or compression, and in the studios, it was usually a pair of Fairchilds and a pair of EQPs, and that was it. Most of the time you just used mic technique to get what you wanted,

Figure 23.5 My favorite kind of gear back then, at that time, Fairchild was my favorite. I loved the Fairchild compressor, and I loved the Pultec EQPs. None of the consoles had any inline EQ or compression, and in the studios, it was usually a pair of Fairchilds and a pair of EQPs, and that was it. Most of the time you just used mic technique to get what you wanted, and occasionally there'd be something that just wasn't going to work, either there were too many guys in the room or too much leakage and you ended up using one of the EQPs.

Figure 23.6 At A&R we had a lot of tube microphones. They had a lot of 251s, C12s, C60s, C37s, Sony Altec salt shakers. And then at some point, the U87 came out, the Neumann 87 came out. The managers of the studio felt it would be a better idea if we replaced the 251s and the C12s with 87s because with the other mics, there was too much upkeep, too much maintenance, and they pretty much took them out of service. We didn't know that they were still in the facility, but everybody started using them, they became an all-purpose mic. And most of the guys pretty much hated it.

and occasionally there'd be something that just wasn't going to work, either there were too many guys in the room or too much leakage and you ended up using one of the EQPs.

I usually used a Fairchild on a Fender bass, you know, just touching. And I used it most of the time on background vocals. Never on a lead vocal, most of the time lead vocals were hand-ridden. But for background vocals, I ended up using Fairchilds for that. I never used it on anything else, it was either bass or vocals or pretty much nothing.

Figure 23.7 Al (Schmidt, l.) and I have done some Steely Dan records together, and Al had mixed one of the songs, and I don't remember which one it was, but Donald and Walter and Gary said they let him have the afternoon to get it and then they would come in at night. And they came in at night and they could see the tape machine rolling, the multi-track machine rolling but there was nothing coming over the monitors, and Al was actually doing stuff on the console. So, they claim, and I think Al says this is not true, but they said he was mixing without monitors and then they said all of a sudden he threw on the monitors, and they said it was brilliant.

The thing about the Fairchild, they were made by a designer in World War II. He designed a lot of warplanes, the Fairchild warplanes. After the war he decided to get into electronics and built the compressors. And I had a cousin who was a famous bandleader, he was the bandleader on the Hit Parade. His name was Raymond Scott, and he ended up working with them, manufacturing these devices. That was about as close as I got to Fairchild. Just the gear that those guys made, it's still here, you could probably buy a Fairchild compressor for about $500 back then maybe. But you know now a Fairchild compressor is like $25,000–$30,000.

I used the Fairchilds for general compression. I never, ever overused anything. Everything was a light touch for me because you can't repair it. If the Fairchild compressor grabs it, you're screwed. So yeah, most of my stuff was hand riding. That's the way you were taught. I remember watching Phil all those years and he was constant. His hands were always moving. He had an orchestra in there, he was always doing something. And like Al said, you could pretty much tell from a meter what was right and what was wrong. There's a great story here about Al, actually. Al and I have done some Steely Dan records together, and Al had mixed one of the songs, and I don't remember which one it was, but Donald and Walter and Gary said they let him have the afternoon to get it and then they would come in at night. And they came in at night and they could see the tape machine rolling, the multi-track machine rolling but there was nothing coming over the monitors, and Al was actually doing stuff on the console. So, they claim, and I think Al says this is not true, but they said he was mixing without monitors and then they said all of a sudden, he threw on the monitors, and they said it was brilliant.

I still use the Fairchilds, I still use Telefunkens and Neumanns. Those are still the best microphones around. AKGs. I actually began using the SM57 back in 1967. I still use an SM57. It's still my main snare drum mic.

I use a Fairchild for kick drum a lot when I'm mixing. I usually use the Fairchilds when I'm mixing, if they're around. I don't own any, but I use it if I'm having trouble with the kick drum sound. There's something about the Fairchild that's magical, and you just put it through there and it's like everything is fixed.

After using the EQPs I remember that A&R wanted to add some more equalizers. And they didn't get EQPs. They thought it would be good to get Langs, the Lang Program Equalizers. I was so used to using the Pultec that when they replaced the Pultec with the Lang it didn't do the same thing for me. The Pultec was really smooth, and the Lang was really hard. Remember when you'd boost the 10k it was brittle almost compared to an EQP1A. So, that was probably the only thing back then that was a little disappointing. I mean everything was pretty much in the microphone and your ears, and the console you used. I got another disappointing piece of gear. When they started to introduce multi-track, 16-track, 24-track machines, I remember the first multi-track 16-track machine that A&R got was an Ampex MM1100, and I remember trying to make punches on that machine, and it was just awful. You had to anticipate ins and outs, and you were always afraid you were going to wipe something or not get out in time. I just hated working on that machine.

What do I have now that I wish I'd had then? The GML EQ. Having something like that would have been really snazzy, considering how we made records then and how we make records now. Yeah, I would have loved to have had that. A 33609. I mean there's a zillion things, a Neve console would have been great. One more thing I wish I'd had, I wish I'd known Al back then. Really. I mean, you learn from engineers, the engineers around you. And I had the benefit of Phil, but I wish I was able to learn from Al at that point too.

What did I have then that I wish I had now? The original Dolby, the first Dolby, the big box, the 301. I wish I had those now. Besides them being unbelievable at noise reduction, we used them to stretch vocals. So you could record through a Dolby and not decode it, and it was like that 10CC effect. I mean you don't really need it anymore there's something, a million things that will give you that, but it was a beautiful sounding piece of gear. Noise reduction was unbelievable.

The changes in the business? Well everything. Because I started analog, now everything is digital, I've seen everything. Went from three-track to limitless tracks, analog machines to digital hard drives, record companies to no record companies, and from vinyl to CD to MP3. I think I've seen everything, pretty much. I wish there was never MP3, ever. It's just the most horrible sounding codec, and it's ruined the industry. Not only in terms of how we hear music. I mean I understand the portability of it. But people have forgotten about quality music and quality recordings. I wish that had never existed.

I still use analog whenever I can. When I can, I use 24-track two-inch. If I'm working with a young jazz act or something, it's my thing, I'll do it because I know I'll get everything on one machine and it's not going to require that much tape. I'll try and do jazz stuff analog. If I had my way I'd do everything analog. But I do use that, and I use Steinberg, the Nuendo system.

I always use a GML EQ, I always use a 33609. I only use analog mics, I never use a digital mic. I still try to do things as much as I can the way I used to. Most of the time it's not that easy. You do what you have to to survive. I wish I'd kept a couple of 49s that I sold, I wish I'd kept those. I recently bought a Brauner VMA. I use it for vocals mainly. I love the sound of the mic. It's flat from top to bottom it's just beautiful sounding. Every artist I've used it on just loves that mic. The last person I used it on was Renee Fleming and for an opera singer who has to stand far back. She was pretty amazed with what this mic sounded like.

I'd like to talk about the mp3 issues and trying to bring back quality and the organization that I'm with, META, and how we're trying to make people and young engineers more aware of quality recording and higher resolution formats that are available. We're trying to get educators and teachers that are teaching courses and training these younger engineers to hold with us on all these issues. So I always want to keep that at the forefront.

We're also working with manufacturers who we feel put out high-quality products that are not selling out. I mean there's nothing against the home studio, but we feel that the home studio guys could be a little more conscientious about quality.

Chapter 24

Bill Schulenburg

Bill Schulenburg (www.productionconsultants.com) is the owner of Fairlight-anchored studio facility Production Consultants, and an award-winning recording engineer/mixer/producer, musician, video director/editor, sound designer, and consultant. He has been recording, mixing, and mastering music for decades, working with artists like Ike Turner, Head East, Stevie Nicks, and Manfred Mann on major record labels including A&M, Motown, Warner Bros., and RCA; designing and editing sound and picture for hundreds of TV and radio programs & commercials, videogames, podcasts, audiobooks, industrial and feature films, and theatre; and teaching Audio Aesthetics at Webster University. An officer of the St. Louis Local of AFTRA, he is active as a freelance voice actor on radio and television, heard nationwide as the syndication promo voice of Mike Judge's long-running animated FOX series, "King of the Hill," and in commercials for Anheuser-Busch, Sea World, CBS, Showtime, and many others. Bill is currently Chair of the St. Louis Section and Regional Vice-President of the Audio Engineering Society.

My whole life has been a fascinating thing for me, and that's what I try to get the students to understand is that even crawling through the rafters in high school hanging microphones becomes part of your experience, part of your perspective.

I'm Bill Schulenburg, born here in St. Louis, Missouri on October 10th, 1952.

I was interested in audio as long as I can remember. When I was eight, nine, ten years old I was very fortunate to have as a friend in grade school the son of the people who owned the biggest studio in town, and I was fascinated by the idea, from the time Mr. Canter at Technisonic took me for the first tour that I had of the place, which might have been 1959. I still have a recording that he made of me doing a Stan Freeburg routine from memory.

And I'll never forget going into the room, the control room, the room that eventually would be my home, and there was a bank of Altec 844s. And they just sounded so HiFi, I can't believe it. I went in and I stood in front of the microphone and I did this little routine, and a couple of my other friends, grade school friends, played the piano. And Mr. Canter took the tape in and went in the next room, and put it on the lathe, at that time it was a Neumann BG 66 with an SX68 cutting head, which was state-of-the-art.

DOI: 10.4324/9781003519829-24

Figure 24.1 And I played the thing, and I remember the thrill of knowing that I was there, I saw this event happen and now I'm reproducing it on a record player. And I think that experience truly just set me off on the path of recreating audio experiences... Mr. Canter was very strict about us not doing that on company time. So I had to do those in the morning, and I worked for my shift, nominally was from 1–9, and so I worked reading scripts in the morning, recorded jingles in the afternoon, made records at night. That's just what I did. And it was really cool because everything that I wanted in my life was in that building.

Figure 24.2 There was lots of equipment around, but you would sort of figure out a way to get some of these effects that you'd get in the old days. You'd think about how can you manipulate the signal. Really, the only things you had was time and frequency distribution, maybe distortion. You'd feed it out to a speaker, that was a big thing you'd always do, feed stuff to speakers and record it again after having done, put a pillow in it or put it inside a drum to make it boomy or have it feed through the piano, all this stuff you'd do, but it wasn't as easy as just pushing a button. So, you had to plan this stuff out. And this is one of the things I think, a lot of these effects-heavy recordings are just so gratuitous. I mean they might be great effects but just because you have a compressor on every channel doesn't mean you should just use it.

Figure 24.3 ...when we opened that place I've never worked harder in my life because his opening promotion in 1973 was an hour of studio time for free, then you had to buy the 45s, that was his deal. You can't imagine, I must have done 150 or 170 bands in the first two, three weeks, fortunately they're all a very similar setups, four singers, bass drums, guitar, piano, that was pretty much it. But still I had to splice them all and mix them all, and get it right, and write the box, document it and it was just constant work. But it was really great fun.

Figure 24.4 And, by that time I had really got an appreciation for these machines that were so well put together, well-designed. They were designed by people who wanted them to be that way. These were people really trying to make the equipment better. This was the goal in those days, and I'm sure you'll understand that everything we did was to try to make what we did better. Not just better than the other studio, which we didn't have that problem because there really wasn't anybody in our category... I remember one of the things that struck me when I was speaking to Alan Parsons was that it was all some of the same stuff. Once you got to this level it was professional equipment and you expected professional equipment to be really great. Yes, there were some esoteric arguments, "well is the Ampex better than the 3M?", or whatever, but these were minor things. It was professional equipment. And you didn't think about an outboard preamp because you had a professional preamp in your board. And it was good. You just didn't think about it.

Figure 24.5 But, Tom Zuzenack and I got this thing, and we hooked it up and we would take turns. He would spend a half hour talking while I would mess with it. And then I'd go in and this thing kept us entertained. I mean when you think about it now, the universe of things it will do is pretty small, but just hearing that stuff for the first time, the pitch shift and feedback, the things that you could make it do with the modulation. I mean it was a revelation. because it was doing things to the sound that you couldn't really understand. I mean with a tape recorder you speed it up, all these things had physics, you know, you could think in analog terms.

And he was proud of it, Mr. Canter was very proud of it. And I remember watching him take the audio disk blank, he put it on the turntable. and I watched the strobe stabilize, and I heard that vacuum go on, and I heard it come out of the speaker, and I'm watching the groove appear on this blank disk. At the end of the thing he gave this memento to me and said, "Bear in mind, he's going to be my boss someday," but he says, "This is the highest fidelity you can get." This is what he told me. Those were the words he used, I'll never forget them.

And I took this thing home, gingerly. And I talked and talked my mom into letting me play it on her Victrola. She had a Victrola, I just had a little Webcor, and I wanted to hear it as HiFi as I could in our house. And I played the thing, and I remember the thrill of knowing that I was there, I saw this event happen, and now I'm reproducing it on a record player. And I think that experience truly just set me off on the path of recreating audio experiences.

So I was involved peripherally with studio operations from then on, from roughly the early '60s on. I bugged Mr. Canter to go down and see the place as often as I could—watch recording sessions and get coffee and that kind of thing. And I was able to meet people, and just to watch and to try and stay out of the way. Frankly, I was scared to death but then on the other hand, whenever I'd go over to Canter's house to play with Charles and Ralph Canter, his sons, I wanted to read comic books into a tape recorder. They had a Wollensac 1500 at their house. And I don't think I've ever seen a more beautiful piece of equipment in my mind. I wanted one of those so badly, I mean I can't tell you, I desperately wanted one of these machines. I hinted to everyone in my family to buy me one for Christmas or whatever. I finally do own one now. It belonged to Frank Harris and it doesn't function. It just says tape recorder, you know what I mean? You know the one I'm talking about? Balance, Tone. HiFi, Standard, I love that stuff. But anyway, that was a big thing for me. I always tried to talk my way into using that machine when I was over at their house for recording bicycles driving by, or birds, or anything.

They also had the first stereo I ever heard at the Canter's house. I heard it in the control room, I didn't really know what I was hearing. It was just overwhelming; the sound that I was hearing. I didn't understand that it was stereo, but when I went to their home, they had one of those big old console stereos, and I would sit in a little chair, you know, I'm 12 years old and I am listening to whatever record they had in stereo, and they were very nice to me and let me do that. And that's when I really became aware of image and stereophony, and creating a space, that the reality of the thing is always what obsessed me.

And when I really got going, I was looking for sound effects records at the county library and I ran across an album, called "Sound 35 mm". It was an Enoch Light recording. It was the mono version of stereo 35 mm. And a blurb on the record said "The first time you hear this record will be one of the most startling experiences of your life." That's what the blurb said. If you remember Command Records, they were always given to this kind of hyperbole. But I put that thing on my little Webcor, and by god it sounded better to me, it sounded better than anything I'd ever played on there before, on my little record player. By this time I had scavenged three-inch speakers from transistor radios, and I had three-inch speakers hanging all over my room. So, I was always trying to recreate what they did in the studio 'cause I couldn't get in there all the time.

We had a cistern on our property and I used to lower a speaker down into the bottom of it and a microphone on top, and that was my reverberation. I was the only kid in high school that had reverb on my recordings. Actually, I was the only kid in high school that cared about recording. We had a live chamber, it was wonderful. And I got involved with the high school audio-visual folks, being the AV guy, always being the one to set up the microphones at the concerts and the tape recorders and the projectors and all that stuff; I was one of those geeks who did that. But I had an interesting perspective because I was also the guy who was the emcee for all the concerts. There's a wonderful photo of me somewhere in my choir robe announcing the next group, and then leaping off to run under the bleachers where the tape recorder was. Over the years I was, my parents were very indulgent in allowing me to get tape recorders and I had a couple of Roberts tape recorders. I was just obsessed with the whole thing. With the idea, I wanted my little audio world to sound not necessarily better than anybody else's but I wanted it to sound as good as it could.

In those days, it was fairly easy. By the time I got into high school I had AR4ax speakers, and had a Dyna Stereo 70. For 99 percent of the people who came to my little room and heard that stuff, it was the best thing they'd ever heard. And I had access to real tapes from the studio; which at that time, having tapes instead of phonograph records was a big difference. Real tapes, not the duplicated kind—safeties and all. And to this day I get a kick out of having the tape that was there, the artifact. This is also something I try to instill in the students is that somewhere there's a box, and it's Sergeant Pepper. Okay, and all of the stuff that I've done there are boxes, this is it, this tape is the master tape. Now, it's all files and numbers and you lose a little of that magic. And that's not necessarily bad in terms of its quality but it's bad in terms of the way you feel about it. I still feel like the idea of the recording being a witness to an event, a combination of events that happened.

Edward H. Canter from Technisonic is mentioned in Tina Turner's book, "I, Tina." The actual fellow who owned the studio was Ed Canter's uncle, Bud Harrison, also known as Charles Harrison. He was a scientist at the Central Institute for the Deaf and a true audio genius and pioneer. He started Technisonic in 1929. As a researcher there, he built a little booth to make recordings, and he bought some disc recorders. He actually started his business by recording network shows for local radio stations for delayed broadcasts. And then he built the place on Brentwood Boulevard in the early to mid-50s. Mike Strube keeps saying he's going to do a documentary about Technisonic. I hope he does. Then that also allowed me to be interested in the integration of the pictures and the acting, because we did so many different things and I loved all of it. And I still don't mind spoken word, as long as I'm not doing audiobooks all day every day, all year. I don't mind doing one here and there. And making sure every edit is right and making it as good as I can.

I went to Northwestern University where I studied radio/TV. At the time I went there, I was still hanging out in the studio, I was doing things in the high school, making recordings, but I really wasn't that interested in going to school. My mom had researched all this and decided that Northwestern had a great, very well-respected program that had both acting and communications, as well. So I went up there and I was the only freshman on the air on the radio station. I did a bunch of technician's technical work on the shows and things. I was in their radio production department, but the radio production department and the radio station had less equipment than I had in my dorm room. In the studio we had two 16-inch turntables, one Wollensac 1500, and an RCA-77 Microphone. So that meant you couldn't record something and play something at the same time. I remember having singers come to my dorm room, we did the jingles in my dorm room. Because I had two Revoxes at the time—actually I had a Roberts 5000 and I had a Revox A77 R4, it might be an R5, my last one. So, we did that and I took the radio production classes. But bear in mind, I had already been operating well beyond that level, and I found it just didn't work for me. And so my parents were very nice and I came back and I went to Wash U to be close to the work. And I will say that I have nothing against Wash U, but I spent as little time there as I could.

I was interested in learning things, but I was reading all the stuff that I was interested in learning, I was just taking whatever I could take that would get me passed without going, without taking my time, and it came to my senior year and I was working 50, 60 hours a week doing stuff, and the Lester family wanted me to help their studio down on 39th street, and Parvin Trammel and I went to my dad and I said,

> I don't want to go back. I don't want to do my senior year. But if you tell me that having that piece of paper is worth it, I will do it. But know that I'm just going to get whatever I'm closest to getting.

And he was very cool about it, he said, "No". I said, "I'm making four dollars an hour, man." That was twice minimum wage, I've got Technisonic pay stubs that said two and a quarter.

The Lester family's studio was called Professional Artists. I have a business card from there. That's down 2000 South 39th Street. I think it's still in audio. We had brick walls that we built inside the storefront and Parvin Trammel, who is now with VSG, he was married to Donna Lester and they were touring, doing gospel groups all over the place, and he conceived this place as a studio where gospel groups would come and do a one-stop deal. They'd come in, record, mix, edit, and we'd go to Technicsonic, cut the masters and then we'd have the records pressed and do the jackets. Thousand records for $12,000, something like that. You know, including all the recording time and all that. He did graphics and printing and he was a really nice guy. When we opened that place I've never worked harder in my life because his opening promotion in 1973 was an hour of studio time for free, then you had to buy the 45s, that was his deal. You can't imagine, I must have done 150 or 170 bands in the first two, three weeks, fortunately they're all very similar setups, four singers, bass drums, guitar, piano, that was pretty much it. But still, I had to splice them all and mix them all, and get it right, and write the box, document it, and it was just constant work. But it was really great fun. And then I ended up sitting next to him and doing gospel records for a couple years while I was still waiting for the right opportunity to come back to Technisonic and fit in there in the union situation.

They were IBW, and the fruits of that are apparent. I've talked to many people who have had similar careers to me, most notably Stewart Sloke in World Wide Wadio in Hollywood. He worked at Universal in Chicago, and he used to talk about how he'd work all night and they'd be stapling stuff on the wall or painting the floor or all the stuff that we used to do. and I said, "Well yeah, at the time it was great. I didn't want to do anything else, and they're paying me this overtime." And he looks at me like, "What?" So I mean I'm very grateful that we got overtime. Mr. Canter didn't mind paying us overtime because he billed the clients for it, so it was great. He loved that we were working overtime.

He would mark it up on top of that. It was an overtime charge. If you wanted to work an extra four hours, you were gonna have to pay overtime, and they did. It was not a big deal. So that early 70s era, I was bouncing around helping people get started because I wasn't really sure if I was going to be able to be a daily guy at Technisonic.

Technisonic was always state-of-the-art. The console was custom-made by Bob Bushnell. He was one of the premiere custom console builders, he did enough of them so he had ads. These were true recording consoles and they were beautiful. We had linear faders, Altec faders. We had EQ on each channel which was basically high and low. And then there were a couple of Pultecs that were outboard EQ you could patch into. And then there were a couple of passive ones, Langevins I believe they were. And you didn't want to use those because you lost like 30 dB of gain. You didn't want to use them unless you had to. And there was no panning at that time, not yet. And you had four buses, four monitoring buses, because you had four speakers in front of you and that sounded really cool at that time.

By the time the late '60s rolled around we had a 3M model 56 in a beautiful custom-made Formica cabinet that matched the cabinet, the board, it was very clinical, the design, but it was all matched. We had this beautiful white Formica with wood doors. If you've ever seen one in a gray cabinet with a white top, that was our equipment. But the series 56 eight-track in this beautiful Formica cabinet with all 8 meters above it was the prettiest tape recorder to this day I've ever seen. Prettiest tape recorder. I used to sit on top of the meter bridge so my head would be against the ceiling so I could listen to the speakers the way I wanted to. It was really nice. It was a great tape recorder.

And, by that time I had really got an appreciation for these machines that were so well put together, well-designed. They were designed by people who wanted them to be that way. These were people really trying to make the equipment better. This was the goal in those days, and I'm sure you'll understand that everything we did was to try to make what we did better. Not just better than the other studio, which we didn't have that problem because there really wasn't anybody in our category. I wanted it to be better because I wanted people, when I would have to try to sell a session, I would just say, "Just come in." And they would come in, and it was only then a question of whether they could afford it. And our boss Mr. Canter said that he doesn't mind hearing that they can't afford us, but they don't want anybody to be better than us. And Mr. Harrison was the same way. He still was, even into his later years, in his 70s, 80s, he was still so fascinated by the equipment. Mr. Canter was more of a businessman but Mr. Harrison was still a real dreamer. And he put all of his money back in the place.

No one was more interested than Mr. Harrison when we were building the automated mixing board, when we were working with automated processes on that. I will give Bob Brose a lot of credit, who is now with VSG, he was our chief engineer at the time. He did so much work on the technical aspects of the automixer because nobody knew what we really wanted to do. And that's when we came up with the idea. Having a completely automated board was just so daunting for the recording side, multi-track side, but it was possible for quad mixing. So, that's why we ended up having two boards. It was an "L" shaped deal. Because we used an API 2488. During the custom-board days, Bob Bushnell was using components made by automated processes. And I remember getting four API 550 equalizers, the original ones. And they were outboard patchable. It was a revelation in those days.

And they were followed shortly thereafter by the 16-track machine. We got a 16-track MM-1000, with 16 Dolbys, the second generation; the 361s. That was the newest, latest thing because the 8301s were huge, I mean they were just huge. We ended up getting a B301 which was the Dolby B duplicator unit. It was a multi-rack space unit for two channels, the same as an 8301. But anyway, we had this machine so we had to modify the board to be a 16-track board. It was all custom done. I have a photo of the middle-aged woman that they sent standing in the middle of the thing with her soldering iron, trying to add buses, and monitor matrix and stuff. This equipment was still very specialized then. You didn't just have a stock board.

Everyone had something that was custom built; either a heavily modified radio console or if you had money and connections, you had a recording console that was built by one of only a handful of companies; Bob Bushnell is one of them. His ads in a few trade publications that there were and had models on them, you know pretty girls sitting there in very sleek looking things, and it was really neat. But that equipment was just solid, it was all very basic, but it was all professional equipment. I remember one of the things that struck me when I was speaking to Alan Parsons was that, it was all some of the same stuff. Once you got to this level, it was professional equipment and you expected professional equipment to be really great. Yes, there were some esoteric arguments, "Well, is the Ampex better than the 3M?", or whatever, but these were minor things. It was professional equipment. And you didn't think about an outboard preamp because you had a professional preamp in your board, and it was good. You just didn't think about it.

We had a Fairchild, we had Pulltecs, and we did have limiters. We had a lot of the Fairchilds, we had several Fairchild limiters; and those always sounded great on acoustic guitars. We had several things that were dedicated mostly to mastering, disc mastering. We had what they called a Conex. Fairchild made it, and I never did understand what it was, but it sounded cool whatever it was.

We had a Moog synthesizer that belonged to Frank Harris Productions, and he was an early pioneer in this electronic music thing; won a Clio for some Annheuser-Busch work where he used the filter, voltage control filter, to make white noise sound like the wind was singing the Busch song. It was a big deal. And I used to play with that machine, and it was just an awesome, awesome piece of gear that was huge, huge, the Keith Emerson deal, multiple keyboards, and giant sequencer bank and patch cords everywhere. One of the things that I do tell the students about effects in general, there were a lot of things you could do with a sound, but you had to really want to do it. So, as a result, you only did it when you really wanted to do it.

You didn't just put a compressor everywhere. A lot of times I'll get a question, "Well, what microphone did you use on the kick drum?" Whatever was left! You have to look at a recording session as a big picture, you have these resources and this recording. You can't just treat it as though you are doing one thing at a time. But I guess, what I am trying to say about that is there was professional equipment that always sounded good when it was functioning. You just assumed that professional equipment was designed at the highest standards that they could adhere to.

And when we got the 1176s at Technisonic, we had dozens of those. We had some LA2As, I didn't like those as well for general-purpose work. Maybe it was just because I had more 1176s and I just got used to using them, but the 1176 was just what we used; they were everywhere. Because it was the professional compressor. It wasn't like "Did it have a different sound than compressor b?" There weren't that many of them that were available. This was the one.

And it's the same thing with microphones. There's a small universe of good microphones. And we had most of them; we had M49 Neumanns, we had U-64 Neumanns, we had 47s, we had Telefunken 47s, and we had Telefunken 251s, which are the ones I miss the most. And then when the tube-type Neumanns came out, we kept buying them. We had 87s and we had 84s, a couple of km86s, and we had a bunch of dynamic mics, some of the older microphones that you still recognize today. But there wasn't this vast universe of microphones. The microphones that you had, these were just really good ones. These are professional microphones. And we learned to use them.

I remember I even wrote a letter to someone early on when I was becoming the music guy, the guy that was doing all the sessions, about how pleased I was with myself that I could really get what microphone I wanted to. I knew in advance what it was going to be when I got out there. It's just something you get with practice, there's no genius about it; it just happens. But again, it was professional equipment that was just really good. At that time, it was so exciting because when something new came out, it came out because it was really better. We wanted the 24-track because we wanted more tracks, it was, when would they get a 24-track that was good enough? And then that happened, that breakthrough happened sometime in the mid '70s I guess. I don't remember the exact date. We got the first MCI JH-114, the first one that was milled out to use 14-inch reels, and we waited an extra six weeks I think, for it. Oh man, it was a long six weeks, a long six weeks.

I went to build the Lester family studio in '72-'73. Parvin had made most of the equipment acquisitions. He had an old, custom-built board. It had Gotham faders, the old belt drive things. It was built by a guy named Norbert Ward and had been in a studio in Atlanta, it was one of the gospel places, and it was a well-known studio. And this thing had all these Langevin equalizers; the two-lever semi-graphic kinds of things, but it was not really designed for stereo, which is why they got rid of it. And it only had four mixing buses. So I developed a technique of doing everything with patch cords, and basically

I made everything into a direct-in coming out of the Fairchild preamps into the fader, and then out of the fader directly into the patch bay and I didn't think of it as any innovation, I'm sure other people were doing it, it's what everybody does now. Because we had plenty of inputs, I would just listen to everything through the eight-track machine.

We had a series 56 eight-track as well, which was in the standard case, which was the vertical. It sounded very good too. And it worked very well. We didn't have any Dolby on it. We had a 440 Ampex and we had two Dolby 361s, and now those exact units are down at Avatar, Jim MacMorran uses them to this day. They were used when we got 'em. And they sounded great. And so I made literally hundreds of these gospel groups, it was a fairly large recording room, and I did a lot of big bands. During that time Mr. Canter and I had a little falling out. He was really leaning on me to be more of a technical guy. He wanted me to be the chief engineer, and he wanted me to take electrical engineering classes at Wash U. and do things a certain way. I was making records, man. That's what I wanted to do.

And the folks at C&C—Steve Litman and Tom Zuzenak—built the thing up at CMC Recording in Lindbergh-Warson. And they were after me to go up there and record up there and the Lesters said, "That's fine." At that time for me, it was worth it to make a stand and say, "Naw, screw it. I'll just do this." And so there was a period there of a couple of years where I was sort of on the outs at Technisonic, I didn't have a key to the place anymore. I mean I had a good relationship with the people there, notably Al Bussen who was my mentor, who was the chief engineer at that time. But, anyway what happened was we were making records, and at that time, Technisonic was really not concentrating on the music business. The music studio was a loss leader.

They were doing commercial work, but not even much commercial music. Frank Harris was there. But basically the big room was there to show people that we're a big-time studio. They had three or four voice rooms and record pressing, there was a motion picture soundstage doing a lot of movie-mixing with an interlock system and all that. So the music studio was just a glamor thing.

But anyway, when I was working with Parvin we had a couple of 1176s, and I remember after meeting George Massenburg at ITI, he was still in recording. He was an engineer at a place called IT Recordings Incorporated. It was in Cockeysville, Maryland, a Baltimore suburb, now I'm talking about '71, '72. He was an interesting guy to watch and I spent a session with him. There's no way he'd remember it, I'm a kid from St. Louis that was introduced to him by Steve Temmer from Gotham Audio because I had helped install the new Neumann BMS-70 lathe that we bought at Technisonic. For some reason Mr. Canter and Mr. Harrison wanted the state-of-the-art cutting equipment. I mean, I was pleased, I was thrilled. Of course it wasn't going to make any economic sense but Mr. Harrison wanted everything to be as good as it could be.

An aside about George Massenburg is that I remember the thing that made the biggest impression on me about him; at the time he had really long hair. He was doing a rock n' roll session and he was the first guy I ever saw that had a gooseneck talkback microphone. It came all the way up to his lips. The music is really loud, screaming, and he would hit the talkback button and say, "Okay, guys". He would say it so quietly, but his lips were right against this Gooseneck microphone. They really controlled the session in a way that the other talkback arrangements didn't. We just had an RCA microphone in the corner, you had to call out to them, so it was a whole different thing—he was talking softly into their ear, a hint of his sensitivity and how far he would go.

But anyway, I mention him because we really coveted what he built; the ITI parametric equalizer. We wanted one of those. And I mean we wanted one of those. We did get one, that was really the extent of our outboard gear. We had a couple of 1176s at Parvin's. We did have an ITI parametric equalizer, the original parametric equalizer. And man, was that thing cool! I have no idea where it went, but I would love to have that thing today. But, no we didn't have a lot of outboard gear, but I would use tape recorders, you could use anything and I was a patch bay fiend. This thing had been custom built by Norbert Ward and I had all the drawings. I spent months with a case of Tun-O Wash cleaning this thing out. It was a smoking studio, we got it working and it sounded really good. We even rigged up a couple of panners, so you could pan a few things. I even had to mechanically remove the interlocks for the mixing buses so that you could feed one and four at the same time so you could have them centered. They weren't even designed to do centered; it was strictly a four-track mono board.

But anyway, we got some very good recordings out of that thing. You'd run microphones out in the street to get a slapback echo, or you'd have all those little things. So we didn't have a lot of outboard gear in the sense that you had a box that you'd patch into and make it do this. There was lots of equipment around, but you would sort of figure out a way to get some of these effects that you'd get in the old days. You'd think about how can you manipulate the signal. Really, the only things you had was time and frequency distribution, maybe distortion. You'd feed it out to a speaker, that was a big thing you'd always do, feed stuff to speakers and record it again after having done, put a pillow in it or put it inside a drum to make it boomy or have it feed through the piano, all this stuff you'd do, but it wasn't as easy as just pushing a button. So, you had to plan this stuff out. And this is one of the things I think, a lot of these effects-heavy recordings are just so gratuitous. I mean they might be great effects, but just because you have a compressor on every channel doesn't mean you should just use it. I mean it does make it easier.

Technisonic had a price per side for cutting lacquers, 30 bucks a side, something like that. I don't know what it was. But there was also an hourly rate for mastering, which was designed to punish people if they wanted to come in and listen while you're mastering. But we got the idea because I knew how to operate the thing, I said, "If I line up all my tones just right and I make everything right, we can go in and cut you 15 sides in a day. And their cost per side is like ten now, it's much less." We book time and materials. So we would book a day of mastering, and I would cut dozens of sides. And it was really cool, and Mr. Canter at that point saw that we were doing a lot of music.

So one day he did say his famous phrase of, "Gotta minute?" I went in, he said, "Here's what we want to do. We want to get back into music recording." Bob Brose had already started the task of assembling this automated plan. He said, "I want to get back into music, I want you to do it." And I couldn't refuse because this was a union job, real money, well it was Technisonic. It's the place. As cool as we were, we were making hundreds of gospel albums but it was all for quartets. And I love those people, they were very nice and we made some good records. And my friend Tom Zuzenack ended up being our commercial client at Technisonic. A lot of things happened. Frank Harris also died, and he was the premiere music recording person in town, and Tom Zuzenack was poised to take over. So by that time I was working with him because C&C had closed and he was working with us at Parvin's. We ended up getting a 16-track machine down there. We did have an MCI 16-track, it was one of those giant, wide things. It had a 24-track electronic rack. But we only had 16 track heads and all these empty spaces.

At Parvin's studio we did Jerry and the Singing Goffs and we did the Lesters, and I did Frankie Ford down there. That was probably one of the biggest things that we did down there, because a fellow named Ken Keene was a producer from New Orleans had the rights to Frankie Ford. He was his manager, somehow, I don't know how he heard about us. So Frankie Ford came up, made an album with us, and we did two or three things for his company. And that's when I got into ASCAP. I wrote the B-sides on some of those singles, and this guy had the publishing company, and he didn't want to miss any penny of revenue, so he said, "Look, I'll put you in ASCAP, we'll publish these songs through my company." And so, he did all the paperwork and the certificates on the wall, and I think I made maybe 50–80 cents. But, to this day I get quarterly reports, "we regret, no royalties this quarter".

So I was overwhelmed that I was going to get to, in effect, be the guy to do the music renaissance at Technisonic. And Bob Brose worked like crazy to make the place as cool as we could, and it was very exciting. So that was probably in early '74 when I went back, full-time, full-union thing. And that was what I was going to do, I was going to be the music guy. I didn't abandon the Lesters because they were clients of ours at Technisonic, so I helped them out. And Parvin was a great guy and the family was nice to me and they continued to make records down there. Parvin had it all set up, we didn't really need to change much from what we had done.

So that all worked out very well and Tom Zuzenack, his company was called "River City Music Works," and we did a lot of jingles and I loved doing that stuff. I really did enjoy that, too. And by that time, I was getting some voice work, too. I was in the union and I was doing voiceovers. Mr. Canter was very strict about us not doing that on company time. So, I had to do those in the morning, and I worked for my shift, nominally was from 1–9, and so I worked reading scripts in the morning, recorded jingles in the afternoon, made records at night. That's just what I did. And it was really cool because everything that I wanted in my life was in that building; we had a movie sound stage, we had moviola editing, we had record pressing in the basement. We didn't do the plate, we did the plating as well. And at one time we did film processing, but that was long gone. But we had movie people, and we had editors, and it was just where everybody in St. Louis went to do commercials and industrials. And it was just a wonderful time—people were really interested in the quality of what we were doing. Our clientele, yes, they were trying to be efficient, but nobody was trying to lowball anything. We were all trying to do professional stuff. And so those times were really great.

And that's sort of when it came into the real modern era when we got the automated mixing. When we went to talk to various console manufacturers, Bob was the main guy who did this stuff, and Mr. Harrison said, "We want everything to come back." And we were going to quad at the same time. We want quad panning, we want echo sends, returns, we want EQ, we want aux sends, we want it all. We want to put our tape on and have it come back. Everybody laughed at us, except Paul Wolff at API. He said, "We can do it." Neve didn't want to do it, they were working on their levels-only system. And Allison had their system that never did work.

We had an Allison programmer. They chose to use the Allison brain to control the API voltage control faders. The problem that we had was our Automix board had so many functions, 24 ins, quad panning, echo, all the different groups, and all the stuff. The original Alison programmer that looked at every function sequentially was too slow. There were too many functions. As a result it was really of limited use; it wouldn't work. The first-generation programmer basically did help you by getting everything reset. But you couldn't really do what you wanted to. It sort of did it. It was so close you could taste it. But you'd do a fade, if you did a fast fade it would go, uh, uh. So anyway, Paul Buff at Allison Research did come up with a second-generation programmer that realized that not every function needed to be looked at on every cycle and he came up with the priority systems so that a function that was changing would get priority. That actually worked very well. And I rigged up on the oscilloscope display because the faders didn't move, it was a learning curve and a sales curve to get the clients to understand; yes, it really is doing it. So I created a display that would show you moving green dots, it would show you that something was happening.

What SSL did later, moving faders on the screen, we didn't have the graphics for. You just had little green dots that would go up and down, and if you moved an equalizer, you'd see it move. And it was very good, but even then, the problem with storing the data and updating it, the latency. You couldn't really do what we freely do today, go back and forth and back and forth. What we would do is I used it pretty much like a pickup recorder, I punched in mixes and then you could do one or two updates and maybe one last one in real-time. You bounce back and forth to generate the data. So, you wouldn't have generation loss but you'd have latency, and you'd have increased latency with too many bounces.

That's what it was, that was the problem. Plus the fact you had to give up two tracks. And we had to have a complicated patching system to bypass the Dolbys for the data track. But when I think, all we needed was time code and a computer, and that board today would still be in use, it would really be fantastic. I don't know where it is. But if somebody has that thing hooked up to a computer, they have a real hell of a nice thing. But this was all part of the idea of being able to repeat a mix. I wrote an article for Recording Engineer/Producer after they started that magazine, talking about how automated mixing was to mixing what multi-track recording was to musicians. You know, you could keep what you liked and mix it. But because of the problems that we had with it, it never became a staple. I mean it was a big, special occasion to use it. But our system was set up so that you'd push a big button and a t-bar relay would switch everything over, so now the front of the room was over here.

We were going to be cutting edge. We had things like the Kepex and Gain Brain, and there started to be a whole industry of people that were starting to build what now we know as outboard gear that did the things that were specialty audio devices. The Kepex was the first one that really comes to mind. But it's also Paul Buff, and I still have the demo record that I gave a copy to Alan Parsons, I still have the demo record with Alan himself narrating. And the idea that you can take a bass drum from *boom boom* to *bup bup bup* was a big deal. And that became an effect that was one of the first devices that you could literally play with all night. Compressors were not in that category. You loved getting them, and you loved messing with them, but they didn't afford you the entertainment value.

We had Fairchilds, we had 1176s, and LA2s, and LA3s, and then we also had an Allison-made product called the Gain Brain, which was very good. And Eventide made the Omnipressor, and then API had a couple of those little ones they still sell today that fit in the 500 rack, I was never that thrilled with them. DBX, we never had any of the 160s, but we had a lot of their 500 series that fit in that rack. I don't know, DBX is another one of those products, like the AKG 451, it's like kryptonite for me. I don't want to badmouth the microphone because I've seen people get great results with it. But don't let me touch it, because whenever I touch it, it just goes bad. I don't know what it is. And it was the same thing with most of the DBX products. The DBX compressors are a perfect example. I've heard wonderful recordings made with it, but somehow I was never able to respond to it, I don't know what it is about it. It's one of those mental things, I guess I got burned by it or I did it wrong or something caused me to get a mental block, so I was never able to successfully use it after that. We had a couple of those, but we had mostly the 500 series DBX units, which are now actually down at Avatar. I traded a couple of them to Jim MacMorran for sound effects years ago.

So we had that, and then we had a little later on when we get into the digital stuff, we'll talk about the delays that everybody wanted to have, but of course, the really breakthrough device was the Eventide H910, the Harmonizer. We had pretty good luck getting our company to buy new stuff that was exciting because Mr. Harrison wanted that stuff. I mean the idea of being able to change the pitch without changing the speed or vice versa, I mean just the idea of it. Well, of course it wouldn't change the speed, but it in effect did because it had an output to a VSO that would proportionally change the tape speed while it changed the pitch.

That was the first Eventide product. Oh no, we had an instant phaser and flanger, though. Those were good devices, too. And of course Eventide ended up being in the avionics business which is really funny because when I had my airplane I would get mailings from them trying to sell me radios and navigation stuff, it was the same company, Eventide Clockworks. We had heard of digital delays, but we had not bought any. We ended up buying a Delta Lab one, we spent big dough for the second and a half or something like that, but, it might have even been more.

The harmonizer, I remember the night that came vividly, because it arrived, and we were one of the early people to get it. I won't say we were the first, we were certainly the first in the Midwest but it was early on. You hadn't really read about it much in magazines yet either. I'll never forget this—the film crew was shooting Colonel Sanders, Colonel Sanders himself was at the Kentucky Fried Chicken there on Brentwood Boulevard and our crew was up there, and it was a thunderstorm. Terrible, pouring down rain, this is at night. They were going to shoot there all night. But Tom Zuzenack and I got this thing, and we hooked it up and we would take turns. He would spend a half hour talking while I would mess with it. And then I'd go in and this thing kept us entertained. I mean when you think about it now, the universe of things it will do is pretty small, but just hearing that stuff for the first time, the pitch shift and feedback, the things that you could make it do with the modulation. I mean it was a revelation because it was doing things to the sound that you couldn't really understand. I mean with a tape recorder you speed it up, all these things had physics, you know, you could think in analog terms. The Harmonizer was the first device, and even the digital delay was easy to relate to. It was just like tape slap.

There was no big deal for it being digital, other than the fact you didn't have to rewind it, and that there was no tape hiss. The fact that it was a digital delay really made no difference. The Delta Labs thing had some good features, anyway the harmonizer suddenly changed everything, it chopped the sound up into numbers and did things to the sound that caused your mind to think differently about how the sound was. That was, in my mind, what mentally prepared me for random access anything. Because once you see that, once the sound is in this form we can do other things to it, other than analogous things like phasing; even with digital phasing it was just easier than putting your finger on a tape flange. But it was an effect we could get, it was just easier with digital. But this harmonizer was truly digital. It could only be accomplished in that way. And that really was all.

Of course now I have to say that then that sort of revelation sort of slipped into the back of my mind because when digital recorders started coming out, people would start doing sessions in digital. The motivation was because it was quieter and better. That's the motivation. The motivation for early digital recordings was not to get it in this form, what we now routinely think of as computer workstations and random access and all that. The original digital recorders were just a natural progression in quality. Tom Stockham and the people at Soundstream, they were just trying to make better recordings, not necessarily create a new way of making recordings.

The earliest digital recorder I used was the Sony F1. And we had a couple of them. We used them on ¾-inch machines, we used them on VHS machines, and some Betamax machines. I still have some of the tapes on my shelf. Why? I don't know.

The first jobs I used them on, well audio-only jobs, we used them on film quite a bit before we started doing them with sound because we had a Nagra IV stereo, which we used to use on remotes. I recorded at the Fox Theatre, right after Leon Strauss bought the Fox, and they renovated the thing down there. I went and made a recording of the organ, just with Marlin Mackley who was the organ restorer and restoration guy. We went down there and I set up, I can't remember the microphones I used. Probably km-84s, and we had an Ampex mixer, but I was just going to do it with two microphones and we recorded it with the F1. That was really the first commercial use that I can remember that I used the F1 for, other than my own personal entertainment. That was the first time I felt like, well it's reliable enough for this job. I wasn't really ready to commit my real professional work to the F1 until that job. And it was really great for theatre organ, as well. It was perfect for that kind of thing. The only problem is you had a big rack full of gear. But again, the fact that it was digital was just supposed to make it better; not different. You see what I'm saying?

It also impressed the client. No question about it. The recording would've been better on the IVs, the Nagra IVs, there's no question about it. But, the Nagra IVs would've required reel changes, all those things, so we had two hours of what passed for "really good recording". And at that point, we just took it on. See this is also part of the thing that's changing here at that point is that we just took it on faith, of course the F1 was never really touted as professional. But you just assume that they would've taken care of all that other stuff.

So this is part of the thing, you just assume that if there's somebody with a major name put out equipment aimed at professionals that it would meet all these standards. So, I can't tell you I ever got burned by it, but I was disappointed by some of the products in that category. But again, the digital revolution sort of proceeded on two paths. One is just in terms of a better way to store and playback audio. And the other is a different way to manipulate the audio. It was not 'til Sound Tools came out, which then turned into Sound Designer, that would be the late '80s, I got Sound Designer in '90 or "91 just after I got my Quadra 700, and it was fairly well-established by that time. So, it was probably late '80s. But if you look at recordings from the late '70s like the "Nightfly" and things like that, there's a digital recording maintenance engineer credited on there.

But the idea was, it was multi-track audio. It was just a natural progression of quieter, cleaner sound. That was my perception of digital as it was coming in, was Hey, these are just better tape recorders". That was what they were selling them to us as. It wasn't a really revolutionary concept in production, because the original Mitsubishi and those machines that came out, they were functionally the same, you used them in the same way. And then Tom bought a Synclavier, that was also in the mid '80s. He was one of the very early adopters and it was a quarter of a million dollars. And it had some Winchester drives record two, three minutes.

And that was our first experience in starting to really deal with what we take for granted today—random access of production. Since we were using it mostly for commercials, we were able to do a lot of things with it. Although today, some of the limitations that that Synclavier had in terms of recording, I'm not talking about its synthesis, I'm talking now about the audio recording portion. t wasn't true random access, you couldn't play two sounds off a single hard drive at once and limitations that you don't even have on Garageband. So, we embraced it. We did, but I got to say that I was slow to really be sold on the random access features. We had had such good results doing it the old way and just making sure it was right. I was interested in the fact that it had no noise and no generation loss.

Generations, this is another thing that was uppermost in our minds. In my mind, particularly was generations staying as true to the original as you possibly could. Anytime, you always go back if you could. Go back another generation. I've said that most people who work in analog have the opposite of a pet peeve, they have one thing that is very important to them. For Dale Manquen, it was scrape flutter. I had a friend, Dan Reed, who was azimuth, and all these things are important, but not one to the exclusion of all others. I would always sort of chuckle inside when somebody would tell me, "Oh, you gotta fix that!" I said, "Well, why fix that if this is bad?" I was a believer in trying to rotate through all the little characteristics and try to get them all better. That was my theory. When I aligned a tape machine, I wouldn't spend any more time on any one thing, because sometimes to get azimuth right, you might pay a price somewhere else. Of course azimuth is something you really do have to have. But, I guess what I'm saying is that the thing about analog is there's so many things you are juggling in your mind to make sure you're optimizing the whole thing. And the professional equipment would give you better, a bigger margin for error.

My favorites among the gear we were using? Well, the 1176 is just your old hand. It just sits there and does what it needs to do. The other day in a music class, they were messing with it and they're trying to record it really clean. On the one end you don't want to over-compress, but if you need compression, you need compression. I said, "I know we're doing it on the record side, but it needs to sound better than this. Just patch it to the 1176." They just patch it. And I didn't really even think about what I was doing. I don't know what I did, they were acting like I was some magic thing, it just did what it needed to do. So that was a device that was always very reliable, didn't worry about it. I really did like the API, all the API EQs. Not the compressors; I was not that crazy about the compressors. The 550 equalizers, well by that time we had them in every module we had 550As and then we had some 565, the graphics, which were really cool. I loved those things. Those things, it's so interesting because of the signal chain. Of course now we have this with the SSL, the preamp is good, the EQ is good, I mean it's just good, Although I would always try to even avoid the mixing bus if I could. I loved patching, I still like patching because it's just the idea. With digital, well I don't know what it's doing, it's going into the digital cross-switcher and here it is. I've got this plugged in.

If I had an 1176 I would still use it. I still use the U-87, and I still have an Ampex 440. I don't use it regularly but it's very satisfying when I use it. I would like to have, I got to say that I don't really covet, I mean I would love to have some of those microphones back. I was very disappointed when Technisonic changed hands and Mike Rosenthal sold the 251s. I can't imagine him doing that, but again, at the time I didn't think of them as anything really that fantastic, but they were professional microphones that sounded great. I mean professional microphones sounded great, so there were just two of them that I used a lot. I used them a lot on vocals. Now I go back and I listen and now I know why people like them. What an amazing thing.

And I will also say I was very fortunate that we had so much stuff. I mean we had those Nagras, they're beautiful, they were like a watch, like a fine watch. This stuff was built so well. I do have a special place for that 3M eight-track; the 56 in the Formica cabinet. Just so pretty. And I mean, some of that stuff, it just means so much to you to have it. I got to say the lathe, the cutting the records was a really neat thing. And I do miss that.

And recently when I was at Capitol, it was just a thrill for me to talk to this guy, and basically, he's not doing it differently. It's the same stuff, same electronics, same cutter, same everything! The biggest leap is the TV camera and the microscope. I told him that was incredible. I don't know how many went there, messed with the microscope, looked at the grooves, but that is something I will say that that particular piece, the system, the mechanical sophistication it takes to do what that machine did. It was something very impressive. A good professional tape recorder is impressive as well, but the tolerances and the physical forces that are being exerted on the stylus and lacquer surface, that is something that is truly the real deal, and I used to really enjoy making records, acetates for people in a way that you don't get for making CDs for people. Well everybody can burn a CD. Dad has one of those. And the idea that the equipment was specially built to do what it did in studios is something that I really miss today.

The Omnipresser was a bit disappointing, the Eventide Omnipressor. They made it sound like "Oh, you could make things sound backward". We had one and when you think about it, the idea is continuously variable from infinity to one to one to infinity. It sounds cool! Functionally, it didn't have much use. It just didn't have much use. We had one and I thought it was going to be really cool and not a knock against the company; it did do that, but it wasn't useful. It wasn't useful. And some of the consumer semi-pro things really, really hurt. When people started having those ½-inch eight-tracks and coming in saying that they had their studio and you'd try to fix it and they'd bring their machine in, it disappointed me that people were referring to that as "professional equipment".

What they're calling vintage now? The idea that something as simple as the 1176 is vintage, it's just a thing. You know what I mean? It's just a professional piece of gear that does what it's supposed to. It's been re-released anyway. It's new again. And so, I don't think of it as a vintage thing. I just think of it as there's no reason you couldn't make it like that. There's no reason for that. And so, I do sort of shake my head at some of these things. Actually, I'll tell you what it was, is the U-67. I don't know if I really feel that way now, but I remember thinking that the 87s, we had several 67s and we had 87s, but the 87s were so much easier to use. You didn't have a dang power supply, they were quieter, everything about them in my mind at the time was better. And then even into the early '80s, people were saying, "Oh you know, I'd give two 87s for one U-67." I would have said, "Call me!" I'll be glad to make that deal! At the time, there were some things, and

I will also say that even the 251 at the time I was using it, I liked it. But I didn't get the sense that it was destined to be some kind of all-time classic. I really didn't. Of course the universe in which I lived was that it was a common thing, in the universe of professional microphones it was one of the ones studios had.

I'll tell you, the Cooper Time Cube was one of those. That box, I think I've probably told you some of my stories about it before, but Bill Putnam knew Al Bussen, they knew each other from Chicago. I don't know, at that time delay was all the rage. But, we really didn't need the Cooper Time Cube because we had rigged up a deal, we had a machine shop in the studio, and we built a capstan that was like an inch in diameter. I called it "MillionIPS." We had no idea how fast it was going, but you could get that kind of 30–40 millisecond delay with that, the tape would only last about two minutes. We called it "MillionIPS", and we had this machine, it was a sleeve that fit on the capstan of a 440C and you'd crank that thing up. So basically we had that effect, but this thing was getting a lot of publicity and it was Putnam and it was Universal Audio. So, we wanted one. We had to get one. And they sent this thing. What the ads showed you was the little black face box, but they didn't show you the big gray thing that's half the size of an EMT, a third of the size of an EMT. Anyway, so we got this device, plugged it in, it was two tubes. One had a 14 millisecond delay, one had a 16 millisecond delay. Together it was 30. The reason I bring that up is that is the key to the one good use that I found for it, and I'll tell you that in a minute. But, we got this thing, and it was a Friday afternoon or something. And for some reason, we're busy over the weekend, but we used to love to mess with the stuff when it came in, and we plugged it in and made sure that it worked. And on Monday we are literally getting ready with our screwdrivers; Bob Brose and me and we were going to take this thing apart and look inside. We wanted to see the tube. There's a letter from Putnam to Al Bussen, god I wish I would've kept it. I wish I had it. Basically, saying "You know, you guys are going to be tempted to open the box up. For God's sake, don't do it!"

It'll go everywhere, it's basically what he said. You'll never get it back together. Here's a Polaroid of what it looks like. He sent us a photo of this little plastic tube coiled up inside the box, and I could see, once we saw it we realized if we would open it, it would've been like a slinky, it would've been everywhere. We would've been in terrible trouble. But, I just remember that, but it never did do what you wanted it to do, which was to do a vocal doubling. That was really what people wanted it for. But it sounded too much like a shower stall. So the one use to which I put it all the time was when I would do television/radio commercials. We did a lot of promotion, similar to episodes that we do now. When you'd have mono bad recordings, I found that if I took the mono recording, put it in the center, and feed the 14 millisecond delay to one side and the 16 to the other side, it would have a nice round stereo-ish effect. And that became sort of my trademark sound for promos. And I liked it for that because you could patch into the 14 millisecond side and the 16 separately. So that was what I did use it for, but they touted it as the vocal doubler, and it just was not. No, it didn't cut that. But the Cooper Time Cube…

Delta Labs had a thing and they had an effect on there. Another thing that, this is pertinent to this, is that a piece of equipment would come out and it would do a signature thing, and there would be one hit record that would use it; very similar to what Cher did with the Autotune. But, there would be one thing, this Delta Lab 8100 or something like that, anyway it was a two-channel thing that had some kind of cross—you could cross from one to another, and it would do a weird kind of like a bounce back and forth. It was very cool. And I hit on the idea just after we got it. We were one of the early people to get it. And I had a client, his name was Carl Leta, his father was Frank Leta Honda. He had a song and I just wanted to do something different with his voice on the hook. So he would sing the hook and it would bounce back. I would use the Delta, I loved the effect, I thought "This was really great, I'm a genius." And not too long later, not too long after that I was driving down the highway, listening to the radio, and Olivia Newton-John's "Magic" comes on. I mean I about drove off the road. I knew exactly how he had set the thing up, John Farrar. But along those lines, this equipment would, in those days if you were steeped in it, you would know "Oh they used this machine for that", "They used that machine," "This is how they set it", there was a limited amount of things you could do. And once you hit on something you could use, you'd use it. I would have to say the Synclavier fell into that category, too. We used it, its hundred presets, almost exclusively to make it sound like a Synclavier. I don't know how many times we would impress the client by doing those first few notes from "Bad".

As mixes became more controlled, as people got more of a handle on these things, you could sense when mixes had been done in layers like that. There are a couple of songs that really screamed out to me, "I am an automated mix." Not necessarily bad or good, but did. One of them that you still hear today is Olivia Newton-John, again, "Please Mister, Please." All of a sudden, the sonic character changes when a lot of things happen, which of course is now very normal. But at the time, that was a very revolutionary mix. And I gotta say that those Olivia Newton-John records that John Farrar did, including the soundtrack for Xanadu, he was getting exactly what he was aiming for. So I really admired the craft.

It's like what Mutt Lange does with Shania Twain, I mean you've got to admire what he's getting, at least the control. and earlier than that Roy Halee did Art Garfunkel's album. "For All we Know" is the name of the song, and I remember that had so much stuff in it. I remember that was another early one that I heard, that felt like it had an automated mix to it. Gosh, there's so much, and I love talking about it because it's something that I wonder if people will have that kind of feeling for these plug-ins. You don't get the same sense as the plug-in is not your partner as much as the machine is. A piece of gear; you nurture it, you take care of it, it's going to live with you for a long time...and I tend to keep the stuff around, not because it's of any vintage value but it works...that McIntosh C28 preamp there, I bought that in 1969. Well, not only has it worked every day since 1969, it still sounds as good as anything you can get. It's probably worth four times what I paid for it. That kind of thing. You don't get rid of tape recorders, you don't get rid of power amplifiers: it's like a musician; you shouldn't get rid of your instruments, you know. And they really are the way we've expressed ourselves. You get a fondness for something. You learn its limitations, you work around those limitations, and I made my living on a Tascam 688 when I first moved here, eight-track cassette with DBX, and if you did everything right it was fine. And you had to do everything right. But it was fine, I made network radio commercials on it. And nobody complained.

Chapter 25

Bob Clearmountain

Bob Clearmountain is an award-winning music engineer, mixer, and producer. He has worked with many prominent names in music including Bruce Springsteen (Born in the U.S.A.), The Rolling Stones ("Miss You" and "Out of Tears"), Bryan Adams, David Bowie, Paul McCartney, Robbie Williams, Toto, Bon Jovi, Altered State, and many others. Starting out as an assistant engineer, he soon became an engineer and then a producer, before becoming perhaps the record industry's first acknowledged specialist mixing engineer.

He has been nominated for six Grammy Awards, winning two, and won a Latin Grammy Award in 2007 for Best Male Pop Vocal Album for his work with engineering Ricky Martin's "MTV Unplugged". He has also been nominated for an Emmy and he has won seven TEC Awards for "Best Recording Engineer", two others for "Best Broadcast Engineer", one special "Les Paul Award," and a Monitor Award for the Rolling Stone's Voodoo Lounge pay-per-view show.

Clearmountain has earned the respect of engineers worldwide and secured a place for himself among the elite few who have entries in the audio history books. In addition to session work, he recently entered the world of product development by designing Apogee's studio management software, Session-Tools.

My name is Bob Clearmountain. I was born in Connecticut. My parents lived in Greenwich, but I was born in Stanford Hospital in 1953.

I started in audio in 1972. before that, I was in some local bands in Connecticut, just little bar bands. The last band I was in, we were doing a demo in a studio called "Media Sound" in New York, with an engineer named Michael Delugg, who had co-written some songs with our lead singers when they were in college together. So while we were doing this demo, Michael was producing the band, and the band split up for various reasons. One of them being that the lead guitar player was messing around with the lead singer's girlfriend. I was like, "Okay that's enough of this for me." I'm not an amazing enough bass player to take this seriously; I hated being on stage. I hated having lights in my eyes. I started hanging around the studio and I convinced them to hire me. I said, "Look, I think I'm going to be good at this. I'm destined to do this job—be a recording engineer." And so finally, they hired me, and that was it.

DOI: 10.4324/9781003519829-25

Figure 25.1 I think a lot of it is the nostalgia factor. And that, I understand. I completely understand there is something cool about a big 12-inch piece of black plastic. And you put it on the turntable, you wipe the dust off, and hope that it isn't too crackly and poppy. Is it nostalgia? There's definitely something to all that. I bought that console from Powerstation in 1977, the Neve 8608, so okay, who's the nostalgic one?

Figure 25.2 I would come in to do a session and I had a two-band equalizer, high and low, and I'd set the high end to 10K and set them all up all the way. And that's where I'd start. And then I'd always show up for my sessions early and collect all the Pultecs I could find in the building. There were three studios, so they were scattered all over the place. And I'd get there before anybody else and I'd stack them up, just patch them all in.

All the gear was analog of course. You know, two-inch tape, 16-track. The consoles that we had, well they were terrible basically. One was an 18-channel homemade console, the other one was a 20-channel made out of these Spectrasonics 101 cards, various bits and pieces. They were homemade console desks. There was a lot of outboard gear. We had a lot of Pultecs and LA2As, and they had some pretty great stuff—1176s, some really great outboard gear. But the consoles themselves, I would come in to do a session and I had a two-band equalizer, high and low, and I'd set the high end to 10K and set them all up all the way. And that's where I'd start. And then I'd always show up for my

Figure 25.3 I still use Pultecs. I love those on guitars and all kinds of things. I don't use LA2As but I use LA3As which are basically the same thing. I have six of them, the original LA3s. I would buy the reissues, actually. A little plug to Urei, the reissues are amazing. They are just as good if not better than the originals. I think they're a bit quieter.

Figure 25.4 It's so funny 'cause my wife, Betty Bennett, for my fiftieth birthday she wanted to get me one because everybody hears about Fairchild, she thought, "Bob would really like one of those". She spent months trying to track a really good one down. And she called my friend, Bryan Adams and asked him if he had one he wanted to sell and he goes "Yeah, I've got a couple of those...but he's going to hate that. He hates those. Don't get him one of those!" She was going to spend like 20 grand. I'm so glad that she called Bryan.

sessions early and collect all the Pultecs I could find in the building. There were three studios, so they were scattered all over the place. And I'd get there before anybody else and I'd stack them up, just patch them all in.

The inboard EQ was just too bad an equalizer, there was EQ in each module but it didn't really do anything. The console had I think 18 dB of headroom, and you had to do all these tricks to get drums to not distort.

So I used Pultecs a lot, EQP 1s and 3s, mostly. They had some MEQs and then these Lang program equalizers, and a few other bits and pieces. They didn't have API stuff yet,

Figure 25.5 I had the same problem when people get into the thing about vinyl. It kills me, these people who say, "The proper way to listen to records is on vinyl." I have a feeling that most of those people have never recorded and produced and mixed an entire record, and then gone to mastering and brought home a ref of their work and stuck it on their turntable, and what would always happen to me is I'd bring the thing home and put it on my record player and go, "So is that it? That's what I get after all that work?" and I would go in a deep depression every single time, "What the hell is that? That's all we get?" It's like the bass gets smaller, everything gets kind of smaller and crunchy sounding. You gotta be careful about how you sequence the album because the last song inside can't be real loud, you can't have a lot of top end, you have to put the ballad at the end, and that's where you want the big rock song. Because it's going slower, the velocity is less so the sound's changing as the needles going into it Give me a fuckin' break. You've got to be kidding with this, and people, you like that?

Figure 25.6 The Grammy thing is not something that I'm all that into. I have a philosophical problem with making records being some sort of competition, I never really understood that. It didn't make any sense to me. And getting the tech awards, I got a lot of tech awards which are great, and I always went along with it because they support the House Ear Institute, they support a lot of good things, and so I thought it was good from that point of view, but it kind of irked me that I was competing with my friends. It would be Ed Cherney or George Massenburg or whoever it was, and these guys are all my friends you know? I don't want to compete with them.

but yeah, whatever was around I would just plug in. They had a bunch of LA2As in the racks and they had some decent stuff. Back then it was just normal stuff to me. A lot of getting the best sound was mic placement and choosing microphones.

Oh, I should say that they didn't hire me as an engineer. They hired me as a delivery boy. I did two deliveries and then it turned out they didn't need delivery boys. They needed an assistant engineer at the time. And so, they put me right in as an assistant and I did that for a number of years. Although I started doing a number of sessions early on, they were really good and they'd put me in the deep end if somebody was sick or something like that.

The studio was great because they'd let us come in on the weekends. Mostly they did jingles and movie soundtracks during the week and R&B records at night. But the weekends, it was open. And so they would let us come in and mess around with the gear and record ourselves. Everybody, all the other engineers and assistants, we'd all write songs and played instruments and so we'd come in on the weekends and mess around. And it was great because I would try every microphone in the place and every instrument I could think of. Because they did all the music for "Sesame Street" there, and some other things like that, they had Glockenspiels and xylophones and timpani, and all kinds of stuff like that. And they had a full set of drums and guitar amps. They had all this gear that we could use, and we could try everything. And we weren't worried about screwing up somebody's session when somebody was paying, we could just make mistakes and say, "Oh that sounds terrible" and "That sounds pretty good". And we'd learn so much, and that's how we got a lot out of the gear and learned proper mic placement, like trying mics in different places and different mics on things. And when you don't have a lot of gear, you don't depend on the equipment so much.

Like the consoles, we had to crank up the input of the tape machine by 10 dB just so we could get enough headroom to record drums at a proper level because of the Spectrasonics cards. It might have just been the way the console was designed. The gain structure was very strange and it didn't really have enough headroom to handle snare drum peaks and things like that.

I still use Pultecs. I love those on guitars and all kinds of things. I don't use LA2As but I use LA3As which are basically the same thing. I have six of them, the original LA3s. I would buy the reissues, actually. A little plug to Urei, the reissues are amazing. They are just as good if not better than the originals. I think they're a bit quieter.

These limiters are what you'd use on vocals, of course. I always found the LA2s and 3s just great for vocals, they were very transparent. You'd control the level but it didn't sound like a lot of compression. I would use the Pultecs on drums. I still use the Pultecs on snare drum and guitars. Later on when we got Neves, they had the built-in E compressors, my guitar chain would always include one of those Neve compressors and a Pultec. I would adjust them for each different sound, but it'd always be going through those.

What's different now is that I don't compress what I'm recording anymore because of digital. In the old days, you had to 'cause if you did it later it brings up tape hiss; a lot of nasty noises, you know, the bad part of analog. So, nowadays, I record more flat. I still EQ to tape 'cause I actually bought the Neve console from Powerstation, the Neve I have in my studio at Berkeley Street. The 8068, I just overhauled the whole thing. But yeah, I'll EQ with that, not in the extreme, just to get it to a point that is pleasant sounding. But I never compress anything to tape. Because with digital on good converters, of course it's all apogee converters so it's the best it can be, I can compress as much as I want and EQ as much as I want in the mix and not bring up the bad analog artifacts that I always hated.

Well, like the Fairchild is a good example of analog gear I never got. I never quite understood why they cost $25,000 for a compressor that I could use maybe twice a year on something, as an effect. To me they're just not very musical-sounding devices. They look amazing, but they take up an incredible amount of room; they're huge. And they have this one sound, it seemed like a very 60s sound because obviously they were used a lot in the 60s and if you don't happen to want that, well it's great if that's what you want; it's an amazing sound. But, if you're going for something slightly different, they're pretty useless.

It's so funny 'cause my wife, Betty Bennett, for my fiftieth birthday she wanted to get me one because everybody hears about Fairchild, she thought, "Bob would really like one of those." She spent months trying to track a really good one down. And she called my friend, Bryan Adams, and asked him if he had one he wanted to sell and he goes, "Yeah, I've got a couple of those…but he's going to hate that. He hates those. Don't get him one of those!" She was going to spend like 20 grand. I'm so glad that she called Bryan.

It's still vintage gear because it's old and it does a very cool thing, but it's built for this one thing. It's not versatile. It's not like an LA3A or an 1176 where it'll just be like a standard you can use on almost anything. Or like a distressor, let's say, you can put anything through a distressor and you're going to find a good setting for it. I sat there with a Fairchild and clicked through that preset knob, "Well, that sounds like shit, click. That sounds like shit, click. What the hell is this? How do you get this to sound good?" It's funny, and every once in a while there'll be one piece of music that's, "Oh, that's pretty cool."

Vintage that was substandard at the time? I'm going to say something very controversial and 99.9 percent of people on the planet will totally disagree with me, but API mic pres, I can't figure that one out. 'Cause man, we had an API at Media Sound, and I recorded the Rolling Stones through APIs, and every time it's like, "What the hell's going on? Why does this sound so bad?" We got this API at Media Sound in the 70s, I was the one to pick it out, I saw it at an AES show and said, "Wow, what a great console that is, we need to get one of these. And this is great, and I loved it for mixing; I mixed a lot of records on it. When we tried to record on it, it was a disaster. "Why does that sound so terrible?" And everybody agreed; everybody was like, "Man, this really sounds bad." It was brand new, it was a brand-new API, so it's not like it needed recapping or something. It's just that everything sounded really sterile and kind of clinical and metallic.

They have such a great reputation; people love APIs. and I've never been able to figure out how to get a good sound coming through an API mic preamp. And I know that people are going to go, "This guy is completely full of crap." It's okay, fair enough. The PCM 41, that's a vintage piece of gear that's garbage to me. Always was. No headroom and it's really hard to set.

I was never really a big fan of analog. I remember thinking, back when there wasn't any other option, I didn't know what digital was other than digital delays but I remember thinking, "Man there's got to be something, I hope something comes along that's better than this." I remember recording bands, bands like Sheik and other bands at Powerstation, and I'd be the only one in the control room because the producers were in the band, you know. And, they'd be out there playing and everything, and I'm sitting there in the control room thinking, "Jesus, this sounds amazing, this is the best thing I've ever done. These guys are brilliant, amazing musicians. They're playing their asses off." And they come in the control room, and I play it back and they're all pretty happy, and I'm sitting there thinking in my mind, "If all you could have heard it while you were playing it, before it hit that tape..." And it just comes back a little distant, a little sort of fuzzy sounding and muddy on the bottom, and just not present. Not like the live stuff I've done so much. I guess that I really like that feeling, that the band's there playing now, in front of me. Having said that 99 percent of my favorite records were all recorded and mixed analog. I've got this huge contradiction in what I'm saying and what I'm thinking, but when I'm doing it, I like it to sound live, like the band is there.

I was an early user of digital. I had an F1 and the second record I did with Bryan Adams, "Cuts Like a Knife," we recorded digitally to it. That was a JVC system they had back then, the Umatic. So, he was really into that pretty early on, and then Robbie Robertson's first solo album, I remember somebody just bought a DAT machine and brought one back from Japan for me. That was before they came out here. I had already mixed one song to ½ inch and then this thing was brought into the studio. I said, "Great, plug it in, where's the record button?" Cool, we got to record digitally. And we ended up mastering that album, except for the first song, off the DAT, directly in the machine.

I liked it better. I mixed it to the 1/2 inch as well so when I assembled the whole album on both and we got to mastering with Bob Ludwig we did blind-listening tests and we both picked the digital. I was willing to say, "Oh forget this," but it sounded good. And now, every now and then, more so a number of years ago, people would request that I mix it 1/2 inch or 1/4 inch and so I'd rent a machine, I don't have one. And to me, going between the output of the converter and that machine, it always seemed to get smaller when I went to the analog. And I don't know if maybe the machine just wasn't aligned right, it's just that I've never had a great experience with analog. And I started in 1972.

I made some pretty good records on analog, and I do kind of miss it to be honest. I miss the tape spinnin' around and the big tapes, in fact, I have a Studer 800 that I'm restoring right now, it's in the process. Denny Buchanan from Henson Studios is rebuilding the power supplies. I got all new caps for it, new brakes, and I'd really like to be able to use it. I got a system at Berkeley Street at my recording studio where I can record on Logic, Analog, and Pro tools all at once when I want to. So I'd like to be able to start recording on both and then go through the tracks and see which sounds better, AB them. Say, "Which sounds better?" and then if something sounds better on the analog, then just bounce it over. Because there is something to it. Definitely on certain things I think it's really good. I think it's real good for guitars, in my experience, it always kind of does something nice to an electric guitar, maybe an acoustic guitar. I don't think much of it for piano, because you always end up just bringing up a lot of noise. I like a nice accurate piano sound. Unless you're going for a really unusual piano sound, then it might be great.

I had the same problem when people get into the thing about vinyl. It kills me, these people who say, "The proper way to listen to records is on vinyl." I have a feeling that most of those people have never recorded and produced and mixed an entire record, and then gone to mastering and brought home a ref of their work and stuck it on their turntable, and what would always happen to me is I'd bring the thing home and put it on my record player and go, "So is that it? That's what I get after all that work?" and I would go in a deep depression every single time, "What the hell is that? That's all we get?" It's like the bass gets smaller, everything gets kind of smaller and crunchy sounding. You gotta be careful about how you sequence the album because the last song inside can't be real loud, you can't have a lot of top end, you have to put the ballad at the end, and that's where you want the big rock song. Because it's going slower, the velocity is less so the sound's changing as the needles going into it—Give me a fuckin' break. You've got to be kidding with this, and people, you like that?

CDs are usually great. Once in a while, you'll have some funny thing happen with the CD playing and that's always been a mystery to all of us. But generally, you get a CD that's mastered properly and all the converters were good, it sounds like what I have in the studio. It's so much closer to what the original thing was supposed to be than any piece of vinyl. That's not representative of what was done in the studio. And if anybody says that it is, it's totally insane. And if there's something very romantic about it, you know, and it's got this big piece of vinyl, and I love the artwork, it was so much better. I really miss that. And you've got to understand, I grew up with vinyls. I should be prejudiced the other way.

I think a lot of it is the nostalgia factor. And that, I understand. I completely understand there is something cool about a big 12-inch piece of black plastic. And you put it on the turntable, you wipe the dust off, and hope that it isn't too crackly and poppy. Is it nostalgia? There's definitely something to all that. I bought that console from Powerstation in 1977, the Neve 8608, so okay, who's the nostalgic one?

I always loved the way that console sounded, and it's been all recapped and the stereo bus is balanced now. Fred Hill came in back in '96 and he redid the whole thing. And now, I just had him come back and redo it again and finish the job. It's fantastic, it just sounds so great. And I have an SSL 4000, and for recording, the Neve beats it, really. It's got better preamps. Everybody knows that Neve preamps, those 70s preamps are amazing sounding. And that combination of them mixing on the 4k, the SSL, it's just great. That's what we always did at Powerstation, too, we had a 4k there and I would record on the Neve and mix on the 4K. I bought my favorite. I got to the point where I was lucky enough to be able to go back.

Changes in the business? Well, obviously the internet's changed everything. Some good ways, some bad ways. There's the whole downloading thing; it's kind of messed up the business a bit. For some reason, people think that music should be free and why music should be any different than anything else in the world I don't understand when people work so hard. That kind of bothers me. That's a whole 'nother topic, but all these people think music should just be free, and they're saying, "The rock stars got plenty of money and the record executives have plenty of money, they don't need it." Well, it's not that. It's no problem for them. The rock stars, people buy their concert tickets, right? Well, what about the recording studios? What about the booking people and the accountants and the runners and the assistant engineers and the engineers and the people that work at the pressing plants? And all these many people that make thirty, forty thousand dollars a year if they're lucky. Just the working class people who've now lost their jobs because you think that music should be free. What if someone thought your product should be free and now you're out of a job? Well, that's what's happened. And people don't realize that, that those are the people—the working-class people—that have been really hurt by it. And a lot of my friends who want to be engineers have said, "I can't even make it as an engineer anymore because there's not enough work. And nobody can pay anything," so now I'm selling insurance, or I'm doing some other thing; and that's not working out too well, either.

So nobody makes money on records anymore. You just don't if you're not a touring band, and that's really difficult too because it costs a fortune to put a band on tour. How do you balance that out? How do you do it? The only way you can make it as an artist is to tour and get your own following. But you have to do it on a shoestring budget, and it's practically impossible. And somehow, bands do it. Some of ‘em do.

I do a lot of mixing for people, now that all this is happening, that artists have to tour more to make money, they are always on the road, so it's really hard to get them to come to a mix. We record an album and as soon as they're finished recording, they are off on tour to help pay for it. So, often I've got a mix up and I'll call them wherever they are on their cell phone and I'll go, "Okay can you plug in your Mac, do you have an internet connection?" Okay, and so I'll stream the mix to them, or I'll send them an AAC or something like that. More and more I've been streaming mixes to people and I couldn't do it before, I can get an immediate response.

Putting the phone up to the monitors worked okay for a jingle, for a pop record it doesn't work so well. And it still doesn't sound perfect to me. It's this pretty heavy digital compression. But it works well enough that somebody can judge a mix, and that's a really good thing. If something has to get to mastering the next day we can post it on our server or post it on the mastering server, and that happens all the time. We're always sending files. And that's always helpful when it works. Doesn't always work.

It's funny because I'm one of those guys where if you unplugged the internet, I'd be fine with that because there's so much crap, so much garbage you hear about; terrorists and pedophiles meeting each other on the internet. You just want to unplug the thing, right? At the same time, our business would have a rough time when the T1 goes down, I'm like "Uh oh, what do I do now?"

It's true, we're totally spoiled with it. With Bryan Adams it's so funny; I'd mix him, did you know Bryan still makes records? He does pretty well in Europe. So he lives in London and most the time he's out on the road, too. And so I'll be mixing for him and streaming to him, and then he's on Ichat. He doesn't even pick up the phone, he just types me little messages on Ichat, and I go, "How's that?" And so I can talk to him on the talkback, you know, and then he can send a message back.

The last piece of analog gear I purchased was probably a distressor. I haven't bought much lately, you kind of get to a point where you say, what else do I need? The Neve console, a bunch of mics. I actually got a really good AKG C24 and a couple of M49s, but I bought a bunch of mics for this studio that we built. Some KM86s and KM84s, this Neumann called an SM2 that not many people know about. It's a stereo, smaller capsule, tube mic, which is really nice. On Ebay, I scored an AKG D12, for bass drum, which is wonderful—more of a bass drum mic. A bunch of 57s, 58s, I just went out and bought a ton of microphones.

Well, something about the schools. There are these schools, recording schools, and I won't mention any names, but it's surprising to me how little these guys know about recording when they come out of these schools. They paid them an incredible amount of money and there's very few jobs available when they get out of school. And most of them don't seem to know that much. I got an email from a guy, not in this country, a German guy who went to a recording school in Germany and he said he was in such shock when he came out and realized that word clock was an important thing because they never even mentioned it. They mentioned something about it but they didn't explain what it was and they didn't explain about time code, especially now that everything is going more to the post-production era. I'm mixing more and more things for concert DVDs.

I did the Stones film where it's about getting everything in sync. Especially when you're on film because there's pull-ups and pull-downs and this really complicated stuff that you've got to know. And especially if you're at that level, you don't just become an engineer, if you're lucky you get to become an assistant engineer and that's when you really have to know all of this stuff because the engineer usually doesn't want to deal with it. They figure, "Oh the assistant, you've got that covered, right?" The whole time-code thing and locking the thing up and they've got to know this stuff coming out. And they don't. It's really weird. You know, they'll know signal flow and they'll know how to mic a guitar amp, maybe, and they'll know how to create a drum loop, okay great, there's nothing wrong with that, you should know all that stuff, but that under-the-hood technical stuff, it's really important.

Some of the schools are really very good. You take University of Miami, for instance, three of my last assistants came from there, and they were all amazing, and they all have gone on to have their own careers which is great, but you have to actually be a musician to even get into the recording thing. That's the other thing, is that to be a recording engineer you've got to know some music. You gotta know something, cause you get to edit things, you've got to know how to count beats and know what key the song's in, just basic stuff. And a lot of these guys, they pay a ton of money, and it's amazing what they don't teach them, and you just wonder what are they doing? Why are they charging all this money to these poor kids, just ripping 'em off. And I get schools asking me to lecture sometimes and I'd like to, I really would, but I don't trust that they are doing their part of it. I'm not going to go lecture at some school that is ripping their students off. I don't want to be part of that. Not only that, but I'm terrible at speaking in front of people. They make you really nervous. That's why I'm a mixer, 'cause I don't like being onstage.

The Grammy thing is not something that I'm all that into. I have a philosophical problem with making records being some sort of competition, I never really understood that. It didn't make any sense to me. And getting the tech awards, I got a lot of tech awards which are great, and I always went along with it because they support the House Ear Institute, they support a lot of good things, and so I thought it was good from that point of view, but it kind of irked me that I was competing with my friends. It would be Ed Cherney or George Massenburg or whoever it was, and these guys are all my friends you know? I don't want to compete with them. It's a friendly competition but I was usually happier when I didn't win 'cause I didn't have to go up there; and I was always happy if someone else would win, 'cause I'd won enough of those things and just the competition thing kind of bothered me.

Chapter 26

Gene Eichelberger

Gene Eichelberger began recording in 1959 in Baldwin Sound in Mechanicsburg, Pennsylvania while working on a radio station in Carlisle. He moved to Nashville in 1969 to work for Wayne Moss at Cinderella Sound, where he recorded Steve Miller, Area Code 615, and cut Anne Murray's "Snowbird". After moving to Quadrafonic Sound in 1970 at the request of Elliot Mazur, Eichelberger worked with Neil Young, Joan Baez, Grand Funk Railroad, John Hiatt, the Pointer Sisters, Billy Joe Thomas, Dan Fogelberg, Buffy Sainte-Marie, Bob Seger, Johnny Cash, James Gang, and many others. Eichelberger was also the first engineer at the Bennett House, where he worked with Jewel, Amy Grant, and Janie Frickey, to name a few. His credits also include live recordings of Neil Young and the Grateful Dead at Winterland, and over the course of his long and distinguished career, he also worked with Steve Goodman, Steve Forbert, Price Jones, Kris Kristofferson, J.J. Cale, Dobie Gray, Van Stephenson, Tammy Comstock, Jimmy Hall, Roger Whittaker, Cat Stevens, Carol Hall, and Bash 'n The Code.

Gene Eichelberger passed away in October of 2018 at the age of 77.

I'm Gene Eichelberger. I was born December 27th, 1940. Well, I got hepatitis my senior year of high school, which was when I really started in audio, because I tore a Silvertone amplifier apart. And that's before they were using permanent magnets. They were using the coil that was the magnet for the speaker as a coil for the power supply of amplifiers. Therefore, if you cut the wrong wire and got to it, you would get 300–400 volts across your fingertips, with just enough amperage to hurt you—not to hurt you bad. I did that the first time out. I have an electric fence, it hurts you but it won't kill you because it pulses; that amplifier didn't pulse, it was just on. It didn't kill me or hurt me, it just scared me. That's why I got the National Radio course; to figure out things.

I took a course while I was home in bed for the whole senior year with this hepatitis, a National Radio Institute course on audio, on how to fix things, not how to record but how to fix an amplifier or build things like that. So, that's when I started, '58–59. And I fiddled with it for a long time. I went to work at a radio station. I was a bad announcer because I hadn't had any experience. But I also worked my way in the next couple years up to having a first-class FCC license so I could operate transmitters legally, or get a job

DOI: 10.4324/9781003519829-26

Figure 26.1 Whatever was on the console is what you had, that's what you used. There was some console equalization, like highs and lows. A lot of radio consoles didn't have any, you moved the microphone to make it "different". Which is what you still ought to do first, and then deal with equalization, 'cause you can fix things since you have the ability to have that now. But you could fix a lot of problems by putting the microphone in the right place.

Figure 26.2 Well you know how mutes are all automated now? Back then we cut tape to make a dead stop from having echo, 'cause you didn't have mutes that could turn off, or you can't get enough people around the console to turn off 24 tracks at once. Sometimes we used cassette boxes taped together and just pushed them so they'd push all the mutes down. They were switches, so we ganged them together using the tape-cassette boxes.

at a station that needed somebody as their chief engineer, who really didn't have to fix a whole lot. The law then was, if a station was directional they had to have a first-class licensed person on the job. So, that's what I did and that's when I started. And also back then, there were high school bands that needed to be recorded or church choirs or whoever to record, and I used the studio's Ampex 601 or 602s to record the groups. That was really my first recording experience.

I stayed in radio on and off for quite a while. I worked in radio even when I was working at a studio, I was working part-time for a radio station when I was at a four-track

Figure 26.3 And then I went to work for Elliot Mazur as an engineer on the road with this truck, "His Master's Wheels" just recording different groups, and did the Grateful Dead. That was a wild week at Winterland. So it was a lot of recording going on, and there was a lot of crazy things going on. Just had to not set your drink down anywhere, you had your cup in your hand all the time. And if you did, don't drink out of it, 'cause you might not remember where you were the next day. You might lose your mind.

Figure 26.4 At Quadrafonic, there was some outboard gear. I also had my own outboard gear, I used to carry a rack of equipment around which had a Dean Jenson stereo preamp in it. We had a variety of kinds of preamps, in addition to the Quad Eight board. But, they changed that board to an MCI, which is when everything died quality-wise. It had VCAs in it, and it didn't sound nearly as good as the preamps, forget the EQ that was on it, but it just didn't sound as good. And when you listened to the cue system preamp prefader, you got your good sound. But then when you went to the board, which is after the fader, it was awful. It didn't have any fullness or quality to it compared to the Jenson.

studio in Mechanicsburg called Baldwin Sound. It had an Ampex four-track and two Ampex 440s, which were a step above 601s. The first console was an old Collins radio console, but Don bought a custom board that was made up of different parts that were custom-built by an engineer from South Carolina. He wasn't an audio engineer, he was a technician.

Figure 26.5 The board we had was a Quad Eight board at Quadrafonic. It had highs and lows and a little bit of mid, I mean it depends on where you go for mids. But it had mostly highs. But it did have some 3k and 5k, but you could only get it to one frequency at a time—2k or 5k or 10k or 12k. It was a good board. It had good preamps in it, and it sounded good. That was the best thing about that board; it sounded good. It worked good most of the time and it was well-made.

There were a couple of UA-1176s which I wish I kept. I had a couple of them but that's the only outboard gear there was. There were no amplifiers, no preamps, no EQ, nothing. Whatever was on the console is what you had, that's what you used. There was some console equalization, like highs and lows. A lot of radio consoles didn't have any, you moved the microphone to make it "different", which is what you still ought to do first, and then deal with equalization, 'cause you can fix things since you have the ability to have that now. But you could fix a lot of problems by putting the microphone in the right place.

After Mechanicsburg, I went to Nashville. In Mechanicsburg Don had a lot of business in the beginning, but then all the business he had gotten in quit because he was not out promoting it. So, everybody, all his friends had made their records, and now six months later he doesn't have any business. I get let go, he wants me to hang around because I do the maintenance, but he can't afford to have me full-time. So I found a job in Carlisle, Pennsylvania at a radio station. I worked there for about six months because after six months of me working at the radio station and at the studio, I figured out that I gotta quit one of these jobs. I didn't want to quit the radio station, but recording is what I wanted to do. I had done radio for ten years now and I don't need any more radio. So I stayed on at the radio station, and I actually quit the radio station as soon as I could and worked at Baldwin Sound, full-time after he got enough business. And there was little or no EQ at Baldwin Sound, you had a little bit in the console but not a lot. It was like a 14-input unit where you could record your drums, and we never filled it up.

I stayed there until 1969. In "68 I came to Nashville looking around at Wayne Moss', at Cinderella Sound and got a job. Three months later I moved down here in the fall of '69 and worked for Wayne. He had an old Collins radio board which had three channels and highs and lows, which was better than some.

We were recording to an Ampex eight-track. I went from four-track to eight-track. Steve Miller's "Five" was worked on there, and Anne Murray's "Snowbird" was recorded there and mixed there. Also Area Code 615, which was all the hot, big, number one record guys, the musicians, that was done there. That's how I met Norbert Putnam, David Briggs, and Elliot Mazur. They were part of the 615 group. Elliot wasn't, but he was the producer of "Harvest", Neil Young's album. That weekend, Elliot asked me to come in and do some work for him, and I did, because the guy they had hired, he could wire but he couldn't put a system together and make it work. So, they hired me, and I went to work for Norbert, David, and Elliot at Quadrafonic Sound. That was the beginning of '70.

Well it was a great studio because we'd try anything, and since we were people who tried anything, we would get people to build things for us to try them out. We had the first parametric equalizer. It was made by George Massenburg and Burgess McNeil. They were up in Baltimore, thereabouts and they'd come down and we'd try it out; they'd change it and we'd try it out more. Anyhow. That's when we started getting peripheral gear. And I built direct boxes using transformers, UTC transformers so that we could hook them up to record out of a guitar or out of a power amp, whichever you felt like doing. This is before there were any direct boxes that you could buy. I built them. That was in 1970.

Equalizers weren't showing up then. They were thinking about it. They weren't doing it yet. The board we had was a Quad Eight board at Quadrafonic. It had highs and lows and a little bit of mid, I mean it depends on where you go for mids. But it had mostly highs. But it did have some 3k and 5k, but you could only get it to one frequency at a time—2k or 5k or 10k or 12k. It was a good board. It had good preamps in it, and it sounded good. That was the best thing about that board; it sounded good. It worked good most of the time and it was well-made. Dean Jenson had designed it, and his stuff worked.

We had two stereo EMTs. We also had a room in the basement. It really wasn't great but it was a room and it was in the basement and it was echo, and that's the way we had echo. We could make it longer or shorter by moving the microphone or the speaker. Depending on how close you had it, would be a shorter time.

I don't really remember everything that happened in the basement. It was a place that some people who were married thought they could get away with cheating on their wives down there but there was no way out. If somebody came looking for you, you were had. Not to mention, they're in a room with a microphone. You'd be listened to at the time, and you never knew who was using the chamber. Well, it was an interesting few years.

We did a lot of demos and masters at Quadrafonic. I mixed Grand Funk there, because I had recorded it at another studio that had a board that I didn't like. It was at the beginning of digital and the board's EQ changed. So nothing you set would ever be reliable. You had what you had while you had it. And then it could change while you were using it. So, that's why I went back to Quadrafonic to mix Grand Funk, the "Phoenix" album. And we were doing John Hiatt then, we were doing "Home Free" with Dan Fogelburg, which was studio musicians, and we did "Harvest"; that was the first album that was done there. And we did Joan Baez's "Drove Old Dixie Down". And a couple of other albums with her. And she was interesting. She was Joan Baez. Whatever that says, she was just off the wall.

At Quadrafonic, there was some outboard gear. I also had my own outboard gear. I used to carry a rack of equipment around which had a Dean Jenson stereo preamp in it. We had a variety of kinds of preamps, in addition to the Quad Eight board. But they changed that board to an MCI, which is when everything died quality-wise. It had VCAs in it, and it didn't sound nearly as good as the preamps. Forget the EQ that was on it, but it just didn't sound as good. And when you listened to the cue system preamp prefader, you got your good sound. But then when you went to the board, which is after the fader, it was awful. It didn't have any fullness or quality to it compared to the Jenson.

When they started bringing in some different types of outboard gear into Quadrafonic, my favorites were the Massenberg and Burgess stuff, the EQ. It was good except for the power supply. It would keep shutting off. It would just heat up too much.

We also had LA2As and 1176s. When they were available they got bought. One thing with Norbert Putnam was he would try it. If it was new and he had used it in another studio we would have one at Quad real soon.

That was nice. And we had Dolbys right away before anybody else did. We were getting $150 an hour, and then with the Dolbys he would charge $165 an hour. So we were very busy at that price, and we would be using them, the Dolbys, and charging extra for them. About the time everybody else was buying Dolbys and raising their price, we lowered the price of the studio to $150 an hour because we had paid for them earlier in the game and we were down below everybody else's price at that time.

The LA2 was used a lot. The 1176; we had a couple of them. And LA4s or LA3s. They worked good. We had some stuff from Paul Buff from Allison. We had them because we could. They worked; that was a part that worked. We would generally use them to turn things off that were noisy when the signal wasn't coming through, like guitars that had buzzes and hums. They would typically be put on a track to stop that noise from being around the whole time. Or on drums, just to turn things off, to kill the leakage.

And we used the compressors on bass and on guitars—electric guitars to change the sound by compressing it more. The LA4s, the LA2s were used a lot on basses to make the signal better when they were being used so the signal would stay up where you could hear it in your face more. I'm an "in your face" kind of recorder and mixer.

We didn't use digital delay a lot in the beginning. We still mostly used tape slap. Used the EMTs all the time. We had an electronic way to change the settings on them, it usually had a wheel on it but you could get a motor on it so that it would change it to what you wanted from a distance. And we had the ability to change it to what it worked for the song. Mostly those EMTs were my echo. Because that room echo wasn't as good as we told everybody. So, we'd just put on the EMT instead. Like the Fogelberg records, we mostly used the EMTs for the echo. We might have tape-delayed it sometimes, but not much.

Some de-essers that started coming in were pretty bad, like the Orbans. They made it big in some people's minds, but they were not used in my mind because they didn't really get rid of what it was supposed to do.

In about '74 I went on the road with Neil Young. So I was out there being a maintenance man on his Master's Wheels truck, it had two MM1000s. We had an MM1000 at Quad, then we kept changing it up to Ampex something else. But when I was on the road with Neil we had a Neve board, a little sidecar which was like a ten or 12-channel sidecar that we used to add more channels. And then I went to work for Elliot Mazur as an engineer on the road with this truck, "His Master's Wheels" just recording different groups, and did the Grateful Dead. That was a wild week at Winterland. So it was a lot of recording going on, and there was a lot of crazy things going on. Just had to not set your drink down anywhere, you had your cup in your hand all the time. And if you did, don't drink out of it. 'Cause you might not remember where you were the next day. You might lose your mind.

I was only on the road about six months. Just enough to like it a lot, but not like it at all. Just wanted to go back home to Quad. So anyway, while I was away from Quad there was another engineer working, and David Rubinson was bringing the Pointer Sisters there to mix something and to record something else and he was thinking I was going to be the engineer so that's pretty much how I got back into working at Quad, because I was requested to be the guy that's engineering the Pointer Sisters. Anyway that's how I got back to Quad and then I stayed there for quite a while after that.

I was really freelance all during this time 'cause I wasn't working, I was just there. Engineers are the last one on the list when it comes to budget, because you as an engineer aren't negotiating with the record company for your pay, you're negotiating with the producer who wants to hire you because you're better than somebody else. But you sort of have to say, "Hey, this is how much I charge, will you pay this?" And you negotiate to get what you can get. Instead of the producer, he's working for the record company. And he negotiates with the record company and gets as much as he can to produce a song or an album. So I negotiated. I tried to get my pay up from $7 an hour to 8 to 9 to 10 to 15 to 25 to 40, and I did. But you worked your way up to that. It didn't just happen because I had figured out that whoever was producing was getting like $50 an hour if you are working by the hour. Or he's getting $5,000 to do the album or more depending on the way things work out. And you were working for $7.50, which was hard to take, because you were doing it as the engineer, because you were making the sounds, you were doing the punch-ins, you were making everybody's voice sound like they wanted it to sound and you thought it should sound. So, it was a lot of negotiating in those days and it still is from what I can tell. Negotiating is a good thing.

I haven't been around engineers that are working for studios these days lately because I'm not really in the business anymore. But I know that George Massenburg works a lot at Blackbird, he's got a room there. But there are engineers who are working there full-time, getting X amount while the producer's working there and they're getting their amount. Then there's other engineers coming in to work for whatever they're getting. But the guy that's working for the studio is still probably making $10 an hour.

He's hoping to get past all that, into a freelance situation where he will make $30 an hour or $40 or $50. So, I don't know what it's like now here, but it's still a negotiating thing. And the guy that's working for the studio; the engineer, he's close to low man on a totem pole. And that's how it is.

I was working a lot at other studios. And then Norbert Putnam built Bennett House, and I went to work for him then to help him build that studio. Went to Montreal, to buy the A-Range and to see if it would work for what we wanted to do there. And it would, so Norbert bought that, but I went up there to tell him it'll work, came back and then we built the Bennett House, which was a studio in a house, and a room that really wasn't any good so we started recording in the house. Which was where some of Amy Grant's things were cut because her producers, Mike Blanton and Dan Harell wanted to record in the house. So, that's what we did. Sounded great in there. It had two MCIs that were locked together.

Then we got the, what I think is a little better, the Studer 800s. And, so we were locking two machines together. We started out with the MCIs but then we were locking a Studer and an MCI together.

We had two Studer two-tracks. And we had half-inch Ampex ATR-100s, lovely machine, great sounding machine. If you made it on that it would sound better when you played it back.

We also had a variety of outboard gear, there were limiters, equalizers, that e900 stereo five-band parametric and we had that there. So, that's where I did most of my work with Bob Montgomery as a producer. Did a lot of albums, Janie Frickey.

Some of Jewel's stuff was done on 24-track digital, and we worked with her and her mother. Ben Keith was the producer, her mother was the person who was in charge of Jewel, so to speak. Jewel was only 19 then and the songs that were recorded on the 24-track Sony were recorded at Neil Young's ranch. We added some guitars and we added a couple of things but we mixed them at Sound Shop, and the ones that were on the eight-track A-DATS, we did at Omni. And we did some guitar stuff there with her playing live, and that we did at Omni in Studio B.

Some other interesting things from back then? Well you know how mutes are all automated now? Back then, we cut tape to make a dead stop from having echo, 'cause you didn't have mutes that could turn off, or you can't get enough people around the console to turn off 24 tracks at once. Sometimes we used cassette boxes taped together and just pushed them so they'd push all the mutes down. They were switches, so we ganged them together using the tape-cassette boxes.

As I mentioned earlier, positioning of the microphones was very important to get what you needed before you had EQ. That's probably changed because most people don't do that anymore, but good engineers do. That's one of the first things you do, move the microphone or change the microphone to give you the sound you're looking for, which you can do using microphone technique.

Chapter 27

Fred Breitberg

Fred Breitberg began his career in audio as an apprentice engineer in 1969 at Universal Recording Corp./Audio Finishers Recording in Chicago. Within a short period of time, he was able to acquire his own budgeted clientele and began to offer his services as first chair engineer to clients around the city. During this time Breitberg also did a great deal of location recording from classical projects to big band and rock/funk, as well as gaining experience in precision mass tape duplication and disc mastering. Over the past five decades, Breitberg has worked staff and freelance positions at Chess Records Recording Studios, Curtom Records (Curtis Mayfield's recording studio), and at nearly every other major recording studio in Chicago. In addition to his studio and audio restoration work, Breitberg currently provides audio services in many custom producers' environments and does audio post-production and mixing for the Owned & Operated ABC and CBS TV stations in Chicago. Breitberg's work has garnered numerous Grammy nominations and he has been awarded three Emmys for his audio work in TV. Breitberg resides with his family in Lincolnwood, IL.

I'm Fred Breitberg, born in Chicago. I started in audio in 1969…Halloween.

I thought I wanted to get into the music industry. I had a cousin who produced commercials for J Walter Thompson. Actually it was my cousin's husband. And I asked him about things and he said, "Well you know, I have a friend in the recording studio that I use all of the time, and I'll see if there's any openings there." And so he got me an interview, and there was an opening for an assistant engineer, and I was trained as an apprentice.

The studio was called Audio Finishers. It was a studio that two fellas that had been very successful at Universal Recording Studios here had broken away and taken their clients to the new studio: the time-honored tradition of stealing clients. They had, at that time, the hottest studio in town. They were very busy, and I signed on as an apprentice engineer.

They showed me how to check a board so that I could make sure the mics were working. They showed me where they wanted the mics, what type of mics they were, what

DOI: 10.4324/9781003519829-27

Figure 27.1 They showed me how to check a board so that I could make sure the mics were working. They showed me where they wanted the mics, what type of mics they were, what they were used for, what kind of cabling to use, how to set up the chairs, the headphones, the music stands. Everything there is to do to facilitate a music recording. I would show up regularly at six in the morning, get ready for a nine o'clock start. I was there until 1 in the morning doing the after-hour stuff. Setting up the tape machine, the console, tape op, patching.

Figure 27.2 I don't hear anybody really thinking this way, but I think air and tape are the same thing. I think they're both mediums for the storage of sound. Air, I feel, has an infinite capacity for dynamics, but a complete inability to store the stuff. Tape has a pretty limited capacity for dynamics, but stores the stuff.

they were used for, what kind of cabling to use, how to set up the chairs, the headphones, the music stands. Everything there is to do to facilitate a music recording. I would show up regularly at six in the morning, and get ready for a nine o'clock start. I was there until 1 in the morning doing the after-hour stuff. Setting up the tape machine, the console, tape op, patching.

We had an Electrodyne four bus console. It had two-band EQ. It was an awful sounding board. We had 16 modules. We were the first 16-track studio in town. They had an eight-track, but they were planning ahead, so they had a 16-track so you could get 16 tracks back in the mix. And I think there were one or two reverb returns outside of that.

Figure 27.3 I think it's real important that the two most important things I think for students especially are "learn to listen" and "don't turn the speakers up with the faders". Realize what headroom is for. Understand distortion. Hit the limiter so hard that it crunches and distorts and it's awful so you know how to work it right.

Figure 27.4 And then they go to work and they got the Kelso going, they got the room going, and I'm telling you, it sounded great. I say, "Guys, it sounds great". They say "thanks". No, you're screwed, nothing sounds great here, let's check this tape. Sure enough, we got it out of there, cut a reel, put it on a 24-track in the other room. It was awful.

And they had an EMT. It was a small unit. Within four or five months, they actually went back to Universal and leased it from the owner with an option to buy. So it was in a couple months that I was at Universal doing the same thing.

At that time, Universal was the biggest studio in Chicago. There were only four or five studios. And all of the bad sessions that nobody wanted were where I cut my teeth at night, all the rock stuff, all the R&B, all of this stuff that the regular guys didn't want to do. Remember, guys like us came through the whole rock thing while we could do classical and jazz and all this stuff. We have a solid foundation in rock and R&B and that sort of thing. When we were students' age, the guys that were ahead of us had no rock sensibilities, there were only a few of them that were sort of forced into it. Most of these guys didn't want to work with those people.

Figure 27.5 When I started freelancing more, and I'd go into these studios that were Mackie-based studios and they said, "Listen Freddie, I'm sorry, I don't even have the Neve or SSL you're used to." I go, "Look, it's just a bigger challenge because I'm not here because of what I do there. I've got to do that here now, don't I?" You can do that here? I can try.

Figure 27.6 I had guys who worked five or six years in post-production begging to be a music guy. I cut into the music scene in two years. Everybody was pissed at me. I had no friends here, but I was aggressive and I had clients, and when you have clients, you're the guy. Hear that? And that's always been the name of the game, and I understood that. I had my first client in six weeks… I had my first unassisted session in six weeks.

Our mentors really weren't interested in rock at all. They were into orchestral and jazz, and that's all they knew how to do. In fact, I don't even think they were that interested in it anymore. So I learned a classic technique from guys that had come up in the 40s and 50s and 60s.

Murray Allen eventually became the owner of Universal, and I was sort of his second. There was another guy, Bob Kidder, who was a big R&B engineer in this town. Bruce Swedien would come through, so I would set up for Bruce. Bruce and I didn't talk too much. He told me what his two setups were and he'd say, "Freddie it's the A setup"—it'd be the A setup complete with the faders right where he didn't have to move them.

Once I studied you I could pretty much do you. And so Bruce liked me a lot from that standpoint. And there was a guy named Doug Brand who did a bunch of R&B stuff. He was quite a good engineer. I'll say the two best guys were Bruce and Doug of the guys I mentioned.

Later on I worked with Malcolm Chisolm and it was funny because Malcolm I had known since I was a sophomore in high school. He was the only guy in the neighborhood with a V12 Ferrari, that didn't work. And so we hung out. All the kids, my crowd of kids, would hang out in the alley where he was fixing his Ferrari, and I sort of got to know him, but I didn't realize what he did and I wasn't that deep into the recording thing then. It was only later when I got into the business I realized, oh this guy Malcolm is, you know, Malcolm. We actually worked together at Chess for about three years. Malcolm was there. If I was working with you today, I'd steal whatever band that you had, you know what I'm saying? It didn't matter to me who you were—if you had stuff that was good and was provocative to me, not only would I assimilate it but I'd work with it. Sometimes I expand on it. Sometimes. I was a heavy chameleon.

I learned a lot from watching these guys—watching what worked, watching what didn't, and seeing all that breadth of 40–60 piece orchestras. You know, the three- and four-piece sections where, "Hey, you know where Jimmy Reed was last night?" "No where?" "Jail." Well, they threw him in jail so they'd know where to find him when they needed him today for the session. And that was a typical way of making sure your blues guy was gonna be there in the 60s.

Remember, this is the city of Chess. And the board at Universal was an original Putnam board. It was a 16 by 8 bus console, four dry, and four wet. And there were still three tracks lying around. By then, we'd use the three tracks for reverb delay. And we had chambers there and it was just a fabulous facility and they got three music rooms. Then there was a point in time where I was the only assistant there, so I would get there, set up two music rooms, sit between the two as the sessions started, then when everybody's rolling run back into another studio and edit Time Life tapes until I got the first phone call to make the copies, and I'd be making the copies, then I'd always get lunch. We can still do all that with lunch. Later on in the 80s and 90s, you could never get out for lunch. Everybody wanted to work through lunch and it was like, what do you order for lunch? What can I eat with one hand?

I was at Universal two and halfish years. I left there and I went to a facility of Sony that they actually owned called Tono Tapes. They're a big duplicator. Reel-to-reel duplicator, cassette duplicator, eight-track tape duplicator. They had all of that. And I was in charge of the reel-to-reel line. I had two women working for me. I've never supervised anybody in my life. I was doing some location recording in churches. It was Christmas carol time, and I could just make more money doing it. So I'd always meet the guy with the gear—the guy had those rollers that you took the groceries off the grocery truck, roll those out of the station wagon and down come the 440s and on to a thing and off you go. And four mics with a Shure mixer, I'd go home and edit on a Studer, deliver to Universal next day for mastering, go to the next place. So I was doing that. Then when that ran out, it made more sense from my standpoint to go to the Tono Tape gig and keep doing the evening thing I was doing. So I did that. And then a job at Chess opened up and I went and got that, as a mastering engineer. Never done it before.

Here, production audio was the entry-level thing. Mastering was already taken seriously enough. Ironically, now the money is in post-production. I had guys who worked five or six years in post-production begging to be a music guy. I cut into the music scene in two years. Everybody was pissed at me. I had no friends here, but I was aggressive and I had clients, and when you have clients you're the guy. Hear that? And that's always been the name of the game, and I understood that. I had my first client in six weeks... I had my first unassisted session in six weeks. One here one there.

That was before Universal when I first started. As soon as I knew I could do a mic setup I knew I could do a session, how hard is that?

At Universal in the big room, it was 16 track by the time I got there because once Audio Finishers got a 16, Chess got a 16-track, Universal got a 16-track. Everybody had it by then. An MM1000. Once I figured out how to give them auto input on the punch in, they never touched it again. Because you didn't have auto input on that, so how do you punch in? Accidentally found that bias is the same as input. It seemed to work and they seemed to love it. I was probably the first person in town that ever punched in a whole band on a 16-track on a... well a 24-track, but an M79. You know, because once auto input, I was done editing. You know, I'm a really good tape editor, but I couldn't cut two-inch tape to save my life. I mean I could cut it and I could make the edit right, and occasionally I could get it seamless enough to not pop across, but I was not that good at that.

So I began punching bands in, and once they got that, they loved it because you gave them the best opportunity to be at the same tempo because they had to play along with themselves in the headphones. And you had immediate knowledge of "Can I save this take?" And so I developed that technique. Actually before timecode came in you'd use tone to lock up, a 60-cycle tone. And you couldn't make a 30 out of a 60 because you had the tone issue. So I would take and record the tone, and we could lock up two 16's, but we weren't using timecode for a film lock. So, first or second it wouldn't matter, but what I'd do is I'd take my client in, I'd punch in the front, where do you want to go to, here? Okay, and I'd offset it, figure out where the offset is, and I'd punch that in. The worst thing that would ever happen is I'd have to go back and maybe re-punch in a cymbal or something, and then I'd take the tone and lay it across on a seamless 30.

What else did they have at Universal? They had the second studio that had almost no outboard. A couple of Urei 1176s, They had a couple of 1176's and then 1176LN's got into the thing. An EMT, a couple of Pultecs, a high pass, low pass. Virtually nothing—a couple of compressors. And when I got to Chess, there was a rack of Kepexes. I thought I had died and gone to heaven, and they had a Cooper Time Cube. What a piece of shit, but they did it. I used that mostly for pre-delay or occasional guitar effects. It was Chess so I was having fun doing anything I wanted to do. I used to take a varispeed tape recorder and crank it, "EEERRREEET, ARRRRARRRR" I love that. Our second room had some kind of rotary board, but by the time I got there they already bounced it out for another Electrodyne. They loved these Electrodynes I don't know why. It's a funny thing. And so they had the Electrodyne in B, and then they had a C room, which was another custom Urei board. And they had an old film side, but I never went over there. For mixing consoles we were monitoring on four A7s or four 844s. That was the typical monitoring then. So it was a crap shoot all the time. And we'd have a little speaker that you could work with, but the sound was there.

I was at Chess for two and a half, three years. I closed Chess. Somebody opened it. I closed it. Someone did the first session there. I did the last session there. It was an R&B session. It was an overdub, a big string and brass overdub. And they came in and said, "We're closing it." I said, "Our client is here. He's got these musicians out here.

Do you mind terribly if we just finish today?" They were gracious enough. Chess at that point was owned by GRP tapes and records. And Chess had moved in 68 from 2120 to 320 East 21st Street. And so by the time I got there, they had a Telefunken Console. Very tubby, weird sounding board. Malcolm took eight or ten Urei mic pre's that were hanging out and stuck them in front. The transistors were breaking down on this board, and so we had the tube mic pre's in front. And then we had a Langevin tube console.

I did a Neil Young session on that board where they came in Thanksgiving of 74 looking at studios. They walk in incognito thing. We were doing a session in the big room, studio manager comes in, "I don't know who he is but you know you got to give him a tour." So I give them a tour, I show them the B room. The B room at Chess was a famous room. Trident modeled the room after it. It was a well-known room, and a lot of hit records came out of it. And this board was a 16 by Langevin with four equalizers—four two-band equalizers for the whole board. Malcolm didn't believe in EQ, he said, 'Move the mic'. And so they came in and they wanted to work there. Elliot Mazur was his producer/engineer, Elliot is a great engineer. Came in, they brought a 16-track, because I told them this is eight-track. So, they had a 16 track there that Monday. They had a Neve console there. We had the weirdest speakers in the world because Malcolm had blown up the tri-amped Spectrasonic speakers, JBL Spectrasonic tri-amped, blew them up one day, which is a whole other story. Put out the crossovers. So they were crazy strange—no bottom end except if you knew where the bottom was, you could hear so well. You could put the pan on the organ with the reverb on the same track and never be wrong, but you didn't know where the bottom was. This guy says, "You gotta listen to these speakers because they're gonna fuck you up". And I go, "Yeah, you're right. These are weird."

And then they go to work and they got the Kelso going, they got the room going, and I'm telling you, it sounded great. I say, "Guys, it sounds great". They says "thanks". No, you're screwed, nothing sounds great here, let's check this tape. Sure enough, we got it out of there, cut a reel, put it on a 24-track in the other room. It was awful. So they, over-reacting, have another Kelso flown now, eight MBM 4s, power amps…and we moved into a room across the hall because they still wanted to use the room. Okay? What an outstanding opportunity to hear the studio, one day in this control room, one day in that one because it didn't matter what the speakers were, I knew what was going on. And that Tuesday, I kind of broke down their session, and I said, "Hey guys, why don't you work out here. I'll do this," and Friday when we compared the tapes, my stuff sounded almost precisely like theirs except for the same VU level and the same crank on the speakers. I was blowing the speakers. So, you know what I'm saying? It's an ear thing. Just an ear thing, and with no outboard gear. I might have used three of the four equalizers that day. I love the outboard gear but without it, you work.

When I started freelancing more, and I'd go into these studios that were Mackie-based studios and they said, "Listen Freddie, I'm sorry, I don't even have the Neve or SSL you're used to." I go, "Look, it's just a bigger challenge because I'm not here because of what I do there. I've got to do that here now, don't I?" You can do that here? I can try. So, outboard wise Chess had those two boards. They had the Kepexes in the big room, couple of 176s, a couple of 1176 low noise, the Cooper Time Cube, that was a big EMT studio—we had four EMTs there, cause we had no live chambers, and I think that was it.

Then, when they closed Chess, Paul Sorano bought the gear, bought all of the gear. I was in the unemployment line the next day and I called home and my wife, my ex said, "Paul called, he says your session's at 1:00." Okay? I go down there, Paul goes,

> Yeah, thanks for coming down. Listen, I've got a new room upstairs, I want you to break it in. We're doing the Chess rhythm section for a Martin Luther King tribute album by Congressman Fortney from Washington D.C. Here you go. Here's the reel and tape. Bye.

Aw, turn the room on. Just turn on the power, I'll figure everything else out from there. The speakers were being held up by 2x4s. The console was MCI, one of those MCI black and red distortion grinders.

I must've been doing a good job that day, that day the chief engineer for Curtis Mayfield studios, which is called Curtom, came in, he had repaired a piece of equipment for Paul. Paul said, "Come on, I want to show you how my room is working." and Roger walked in because he got a load of Paul's stuff, Roger Anfensen, he looked around, he looked at me, and said, "Would you give me your phone number?" And six weeks later they called me and hired me at Curtom and I worked for Curtis Mayfield for five years. I did the Staple Singers' stuff, the movie thing, an Aretha album. I did Natalie Cole's second record there. It was a great gig, especially for Chicago because in New York you got big acts, Chicago you got some Blues, but you only really have that. I was really in a nice spot. Speaking of not doing jingles, I like jingles, but I wasn't doing them if I didn't have to, I was doing this.

And so that was great for five years, and then they were getting a divorce, Curtis and his manager, so I dove out of that and went to Streeterville Recording Studios, which was built in 69. Swedien had a hand in it as well as a guy named Ron Steele, who was a former RCA engineer, but is a session guitar player. His brother-in-law is Brian, the RCA guy who did Kiss, and Guess Who, who did all the Jack Douglas stuff. He was in the business and so they built this studio. It was like the third of the big three recording studios—Universal, Eight Track, which was Dick Marx's place. Dick Marx was like the king of jingles, and he started Universal and then he opens his own studio. Bruce built that big Helmholtz resonator thing, beautiful, sounded great, terrible board. Again, terrible control room, great studios, these guys build great studios with terrible control rooms.

It had an Electrodyne. They eventually got rid of it. This was an Electrodyne town and those things were terrible. They sounded like crap. They had an Audix at Streeterville originally. That was another terrible sounding board. Then they got an MCI black and red, Curtom had the MCI black and red thing. Sigma Sound had those, but they had them reworked. They had the kind that can actually work. They were souped.

I really liked the MCI 500 series—that was a great board, it was tan, but the SSL and Neves were beginning to heat up by then and of course Neve was here in town, there were a few Neves, but I couldn't get my hands of them because it wasn't a freelance community at all.

So I took the job at Streeterville and they had jingles, and I was bringing my record work there at night. I was doing a lot for Alligator Records, and I had a strong blues following of stuff and R&B still. By then they had an SSL. They had two Harrisons. Then they got a Neve. Then they got another Neve to replace the Harrison. So we had two Neves and the SSL. That was in 81. I had an opportunity to go and run a studio, so

I took it in 82. It was a vanity studio, I stayed away from these vanity things, but this guy I couldn't resist. His wife was a bad one, but I had enough business that I knew I could support myself with my business at his place. And he had a Harrison, and I had to redesign the acoustics of the studio because the guy who rebuilt it, I don't know if you're a fan of that pressed fiberglass. Most of the studios use them, I hate it, I just hate it. I replaced it all with regular fiberglass because pressed fiberglass never absorbed it—oh yeah, it's fiberglass it absorbs. No it doesn't absorb. In fact, if you get next to it, it reflects and it's an ugly-sounding reflection.

We did the super bowl shuffle there and it was going good, but then, his name was Dick Meyer, he was the CEO at Jovan. In 81, wherever you were, Jovan brought you the Rolling Stones. The first corporate sponsorship of a major rock tour ever. He also invented the talking box, he was a genius. You know, the talking box was the musk oil thing, "This musk oil comes from blah blah blah," and it sold a gazillion boxes of musk oil because the box talked to you... seriously. He was the inventor of the talking box. He's a great guy. He went off when we just finished the shuffle, and there was a hole at Streeterville and so I called him up and I said, "Hey, I'd like to come back if you'll have me." And so they had me back. I worked there from 86 through 94 then. That was when they replaced the boards. They didn't have the SSL, they had Harrisons everywhere. In 80, they had the red and black MCI and Harrisons. By the time I got back, they had one SSL and they were replacing the other two with Neves.

I stayed at Streeterville until 94 when the fun ran out you know. When so many commercial guys got their own studios, you know, you had to start going and working there. And so I went sort of freelance in 90; 94–97 was sort of my transition out of the Streeterville period. And in that time I found TV. I worked for a variety of guys in their home environments, which I still do. And I got one guy who's got a full Sierra Audio in there. I've got guys that we've built them or I've helped them, I've got guys that are just working in closets, not closets, but they're like the Stroh's thing, that Coors thing, that's a big loft, all wood with the columns and stuff, and they got a big iso room. It resonates so I won't use it, so I stuck them in the hall, in the office with two 77s in figure eight and a 414 in figure eight for some top end. So I'm already blocking out a lot, and that's 24 tracks of stuff, and very articulate. So, I used the splash, the extra splash of the wood against the ribbons. I knew it was happening so I brought my ribbons. I had ribbons, that's my gear collection.

I wasn't one of these guys that had a rack with mic pre's. First of all I used the variety of mic pre's. I'd rather have a board with one set of mic pre's on it because for me, from a textural standpoint, one set of mic pre's puts everything in a similar thing. Now when I start using this, using that, you gotta be sensitive to, does it sound like it's coming from the same spot? So, I always really liked using a board, and as the boards had their own compression and places got more compression, I didn't feel I needed a reverb, with the typical racks, a couple of Pultecs, and some reverb, a PCM 70. Just garbage.

So I bought mics, but I couldn't afford Neumanns, I just never could. So I invested in ribbons. So I got two 44s, seven 77s, and a BK5. I can do a complete big band. Horns, brass, and reed on the ribbons. My ribbons are all tight. You know, I had Clarence Kane, Enak? I had Clarence do my stuff. In fact I gotta go through my mics real soon because this guy's in his 80s and if he's still doing it, I better get the last of it. I have about 25 mics now. I got a couple of Chinese knock-offs of tube 47s that are really good. They are really good. Call me unreliable, I like 414s. Everybody says if I had one mic, I'd want a 47 or this or that, a 414, it'll do everything. I get more jazz vocals out of them when I have to. They're not a cold mic to me. And I'm not a dynamic mic person. On anything, except kick. It'll be an element of it, but I'm a condenser or ribbon guy. And so you know, a 414 is like the one. I am not an 87 guy. Unless you like a lot of distortion, and so what do I use 87s on? Guitar amp, when I want the distortion, and organ top, when I want the distortion to thicken up that thin ass organ occasionally on congas if I want distortion. Because again, I want the distortion to fatten it up a little bit. But I'm not an 87 guy, especially on vocals. He'd break them right up, and these guys love them. Maybe I got bad 87s I don't know is it me? So fet mics.

I got a couple of RE20s, they're fabulous. I like that MD series, EV stuff, so for kick I use the MD thing that they got. If I got a location with a voice-over or if they need a good voice at the TV station, I'll bring my RE20s down. But I collected mics. I felt that that was where I was gonna get the biggest bang for my buck in terms of controlling my audio. I think it's funny in terms of coloration, people put such a premium on mic pre's I find them having the least impact in the color change.

I have no idea why it is, but it is. When you take that Neve pre and you put in next to that SSL pre, the V pre, those two pre's, it's identical. The older Neve pre's are great, but not that much greater. The tube pre's versus the transistor pre's has got the biggest difference. I loathe these Hardy preamps. I can't stand them. People love these. Hardy, I don't get it.

I was a Lang guy. I preferred Lang over Pultec. You could do more. I never understood the detent on the Pultec, which seemed to be at the same select level as the attenuation. So, could you use them both at once? No, so what's it doing there? With the Lang you could because it had a separate control for each thing, and I thought it sounded better. What don't I use? I almost don't use anything. I use whatever you got.

I'd be least likely to use the Hardys. I wouldn't use an LA3 or an LA4. I'm not a big LA2 guy to tell you the truth. I find the lack of ability to adjust attack or release bogs me down on an LA2. I'd rather have an 1176 because I can keep it out of distortion, and it's as simple as that. And the LA2s are for lazy people because it distorts so much later. But I'm not that persnickety. Yeah, whatever's there.

Everybody's ear is different. You hear things differently. Your perception is different. Your choice of how to handle the headroom is intrinsic, so that's always different. We were talking about headroom with this, for the students. If you start bringing your fader down, you're a rookie. You know, my fader never comes down. In analog, my fader is always up there and I don't even have to look at it anymore. It's there. The way I trained myself for that is when I worked for Curtis, Curtis used to love to do his own mixing, so what he had me do is "Set up my mix for me. Get a mix." And Curtis would come in and pull it right down. So your EQ and your reverb and all of that would be there, then he'd start putting this balance to it. And sometimes I have to reach over and go, "Curt. Let me change this for you because you're doing this and it wants this. Now let me help you here." But the fader would be down at minus 20 because he was turning up his speakers with his faders, and that's where it dawned on me. When they came down I had that monitor all the way up. Sure enough, the fader came down 5, 7.

So you start loud. Now, I start loud and I get all of my determinations loud, but I mix real soft, so I mix it at about 92, 93 dB. But I'll get you though. I'll get you 106, you know, on the front end of the stuff. And, checking, and where's the inside of the noise and all of that stuff I'll listen loud, but when I'm mixing, I'm generally moderate at 97,

93, 95, whatever is soft, super soft. And I want you to talk, I don't want a quiet control room because the noisier it is, the more distractions I can get my mix through, the more I'm going to rely on the fact that it's going to sound good at all, through all of the other crap. So I figured that out. Other than staying away from Hardys, I'll use everything.

There's almost nothing I have now that I wish I had then because I don't care. I personally think that digital compression works better than analog compression. So, the closest answer would be, the compression working more like compression is supposed to work, which digital actually accomplishes. All digital compression works better, works like compression is intellectually explained to us as it's supposed to work. You can use more of it with less pumping issues and impact.

So many people say that analog compression is much more forgiving than digital compression, but not to me, I don't agree with that. I used to do a series compression thing, two compressors at once. You ever do two compressions in line? Of course you did. So which compressor was compressing first? The way I'd set it up was always the second one. The first one was just there to protect the second one. How hard is that? It makes the most sense, and then you can get 14 dB of analog compression without it going "shhhhooooawwoooodll," you know? And I do that with digital, but I could be way sloppier. In post-production. Sometimes over compression, digital is the way to warm it up.

Some people say they want to put the crunchiness on it by running it through analog, but that's not necessary. It's how you hear it. If you hear warmth, and you know how to manipulate, and you've taught yourself to manipulate. I don't think students sit there enough and just diddle. How much time is mixing an hour of snare drum for reverb, that's the first hour. That may be the sixth hour. I did a spot for Jovan when I was working for these guys, it was Kenny Rogers and Lionel Richie's studio when he owned Lion's Share, which is the old ABC Dunhill, where they did the Steely Dan records. All I remember is everything's out of phase. I was taking out of phase patch cords and phasing it in—I mean it was just crazy. They were mixing a Lionel Ritchie thing down the hall, and I walked in in the morning and it was snare okay? And throughout the day, I'm walking in and out, and you hear the mix in various stages, end of the day I'm walking home, snare. And many times, I've sat with the digital stuff and just put everything I can possibly put through everything because I had the time and the breath to be able to do it, with analog you can't do that. So I'm okay with digital, I'm completely okay with it. And I understand what your students are saying about needing an analog box, but here it is, and they each own two. (He's pointing at his ears). And that's the only analog box I think you really need because forever, the ear will be an analog device.

There's nothing I had then that you wish I had now? Nothing. I have a great mic collection, so I never had to want for my collection. As I saw the diffusion of the studio scene, I acquired enough of a mic collection to always be able to augment the studios. I can make an M49 on an acoustic guitar with a 414 and a 44 if I want. I'm very flexible. Do I miss punching in? Hell no. I had a great punching technique, I never missed. And I'd sit there an hour, hour, hour, hour, punching in your vocals, you suck. I want to shoot myself. Great, you built up a technique that now they're taking advantage of because you can do it. So they'll do it with you. And okay, I want to bill hours, that's great.

It causes the talent to be lazier and have less talent. I've always told my children, "You want to hear really good music? Here" and I'd give Carl Stalling, all of the cartoon music. It's in tune, he'd play great, he needs more bass he'd hire three more guys. My kids don't get it yet, but what a wonderful history of recording from wax to direct to disc to eight, they're pretty consistent in terms of the music. But these guys play. And even the guys in the '60s, and there's guys that can play now, the guys that can play are in the serious big bands that are jobbing in the theaters. I mean all of the guys that are in rock bands and stuff. Is Fallout Boy really great? I mean, when you go back and listen to a performance from Monterey Pop, even Big Brother, who was making mistakes all over the place and out of tune like crazy, is great. And I'm not just, Fallout Boy, and I know they love them.

There was a point where people would get together and they would play together, and that was how it was always done. Now that's just not the normal thing anymore. They want to do the drums, then they want to redo the drums, they record together and then they replace everything separately. I won't record like that. I make them work loud, I produced them right in their rehearsal space. I got them tight in the rehearsal space. I said, "When we walk in, we want to be tight". They were very grateful for that. Yes, I redid the vocals because it's so loud or whatever, but you heard that guy screaming in that vocal. Was that the cleanest scream you ever heard? You know what I'm saying? I caught that screech clean. Oh, I try.

It's about the ears, it's about the attitudes, it's about the musicianship, and it's about what's available. Right. Who you're working with. If the guy on the other side of the glass ain't great or ain't putting it out, forget great. If they're not putting it out, then it doesn't matter what gear you have. A musician that's out of tune, an instrument that's out of tune, piano's a classic example, you can't get the right piano sound when it's out of tune. The math don't work and the harmonics, it's just a whole nother thing. I was playing a thing for my kid to show him something I am working on in my basement because I've got guys that bring me their stuff, they work up in their rehearsal studios, and I mix it in my basement. I've got a surround theater, really decent, translatable. The horns were way out of tune but in the track, I got them sounding like they're in tune. And how do I do that? I just do it. I don't know. I wasn't even aware that they were that out of tune when I popped them in. I just kind of put enough verb and delay on it to soup it right in. Unless it's terrible. It's just how you hear to me. It always has been.

Again, I think it's real important that the two most important things I think for students especially are "learn to listen" and "don't turn the speakers up with the faders". Realize what headroom is for. Understand distortion. Hit the limiter so hard that it crunches and distorts and it's awful so you know how to work it right.

I don't hear anybody really thinking this way, but I think air and tape are the same thing. I think they're both mediums for the storage of sound. Air, I feel, has an infinite capacity for dynamics, but a complete inability to store the stuff. Tape has a pretty limited capacity for dynamics, but stores the stuff. Digital replicates the storage of audio in air more because of the greater dynamic range, however, air has pressure and density and humidity, and all sorts of stuff going in it that will dampen or cause a dampening factor to sound. I don't believe digital does that. So, because your harmonics are not automatically dampening and are attenuating down through distance, first of all, the only thing that we're manipulating in audio, beyond storage, is time. That's the only thing you've got. EQ is a function of time. Reverb is certainly a function of time. Delay is a function of time. Chorus and modulation of all sorts are a function of time.

I'll get back to the digital business with the harmonics, but you look at a mono signal. In EQ, guys that go right to use EQ, EQ causes stuff to go out of phase, right? EQ changes the phase causing it to go out of phase. Who said it was in phase in the first place? What if you're EQ'ing it into phase? Okay so, forget stereo, in this example, let's talk about a mono signal, which has its own relationship so it needs more top end, add some treble. Isn't that taking the treble and juicing it out in front of the time, of the median time of all of the frequencies? Isn't attenuating taking the behind, and that's time. So what's time? It's all time. It's all time-based. And if you say it can take it out of phase, I say it can, if it's moving phase, I agree, it's moving phase, but not necessarily out. It could be moving it in. The dampening factor thing is again—it's sound traveling in air over time or tape—was dampening in its own right. So with digital, you've got no dampening. So what do you do in digital to replicate dampening? That's your question.

Chapter 28

Frank Filipetti

Multiple Grammy Award-winning engineer and producer Frank Filipetti was one of the first engineers to embrace digital. His credits include James Taylor, Kiss, Luciano Pavarotti, Vanessa Williams, George Michael, 10,000 Maniacs, Courtney Love and Hole, Barbra Streisand, Dave Grusin, Korn, Carly Simon, Elton John, Mariah Carey, Rod Stewart, Paul McCartney, and Bob Dylan, and mixes for such number one singles as Foreigner's "I Want to Know What Love Is" and "I Don't Want to Live Without You", which he also produced, along with Kiss' "Lick It Up" and The Bangles' "Eternal Flame."

Among his seven wins and ten nominations, Filipetti produced, engineered, and mixed James Taylor's "Hourglass", winning Grammy awards in 1998 for Best Engineered Album and Best Pop Album.

He has also produced film scores and Broadway cast albums and is a major figure in the world of 5.1 surround mixing, with numerous 5.1/DVD projects under his belt, including works for Billy Joel, James Taylor, and Meatloaf. He has also delved into live shows, recording and mixing numerous live albums including the Pavarotti and Friends series, last year's Minnelli on Minnelli, James Taylor's Live at the Beacon, and most recently Elton John's One Night Only. He's also recorded original cast albums for A Funny Thing Happened on the Way to the Forum (featuring Nathan Lane), the Grammy-winning Annie Get Your Gun, and Tony Award-winning and Grammy-nominated Aida, among others.

My name is Frank Filipetti, I was born in Bristol, Connecticut in 1948. I started as a professional in 1980. As a non-professional I probably started around 16 or 17 years old. Somehow or other I developed a real interest in tape machines. I also started playing drums at that point. I guess I was about 15. My dad got me a very rudimentary drum kit at the time and we formed our own band. That had to be around '62, '63 maybe, '63 actually because it was around The Beatles. We had a band based on The Ventures at the time, and when The Beatles came out we went to vocals. And about a year or two later I got into tape machines and being able to record the band.

DOI: 10.4324/9781003519829-28

Figure 28.1 Vintage is a "beauty is in the eye of the beholder" kind of a thing. Vintage is... vintage sound, vintage this, vintage that, that's a marketing thing more than anything. If someone wants to call an 87 vintage I guess that's up to them. That's fine with me, to me it's not vintage. A 47 is vintage, a 49 is vintage, an 87 isn't vintage.

Figure 28.2 Everything else, there were great points about both eras. We made great records in both eras. I just wish we didn't have to go through the period of converting to digital, the period of ten or fifteen years we went through with bad converters and bad bit-rates, 16-bit, and all that stuff. I wish that we could have gone directly from analog to 96 or 192 audio with great converters. It would have made everybody's lives a lot better.

So, as a non-professional I was right from the late '60s through the early '70s very much into taping my bands and doing stuff like that. It got to where I had reconfigured a quarter-inch four-track to be a four-track all in one line. I made a quarter track into a four-track. And it was a real beast. It was a Teac machine before they came out with their version. No it wasn't Teac, it was a Roberts machine. Yeah, Roberts, which then became Akai. Me and this friend of mine built an actual sync head thing, the whole machine looked like a Rube Goldberg apparatus but it was fun. I did it for a while, and about two years later the Teac Simul-Sync four-track came along, and I started working with that. But I was always working as a band or a musician until 1980, when I went into this side of the business, the engineering/production side full-time.

Figure 28.3 I do think that the current digital technology that we have, when used properly, is the highest resolution audio and the best sounding audio that the consumer has certainly ever been able to have for the least amount of money that they'd ever been able to pay. Unfortunately, while that's going on, we're also compressing and smashing and doing all that. What I would wish is not any piece of gear, but it's a mindset that we don't have today. It's the mindset that, yes, this walkman or this iPod or whatever you want to call it is very convenient and it's really great to listen to while I'm jogging or doing my homework; but tonight I'm really going to get into listening to this on a great system under great conditions and really experience music in a way that other way is never going to give me. So I'd say it's a mindset that I wish we had today, I wish we had the gear of today with the mindset of the 1970s and '80s.

Figure 28.4 ...it took us thirty or forty years to get analog to sound really good. We had to learn all of the tricks of the trade and the different biases and tape formulations and the differences, and high output and low noise and how far do you saturate a tape. Do you go to 250, +3, do you go to +5? The bass drum, you can record that at -3 but you better not record the tambourine any higher than -18 otherwise.... All of those things, you know this is going to bleed through to the next track, okay let's move this over. Come on, we spent years perfecting all that stuff. Then they suddenly want to go into a studio and they just set up the microphones, they just record the digital thing the same way which is a totally different recording system, say, "Oh, this sounds harsh, it's not this it's not that". Of course.

Figure 28.5 And the one thing, more than anything else that separates digital from analog is not the sound. To me, it's that analog is so much more forgiving than digital. If you screw up analog, you can get away with it because if you overload it, it actually can sound cool. If you record something in the wrong way or there's a little too much print through, some of that stuff actually works out okay and you can get away with it. In the digital world, you can totally destroy by doing something wrong. You cannot be lazy in digital.

Figure 28.6 The simple fact is that you've got to do it right just like anything else. And I learned this back when I heard these great records on digital. Never say that this format sounds better than that format because I can guarantee you, just as there are women that are stronger than men, and some men that are brighter than some women; the simple fact is there is always going to be a better sounding digital recording than an analog and vice versa. Anybody that starts talking about what you can accomplish with a format or a console or with a piece of gear or using a class A versus.... it's all bologna because a great driver behind the wheel will make it sound great. Simple as that.

I had been a signed songwriter to Screen Gem's, Colgems as one of their stable songwriters. And they paid my weekly salary. And it was in 1980 that I was under their contract with them for two or three years. The third year, they did not pick up my option. I guess I didn't make 'em any money is what the problem was. But I used to do all my songs, back then you didn't record your songwriter demos with your DigiDesign Pro tools rig, you went to the studio, you went to what was a demo studio, and that's where your songwriter demos were done. They'd be $50 an hour or something like that. Screen Gems would pay for the session and the place that I had done all of that was what was called Right Track Recording back then. It had a 16-track MCI with dbx noise reduction and we used to do the songwriter demos there.

So, when Screen Gems didn't pick up my option and I had just finished a recording for Lifesong Records, but Lifesong Records went bust, at that point I had no income and really nothing to do. I went to Simon Andrews, who was the owner of Right Track at the time, and it was on 24th Street and said, "You know, I'm 30 years old (I think I was 29 or 30 at the time), I know I have good ears. I've been working with tape machines all my life and I think I could be a really good engineer, but I am too old to be an assistant for two or three or four years. I need to start doing something right away, would you give me a chance?" And we knew each other because I did all my demos there. And, he said, "Sure." So, I worked there for about 30 days before I did my first four-track session and within about six months I was doing full 24-track sessions. By the end of the year I was a chief engineer at the studio. And, it was at that time that we then built the facility on 48th Street. Simon built what is now Right Track or Legacy. We built that back in 1981. And, I've pretty much been working there ever since.

On 24th Street, there was a thing called the Auditronics console, with Allison automation, where you recorded the automation on one track of the multi-track. And they had the MCI 16-track, which then became, somewhere during that period, a 24-track. We bought a 24-track headstack. It was 16-track, two-inch that eventually became 24-track two-inch with dbx noise reduction. We had things like an Eventide 910 harmonizer and a couple of other things. But, as I said, it started out as not a major studio; it was a demo studio. But, within a year or two when we built the room on 48th Street, we purchased an MCI 56 channel console, and we also by that point had two 24-track machines and started to put together a fair complement of the LA2As and the 1176s. By then we had a pretty decent tracking room and mixing room going. We obviously did because it became very successful very quickly. Within two years we built a second room, which is now the room that actually is my room at the studio. And, we purchased the second SSL in America. From the day we put the SSL in, it was a monstrous success.

The MCI still was in Studio A but when we built the second room, Studio B, which is my room, we put in an SSL, and that became monstrously successful. I did Kiss there, and I had my first number-one single there with Foreigner's "I Want to Know what Love is." Things just took off from that point, James Taylor, Carly Simon...

I didn't have an Al Schmidt or an Ed Cherney or Phil Ramone or anybody like that to work under. I wasn't an assistant. I was an assistant for 30 days in a demo room. So I had to learn a lot of this on my own. And if I have a regret, I don't have very many, but if I did have a regret it was that I didn't get a chance to work under these guys. So, a lot of the stuff that I learned, I had to learn on my own by trial and error. And it was just a process of tweaking these boxes and working with the things and finding out that every box has a sweet spot. Especially when it comes to preamps, compressors, faders, EQs. There's always a sweet spot where they do what they do the best. And then there are deviations from that sweet spot where they may still do what you want them to, but not as effectively. And so, what I built up was a mental database of all this gear and where their sweet spots were, so if I needed a particular thing I could pretty much know how to dial in to get it. Some devices like an LA2A for example don't sound anything like an LA3A, but there are places where one or the other would suffice under the same condition and then you'd just say, "Well, you know they have the sweet spot, which would give you a little more of what you're looking for." You always have devices like a 910 harmonizer where if you had it at like 1.002 on one of them and you had .997 on the other one you'd have this nice little thing happen. But, if it went too far it sounded a little too far off, and if it didn't go far enough it wasn't enough. So, you just developed these things.

One of the things that I think is interesting between the analog and digital world is digital gear doesn't really have a sweet spot. Digital gear pretty much acts at -20 as it does at +4, you know? I mean, it's not like there's an area where suddenly all of those little elements come together and coalesce. With digital, you just put it in. You get the sound right. But it's not like "Wow, suddenly it becomes this". And, with digital gear you can kind of move up and down that spectrum. Digital doesn't quite have the personality. The SSL console is a perfect example. There was a spot where you'd see those meters wrapped around the edge, way beyond +3, but there was something really cool about the sound of it. And once you hit that sweet spot with guitars or with drums it suddenly transformed an ordinary thing to an extraordinary thing. And the same thing with the Neve consoles. The new generation, even of analog consoles. My main peeve with them is they are cleaner and they spec out better and have all this new stuff, but even in the analog world, they've lost some of that sweet spot characteristics. Like the 9k, which I thought was a really good console, but I couldn't really mix on it properly because I found that it didn't go from "okay" to "extraordinary" to just "over the top". It went from "okay" to "over the top." And I couldn't find that sweet spot. I think that's the thing about the analog gear, especially the really good stuff. Is boy, you go along the dial and it's sounding good, and oh man, that's it. And it's there. And that's what I found very interesting versus the digital world.

My favorites from back then, there was an old box that Lexicon made called the "Delta T". It was one of the early, early digital boxes. I was fascinated by it because it was one of the few early boxes where you could get an incredibly quick delay. If you fed it back on itself you had this really interesting effect. And the delays were much quicker than you could get in any analog device. You know, because usually you'd use a tape machine or an Echoplex, and those were slower, nothing like this, nothing like a flam. And, so you'd get these, you can set up these things with a Delta T on a snare drum, you could get seven or eight flams in a row on a drum as opposed to just a hit. So I was fascinated with that. I always loved the original Lexicon Primetime, the first 224 that came out.

I thought it was a wonderful box, but also there was all the analog gear, obviously the great tube stuff from the '50s and '60s, Pultecs and the Teletronics, LA2As which later became Urei boxes and all the great limiters, and obviously the Fairchild's 670s, the great microphones, the tube microphones. I was a big tube microphone fan. I would never use an 87 where a 67 or 47 was available. We had an awful lot of very colored, very personality-driven boxes and microphones, but that really did have a personality. For example, once you went from a 67 to an 87 it was more neutral but it didn't have that personality that the old 67 did. I found lots of pieces of gear that I really enjoyed. When the first A800 tape machine came out I really enjoyed that, even though it had one incredibly disturbing feature on it, which got me into trouble a couple of times.

It had a thing called a SMPTE reader. You could switch this button and it would read the SMPTE of say, track 24. The problem is, it didn't follow when you put the machine into repro or into sync. It didn't follow that All Repro or in sync button. So, many times when you were locking up to film you'd be listening off the sync head, but the tape machine would be coming off the record head, but that was a wonder of the analog world. You just had all these kinds of things that made it interesting. But yeah, I had all kinds and boxes and things that I was very fond of, microphones and so forth.

Yeah, if you listen to the first Foreigner album I used the Delta T on it. But I remember another box that I used on that record which was the Publison—the Publison harmonizer. I'll never forget this because it's one of those things that's just the magic of the timing. I used to use a Publison harmonizer and I came across this thing where if I took the drums after I compressed them and tuned them down and used the cross points right, it sounded like this massive room distort-o kind of thing. And I used it on a song on the first album, the last song on the vinyl disc, the inside band, and it was really cool. But the band thought it was too over the top, so they had me dial it back. And, a couple of months later after the album was released that same effect appeared on somebody else's album; the Powerstation band. And he used it, Jason Corsaro was the guy, and he used it, really huge and so everybody thinks that was the first time that was done with that, but I actually did it earlier. But nobody heard that one because it was subtle as opposed to being out there, because that band was saying, "I don't know…it might be too over the top." Also, being the last cut and on an inside band on the vinyl, that's why I was never that enamored with analog discs, a lot of people wax rhapsodic about how great vinyl discs sound and all that, and I'm saying, "Yeah, if your on the outside band." But as soon as you started to get to the middle or end of the record you were screwed. I was not a fan of that at all.

I never stopped using LA2As, Pultecs. There's a program on the Lexicon 480 that, even though the 480 isn't in use anymore I still use it 'cause nothing else sounds like it. It's called buckram and they've tried to emulate it on some later devices but doesn't quite work. I've never been so enamored with a piece of gear that if I didn't have it I couldn't get it with something else. I think the thing that I never stopped using is some of the great old microphones. As far as gear goes, you know whenever I can get a Fairchild 670 of course I'll use it 'cause it sounds amazing. There's nothing that duplicates that. In my room I don't have a Fairchild, but I do have a couple of LA2As, I have a couple of 1176s, those are great boxes that'll never be duplicated, and so there's that. But mostly it's microphones that I stick with, that I know how they sound, I know what they do.

And now I do the majority of my work in a digital domain, especially my mixing, I do all of the mixing digitally. I only go out to some of these older boxes before I go into the digital domain. Once I get to the digital domain, I don't mess with it much. I try not to do too many A to D conversions and D to A conversions. But I do like to go back to my Marshall Tape Eliminator and the Marshall Time Modulator, which was an amazing box which I used to use as well. Now I am thinking back to these old times, and every once in a while I'll go back to that. I still think the original Primetime was one of the coolest delays and had one of the neatest sounds of all of them. So, you know, there are still things that I do like and go back to.

In the sense that the only thing I do differently now is if I'm going to go to an analog device, I tend to want to do it before the digital conversion, whereas earlier I might wait until after I go out to tape and wait 'til the mix stage. Now, if I'm going to do something in analog and I'm going to store it on a digital device like a hard drive or whatever, I tend to want to put that on now, before I go any further with it.

I was never disappointed with analog gear, is there is any piece of analog gear that doesn't do everything, yes. Even working with the little Korg and stuff, even the little old analog stomp boxes and stuff from the '70s and '80s. A lot of things are noisy. But boy, on a particular thing they are magical, I mean you can't get that sound any other way. So no, I'd say that there are a lot of boxes that never lived up to their hype or that I was told, "Oh god, when you listen to this you're going to love it." And then I listened to it and I don't love it. But then I say, "Well, yeah but you know it might work here." So, I think they all have their uses. Oh, and one of the things I still use to this day is an EMT 140 Plate because again that's something that just has a magical thing and it's frustrating sometimes because every day it sounds different. And the days of recalls, and all that, the plates tend to cause a problem because with the humidity in the air or the temperature in the room or whatever, you can try and stabilize these plates as much as you can but from one day to the next the tension change is just enough that it sounds different. But I still try and do a lot of stuff with plates. I think that there are devices that I pretty much didn't use, what they were? I mean obviously they don't stay in my mind because I didn't use them. Most things I just find that one little thing they were good for. Some boxes that I would use did one thing well. And, okay, that's good enough for me.

Vintage is a "beauty is in the eye of the beholder" kind of a thing. Vintage is... vintage sound, vintage this, vintage that, that's a marketing thing more than anything. If someone wants to call an 87 vintage I guess that's up to them. That's fine with me, to me it's not vintage. A 47 is vintage, a 49 is vintage, an 87 isn't vintage. We all have our views on this kind of a thing. I don't know, is a Lexicon 224 vintage? At this point it is, but for me? What someone labels something doesn't matter to me. They can call it whatever they want, I'm gonna listen to it. I'm not gonna read the specs because that's the other thing, is the obsession with specs nowadays. Back in the '70s and '80s there was no obsession with specs so you'd use your ears all the time. And so many times now I'll say, "This mic doesn't sound as good as my 47 here sounds." And they'll say, "But oh, look at the specs." And I'll say, "Hey, if I showed you the specs on this 47 you'd laugh me out of the room." Because if all you had with those specs, there's high-end distortion all over the place, there's all kinds of things going on inside the capsules, there's fluctuations, there's frequencies, anomalies, that would take your typical mic manufacturers today's breath away. It sounds good. Which only shows me the specs that we've come up with. We haven't figured out what we do when we listen. And so the specs to me are guidelines, and words like "vintage" or whatever they come up with, just the latest marketing thing just doesn't mean anything.

The first thing when someone says, "Oh, this simulates tape." You can call it whatever you want but I want to see if it simulates tape. And it doesn't. And today I went to see a box, it has bias control and all of this and it "simulates tape" if you're not going to tape. And I listen to the demo and say, "That's fine" but I can't tell on this material. You want me to take the box into a studio? I'll see if it simulates tape. I'm going to send the microphone signal in there and have a drummer play and I'll see what happens then record, playback then I'll tell you if it simulates tape. But, just because you have the graphs and frequency response and all that doesn't mean anything to me.

What I have now that I wished I had then is my console. I know that people really do go on and on about analog consoles and how great they sound. I never got that. I have a Euphonix Sysem 5. My problem with every analog console I ever had, and I loved the old SSL and the old Neves that had the sweet spot, which was magical. However, when I was tracking, and I was going to an analog console and going to tape, and then I'd play it back the analog, the one coming off of the tape didn't sound like what I sent going in. And two, the analog monitoring in many of these, like the older Neve consoles, the monitoring section was a jukebox section where they didn't spend as much time as they used to on the faders. There'd be crackles, you'd have spots where you turned the dial the signal would go away for a second and then come back and you'd have all this stuff going on. You'd hear the tape hiss and all that, all the stuff happening in the analog world and I said, "Oh god, I just wanted the band when they come in the control room to hear it the way I heard it when they were running it down!" And when they came in, there was a tape compression, there were the little ticks and pops and dings and all that stuff was going on, and then you'd come in the next day and the bias would be slightly off on the machine, or the assistant that did the alignment in the morning didn't do it quite right. And then, you'd have to move from this fader to this fader because that one wasn't working, but then this fader didn't sound anything like that fader. And you'd have artists like Foreigner who are extremely nitpicky about it, "It doesn't sound like it did yesterday…" so you spent all this time chasing things down and dealing with the fact that it never sounded today the way it did the day before.

So, for me a great digital console where you could rely on the fact that everything you did today—you will get that back tomorrow or a week from now or a month from now or a year from now. And also, the ability to mix an album as an album, which you never had in the analog world. I can sit down now and go through six songs in a day. Everybody used to talk about the rough mix and the great feel that you always had in the rough mix and how when you got into the final mix, you never got that vibe back. That's what I do. That's how I mix, I mix the rough mix, I spend two or three hours on it, an hour, until I'm tired of it, and move on to the next song. And then I do a rough mix there. And then if I want to go back to the first one, I hit a button and I'm back to the first one. I don't have to walk out of the room, I don't have to have the assistants go for 30 or 40 minutes and change all the faders, EQs and all this; I'm back. So I'm always working on a rough mix. And I'm constantly upgrading that rough mix. Unlike the analog world where you have to do the rough mix, but obviously you got another; you've got ten to do that day so you can't write everything down so then you do the final mix and you play the rough mix back and you say, "Oh god that sounded good. How did we do that? Oh well, we don't know."

So if there was one thing that I wished we had then, I wish I had my console. Everything else, there were great points about both eras. We made great records in both eras. I just wish we didn't have to go through the period of converting to digital, the period of 10 or 15 years we went through with bad converters and bad bit-rates, 16-bit, and all that stuff. I wish that we could have gone directly from analog to 96 or 192 audio with great converters. It would have made everybody's lives a lot better.

I still have the old gear but I really don't miss when vinyl was king or having to get five or six albums that I could actually play without the needle popping out or where it wouldn't tick and pop. I don't miss aligning tape machines. I don't miss the vagaries of analog gear. I guess the one thing, if I had one thing I wish, it's that we had given DSD and one-bit audio more of a chance. I think it was a magnificent format. However, I do think that the current digital technology that we have, when used properly, is the highest resolution audio and the best sounding audio that the consumer has certainly ever been able to have for the least amount of money that they'd ever been able to pay. Unfortunately while that's going on, we're also compressing and smashing and doing all that. What I would wish is not any piece of gear, but it's a mindset that we don't have today. It's the mindset that, yes, this walkman or this iPod or whatever you want to call it is very convenient and it's really great to listen to while I'm jogging or doing my homework; but tonight I'm really going to get into listening to this on a great system under great conditions and really experience music in a way that other way is never going to give me. So I'd say it's a mindset that I wish we had today. I wish we had the gear of today with the mindset of the 1970s and '80s.

I was anti-digital for quite a long time. I kept trying them out, when the first 24-track Sony came out I tried that. I tried the 3M machine. I was requested to do a 10,000 Maniacs album on a Mitsubishi digital. I was just not fond of any of them. Then, I went through a couple of transformations. One was hearing what I thought were great sounding records that other people have done that were stored on these machines. Peter Gabriel was one. Kevin Killian and some of the fellows involved in that had done an amazing job with it, also some of Steely Dan records, "The Nightfly," those things, stuff that Elliot had worked on. And I said, "Well, you know what? Digital can obviously sound good with the right driver behind the wheel." So I slowly got into doing it and over the course of the years, I realized that all the people that were complaining about digital were complaining about it because they were recording it like they were recording analog. And, if you record digital like you're recording analog, it's going to sound dreadful.

And also, you know, it took us 30 or 40 years to get analog to sound really good. We had to learn all of the tricks of the trade and the different biases and tape formulations and the differences, and high output and low noise and how far do you saturate a tape? Do you go to 250, +3, do you go to +5? The bass drum, you can record that at -3 but you better not record the tambourine any higher than -18 otherwise.... All of those things, you know this is going to bleed through to the next track, okay let's move this over. Come on, we spent years perfecting all that stuff. Then they suddenly want to go into a studio and they just set up the microphones, they just record the digital thing the same way which is a totally different recording system, and say, "Oh, this sounds harsh, it's not this, it's not that". Of course.

I do everything differently, there's almost nothing that I do the same in the digital world that I do in the analog world. I'm talking about levels, EQs. When you EQ, how you EQ. I would always compress a signal before the EQ in the analog world. I almost always compressed after the EQ in the digital world simply because of the way the bits are being treated. The levels that you record these things at, the accuracy of the metering, sometimes it's totally wrong. You've got to be very, very careful about your levels in a digital world because in the 16-bit world especially where a lot of people gave digital a bad name they were just recording it wrong. They were overloading or being so careful, they weren't recording in 16 bits; they were recording in 11 bits.

I mean literally, I got things in, orchestral things in that were -20 and -30 and these guys, that was like 10 bits, 11 bits, come on. You learn these things, no one, NO ONE ever talked about jitter when digital first came out. It wasn't even a concept back then. People were daisy-chaining, word clocks and AES lines and using mic cables instead of AES cables, all of this stuff was being abused terribly. And, so now there are a lot of ways to refine this to a point where it becomes absolutely sonically stellar. But, there are an awful lot of ways to really screw yourself up. And the one thing, more than anything else that separates digital from analog is not the sound. To me, it's that analog is so much more forgiving than digital. If you screw up analog, you can get away with it because if you overload it, it actually can sound cool. If you record something in the wrong way or there's a little too much print through, some of that stuff actually works out okay and you can get away with it. In the digital world, you can totally destroy by doing something wrong. So it's much easier to really, using the French, easier to fuck yourself up using digital than it is in analog and so you have to be a lot more careful. You cannot be lazy in digital.

The simple fact is that you've got to do it right just like anything else. And I learned this back when I heard these great records on digital. Never say that this format sounds better than that format because I can guarantee you, just as there are women that are stronger than men, and some men that are brighter than some women, simple fact is there is always going to be a better sounding digital recording than an analog and vice versa. Anybody that starts talking about what you can accomplish with a format or a console or with a piece of gear or using a class A versus.... it's all bologna because a great driver behind the wheel will make it sound great. Simple as that.

Personally, I am using the System 5 for console and for automation. I am using Nuendo as my main machine for running and storing audio. I do have a Pro tools rig which I also use because a lot of stuff come in that way. I have a Logic rig again because more and more are starting to come in that way. My preferred format is a Nuendo format. And I use analog, great analog gear and digital gear for everything, I have some really good converters and all that, and I think at the end of the day that's what you want. You want a good preamp, you want a good converter. And then the storage format is up to you.

I'm always buying microphones. And I've tried a couple of digital microphones unsuccessfully. Not very pleased, so far that's been a no-no. As far as analog gear goes, I love my dbx 120XP. I am building up a rack of them. I bought another one of them recently, oh about a year ago so I have four of them now. I love subharmonic synthesizers, it's a fantastic piece of gear. I have the digital stuff, I've got the TC 6000 and all that, the new 96. But I have to say that the last piece of gear that I really spent a lot of money on that wasn't digital was the Chandler stuff, some Chandler preamps about a year and a half ago, two years ago. Chandler preamps and the Chandler limiter are just fantastic. So I'd say probably I still buy analog compressors and limiters and preamps because they're still great stuff.

When I think about analog there's a story that I always thought of as funny but I was quite agitated at the time. I was working at a studio, a very good studio which will remain unnamed, but it was a James Taylor project. We were listening and I was getting the mix up 'cause we were going to do some recording and getting a rough mix up and it wasn't sounding good at all and I kept looking at the machine thinking something's not right. It's not sounding right. And I said, "Did you align the machine this morning?" "Oh yeah, we aligned it." It just doesn't sound right. So finally I said, "Look, let's put up the reference tape." We stopped the session, we put up the reference tape and everything came back at the right level, but throw up the 15k for a minute." We threw up the 15k, and it was like wobbling all over the place. I said, "How did you set the azimuth?" And they said, "We don't set the azimuth." I said, "What are you talking about you don't set the azimuth?" "Oh, no no no, our azimuth is correct. If you bring something in that's not the correct azimuth we're not going to change our tape machines to fit your azimuth." And then he said all kinds of things, and I tell you, this is a high-end studio and I just said, "You can't be serious." He says, "No, I'm serious." I say, "Well change the azimuth right now, I'm not recording and then having to set two different azimuths because I can't do that physically, so either I get to change your azimuth or we leave now." So I took a screwdriver and started adjusting the azimuth, and you know - that was their policy. I look back on it now and it's really quite funny. That was the thing, you had to deal with those kinds of things at the time.

Chapter 29

Jim Anderson

Jim Anderson is a New York based recording engineer and producer.

Specializing in jazz and acoustic music, he has worked with producers Bob Belden, Michael Cuscuna, Dr. Mark Feldman, Tommy LiPuma, Delfayo Marsalis, Richard Seidel, Kazunori Sugiyama, Akira Taguchi, Creed Taylor, Matthias Winckelmann, among others, and has recorded projects for Toshiko Akiyoshi, Patricia Barber, Terence Blanchard, James Carter, Ron Carter, Jon Fadis, Joe Henderson, J.J. Johnson, Lorin Maazel, Branford Marsalis, Christian McBride, Gonzalo Rubalcaba, Maria Schneider, McCoy Tyner, Phil Woods, John Zorn. Four of his recordings have received Grammy awards and 18 have received nominations.

In television, he has worked with the Muppets and has been the Audio Producer for "In Performance at the White House" and "The Kennedy Center Gala with the National Symphony" for PBS, among others. Emmy nominations have been given to many of his television projects.

A graduate of the Duquesne University School of Music in Pittsburgh, Pennsylvania, he studied audio engineering at the Eastman School of Music and Sender Freies Berlin. During the 1970's, he was employed by National Public Radio (NPR) and engineered and produced many DuPont and Peabody award-winning classical, jazz, documentary, and news programs. Since 1980, he has had a career as an independent audio engineer and producer, living in New York City. During the years 1999 and 2000, he was the Chairman of the New York Section of the Audio Engineering Society (AES) and served as the AES President. Anderson was chair at New York University's Clive Davis Institute of Recorded Music from 2004–2008. He is currently a professor in this program.

I'm Jim Anderson. I was born December 23, 1951 in Butler, PA which is a little town north of Pittsburgh.

I started in audio when I was a kid, doing anything that made sound, anything that made music that totally fascinated me.

Professionally my first job was really at NPR. If we back up a bit, in music school when I was at Duquesne University I was given the keys to the recording studio. I had read the

DOI: 10.4324/9781003519829-29

Figure 29.1 I actually dropped a C12 from the roof to record a recital in the recital hall and I just couldn't believe the quality of sound. You know it was sort of like I was doing the equivalent of Mercury Living Presence record. I used one microphone because that's the only thing that worked. And honestly, we had just kind of hit the right spot instantly, said that seems about right, and it just covered the entire stage. It was perfect. And I saw really what you could do with just a single microphone.

Figure 29.2 So about two weeks after the broadcast I get this call from Michael Brecker and he said, "Hey, just wanted to call and tell you this is a great recording. This is really nice." He said I'd just broken up with the band and this was a really nice memento of what this band was like live. And I said, "I have to ask you Michael, a couple of years ago we did a recording for NPR called Steps Ahead in Boston. And I said, "it was approved, it was every bit as good as what you just heard." And he said, "Ah, we were probably just being assholes."

Alec Nisbett book "Technique of the Sound Studio" and taken it out of the library, and if you read that book from the Duquesne library, looked at the card in the back, it had my name on it front and back. I would check it out and read it like a novel, read it over and over and I was just doing this for fun. So I was handed the recording studio keys at the university along with another friend and what was there was an Ampex 440 with an MX 10 mixer and a couple of microphones, a C12, there were two, one worked. And then there were two Sony 37Ps. So the first recording which I think was for me, my first

Figure 29.3 I would complain mightily that there's nothing in the midrange. There's something in the bottom and something in the top but there are times I know I have to do something in the middle, what can I do here?

Figure 29.4 I remember once I was recording the sound of oxen plowing in a field in Somalia and the wind is like crazy. And I had various sizes of windsocks I had built out of foam, and they still weren't enough. And with those mics you had the roll-off and I got the track. So you learned every inch of every piece of gear you had.

milestone, I actually dropped a C12 from the roof to record a recital in the recital hall and I just couldn't believe the quality of sound. You know it was sort of like I was doing the equivalent of Mercury Living Presence record. I used one microphone because that's the only thing that worked. And honestly, we had just kind of hit the right spot instantly, said that seems about right, and it just covered the entire stage it was perfect. And I saw really what you could do with just a single microphone.

That would have been 1970. So we slowly got this recording studio going. Much of what we did and many of the tapes that I had done, I had recorded the big band at the university. I had six channels, it was an MX10 mixer so there were no panpots, it was left, center, right, that's all you had, if you wanted to move something you had to take a pair of microphones and kind of fix your stereo that way. So, some of these tapes made it to the radio station at the university, WDBQ, and it was one of the first NPR stations.

Figure 29.5 I was doing a John Fadis record with Ray Brown and Harold Land and Kenny Baron and Mel Lewis on drums. And John said to me "Here's how I'd like to do it. I want to do it where I'm standing here and the drums are behind me". And in a studio, you kind of go "Oh no" and also it was two-track. Two-track digital, Mitsubishi X80. And I thought wait, I've done live recordings. Yeah, it's just like a club, we'll make it sound like a club. So in the recording studio John's happy, I remember we did the first playback and Ray Brown said, "Ehh, tweak it here, do this" and second playback Ray came in and said, "Yeah, when you get it you get it. It takes you a while to get it." So, thanks Ray.

Figure 29.6 I was just getting my sounds. And so then Kenny said, "Let's run that tune down" and I hooked it up and rolled it. We rolled it and Kenny at the very end, this is Ann Hampton Callaway, they did this beautiful song. Kenny said, "aww damn, too bad we didn't get it" and I said, "Let's see if we didn't get it" and Kenny says "You got that?" "Yeah". And that's the take, the take is that rehearsal, that's the first thing we did.

And they said to me, "if you'd like to have a job after you graduate go get your FCC license and you'll have a summer job."

So I got into this situation where at the radio station nobody had any kind of production sense and I had a recording studio. I still had the keys to the thing. I had graduated but I still could get access to it. So I took all the talent over and started producing spots and producing material for the station like we never had. So eventually I turned that into a graduate assistantship and slowly realized radio was where I wanted to be. So to make a really long story very short, a position came up at NPR, and I had a chance to go to NPR when at that time there were only three studios. There was just All Things Considered, and Weekend All Things Considered had just gone on the air and they were looking to expand their engineering talent pool. And I think at that time there were four recording engineers period in the studios, and I was brought in to be one of them. And the best thing about all the NPR days were you learned to do everything.

I was doing spot news, I was doing live, in fact All Things Considered at that time was a live 90 minute mix, 5 o'clock, you go on the air and the tape doesn't stop rolling until 6:30 and you learned how to have kind of grace under pressure. And you knew anything you did at that time, if you screwed up you had to be able to figure out, all hell could be breaking loose in the control room, but on the air how can you make it sound like everything's seamless? So you know, everything happened that you could ever imagine, and you would try to make sure on the air, nothing was ever untoward. That was just news.

I might have been the only engineer at that time who came there with a music degree and could read a score and all this kind of thing. So I was brought in to do a lot of the jazz recording for them. We started a show called Jazz Live. So the first recording, another milestone, the first recording I did for them was Ella Fitzgerald, Stevie Wonder in New Orleans. Eventually, that track actually just got released last year on a Phil Ramone album, We All Love Ella, there's that track I did in 1977. The one thing that I learned in all of this was live to two-track and how to literally hit the mix, literally from the first note. Because you didn't have ten minutes to kind of get the mix together, if at best you probably had 10 to 15 seconds to get the mix together. And we would do it as, you know, full-blown out 24, 36, maybe even 48 channel recording, but it was live either to tape or live to air, and it was the best experience.

I still do live to two-track, I'm doing some next week, and it's all based on the radio experience. I also came up with, I had a love of radio documentaries. And so I'd do a lot of post-production, radio drama post-production, radio documentary post-production, and would go off and do the outside recording, bring it back, post it. And sometimes also be like an assistant or co-producer with the talent you know. What I tried to do was establish the engineer was as important as the content producer and the on-air talent. And to say my contribution is just as big as yours if not bigger actually, and to get recognition for it. So I fought for that at NPR. So we did, we went to Daytona Beach and did the Firecracker 400. It was a one hour documentary in stereo on stock car racing. And it was Scott Simon's first extended piece, and that aired on Labor Day weekend, 1979 something like that. And so you know I just kind of did what I always thought, what I was interested in. I had a chance to leave NPR and go freelance, essentially take my savings and invest it in myself. That's when I moved to New York and really started hitting the streets, and the thing is, I'd never worked as an assistant in the studio, I've always engineered. So in the recording studios I've had great assistants who've gone on to be terrific engineers, but I always walked in with the client in the studio and I was in charge. So I never had to go that assisting route, because when you move into a new city you start sort of at the bottom again, start all over again and kind of re-establish your credits. But I was, for the early 80s, always going back to Washington to do the occasional radio show. I was producing one with a couple of other guys, a series on Segovia, so I had that to work on. It was one of my little brainchilds. But at the same time I was establishing myself in New York City. The thing you would find is that the work really was exponential you know, and sort of like coming to a conference like this, someone looks and says, "You could do that." And the guy saying "You could that," it was a record with Bud Shank, Ron Carter, Al Foster, Kenny Baron called This Bud's For You. And it was recorded in one day, multi-track, and mixed that evening. So we started recording about 10 or 11 in the morning and I remember at 3 o'clock in the morning going home. And there I'm thinking I've just been working with giants from the world of jazz, and now I'm changing my baby's diaper.

And then there was no automation on the console, so you were expected to do live mix straight to the two-track, and then you would even do the assembly of the two-track master. So at 3 am when they walked out, they had a master and a safety, and it was going off to mastering the next morning. So that was the aesthetic I came out of, and the one thing I always found was I wanted to be in a situation where I was working with people I wanted to work with, and working on projects and music I wanted to work on. That was my goal. People would always say to me, "Why aren't you doing commercials, why aren't you doing this?" Jingles were really big.

When I would go into the studio, and the way studios used to be, jingles would be from 9 am until about 3 pm, and then the album work would start from 3 pm and go on. And I remember so many times I'd walk in there and somebody I had known from the jingle session saying, "Who you doing today?" I'd say, "Well I've got Frank Foster, Rufus Reed, and Smitty Smith, and Kenny Baron," and I could see they were so jealous. And obviously, I'm working on the better project. They might be making more money in the short term, but I'm having more fun. And my material was going to last, I hear it on the radio today. I hear stuff I did 20, 25 years ago and it's still on the air and it sounds just as fresh and live as it did then, and those jingles died years ago.

I did a couple of Chiquita banana spots but it was only because a friend of mine, a jingle engineer, had asked me to do it. And I found myself doing the same usual thing, there I was, I'm just cutting a voice for Chiquita banana. And I've got the perfect mic and I'm running to cable down the corridor into the perfect mic preamp and he said, "You can't stop that." And I said, "No this is how I've got to do it, it's got to sound like that". Hilarious.

But I did a fair amount of radio. And sometimes I just did it for practice, just to keep my chops up. For almost 20 years I did the Detroit Montreux Jazz Festival, which was four days of live broadcasting from noon until midnight. At the end of four days over Labor Day weekend, we would have done somewhere in the neighborhood of roughly 40 bands. I remember once Michael Brecker was going to be on the Sunday. And he was touring, we would go local until 6 pm and then at 6 we'd go national. And he said, "You know" he was doing two sets, he was doing an afternoon set and an evening, and the evening set was our highlight for that broadcast. So he said, "Do the afternoon, let me listen to it a little bit, and I'll give you the approval if I like it." And at that point, I was not that well known in New York City, I had done some work with Randy (Brecker) and I knew some of the other guys in his band, but I didn't know Michael at the time. So we did the recording and at that time I carried a cassette machine over with a pair of headphones, and Michael listened to it and said, "Yeah, sounds pretty good. Just a touch more cymbals, that's I think all you need." I said, "Fine." I don't know what we would have done otherwise, because we would have had two hours of no air if Michael had said, "No you can't use it."

So about two weeks after the broadcast I get this call from Michael Brecker and he said, "Hey, just wanted to call and tell you this is a great recording. This is really nice."

He said that he'd just broken up with the band and that this was a really nice memento of what this band was like live. And I said, "I have to ask you Michael, a couple of years ago we did a recording for NPR called Steps Ahead in Boston. And I said "it was approved, it was every bit as good as what you just heard." And he said, "Ah, we were probably just being assholes."

So with that experience, Michael said, "The next time like a public radio thing comes to me and asks, you know what? I'm not going to be as snooty about it next time." And after that Michael and I were very good friends, we did a lot of work in the studios. It's that kind of trust that you have to develop sometimes, some fairly big names, you have to prove to them that you can do it. And again that was two-track, that was live, I'm laying in all the effects, all the EQ, any limiting I'm doing or anything like that, at the time. And the thing was, this all developed out of you know, we tried to be very light handed and audiophile like when we first started at NPR. And I would hear it on the air and I would say, "Oh it just sounds wimpy, sounds namby pamby. It didn't have the guts that recording would have." And so I started listening to records and comparing them to my recordings and thinking, "Ok, what's the difference here?" I did something almost like 20 years' worth of the New Year's Eve broadcast for NPR. And I'm on year two or three, maybe year two in Washington and I've got the recording truck in there.

I had a 12 by 2 Neve console. Very nice, heavier, it took like four guys to carry this thing, so bloody heavy. And you know, typical microphones, but here's the thing—normally, what they would have done is they would have just gone in and recorded like normal. Since I was in Washington, I could load up from my studio in NPR all the goodies. So I took in there the first little portable AKG BX10 reverb.

We had the first one. And I took in there a couple of EQs and a couple of dbx 160 compressors, things like that. So, before we're doing the test run broadcast the night before, we would always do a full broadcast on December 30, and then on the December 31, we're ready to go. And so I had done all the processing, and my friends, the other engineers had gone out to San Francisco and are sitting at Kingston Corner listening to the broadcast out there, it's like 5 or 6 o'clock in the evening out there. And I get this phone call from one of the guys and it's like, "You son of a bitch, you've got the BX10. You're...you're processing everything. You know we're never going to be able to come up to that energy in our mix." And I said, "Yeah, because nothing can sound that good." You know what? I'm the first one out of the gate and I've got the east coast feed and damnit I'm going to hit it with everything I've got. So that's what I did, and that's when I started thinking I could do all of this stuff that I would normally do maybe on a remix or in posting, but I could do it live if I really approach all my EQ and all my reverb and all that. And really think about the total mix immediately, and that's where that whole thing kind of started.

You know, with radio you would tend to sort of do the best job you could, and you'd be very light on the EQ. It was really considered early on kind of documentation. I said let's take it beyond documentation, let's make it sound like a record. On the radio stations they're playing records, and our stuff needs to sit right next to it. So we started changing that approach, and it started making the air product sound much better, much more listenable. So I wanted to be able to take these tapes away, take them home. And that was the thing, all of us had professional tape machines at home. So I could take home ten-inch masters and play them on my system at home and really listen to them, really get in there and say, "Okay, I could have done this, I could have done that." And there was a lot of give and take with the music engineers at NPR, and we would sit around a lot on off hours and listen to each other's work. It was a lot of healthy competition.

It was healthy competition because you were fighting for these jobs. If I knew say, oh like a Dexter Gordon recording was coming up I knew I wanted to do that. And also, manufacturers were very good at getting us the latest and greatest. So we had the first set of portable Studer mixers, we had the first pair of B67s, and so we were always kind of testing stuff. We had the first set of I think dbx 160s. The only multi-track we had in house was a set of 3M four-tracks, we had a pair of those and they were really cankerous or persnickety or whatever you want to say. But when they worked they were great. More likely they didn't work. But we had the first set of Type 1 dbx and we used that on those tapes and the stuff was outstanding.

But again, most of our post-production in documentary was two-track, live mix two-track. And so of all the mixing we would do on the documentaries, I think the biggest one I ever did was ten two-track machines, and nothing was ever running in sync. Everything was self-timed. So you were always playing the console, playing the tape machines, all the starts and stops and that thing, doing a live mix, and then you would do an intergenerational cut. And that was the thing, we were always cutting two-track mixes, we were cutting masters, intergenerational masters, so I had my original recording. I had one chance to make that edit and that was going to be it. It had to match, and we had to worry not only about levels but you had to worry about azimuth, about how all these machines had to line up and you sweated bullets. Making sure all that stuff works. And unity, you knew where unity gain was on the console for every single device so you could do a match, and if you had to go back you knew where everything was. But that's why I say that was great training, that's the kind of training I don't think people get these days.

Also, in the studios, there were no assistants. It was me, I had the room, I had to do everything. The only assisting routines were in All Things Considered, like the large shows where you would literally take half the show and then somebody would trot up to the machines and then you'd switch off, so you're really only live for 45 minutes, but it was a straight 45 minutes.

I remember the first time I sat down at the console, I was driving the show and Susan Stanberg looked up and said, "He's driving the show?" and she's like (rolls eyes), and that gives you all the confidence in the world right there. And you had to prove, I can do this. Don't worry lady, everything will be fine. So eventually they forget you're the new kid and new kids come in, so you're always trying to kind of prove yourself, trying to better yourself.

I was always looking for other outside places to learn from, and that's when I went to Eastman, did some courses up there, in music recording in that program up there for a long time back in the '70s. And it was funny, my teachers at that time were Val Valentine who did all the Sinatra records, Ed Green, Gil Muncie, who else? Sid Feldman in mastering. You know we got a great education up there and I remember I brought up a reel. I think I was the only one that had one that had a reel, Detroit Symphony, Jonathan Edwards, real stuff that I could take to each instructor and say, "Here's what I've got, what do you think?" and got good feedback from all of them. And the other thing I learned is, some things you might be doing right. That's good, that sounds great, keep going in that direction. So I used that time with those instructors to also further myself. So it was really a fertile time for a bunch of us down at NPR.

You had to use everything you had because there wasn't much. Each studio had a pair of dbx 160s, that was your limiter, there weren't many others. We had some Pultecs, Lang Program EQs, and we had a pair of those. And that was essentially it. So you had to do everything with shaping that EQ. We had two per machine, and we had two limiters for each machine. And the limiters weren't ganged, you had to set them so they would track stereo, but there were no stereo limiters. In fact I don't think at that time they had stereo ganging on the 160s. So things were pretty crude back then. I took over what was Studio 3, and that was my room basically, or I considered it my room, and I was the first one to take a graphic EQ and do a sweep in the room and kind of set the EQ for the room.

People thought I was crazy but you know what? My stuff sounded like nobody else's. And you know, I would mark the graphic, and if I was in the room, the graphic went on the speakers. I tailored everything to the graphic, so I had some Tannoys, concentric Tannoys, soffit mounted, and those were my mains. We had no small speakers at all, we just had the mains. And I always felt you know it's not quite sounding right, "What can I do to fix it?" I was always thinking in that direction, what pieces do I have that will do that. So our consoles were eight-bus consoles, and you had to think about how you would route signals. All the studio mics were Neumann U87s, but they were used with the rolloff. At the time, that's what you had to do, you were told, you will use this rolloff.

We had a fair amount of on the job training, especially in remote land when you could use condensers, you could use large diaphragm condensers. And you learned when, you learned the hard way sometimes, you were stuck with, "Oh geez I'll never do that again."

That's the thing, you learned when, where, and why you should be using things. We had engineering management that would come down and say, "Why are you doing that?" and if you were doing something you had to justify why you were doing it, why are you using that EQ, why are you using that limiter, this doesn't need limiting. Of course you're a young engineer that wants to play with everything, and try this and try that, and you learned when not to do things. And because you had to justify everything you were doing, that was just out of fear. Because you knew people were going to listen to it, people were going to hear it, it's not like it was just going out in a vacuum and you'd never hear it again. It was going to be heard the next day or even that very day. We had times when we would be going up to New York, doing a recording and we were posting that show the following Monday. We had literally a two-hour slot to fill, we needed every ounce of music that was coming off the stage and you had the pressure of knowing that there was nothing to waste there. And so also, that was the thing, you went off and did the recording, you came back and had to post it. So you would have to live and die by the recording you made. And also, your success rate would determine whether you got to go out on the next job too. So you were always trying to make sure that your stuff was always on a level that it was going to ensure the next job. There was a subtle pressure that was there.

I still mix on a console, I still do it by hand. I now use automation, certainly, but I'll still approach it like a live mix. Like a live two-track mix. I don't like the sound of mixing in the box, I just don't like that sound. So if I have a chance to use a pro control what I'll do is maybe a level automation, but have it come out in say eight stems, put that through a line level mixer like a GML or a Millennia and have that be my two-track, and add my reverb there. So I'm really spitting this out in 8 or 16 channels and just doing the combining. I don't like the way the computer sounds still on combining networks, on the bussing. I don't know what it is, they haven't quite gotten that together at all.

My students still try to figure out, "Why does your stuff sound this way and why does my stuff sounds this way?" Also, I like the tactile feeling of being able to listen to something and I can pretty much with my hand know just a slight little pull here or there is all this needs. Or I can kind of ride it. Especially transversely, if I go back and do an edit on a Pro tools session, how would I have done that if I'd had two tape machines and I was doing a crossfade between them? I'd have the one up, and then I'd sneak the other in and do a quick over. Now in the envelope, I know what I'm going to do is have this one go long, this one stick in and go. So I'll tend to imitate in my mind, here's how I would have done it with my hands. And so that's how I'll look at these fade curves, I'll tend to approach it that way. Having that tactile feeling really helps me with Pro tools.

What else am I doing, using these days? Microphones haven't changed. I do a lot with the B&Ks. My favorite vocal mic is the Dirk Brauner, but it's really based on a 251, it's just quieter and its under warranty. And the Sanken microphones. So I had my sort of, my palette of microphones I use all the time. And I know they're going to work, I know where they are, I know the placement on them, I have some consistency that I can work with. The one thing I've gotten into over the past 20 years are mic-pres, which before, at NPR, we had two flavors. If you are on remote, it's a Neve, if you're in the studio it's a Spectrasonics. That's the choice you have. Or if you're using the Studer consoles, you were using Studer mic-pres. But you learned on those things, you learned gain stage, how to literally maximize your gain staging. So the training was unbelievable, where could you have been thrown at so many different projects? And I remember once when I was off, when I was a newbie basically, I went off to assist the original music recording engineer at NPR back in like 75 I think, I was there only for a few weeks I think. I went off to Chicago to do the Chicago Folk Festival. I was manning the stage, I was doing everything stage related because there was nobody out there doing it, period.

Also the hall had nobody and the folk festival had nobody. Okay if we're going to do this I'm going to need to know xyz. So I would go back into the truck during the one act and say, "Okay, here's what's coming up." Blank blank blank blank blank. Done. So I was stage managing, I was doing everything. Came back, we had driven from Washington to Chicago and back, so I sat down in my supervisor's office and ask, "What's coming up this week?" He looked up and said, "What are you doing tomorrow?" I said, "Detroit symphony, okay?" and he said, "Okay tomorrow we leave for Detroit." Same truck, traveled up to Detroit, but this time he said "I understand you're a pretty good mixer. It's your job." So he basically watched me work. Interestingly enough it was the Detroit Symphony and the Billy Taylor Trio. It was for Black History Month in February. And then Billy became one of my closest friends, but that was my initial meeting with Billy and the trio. And 15 years later I'm working with Billy in the studio and we're cutting tracks for an album with Billy. All that work experience really paid off.

There was some gear that didn't do enough, like the Lang Program EQ. I would complain mightily that there's nothing in the midrange. There's something in the bottom and something in the top but there are times I know I have to do something in the middle, what can I do here? And that was all we had for a long time. There was nothing in the board, so that was on everything you were doing then, you were really missing the mid-EQ. So you shaped, you tried to figure ways you could bring out things by shaping the bottom and shaping the top and maybe bumping, you did the middle with levels. So you learned all that stuff. So you make it louder and add compression. So between EQ and compression you had the tools you needed. Eventually they got into more of that kind of stuff. And you know at that time the parametric hadn't been invented.

The Orban was the first one we had. And you know Bob Orban brought it in and said, "Here guys, try this. I just made this." Yeah, we had one of the first ones. You did more with less at that time because that's all you had and we had to figure out how to do it. I was just telling my students two days ago, I said, "You know you're in a room, you're lucky, this is probably the best room you're ever going to work in, where everything works. I can guarantee everything works." I said, "I just came from two days of mixing in a studio where if I wasn't careful, something I had panned to the left actually would go to the center because the switching was so funky that you have to be aware." I said, "I would love for you to work in a room where half the stuff doesn't work." In fact I used to give my students a snake and say, "Mic the drums," but I knew half the snake wasn't working. So they would plug everything up and think everything was okay. I'd also have it misnumbered, "No, that's not number 1 that's number 7!" and I would do it on purpose. And I said, "I'm not going to do that to you people," but that's what I used to do to these guys. It's almost like you have to design traps to show them what could happen.

The one thing I learned to do at NPR was signal flow and the patch bay. I would go in on weekends, especially when I first started, and I would set myself a goal. I would say today I'm going to get the signal from here to there, how do I do it? Or coming up, for example, I had to create the sound of a grocery store PA system. And the compressor needed to act as a ducker. How can I do that? So when the voice would come in the music would slam away, so you learn how to set that threshold really tenderly, and then all of a sudden the voice comes in and everything pops out. So you learned to use these things as creative devices, I'd take a Saturday, come in and just do that.

Things I can't believe anyone is calling vintage? There's the PCM 42s, and the price those things go for, I can't believe it. You've got those, you've got the Lang Program EQs. I still have a pair of those lying around in my basement, someone says, "I'll give you a ton of money for those," I say, "You can have them." I'd be happy to get a lot of money for those things. You know once someone asked me, "How do you emulate analog?" I said, "I use analog, that's how I emulate it." Like my latest Patricia Barber recording. The final that we mastered from is actually half-inch, 15IPS SR, which I then bumped over to a digital file. I made the transfer immediately, didn't leave it up to anybody, didn't have to worry about the cards, and the mastering engineer had a choice of the original digital transfer or the one that went through the half-inch ATR100. And he picked blindly the ATR consistently.

And it just sounded grounded. So you know I'm still using two-inch or at least a half-inch master. So analog tape is still the best, well, for example, my little quarter-inch Nagra, the stereo Nagra still works like a champ, and the tapes sound great. They sound better than a DAT for sure.

I carried those around, we haven't talked about any of that stuff, but I used to do a ton of outside broadcast. And I learned a lot about going out in the field and gathering sound. I did it in Africa, I did it in Japan, I did it in Europe, and literally for a long time you carried a stereo Nagra on your shoulder and developed ways of carrying stereo pairs and things like that. And I created a pair of what some used to call Anderheisers because they were Dean Clark hearing protection cups that I would put Sennheiser headphones inside. So, when we did the Daytona Firecracker 400 on the Fourth of July, you were standing beside 40 stock cars at 200 mph. You could put these on and hear what was coming in through the microphones and you were protected and you heard all that. So again you just had to be creative as hell. So I had a pair of 421s mounted on a handbar and that's how you went around and got the sounds I needed, and you had to create all these things.

So 421 s everyone thinks of them as a tom mic, that was my main sound gathering mic. And as a studio pair they're a beautiful sound. Also I remember once I was recording the sound of oxen plowing in a field in Somalia and the wind was like crazy. And I had various sizes of windsocks I had built out of foam and they still weren't enough. And with those mics you had the roll-off and I got the track. So you learned every inch of every piece of gear you had.

I've talked to some of the guys on the jazz show we did and I said to them, "I wish we knew then what we know now." And had the experience and knowledge, we could really go in and do a serious kick-ass show.

As far as the gear, I could still do the same show with the same mixers. It translated very nicely from one stage to the other. I can still sit down and mix a two-channel show with a pair of Studer mixers. Or I can do it on a DM 2000, because of having that experience of running that to this. For example, on the Patricia Barber live CD, there's an instrumental track on there while everything else is multi. One of the machines had died, and we had an audience upstairs that was rhythmically clapping. We had to let them go and we weren't ready in the control room. They said what are we going to do? I said, "Well, you guys get this thing fixed and get it rolling, I'll sit and do the best live mix I possibly can." And out of that one set there's one tune and that's the version. And that's about it, the effects are all a DM 2 or DM 5, whatever it was before, it might be the DM 1000, the early version. And so everything, the mix, the effects, is from that desk, that digital desk, to an HHB CD cutter. And so when this comes out on MoFi and all these esoteric XRCDs and they get the masters, they say "Well where's the master of this tune?" What's that CD doing? That is the master. That's it. And that comes again from that, "I'll sit here and just do everything right now," bang. And that's the live mix I did in the basement of this club, and it's been released in five formats in two types of LP and two types of CD.

There were actually some guys up in Canada that had a system where they made it sound like the audience was behind them in surround. But that again comes from using a lot of the studio techniques I have now, but basing it on that radio technique that I developed. In fact it's the reason I sometimes feel like I have trouble instructing students, because for me it's so innate, I don't have to think about it. And what can I tell you, all you have to do is sit and listen, this is all you have to do. And when I mix that's what I do, I sit and listen. What's wrong, okay it needs a little bit of this, a little bit of that, and you concentrate solely on one element at a time. And when I'm doing a live mix, I find if I can shift my focus around the mix then the mix is okay. If something's grabbing my attention it's saying that there's something's wrong over there. And that again comes from being in the moment and doing radio.

It takes years of experience, but there's an innate talent too. And it is the kind of thing you either have or you don't. If it was that easy, everyone could do it. But it's not that easy.

The other side of it is sometimes the project, doesn't matter who's sitting there, it's still going to suck. And there's nothing you can do about it, you wish you could be the magic guy that can do everything but you can't. I've heard stuff that George has done that I've thought, "Wow, I can't get a bass sound like that." And George says, "You can't do everything." But we're all human and there are times when it ain't your day. I've had plenty of those days where it wasn't my day but you just make the best of it. For example I would do some TV shows where it was a student orchestra, 160- or 180 piece student orchestra, and I would be beating myself up over the string sound. And then there's a point I have to say, "I've done the best job I can, it's a student orchestra." I'm so used to working with the best players in New York City, I can put 12 New York string players out there and get this incredible string sound. You know it ain't me, it's the players. I just happen to be putting good mics set in the right place, I'll get the sound. But if the players aren't happening, you are going to have a hell of a time getting the sound. And so you always have to look at the situation and kind of assess that and try to figure out what's the best thing I can do? Maybe I'm doing the best I can right now.

So much of the old gear keeps coming back, the 1176, the LA2. Well you know I wish RCA was still making RCAs, the real ones. Because all these others, the Royers sound like Royers and Coles sound like Coles, RCA sound like RCAs. And that, I think that's the one thing I miss. So I love when I can get a 77 or a 44.

If they're treated well they tend to do okay. And in New York at Avatar, we've got I think easily four, six, eight of each one. And they're all in pretty good shape. The thing is you do have to be careful and really audition them when you listen to them. Also, you never know if they're going to be in polarity, you've got to be very aware of all that stuff.

You've got to get your ear trained for that stuff. The one thing I've been able to do is to pre-conceive a session, if you know the players you have a sense that this microphone will be fine for this and this will be fine for that. You already know what it's going to sound like before you hear a single note. And so if you can get to that point where you know the gear inside and out, where you can understand if I choose this microphone, I put it in this placement on this kind of instrument, I'm going to get this kind of sound. So I can pick, choose. And many times I'll send in my setup for the sessions, and on my short walk from the subway to the studio I'll say, "What if I did this?" Or I'll walk in and I'll say to the musicians, "We're not going to use these, we're going to use these over here." And they'll swing with it, and it's usually the right decision. It had to percolate a little bit. And it's generally the right approach.

Besides the 77s and 44s, I wish we'd bought 56s and 67s when they were new because they were about $400, something like that. But I'm still using many of the microphones I bought 20, 25 years ago, so it's not like I've given any of this stuff up. The only thing I've tried to do is make sure my collection is a collection of gear that I know the studio won't buy, it's either too expensive or too esoteric. I can always get an 87, studio's got a hundred 87s. But they're not going to have ten 4007s. I can do that. Or 4006s or any of that stuff.

I've got almost the entire Sanken collection. And I've got it all there, I know exactly what it sounds like. And that's the kind of stuff, sort of like I wish I had this mic package then that I have now. It's taken all these years to develop this package.

You know, but you know, I was doing a John Fadis record with Ray Brown and Harold Land and Kenny Baron and Mel Lewis on drums. And John said to me, "Here's how I'd like to do it. I want to do it where I'm standing here and the drums are behind me". And in a studio you kind of go "Oh no" and also it was two-track. Two-track digital, Mitsubishi X80. And I thought wait, I've done live recordings. Yeah, it's just like a club, we'll make it sound like a club. So, in the recording studio John's happy. I remember we did the first playback and Ray Brown said, "Ehh, tweak it here, do this" and on the second playback Ray came in and said, "Yeah, when you get it you get it. It takes you a while to get it." So, thanks Ray. But you know, he understood. Because it's live to two, and that record still sounds pretty damn amazing. But then I'm cutting the X80, you're cutting that with a razor and assembling that tape.

I guess the thing is, back then I would love to have had the experience and knowledge I've got now. I'd like to have my mic package, you know I'd love to have some of this new convolution reverb stuff like the Sony 777. Some pieces like that would have been really cool.

The last thing I bought would have been some Radio Shack PZMs—the boundary layer mics, they were closing those out and I thought, "Oh, got to get a couple." But the last would have been a Sanken CUW-180, which is a stereo mic that they developed based on my technique, so I loved that. And you know most of my purchases have been microphones or mic-pres.

People would expect our recordings to stand up against Al Schmitt and Diana Krall. You're expecting it to play, you've got a girl singer and a piano. You know, you can't just sit there and spend hours on a drum sound. But also the musicians appreciate that too. The fact that pretty much we have an 11 o'clock boundary, we're willing to take an 11 o'clock. 11 to 1. The new Kenny Baron that's just coming out right now, while they were running the tune, I didn't say a word, I was just getting my sounds. And so then Kenny said, "Let's run that tune down" and I hooked it up and rolled it. We rolled it and Kenny at the very end, this is Ann Hampton Callaway, they did this beautiful song. Kenny said, "Aww damn, too bad we didn't get it" and I said, "Let's see if we didn't get it" and Kenny says "You got that?" "Yeah". And that's the take, the take is that rehearsal, that's the first thing we did.

Everyone goes wow, and you are their hero. Michael Brecker, there's a version on the Charlie Brown Christmas with Cyrus Chestnut, they do a duo, O Hark the Herald Angels Sing, and on this record especially I thought I should roll all the time, this is 3348 Sony. And so again, at the end of that Michael says "Geez, how long was that?" I said, "Let's roll back the tape and see." He says "That's on tape?" and you know what, it's so innocent they just play the melody they're not thinking and it's incredible, it's Michael Brecker at his peak. And again, they look at you like, "You have just saved my life, you have shown what I can do." And time after time after time that's the kind of thing, you can't be sitting back there not engaged in what's going on in the studio. You have to be completely on top of your game and completely involved with these people. You have to think of it as a documentary, you're not just making a record. So it's not the rolling but that you're aware, because digits are cheap, you can throw them away if they're no good, but if you're not recording you can't get it. That's like my radio experience. I did a solo album with Gonzalo Rubalcaba, and I said, "Look, when you leave this room you will never have to worry about am I rolling, are we ready, is it a take? You leave this room, tape is rolling. So if you're sitting there, you're playing, you never have to worry about anything. Don't worry about it." So for three days, he'd leave the room he'd play, he came in, that's when we stopped. I also set him up so he couldn't see me, he was off on his own, so it was him with the piano. So if I'm doing a solo album I'll tend to approach it that way. Don't worry about us. You're there, you can play anytime you want. So it's again kind of documenting this process.

Chapter 30

Bil VornDick

The successful musical career of Bil VornDick covered well over five decades. As a youth, his musical education and private tutoring on various instruments excelled his performance in a leading band in the Washington D.C. area. When Bil was a teenager, he enjoyed recording his songs in the studio, and that led him to record and produce other groups in his region. Signing his songs to a publisher in Nashville at 19, Bil was able to meet the heads of the music industry in Nashville who encouraged him to attend Belmont University where he gained a B.B.A. in Music Business.

Directly after graduation, Bil was hired by Country Music Legend and Country Music Hall of Fame member Marty Robbins to be his Chief Recording Engineer. This position made it possible for him to work with the leading stars in Country Music. Over the years in Nashville, Bil became known internationally as one of the leading Engineers and Producers, developing and producing the career of such acts as the multiple Grammy winner Alison Krauss. Bil's work with other artists has resulted in 42 Grammy nominations, eight Grammy wins, and various multiple Gold and Platinum albums. Around 600 albums have his credits. Bil's accomplishments have led to number-one records in five different styles of music. When it comes to awards in acoustic music, Bil has received every one that can be won and in most instances, he has won repeatedly.

The artists that Bil has worked with in the studio read like a who's who...from Bob Dylan, Bela Fleck, Jerry Douglas, and T.Bone Burnett to Maura O'Connel, Mark O'Connor, and Ralph Stanley, to name a few. Bil's life in the studio has been very rewarding. An album he produced "Clinch Mountain Country" and released in May 1998 is one of the largest collaborative recorded projects in Nashville, with 36 songs, 32 artists, and won Album and Recorded Event of the Year at IBMA 1999, plus number-one Country Album of the year 1998 in Rolling Stone. The album "Sweethearts" by Ralph Stanley was a Grammy Finalist for the year 2001.

Drawing from a background in music composition and arranging, Bil produced and/or engineered soundtracks for a documentary film with James Taylor, movies

DOI: 10.4324/9781003519829-30

(Twisted Justice, Outlaw Force, The Loner, etc.), and jingles for major corporations (McDonald's, American Airlines, etc.).

Bil's dedication to the music industry has placed Bil on the Board of Directors of Belmont University's Advisory Board, South Plains College, North American Folk Alliance, a Who's Who in American Entertainment and in Europe, a leader "IN CHARGE" in the Nashville publication Music Row, and served as Chairman of the Nashville Audio Engineering Society. He was also a P&E Wing committee member of NARAS that set the delivery and archival standard for digital recorded media. He also gave back by giving of his time by lecturing at Middle Tennessee State University (MTSU), IBMA, MerleFest, South Plains College, Telluride Music Festival, Swannanoa Gathering, and as an adjunct professor at Belmont University. He also offered internships each semester to qualified recording arts students at MTSU and Belmont University. He was a member of the CMA, IBMA, BSA, AES, Folk Alliance, National Academy of Recording Arts and Sciences, F&AM, A&ASRF, and the Shrine.

Bil VornDick passed away in July 2022 at the age of 72.

Figure 30.1 Music is an art, not a science. Even though there is the National Academy of Recording Arts & Sciences, it's an art. No offense to them, but the young students need to know that they need to get a performance, and they don't need to treat it as a science, as a computer science. It's not computer science.

I'm Bil VornDick and I was born in Washington D.C., March the 9th, 1950. When I was a teenager, I wasn't even old enough to drive, I had a Wollensak tape recorder and I was in a rock and roll band, and when my band wasn't working I would go out and record other bands in the northern Virginia area. And, I got my mics…I guess it was from a store called Lafayette in Seven Corners. And then after that, I started hanging out at studios up near D.C.

George Massenberg was working there; it was in Bethesda. But I always had a small studio, and then I got encouraged to move to Nashville by Chet Atkins. Chet Atkins mentored me, he started mentoring me when I was about 19 and then signed my paperwork

Figure 30.2 I got a call from Don Wershba at SSL at the beginning of the week, and it made me feel really good because he just took the time and I've known him forever and he goes, "I just picked up Jerry Douglas' album, and thanks Bill, I'm listening to music again." Because I made it to a point where it wasn't slammed—it was loud but it had distance, there were notes that were expressive that weren't brought up on a Waves Leveler. Takes all the emotion. He said, "It's an album that gave me emotion again." So that meant a lot. They're not gonna witness what happens in the control room and then after it's processed and out to the market, they're not going to actually be able to feel the hairs going up on the back of your neck while it's being recorded and you know which ones which will be the singles by how many hairs rose up on the back of your neck and the little cold chills. The general public I'm afraid are not going to really witness the emotion that was there in vinyl, everything that has to be so correct now. And in this town, they'll take a drummer that's making $800 for three hours to play on a song and then strip him away and grid him to the click and then replace all emotion and dynamics that he performed so that it would be absolutely, perfectly correct. But that "perfectly correct" is just an opinion.

Figure 30.3 About three weeks ago I recorded a group; 16-track, two inch in RCA Studio B. And we were cutting through an old API console. It doesn't get any more warm and fuzzy to me than that. And I think it's the reality that you're actually hearing the sine wave 'cause it's creating a sine wave, and you're actually hearing back the sine wave without the pixels and the analysis. And on those machines they still go up to 30some k. So you've got those overtones, and it's the overtones of the instruments that, for me, make the tone color. So I try to record analog as much as I can. And, I just mixed a couple projects to 1/2 inch. We recorded digitally but I haven't mixed in the box yet, not even demos. I still go through a console. And maybe it's the old me, but to me it still sounds better.

Figure 30.4 I have a Lexicon 200 still, and it's running. And nothing's got those sounds in it. Nothing sounds the same as that, it's a little gritty and it has its own uniqueness. No different than the 240 or D2. But through the whole process, it's the microphones that I think that have lost. And now pretty much everything's made in China. So, the Neumanns and AKGs and the Telefunkens, nobody's really the same anymore. Neumann is owned by Sennheiser, I don't know where their product is made, but if you stick a 149 up against a 49, there's no comparison.

Figure 30.5 And I have tape, a little white console tape on each one of the 84s so I know which one is which. And I have little notes on it. So when I grab it, I don't have to memorize the serial number, I just put white tape on it and my interns and assistants go, "Man, you've got tape on your microphones." And I say, "They're my tools." When I'm gone, if someone wants to buy them from me, my family, if they want to sell them then they'll just have to deal with it, either they're going to buy it or they're not. For me, I know I can go there, I can open up my case and go "BAM!" That's the one that I want for this and that's the one that I use on Sam Bush because they're all different.

so I could get into Belmont. Back then you had to be endorsed by somebody to get in, it was such a small program. So coming up through that era there was a lot of acoustic musical festivals, bluegrass music festivals, and I was always there with, I guess it was a Teac at that point, or the Sony cassette machine, recording those festivals. And then doing different bands in the area. But, at that point it was still to stereo. I did my first recording in mono, that would have been '62ish.

Figure 30.6 Marty Robbins was extremely consistent. Of all the vocal stylists that I've worked with, he was the best. And intonation wasn't an issue. I mean if he was a little flat it was my job to tell him. And he would come in and listen, and he goes, "Well, yeah I am a little bit, but it feels really good, Bill." And we left everything with the definition of "feel". Intonation wasn't as important as the feeling and the emotion that was being represented. You know, where nowadays everything has to be in tune, and I think the kids look at tuning more and they're not listening to the performance that's actually being recorded.

It was a few years later when the Sony machine came out, stereo. I want to say that machine was a 530. I wanted a Tandberg so bad, I just couldn't afford it. Studer was out of the question.

So I came to Nashville and after Belmont Marty Robbins grabbed me. It was my late teens that Chet Atkins, when he came to Washington D.C. he would invite me over for dinner before his performance. And then I signed with Cedarwood Publishing Company as a songwriter when I was 19. But when I graduated from Belmont, Marty Robbins grabbed me. And I worked for him for three years until he passed away. And then Ken Laxton was an engineer at CBS, and CBS had closed their studios. And he went independent then. I engineered a lot of his stuff for about a year, then I built a studio on the corner down here called Curb Studio now, for a company at that point. So, it gave me the opportunity to build something from the ground up. And, what's neat is it's still operational.

It was called Stargem, originally, and it was the first all-Sony studio. With the MCI 600 and the JH-24, Sony had just bought MCI. And the president of Sony happened to be coming through doing a tour of the United States and he had come by, I forget the guy's name but he bowed a lot. It was pretty basic, even back then. I think we had an LA2A, a couple of 1176s, four 160s. At that point, I started buying a lot of outboard gear, Lexicon gear. Because none of the studios, well none that I knew of, had other outboard, besides the compressors, or maybe a Space Station or TimeCube or the flanger and phaser, Eventide, an Eventide 910. And, if you were really lucky you had a 949. They were pretty sparse, so I bought equipment and then I rented it out when I wasn't mixing. I would rent out the rack for a 100 bucks a day. And that did very well. And then that rack grew into other racks. And I collected, I remember back in Marty Robbin's days, everything starting to go transistor for microphones, and I started buying up the tube microphones that people were selling so they could buy the new transistorized microphones, so they didn't have to replace the tube. I know I have a nice collection of tubes. And they're still a little noisy but man, they sound really good.

So about '84 I went independent. And then a few years after that I just had my own room across from Sound Stage and Ronnie Milsap's place for a long time—until the A-DATs came in. And then it was more cost-effective, tax-wise, for me just to hire studios. And I've always had a studio at home.

Favorite pieces of gear? Oh, LA3A. It's always been one of my favorites. There was a vocal stressor that I now own, but we had one of those at Marty Robbins'. It had just come out. It was made by ADR. I really like that, and that was about it. We had two plates, and we had an extra B67 that had a variable speed on it so we could use it to slap the plate for delay. 47s, 67s. Yeah, C12s. It's all down to the performance. We didn't have that many choices. In this facility you have so many different choices. Marty Robbins' studio had a limited amount of mics, and that's when we stuck the ECM 50s, the Sony's inside the acoustic guitar because the acoustic guitars…we usually had two acoustic guitars in the session, so they sat right across from each other in the live room. And we didn't use headphones.

There was a 610 that I really liked; a mono unit. I liked it on bass instead of the LA2A. But back then we didn't compress a lot. If we did we did it very slightly; if the singer was uneven. So at Marty Robbins', I had the LA3A then we went to the vocal stressor. But mainly I used it so I could use the high-pass filter 'cause it had a side chain EQ and I could get the air conditioning out 'Cause you could hear it a little bit.

When I first started seeing these compressors I mainly used them to keep everything sort of leveled. Especially the bass, I used them more on bass than anything else. I would ride vocals instead of compressing vocals and then in the mix, compress them to have them hold their position. Back then we didn't have automation, so the more that we could do to get everything settled while we were tracking, the easier it was to mix. And tape, marking the tape and knowing where you're at, we didn't have any more than maybe half an hour at the most to mix a song.

Marty Robbins was extremely consistent. Of all the vocal stylists that I've worked with, he was the best. And intonation wasn't an issue. I mean if he was a little flat it was my job to tell him. And he would come in and listen, and he goes, "Well, yeah I am a little bit, but it feels really good, Bill." And we left everything with the definition of "feel". Intonation wasn't as important as the feeling and the emotion that was being represented. You know, where nowadays everything has to be in tune, and I think the kids look at tuning more and they're not listening to the performance that's actually being recorded.

I liked the Space Station when it first came out. Marty didn't know what it was. I remember one time on a playback, during his sessions, he was always making jokes and kidding around. So I thought on a playback that I would patch in the new Harmonizer 910 and detune it a little bit and play it back, and that got about four bars, and Marty goes, "I couldn't possibly be singing that flat." And everybody else in the session started laughing 'cause they knew I was playing a joke on Marty. And then I bypassed it and kept throwing it in and he goes, "Bil, did you do that on that box I just bought?" 'Cause he always called them boxes—and I went, "Yes, sir." And he goes, "Don't ever do that again." But there really wasn't that much, I used the delays on the 910 a lot, and we had one machine for slapping, and if I wasn't using the 910 for anything like if you got a double acoustic guitar, if you had one acoustic guitar, I would use that as a delay line with another plate.

I never stopped using LA3As, LA2As, 1176s, dbx 160s—they're incredible. I use them for kick and snare. LA2As are mainly used for bass. LA3As for vocals. My vocal path right now is Martech and an LA3A, no high-pass filter or anything. Plates...I love the sound of plates and I haven't heard a plug-in that sounds like a real EMT 240 gold foil yet. I still have a plate at the house. When I closed the studio, I moved the plates to the house and one of them took too much room so I couldn't put the car in the garage, so I sold one, and I still have one.

They stayed pretty consistent. I mean you have to do the maintenance on them. I just like the way they sound. There's a couple rooms here in Nashville that have live chambers and I tried to use them. You can't use them as much on vocals anymore because they wash so much, but for effects, on Bela Fleck's albums I've used the chambers quite a bit.

I still ride the vocal on a fader. I have four Neve faders in a pack that I carry around. And sometimes I'll ride guitar solos instead of having to over-compress them later. I would much prefer for the listener to feel that they're part of the group, what they're listening to, instead of having it slammed into their face. Nowadays pretty much everything is so loud and slammed to compress that the tones of the instruments are being forsaken for space. So I don't compress a whole lot, I don't compress drums onto tape. Why interfere with the performance? The nuances? I might compress a kick or snare later if I need it to be a little more solid or it's starting to drop. I don't normally record bass anymore with a compressor. I let those nuances happen, and then figure out if that's going to translate in the mix that I'm doing on a particular song. You can always damage it later, so why compress all the transients when you don't know exactly how they're going to be coming at you from song to song? A lot of people set up their compressors, especially their attack and release times, and I try to be very conscious when we're changing a song on a different tempo to relate those attacks and release times to the tempo that we're in. So, if I don't have to think about that, I can always do that later. Especially in digital. I mean, digital does so much harm to the analog signal path, anyway. Just my opinion.

About three weeks ago, I recorded a group; 16-track, two inch in RCA Studio B. And we were cutting through an old API console. It doesn't get any more warm and fuzzy to me than that. And I think it's the reality that you're actually hearing the sine wave 'cause it's creating a sine wave, and you're actually hearing back the sine wave without the pixels and the analysis. And on those machines, they still go up to 30some k. So you've got those overtones, and it's the overtones of the instruments that, for me, make the tone color. So I try to record analog as much as I can. And, I just mixed a couple projects to 1/2 inch. We recorded digitally but I haven't mixed in the box yet, not even demos. I still go through a console. And maybe it's the old me, but to me it still sounds better.

It sounds more "musical" to me. It's the overtones. The processors are not fast enough yet; it's still only 2008, and it's getting better. I was at the first mastering of a digital mix, and I think it was eight-bit and on Soundstream and the equipment took up the whole wall at Masterphonics just to play back a three-and-a-half-minute song. And it was Mack Evans, Glen Meadows, Jimmy Bowen and me, and the team from Soundstream, trying to keep all the processors going. And then, two years later a DAT machine came out. But even then it just sounded small. There's something about analog that makes everything sound real. And I don't think anybody driving down the road really knows the difference. They like what they like.

Everything was so new back then and I never thought of it as being disappointing because I didn't know what they were missing. You really knew when you went from the 910 Eventide to the 949, that was another incredible box that did so much more. The Eventide flanger and phaser did what it did. I had an old Maestro, I've still got it, the pedal that you got back in the '60s, that had speed and balls on it, I used to use that, I used to put that in our mixes because that was like the first phaser kind of thing. A lot different from the Fuzz Tone that came about here during Marty Robbins' "Don't Worry About Me," when Grady Martin overdrove the pre-amp. And they're smart enough to make the box. If Marty hadn't said "Man I think that's cool," then it would've been just considered a mistake.

Talking about that era, API and Neve, you can never go wrong. Until they started making the fixed consoles, the MCI I guess was the first one.

I never got to work with Fairchilds until I came to Oceanway, so I didn't really get to experience them. Oh, the Flickenger. I liked Flickenger. There were a couple of rooms that had Flickenger.

In the "what were we thinking" category? Oh, every plug-in, probably. Really, if I thought back when I was a teenager that we would actually be spending our time looking at computer screens, which I don't, I look at artists have an assistant doing the typing and stuff normally, unless we're on a one-on-one doing overdubs. I would have never thought that it was going to come down to zeroes and ones.

Even as late as 1980 I don't even think we were really thinking that. And a lot of people here had the JVC U-Matic, we had it in a rack, we'd mix everything to that because Masterphonics did a lot of our mastering, so they had quite a few. And there was the Sony F1.

The Altec was popular in a lot of rooms here. There were some gates, compressors, as a matter of fact I just sold one of my Gain Brain racks to one of my past interns. I still use the Valley People 730 a lot. I like that. But the Kepexes, when they first came out, I can remember going to England to visit my wife's relatives and Drawmer had just come out with a gate. I was in London getting off the train coming back from Cornwall and getting there just in time to pick up the gate. And I put it in my suitcase and carried it back with me, and I was gating the returns to the plates, and I remember over at Masterphonics people going, "How are you doing that?" And I had the Drawmer gates. And then I bought some more. But, back then we didn't have that in Nashville.

That's why in the early '80s I put together that rack, because rooms didn't have that Primetime, they didn't have 42s. A harmonizer was kind of normal here, but I had the Aural Exciters, I had compellers in there, MXR, the first thing that we talked about earlier, you had the four buttons you could change the pitch on each one so you could tune things. Things that weren't normal in Nashville, I just put in a box with a patch bay and you could roll it up to anywhere. So Nashville was probably a little bit behind the times, but we had really nice rooms here. It wasn't until the early '80s when Nashville was probably the town that took digital and embraced it. During that era, the producers that were here, I think we probably at one point had more digital machines than New York or LA.

Mitsubishi got a big hold here, and Otari, I mean real big hold, everybody switched over, so at that point we kind of switched over with the cutting edge of digital, and at that point Country market share went up tremendously. I mean, there were 22 labels here at one time! Every major label had multiple divisions.

It's just that it happened so fast here. Everybody made the transition so fast. So we're very used to doing it. Some of us still ran digital multi-tracks and analog machines at the same time. I'd do an album where there's a 32 Mitsubishi and a Studer 827. And trying to get them both to punch in at the same time didn't happen. So you had to do each machine manually. Back then there weren't assistants. Assistants really didn't do anything. It was the first engineer that did all those punch-ins.

The unions were gone by about '82. CBS was closed and RCA studios were closed. Yeah, there weren't assistants. It wasn't like you had to have a tape op and a maintenance person there at the session. If there's anything, there was an intern there from Belmont, either for the studio or for the engineer.

Looking back at what they're calling vintage? LA2As and 3As and 1176s because they are still such good units. On the other side of it, Fairchild. I really don't use it that much unless I really want to slam something and make it less defined.

I have a Lexicon 200 still, and it's running. And nothing's got those sounds in it. Nothing sounds the same as that, it's a little gritty and it has its own uniqueness. No different than the 240 or D2. But through the whole process, it's the microphones that I think that have lost. And now pretty much everything's made in China. So, the Neumanns and AKGs and the Telefunkens, nobody's really the same anymore. Neumann is owned by Sennheiser, I don't know where their product is made, but if you stick a 149 up against a 49, there's no comparison.

But then if you took every one of those, if you line up all those 67s here at Oceanway, each one of them sounds different. And all the C12s sound different, I have a pair of U47s and each one of them sounds different. I have a 67, a pair of 54s and 64s, RCA 77, 74s, a bunch of km84s, got about six of them in my arsenal. And each one of those sounds different.

And I have tape, a little white console tape on each one of the 84s so I know which one is which. And I have little notes on it. So when I grab it I don't have to memorize the serial number, I just put white tape on it and my interns and assistants go, "Man, you've got tape on your microphones." And I say, "They're my tools." When I'm gone, if someone wants to buy them from me, my family, if they want to sell them then they'll just have to deal with it, either they're going to buy it or they're not. For me, I know I can go there, I can open up my case and go, "BAM!" That's the one that I want for this and that's the one that I use on Sam Bush because they're all different. I think the microphones are what's taken the biggest hit. Unless the kids that are in school right now actually get to experience a good C-12 or a 67 or a 47 or a 48 or a 49 or 50, or the 54s, and then the 64 and how the 64 sounds against the 84. How can they possibly know unless they witness that, to have that paintbrush, that sound paintbrush? We talked about outboard gear, but the microphones and the mic pres, I used to love every opportunity I had to go work on an 8068 'cause it was musical to me.

And the Sphere would have probably been second. Even the Neoteks were kind of popular here in town, and they were pretty much around class-A. And they sounded nice and warm, like the 9098 was probably the last console I could think of that sounds that way, that close to Rupert Neve, probably because Rupert Neve designed it. The API and the Neve will work now, ten years from now, twenty years from now; all the others come and go.

But I think if they can invest wisely and invest in vintage mics and original 1176s or LA3As or 2As, There's going to be things that are not going to go down in value. The reissued ones, I don't even think they're going to go down. The little switch, the new mod on the LA3A, brings the noise floor down 3 dB. It's incredible. I think if they were to invest in mics, get their vocal chain and their mic pre, and then work from there it would help.

What I have now that I wish I had then? Martek. I like the B76s and the B72s a whole lot. I'm a big proponent of 1073s 1081s, 1060, and the 1084s. Great River, I wish I had a Great River mic pre, stereo mic pre, and equalizer back in the '70s. It's an incredible mic pre; you have the loading switch, you have the impedance switch. I used it on bass. I used it on Jerry Douglas's dobro. It's transparent with the warmth of Rupert. It's the only mic pre that you could take a 57 and mono mic a Conga and have the bottom end roll your pant legs. That mic pre is incredible. Maybe a Mercury, the Mercurys are like 76s. Of all of them, the Great River. Back then, unless you worked on a Neve console, there weren't rental companies where you could get pres. I had Sontec mic pres; I had two stereo pairs Sontec mic pres. When I would go to studios like Mike Bradley's down at Soundshop, when I'd bring in my rack and my mic pres and my mics, he goes, "Bill, what are you bringing in them crutches for?" It was kind of a running joke. But I wanted to have different choices and have consistency. And maybe I liked the old 1960, which is now a 1968 Drawmer. I used to use that a lot. But I guess overall, probably the Great River and the Martech.

The other way around, what I had then that I wish I had now? Because I do everything in stereo, I sold the 610 Urei, I guess it was Urei 610. I sold it to somebody because I hadn't used it in a year and a half. And at that point I was doing the basses sometimes using the LA2A, and it also got to a point where I was doing so much acoustic music that everything was stereo. And I only had one 610. So, I got rid of that—wish I hadn't.

One of my partners traded in a pair of LA3As for a pair of 4311 studio monitors for the studio when I was out on a Boy Scout trip for three weeks. And I'll never forgive him for that. He just didn't use them. And the guy came in with the speakers, and he goes, "Well, here what do you want for 'em?" That gentleman that came from Texas didn't have a whole lot of common sense. And I couldn't buy them back; the guy had already sold them. His first name was Scott, and it was a three-way partnership that didn't last very long, but Bruce Dees and I were friends since the late '70s—we had lunch the other day—we were in a partnership with the guy in Texas and he didn't last very long.

Changes in the business? From Mono to too many tracks, to an industry that was an art form that's now become a computer science. The lack of quality over loudness, even down to the iPods. My children fortunately know the difference between a 16-bit mix and what they hear in their iPods. But the general public doesn't. I'm afraid they're losing their gift of hearing and their gift of performance to loudness and over-processing.

Music has always been something for me that you felt. Where now, it's something that's slammed—that you can't get back of. I got a call from Don Wershba at SSL at the beginning of the week, and it made me feel really good because he just took the time and I've known him forever and he goes, "I just picked up Jerry Douglas' album, and thanks Bill, I'm listening to music again." Because I made it to a point where it wasn't slammed—it was loud but it had distance, there were notes that were expressive that weren't brought up on a Waves Leveler. And now they have that new one that just levels everything. Takes all the emotion. He said, "It's an album that gave me emotion again." So that meant a lot. And I'm afraid the kids are not gonna really witness that many albums. They're not gonna witness what happens in the control room and then after it's processed and out to the market, they're not going to actually be able to feel the hairs going up on the back of your neck while it's being recorded and you know which ones which will be the singles by how many hairs rose up on the back of your neck and the little cold chills. The general public I'm afraid are not going to really witness the emotion that was there in vinyl, and it wasn't there as much in vinyl as it was in the earlier digitals, too. I could go forever, everything that has to be so correct now. And in this town they'll take a drummer that's making $800 for three hours to play on a song and then strip him away and grid him to the click and then replace all emotion and dynamics that he performed so that it would be absolutely, perfectly correct. But that "perfectly correct" is just an opinion.

When it comes down to it, there aren't any pop radio stations hardly anymore. And the majority of the stations that are out there are playing the hits that we grew up on where yeah, the bass is slapped, the guy sang a little flat or sharp, or the B string on the guitar was out of tune. Mick Jagger got close to the beat with the tambourine; it was a feel, an emotion that was there. It was a performance, now it's an analysis.

There's an album coming out in February that I produced and engineered; on a girl from Nashville that everybody loves but she's just never been able to escape to the marketplace. All of her vocals on that album are her scratch vocals going down with the tracks with the leakage coming into her booth. There are three lines that we fixed, and if you listen to the album you'll definitely tell that there isn't any leakage in her vocals. But the only reason why we fixed those three lines was the lyrics of the song had changed because of the era that we're in. But that's it. And the band played, I didn't have to fix anything, everybody was in the moment, where now, everybody is into what session they're going to do next week, what's my pager, what's my PDA, how's my iPhone? Did I get any messages while I was working for three minutes on this song? They are more interested in what's happening next week than where we grew up. It was all about the song and "right now."

And a musician, when we made records, if they made a mistake, they had to be embarrassed, they needed to be embarrassed. They weren't paying attention. Where now, how many times can we duplicate or bring up a new track for them to do a simple eight-bar solo? I mean, it's ridiculous. The musicianship, well, we grew up in an era, too where we didn't have the video games and everything that can cause someone from practicing. I mean we grew up in an era where those musicians, the A-Teams were a perfect example; they didn't have a whole lot of TV—they definitely didn't have any video games, what did they do for entertainment? They learned their instrument. And they learned their instrument in every key. They could go into the next town and pick with a musician there and spend the evening; instead of watching the news and *The Simpsons* or whatever and actually take that time and learn their art. Where the musician now—it can be fixed, it can be cross-faded, every note, every syllable.

There's actually budgets for autotuning in this town, and I don't like autotune. I'd much rather have the person sing it again and comp it. Maybe when we had 16-tracks we had an extra track for vocals, but when we got to 24-track I would always have another track. All that Alison stuff, it was one vocal track that I would really like and then try to do another one to beat the other one, and then have two really good choices. Two choices, not fifty choices.

Oh, and there's one place I walked in mastering, and he goes, "I brought in the CD 24s that had gone through Apogees, which is so much better than going through Pro tools", oh gosh. Benchmarks if I can get them. He goes, "Did you bring your stems?" and I was the engineer, and the producer goes, "What do you mean, stems?" And he goes, "Well, you know, in case I want to make changes." The producer goes, "You're not going to make any changes. The only thing you are going to do is even it out and you might have to add a little shelving at 12k maybe." And I never worked with this mastering engineer before. He goes, "Bil you didn't bring any stems?" I went, "No. We like it. We mixed it. We like the mix. We don't want it really loud, and we were very careful in making sure we had no aliasing feedbacks everything is mixed it between -6 and -10. And we still held our 24-bit".

Music is an art, not a science. Even though there is the National Academy of Recording Arts & Sciences, it's an art. No offense to them, but the young students need to know that they need to get a performance and they don't need to treat it as a science, as a computer science. It's not computer science.

Chapter 31

Leslie Gaston-Bird

Dr. Leslie Gaston-Bird CAS, MPSE began her term as President of the Audio Engineering Society in 2024. As Supervising Sound Editor and Re-Recording Mixer, she was nominated for an MPSE Golden Reel award for Outstanding Achievement in Sound for a Non-Theatrical Feature for her work on Publish or Perish, a dark comedy by David Liban. In addition, Leslie is currently a Senior Lecturer in Sound Recording & Music Production at City University of London. She is the founder and director of Immersive and Inclusive Audio, CIC, which provides training in Avid Pro Tools and Dolby Atmos certification for underrepresented groups, an initiative that she created as part of her PhD at the University of Surrey. Leslie is the author of the books Women in Audio (Routledge) and Math Fundamentals for Audio (A-R Editions). She is a Pro Tools Dolby Professional Avid Certified Instructor and Dante Level 3 Certified audio engineer specializing in re-recording mixing and sound editing. She is a member of the Recording Academy (The Grammys), BAFTA, Cinema Audio Society, and Motion Picture Sound Editors (MPSE). She has worked for National Public Radio (Washington, D.C.), Colorado Public Radio, the Colorado Symphony Orchestra, Post Modern Company, and was a tenured Associate Professor at the University of Colorado Denver.

I'm Dr. Leslie Gaston-Bird. I was born in Dayton, Ohio, U.S.A.

One of my earliest memories is my dad showing me how to thread a tape machine. And that was around the same time I was learning how to tie my shoes. And for some reason, the memory of tying my shoes, Dressy Bessy, and threading a tape machine are all kind of commingled in my brain. I remember the little rubber stoppers on the reels. I remember the smell of the machine. And I remember this little carbon microphone that I love to just whap with my fingers. This is probably why he gave me the crappy microphone because he knew I was going to try to destroy it. But you know, I was curious just listening to how tapping the diaphragm of the mic could make this huge sound to the speaker. So that's really when it started.

It was a prosumer home, late 60s, early 70s Ampex machine, and it has speakers on the machine itself. And you could choose, 7 1/2 or 3 3/4 inches per second. So it was 30, 15, 7 1/2, and 3 3/4. I think he had the bottom two or three speeds on there. It was crazy.

DOI: 10.4324/9781003519829-31

Figure 31.1 One of my earliest memories is my dad showing me how to thread a tape machine. That was around the same time I was learning how to tie my shoes. And for some reason, the memory of tying my shoes, Dressy Bessy, and threading a tape machine are all kind of commingled in my brain.

Figure 31.2 There was a Klark Teknik reverb unit that we used in school that I loved. I think it's a 700 series digital reverb. And the crazy thing was it didn't sound digital. We had Lexicon right with the faders but that Klark Teknik digital reverb. Really nice.

I started at Indiana University and we had a Sound Workshop console and we had an MCI 16-track, two-inch machine. And we had the MCI quarter-inch reel to reels. And then I was also working at our campus radio station. We had the Atari 5050Bs that were recording Morning Edition and All Things Considered from the satellite, and Marion McPartland's Piano Jazz, and music from the Hearts of Space. We were recording that on Otari 5050s on quarter-inch.

We were running at seven and a half because you wanted to record an hour-long show on one reel of tape. We were not using noise reduction. It sounded pretty good, it sounded pretty clean. It wasn't hissy or anything. It was coming from a satellite, and this was before MP3, so it wasn't like data compression or anything. If there's anything that's going to degrade the audio, it would just be tape noise. But we had good signal-to-noise ratio and it sounded good.

Figure 31.3 National Public Radio's Performance Today had really high standards for being aired on that program, which was a classical music program that featured orchestras from around the world. And Colorado Symphony Orchestra had wanted to be aired on PT, and their recordings kept getting rejected, and so they asked me to come in. I went to Boettcher Hall, which was where the CSO recorded, and I said, "So where are the mics?" And the stage manager pointed up into the catwalk. And I'm like, well, they're too far away.

Figure 31.4 I was watching Midge Costin's Making Waves, the Art of Cinematic Audio. They were talking about sound design with Ben Burtt and all the big name Hollywood sound designers. And they had a section where they talked about women in sound design. And it was at the end of the movie and they spent a good deal of time talking about women and audio. But something was nagging me and I'm like, it's not quite tokenism because they gave it space and what is it? And it occurred to me it's because they didn't talk to the women about their curiosity at early ages. So the way the movie went, the way the movie told its story, they said when Ben Burtt was a kid, he used to like to take things apart. And he took apart his transistor radio and what a curious child. And so that curiosity as a child burgeoned and blossomed, and I didn't get that story from the women.

There was a Klark Teknik reverb unit that we used in school that I loved. I think it's a 700 series digital reverb. And the crazy thing was it didn't sound digital. We had the Lexicon with the faders but that Klark Teknik digital reverb. Really nice.

Figure 31.5 ...when I went to NPR, we were half women and half men. We were half people of color and half not people of color. In those early professional days I saw somewhat of a balance. And when I moved to Colorado, I became the unicorn. It was from then I started paying attention, not that many years later, when WAM (Women's Audio Mission) started in 2004, I'm like, oh, what's this thing? The more you learn about other women's stories, the more you see yourself in those stories and the more you realize, oh, shit, I've been going around obstacles my whole life. It's never been a straight path for me. Why is that? That's what it's been like. Once you see it, you can't unsee it.

Figure 31.6 If you're a lawyer or a doctor you'll always have work, but where's the beauty and joy in that. So just in terms of how it's helped me, I think I've had a career that has put food on the table, that has been creative.

We're talking late 80s, early 90s. We had Schoeps microphones, so we had the cardioid and Omni capsules for those which were beautiful. We had the B&K microphones, which were nice. But yeah, the Schoeps were something special.

We recorded the school operas there and then, I remember using gaffer tape to tape the Neumann 84s to the foot of the stage. And then we had a pair of Schoeps XY that we flew in. And, yeah, that sounded like you might think, with lots of footsteps as the singers crossed the stage. It wasn't too bad, though. And during that time, I was just doing school stuff, and then I went on to record the Colorado Symphony Orchestra (CSO). In that case, we had Schoeps in the house, ORTF. And then we had MKH flank microphones. National Public Radio's (NPR) Performance Today (PT) had really high standards for being aired on that program, which was a classical music program that featured orchestras from around the world. And CSO had wanted to be aired on PT, and their recordings kept getting rejected, and so they asked me to come in. I went to Boettcher Hall, which was where the CSO recorded, and I said, "So where are the mics?" And the stage manager pointed up into the catwalk. And I'm like, well, they're too far away. As I look up into the rafters, shielding my eyes, with those mics way too far away. I worked with, I'm trying to think if it was Steve Zakar or Ben Rowe who were doing PT production at that time as producers, and probably Suraya Mohamed. And I was sending some test recordings to them, and we finally got it like we wanted it. We put that together pretty meticulously. And as far as I know, they used it for at least four years. I don't know if they're still using that setup but yeah.

I never stopped using Pro Tools, because I got away from recording and got into editing, so in terms of my freelance and professional work, I'm just using Pro Tools to edit. I left NPR in 95, went to Colorado Public Radio, left Colorado Public Radio in 2002, got my master's degree, went to teach, and with the exception of the Schoeps we had pretty much the same arsenal of mics there. For teaching we just used the AKG414s, the RE20 on the kick, SM57 on the snare, MD421s on toms. We just used the standard stuff. But then I got invited by Dave Malan from the University of York to do some ambisonics research and started using the Soundfield microphone. So the Soundfield microphone has four capsules, an ambisonics microphone, and I recorded Christian Wallumrød, who was a Norwegian composer. I still have those recordings. When I want to go back and test equipment or test a playback system, I use those recordings from 2009.

As far as analog gear, with noise reduction, you had to have calibration tones and, you know, you had to have the little Dolby lights light up. And if you wanted to play that back you had to make sure you had the calibration tone. It wasn't that it didn't work. It's just that some of that stuff was just fidgety. But we got good results. And I remember that we were recording double bass using that technology and it sure did keep the tape hiss down, and it sounded fine. That was right before people started getting into digital. So that was 1988, and that was right at sort of the birth of digital. So we really didn't have to worry about noise reduction for long. After that came noise shaping, which is a whole other thing.

It would have been really convenient to have Pro Tools in those days, because I remember being at NPR and people were slicing their fingers with these razor blades. So, yeah, digital editing came too late for some. I hope everybody had their tetanus shots because that was a drag.

I wish I still had the Klark Teknik Digital reverb. I still go on Vintage King once every two years, and I'm on eBay trying to see if anybody has one. I think they're like 700 bucks.

This is a great historical perspective, isn't it? Because I feel like when I started in as a student into audio, it was MTV, right? MTV caused a new kind of renaissance in terms of music recording because we had bands like Devo and all these synth-pop groups and new wave groups who were using synthesizers. We started to see an explosion of music recording programs, which I still think is kind of irresponsible because we went from having five audio engineering programs in the United States in 1987. There were more electronic music programs, because you had Berkeley and Ohio State and Ohio U and

Oberlin, and everybody had a synth lab. But if you wanted to do audio engineering, microphones and acoustic recording, there were maybe five places where you could get a degree in that, and now there's five per city. It's kind of nuts. So that's a big change. The other thing was in terms of radio. When I was working at NPR, starting in 1991 when I joined, if you wanted to go out in the field, you had a Nagra, which was a portable reel-to-reel tape recorder and workhorses, and everybody loves the Nagra. But then we went to digital audio tape recorders. We went from, you know, 20 pounds to 3 pounds, so not breaking our backs anymore. And then here comes digital audio and what started to happen was people started to lose their jobs. Just today I read that iHeartMedia was cutting 10,000 jobs.

Well, this actually, in my view, started in say 1999. I had friends who were radio announcers who were getting fired, laid off because Clear Channel was doing voice tracking. And what that means is if you're Clear Channel, you can have an announcer in New York reading the weather for Denver or Grand Junction or Bloomington, and they would just drop these tracks in and they didn't need local announcers anymore. So tons of people were getting laid off right there at the turn of the century. And that's when I started thinking I need a new job because I was an audio engineer. And now news departments were getting smaller and I was training announcers how to use Cool Edit Pro, which became Adobe Audition. So I'm training announcers how to cut their own stories. So what am I here for? I thought I better learn what the hell MP3 is. Like what is data reduction now? What is data compression? What is normalizing, all of this, all of these new digital ways to save bandwidth and save hard drive space. So I decided to learn about those. Those trends put a lot of people out of work and are still putting people out of work. And of course, home recording, the big recording studios are disappearing and have been for over a decade as people start to record in their homes. So those are the biggest changes I've seen.

There's a line from a song from Utopia and the lyric goes, there's a million extended mixers we're ready to retire. And I think that that lyric was written in 1986 or 1985. And I didn't know what it meant. I didn't know if they were talking about hand mixers, you know, Oster home blenders. To my 16-year-old mind, "there's a million extended mixers we're ready to retire" just meant something is obsolete. I don't know. I didn't know they were talking about me, or I didn't know they were talking about what would eventually become my job. So a lot of mixers went out of work. And however many years later, 30 years later, we're seeing the effects of the writers' strike and digital audio and artificial intelligence putting people out of work, including me. And so the line follows, we all face obsolescence sooner or later, right? I mean this is, this is 1985. Of course, it's Todd Rundgren who's one of my heroes. And he was, as always, predicting whether future technology is just displacing so many of us. If I had to do it all again, I would have thought, you know what? Lawyer. Being a lawyer isn't bad. You know, studying law because we're always going to need lawyers and politicians. Have you ever met an out-of-work politician? Not to get political. I'm serious though. If you're a lawyer or a doctor you'll always have work, but where's the beauty and joy in that? So just in terms of how it's helped me, I think I've had a career that has put food on the table, that has been creative. Some technical, some creative, and allows me to enjoy a hobby which relies on technology. So that's a nice thing to have. So I think it's better than digging a ditch to quote yet another song lyric.

I don't teach synthesis, but there are a lot of music programs, and I'm talking about degree-granting university programs that still use analog stuff, synthesizers and the like.

You don't see many reel-to-reels, although some colleges and universities have them. No, I don't have any analog gear that I still use.

I use an analog console to teach, and it's a shame that a student can't buy one at Guitar Center. You can buy a console at Guitar Center, but it's easier to buy Pro Tools.

But the thing I like about analog consoles and hitting tape is that you don't have to worry about a converter getting in your way. It's just electronics. It's an electric signal that you've got, inductors, capacitors, shaping the EQ. You've got transformers making it louder and softer. But I was just talking to a class about jitter because I teach a mastering class and on Monday I was trying to explain to them what jitter is and how jitter sounds. And that's the example I use: If you're setting up a tracking session and you got all the mics coming through the console, it's beautiful. But if you go to play back the tape and it's less beautiful, that's a clocking problem and that's a converter problem. Making sure that you keep the integrity of your signal once it leaves the console.

I guess one thing that I thought about, let's see if I can put this in a pretty box with a pretty bow on it, was when I was watching Midge Costin's Making Waves, the Art of Cinematic Audio. They were talking about sound design with Ben Burtt and all the big name Hollywood sound designers. And they had a section where they talked about women in sound design. And it was at the end of the movie and they spent a good deal of time talking about women and audio. But something was nagging me and I'm like, it's not quite tokenism because they gave it space and what is it? And it occurred to me it's because they didn't talk to the women about their curiosity at early ages. So the way the movie went, the way the movie told its story, they said when Ben Burtt was a kid, he used to like to take things apart. And he took apart his transistor radio and what a curious child. And so that curiosity as a child burgeoned and blossomed and I didn't get that story from the women.

And so this thing that I think was nagging me is women who are in sound didn't get there because of a DEI program because there weren't any, or any of this uplifting in the 70s and 80s. And earlier than that actually, women had the same curiosity about sound. And just like thinking about me threading a tape machine with my tiny little six-year-old, five-year-old fingers, however old I was. And I think that's what seems to be missing from most narratives. When we talk about the big mixers and the big names we leave out the little girl in the story. And so I think that's one thing that was missing. And I think that's another reason why organizations like Women's Audio Mission (WAM) and SoundGirls, and there are 70 of them on the planet, We Make Noise, Beats By Girlz, Girls Make Beats, all of these women's organizations recognize the little girl in themselves and reach out to recapture whatever is happening. And there's been papers written about it, whatever's happening between the ages of 9 and 15, where we lose little girls and young girls and teenagers from STEM and from recording. And so that has been part of this story.

And just in terms of talking about what it's like to be an audio engineer who happens to be female and a black woman, in 1987, when I got into audio, my dad might have, hinted at that, why do you want to do that? And, I think he might have worried. Well, you know, studios are notoriously misogynistic. I mean, he didn't say that, but I think he might have said, "Be careful in those studios at night. You never know what kind of people are in there." And I never had a problem with people in recording studios. But there was the worry. And there were 5 girls with me in a class of 15 when I studied. And then when I went to NPR, we were half women and half men. We were half people of color and half not people of color. In those early professional days, I saw somewhat of a balance. And when I moved to Colorado, I became the unicorn. It was from then I started paying attention, not that many years later when WAM started in 2004, I'm like, "Oh, what's this thing?" The more you learn about other women's stories, the more you see yourself in those stories and the more you realize, "oh, shit, I've been going around obstacles my whole life. It's never been a straight path for me. Why is that?" That's what it's been like. Once you see it, you can't unsee it. I think that that's basically what I have to say on that subject.

Chapter 32

Phil Ramone

For six decades, Phil Ramone was a force in the music industry. He produced records and collaborated with almost every major talent in the business, with 14 Grammy wins and 32 Nominations.

As a young child, Ramone was a musical prodigy, beginning to play the violin at age three and performing for Queen Elizabeth II at age ten. In the late 1940s, he trained as a classical violinist at The Juilliard School, where one of his classmates was Phil Woods.

In 1959, he established an independent recording studio, A&R Recording. There he quickly gained a reputation as a sound engineer and music producer, in particular for his use of innovative technology. Among those whose music he has produced are Burt Bacharach, Laura Branigan, Karen Carpenter, Ray Charles, Peter Cincotti, Chicago, Natalie Cole, Bob Dylan, Gloria Estefan, Aretha Franklin, Billy Joel, Elton John, Fito Páez, Quincy Jones, B. B. King, Diane Schuur, Julian Lennon, Madonna, Richard Marx, Paul McCartney, George Michael, Sinéad O'Connor, Luciano Pavarotti, Andre Previn, Carly Simon, Paul Simon, Frank Sinatra, Rod Stewart, James Taylor, Olivia Newton-John, Liza Minnelli, Barry Manilow, Clay Aiken, Peter Paul and Mary, and Melissa Errico.

He is also credited with recording Marilyn Monroe's rendition of "Happy Birthday to You" to President John F. Kennedy.

Among the technical innovations he introduced at A&R are four-track recorders, optical surround sound for movies, and digital recording techniques. His studio was the first to release music commercially on compact disc; Billy Joel's 52nd Street was the first album to be broadly released on the medium.

He was also on Berklee's College of Music's Board of Trustees, and his book, Making Records: The Scenes Behind the Music, written with Chuck Granata, was released on October 9, 2007. Phil Ramone passed away in March 2013 at the age of 79.

My name is Phil Ramone. I was raised in New York from a youngster.

I really got interested in audio at an early age, 13 or 14. I started to really try to understand, because I played classical violin, and I was lucky enough to be asked to record.

DOI: 10.4324/9781003519829-32

Figure 32.1 Positioning, understanding, I got to be well-known because I got on a high ladder and found the focal point of where the strings sounded really good, then locked the mic in because we had an old film boom, you could ride the thing cause it was so huge.

Figure 32.2 As far as the equipment, the classic compressor would be a Fairchild. Sherman Fairchild used to come over because he loved the jazz content at the studio. And I would tell him what I liked about something, and then he'd get his guys on it because they made aircraft.

I heard records of me as a child with an orchestra and you know that's pretty much a single mic, maybe two mics. Once I got in the studio, I realized this art needed to be amended, and a lot of engineers—because I was still at a youthful age—would let me come in the control room and see how things worked, and I would get invited to other dates. Once I got involved in pop and jazz music, I was really young—I was probably 15, I was a huge fan of Les Paul. I just was fascinated and thought, "Wow, if I could learn how to do what he does with guitar on the violin, and it was like a mantra for me."

I was lucky enough because some contractors in New York would use me in the orchestra in the string sections. I was probably 15 or 16, but I was already a "tea boy" in the studio, working in the studio, cleaning until 6, 7 o'clock at night, at one place they said, "Okay now at 7 we like to give our clients a martini. Why don't you learn how to make a

Figure 32.3 Every teacher in the audio world will tell you, "Get your ass out there and go and stand in front of the musician and listen to what they're trying to do." But if you don't know where the sonic side of it is what difference does it make? They just keep reaching for EQ knobs and hoping that something's going to work. I would have been disgraced if I walked up to a Stan Getz and didn't have that sound.

Figure 32.4 And all it took was one big hit one after another, and then they said, "Oh yeah, that guy Ramone, he makes you sit in circles." And, to break the tradition of sitting in rows, I said, "That's what they do when you play clubs or theaters." It's economical sound, whatever you want to call it. I said, "But I don't have enough..." I didn't say it to them, but I didn't have enough microphones and inputs to put one by every sax. I did afterward. Built bigger boards, and had our guys who understand I had to premix, that word, but the gear was good mics. I was a nutcase for good mics.

martini? And I'll teach you how to cut a disk." And this was in the late '50s and I'm saying, "Huh, okay." So, it led to more than idle curiosity. I was mentored by Tom Dowd, Bill Putnam, and people who were incredible mixers, and I started to realize that, as a player, there was so much to accomplish and so much need. That "Charlie Parker" kind of saxophone playing, you know, things like that, and Dizzy Gillespie and Louis Armstrong, I needed to know and wanted the chance. And I went to work in a studio when I was about 20 years old and a lot of those guys came to that studio. It opened a door for

Figure 32.5 I think our job is to know your role, "check your ego outside the door", Quincy Jones' famous phrase. But the producers have to do that, too. Because you're there to inspire, to perspire, settle on nothing, and make the gear work for you rather than always saying, "Well, it never did this before." Give it a break, you know?

me, I met Quincy Jones when I was working, and that started a whole other cavalcade of the next generation.

The early '60s was really the height of a lot of recording by a lot of independent companies. The traditional union studios were pretty much RCA, Capitol, CBS, Colombia, and Decca. So you couldn't touch anything; you had to be a member of their union. I felt the only entrance into the studio work was through seniority and years and years of apprenticeship. And the small independent studios were sparkling because there were lots of independent labels, and having worked in a demo studio for quite a while I got the late-night shift, I would cut disks until 3, 4 in the morning, and then maybe have a session from 2 to 5, and come back at 7 or 8 o'clock. You learn from songwriters, you learn from demo makers. I mean Paul Simon was a demo singer for Bacharach or other song publishers. It was a very flourishing time, and speed and accuracy were probably the byword for success.

You learned your aesthetics on the fly. You just had to get there in a hurry, and musicians talked about you if you were good. References from arrangers, I mean once you got past the rhythm section you really had to be beyond good, you know? We got three hours, we got to do four songs, and we got six horns and background singers and eight strings. Not the biggest band you've ever seen, and certainly not balanced, but in those days, I know people used to put up screens, sound screens, gobos. And finally, I got to work in Bill's studio and I said, "We're going to build that into the room." Rooms with a door on it with glass so they could look out, the conductor could see them and could keep a private cue going to them, one to the singer. So many records had vocal groups on them, you don't think about it, but if they didn't sing in tune or do things exactly the same, that's a whole other story about how that got to be made.

A lot of stuff then was altered consoles; radio consoles: GE, Altec. They were pretty much all mono, and I sat down with a couple of these guys who worked at NBC and other places and independents like Bill Schwartz, and they would show me the possibilities of what we could do with stereo. Most of the producers did not want, nor did the record company want to even run the cost of a second tape machine because I'd figured it out with a couple of technicians how to make stereo, three mixers, four channels each, a total of 12, and then two spare four-channel mixers in case I had strings. Nobody put 24 mics up, that's a lot, it would have been a lot then. I put a left, center, and right format using a three-track machine which a guy loaned and after six months he said, "I'm taking my equipment back, you guys will never be successful, this is crazy what you're doing." Stereo. It's a nice idea but, he said, "I like what Toscanini does and you're not capturing him." I said, "Well, we're not recording him." That was David Sarser, a concertmaster for years, he was Toscanini's audio adviser. He was a great guy. I talked to him last year. I said, "I just wanted to let you know I did okay." He just laughed.

You always learn, try to learn. Preamps were the key to what the signals flow was going to be. A good preamp, a good mic, if you had a good U47 you could cover a lot of room in the room. And, I worked in a room that was about 38 feet by 40 feet by 14 foot ceilings. Nothing terrible but some of the biggest records that ever came out in the early '60s were from indie labels, Mercury and all these other labels were pretty much independent. Bob Fine was a good friend. You know if there's more than one mic on the string section, other than the lowest strings maybe and one for the high strings, it's all you have for inputs.

Positioning, understanding, I got to be well-known because I got on a high ladder and found the focal point of where the strings sounded really good, then locked the mic in because we had an old film boom, you could ride the thing cause it was so huge. It was left over from a guy who had kind of donated it to the studio. Some of the circumstances work for you or against you. We had no air conditioning, sometimes I had to open the doors, it was so intolerable. And the dust from the floor, which turned to be vermiculite and cement, but it had no sealer. If you rolled a piano over it, it would cut the floor up, or guitar amps or anything else, so you'd get dust. And musicians used to dress up in those days. They'd say, "I don't know if I 'm going to work an A&R recording date, they have dust all over their floors." So I found a guy and we patented a new floor that could breathe and still not put out dust.

You know, through trial and error we have to survive and the pop and the rock era was upon us. Once the Beatles hit, everybody in New York said, "I've got to have sounds like that." They obviously realized that George Martin had a lot to do with how they were going to sound. And you know that a certain engineer catered to what the boys wanted. The boys were thinking forward of the classical style so all of it was changing and the more you added, if I didn't have an input and then you needed to get two mics, I got the extra mic but I had to figure out how to cascade them together so they worked off the one fader. Then, the height and the width of that space had to be right. So, survival was important, because you wanted the business, you wanted people to love what you did. Did a lot of free dates to get the room known, and when the room had a hit boy, the calls came in every day.

Quincy Jones and I reminisced the other day. We made a record called "Big Band Bossa Nova" in 1964. And in the comedy picture Austin Powers the main title is exactly that track. They've added over it. They couldn't copy it, they couldn't cut the echo the same way. They tried to copy the chart, but nothing worked.

As far as the equipment, the classic compressor would be a Fairchild. Sherman Fairchild used to come over because he loved the jazz content at the studio. And, I would tell him what I liked about something and then he'd get his guys on it because they made aircraft. But the competition between the professional audio guys was also like that. You know a guy named Koss that built an earphone? Well, I kept complaining. I thought if I could get the musicians to hear themselves, instead of thinking of it as an army, air corps piece of equipment left from landings and takeoffs that you could possibly give the guy a chance to hear, 'cause you know, a CB radio is about the quality of what those headphones were in studios. They were all Army used equipment that everybody bought. There was no such thing as recording with those kinds of headphones other than click track if you were doing film but we weren't doing big films, New York wasn't a big film town at the time.

And limiters and compressors came in, especially simple ones, I mean in the beginning, just to have a Pultec, maybe three or four of them, you patched them. You didn't have it in line in your console. The bigger manufacturers which were coming were Neve and other people like that. RCA made their own consoles. Colombia made their own. The components, if you were lucky you'd find something they were getting rid of at a radio station and then sit and have a backroom where all of us would keep wiring, adding inputs, changing the balance on how to get a simultaneous two-track. Probably, for me, stereo was one of the first changes that certainly wasn't accepted. But when I'd go and play it back, I said, "You'll never have to remix this, this is your sound on the mono." And, it's just dividing up where we put the band parts. It was minimalist every time, all the way.

You know, I remember the first time a guy came around and he had figured out a way to get rid of sibilance, which was the enemy. I had made this bossa nova record for Astrud Gilberto and Stan Getz and in it a very soft, sweet kind of vocal. But when you have a wide-open preamp and microphone working hard and it's so close, you now subject yourself to things that are the particles of sound, it's soft and sss and a lot of "s"s going on. So, I was looking for something that could work for me, I'd figure out a way that I could catch that "s" yet not destroy it. Those weren't common pieces of equipment. Most equipment were crushers, I called them. They sounded like radio stations crunching in AM format, and some of the early clients came to us because our stuff on the air sounded better than some other studios for the mix.

And I just heard one the other day, Hertz has put it back on their campaign, "Let Hertz put you in the driver's seat" probably made in '67 or '68--somewhere in there. It may have been older than that, could have been '63 or '64. It was the same jingle, it's not a great revitalization because I know what it originally sounded like but the stuff that came out of the room with all the different engineers that worked there established a really good sound, and it could go from this light bossa nova to a big band screaming Quincy Jones or Count Basie. The room would take it, and you could learn your trade by not trying too much.

Sometimes if you try too much you actually defeat all of what the music is about because you're not listening to see what it really is and why it doesn't work for you and what it is you're doing wrong. I used to scream at engineers because they would sit like the king on their special throne and they never left their console seat. Especially when it became individual EQ compressors, gates on each fader. And I think, as you fast-forward that into today there is that habit. Every teacher in the audio world will tell you, "Get your ass out there and go and stand in front of the musician and listen to what they're trying to do." But if you don't know where the sonic side of it is what difference does it make? They just keep reaching for EQ knobs and hoping that something's going to work.

I would have been disgraced if I walked up to a Stan Getz and didn't have that sound, and that's really what you did. And the singers and most of the A&R producers really knew what they were coming in for. Whether it was Gerry Mulligan or Chet Baker, Miles Davis, you know we did some very eclectic jazz bands, which is a discipline where you learn how to surround yourself when the guy says, "I want another mic, I want two mics on my instrument. Two." How am I gonna? Should I tell him that I may have to mult them together? No.

You know, of course you had outboard equalizers, even buckets of two or three inputs that you could change the preamp or have a spare box. I mean if somebody lugged an API board, those things were starting to be made, and film boards where everything was patched. Any good film board had good preamps, good line amps but you patched everything. So, it looked like you were calling across the world.

You learn something because the first time an outboard piece of gear, and that wasn't even a word that was thought of yet, the owners, the people you were working for didn't want it to look like you weren't ready and so when they started making separate boxes of gear, it was much later, and that ends up in the '70s. Especially with rock n' roll. And then you'd build two small limiters of different brands. Guys were experimenting with what we call line-in products. I always had experimental racks. I didn't have to tell you what I was doing because I'd say, "Hang on a minute," and then I'd go over to the rack. If I hated what I just heard then I would unpatch it and go to the next one. We were always building or buying.

Pultec was a really wonderful, warm sound that you could add, just add a little bit of this or that and vocals sounded pure but it had this sweet little edge if you knew how to do that. We were totally about making sure the record worked on radio, and that the HiFi buyers—or what we called them - "quality people"—heard what they paid for. It was the Motowns and other companies that figured out how to make a great record sound, Atlantic. That's why I was so close with Tommy Dowd. 'Cause we knew if we made a special 45 for radio we'd take out a lot of the silly bottom that wasn't gonna do us any good, but when you played it on your new high-fidelity system at home it better be there. And it's easily traceable now if you listen to Motown records, how great they sounded on the air.

And our game was to sound as good, or as Pepsi once paid me, "to make a commercial sound like it was a record." They bought a standard song, Makin' Whoopie, and they got a young, talented girl, Joanie Summers, and she was 17. And when they were singing, "We love Pepsi—for those who think young" that was the title of it, "For those who think young," and it started with a big band arrangement or a Latin version of it. The whole purpose of it, my job, was to make sure when they sent that disc over, that if you came out of a big band record and went into our record, you didn't realize it was a commercial. Point of interest, point of sound, because agencies had a lot to do with what we were going to do. They'd spend the money, but if they'd wanted that really typical, what I call "overEQed" sound to make sure that their commercials sounded louder, brighter, we gave it to them. Whether it was cigarette commercials, those were big. If you did jingles all of the time they didn't want to be in your studio. So, you know, 9 in the morning until 4 or 5, I lost some clients because they couldn't get in from 2 to 5, 7 to 10, and these were comfortable working hours and the outboard gear was available because we were trying to make good records, and it became more available to the jingle guy who would come and say to me, "What was that sound you used?" I said, "Oh, you know I used this, don't tell anybody, it was a guitar pedal, something that I found with some phaser on it and it just created this great thing on the echo chamber". "Oh yeah, well what'd you do it for?" "Well, I used it around the boys, it just kind of sounded a little bit of Elvis and something else."

You know, invention was the name of the game. You had to know what you had and what limitations there were. Once the Coca-Colas, which they've always done, they've been in the radio business for years, and airline commercials, they always made vocal spots. And then cigarettes, Kent, Marlboro was a big deal. And then, I always thought if you could get through that and keep your patience level, you certainly should have extreme patience because they rushed you like crazy to make a record. They thought that you were an amateur if you couldn't get four songs in three hours. Union guilds were set up, and then there was a five-minute break per hour, except for the last hour. A different scale of thinking, too. The pros would sit down and read. They never had the kind of scrappy bands that we had later, 'cause they couldn't read, they couldn't get a gig. They worked in a band and we were in a garage band and they're getting better and better. The labels loved to tie them up with a real pro drummer, and for me that's what changed a whole life for me with Billy Joel. He was in and out, a lot of composing, arranging. But his band was dependable and not on a metronome, and nobody read. Notations on sheets looked like a little bit of kindergarten and some musical symbols, whatever you wanted to call them.

For the first ten years of making records, I'll call it that, finding the right microphones, doing things in the positions based on having to share two mics with four people, and how did you make that work? I got well known for sitting the trumpets in a circle and the trombones. But, I think they probably did that in the '30s, due to lack of mics. I knew that if I had the trumpets and the 'bones in two circles and maybe the saxes in a circle, so there were three circles in a room and the drums right smack next to them. And people wouldn't have done that because they didn't want the leakage. But a band lives on the fact that it has great leakage, and the arrangers, you know some musicians would complain and say, "I can't see the arrangers". I said, "You shouldn't be. You should be playing what you see in the music paper." And, in a circle it doesn't make a difference, as a matter of fact, you can hear the fifth trumpet because he's facing you.

And all it took was one big hit one after another, and then they said, "Oh yeah, that guy Ramone, he makes you sit in circles." And, to break the tradition of sitting in rows, I said, "That's what they do when you play clubs or theaters." It's economical sound, whatever you want to call it. I said, "But I don't have enough..." I didn't say it to them, but I didn't have enough microphones and inputs to put one by every sax. I did afterward. Built bigger boards, had our guys who understand I had to premix, that word, but the gear was good mics. I was a nutcase for good mics.

I was doing stuff like Burt Bacharach and Hal David. They had done a couple of albums at Bell Sound, and then we started with the "House and Not A Home" and "What's It All About, Alfie" and one hit after another. You know, "Do You Know The Way To San Jose". Just four or five years straight, and then made an instrumental album with him and then I made an album with Midnight Cowboy, where "Everybody's Talkin'" was the first John Barry let me produce, then I made records for Peter, Paul, and Mary. All of that was engineering, long before I was being asked to produce. Of course, someone asked, "Can you produce this while you are engineering?" I said, "Yeah. I just don't have anybody to talk to. Just you guys, it's okay."

Talking about the equipment though, I think the Fairchild was perfectly adequate, more than adequate. But it was built as a cutting amplifier. It wasn't built to be an audio piece in a recording studio. It took care of the two channels. In the beginning, they made one channel, and then they made a two-channel version. Vertical and lateral—those words are still on there. There weren't that many good compressors on the line. A lot of us would take an old radio station's compressors or RCA or one of these companies that made their disc compressor and readjust it and change the tube values so we could be more subtle. And then there was the group of people who loved heavy compression, not like it is now. Well, there were Putnams moving forward. When I met him and I saw him record Sinatra, I said, "Bill, what is that?" He said, "Oh, it's something I'm trying to mess with. I'm designing stuff." Well, that's where it starts.

Universal Audio. Any of that Universal Audio, 1176s, LA3As, 2As, all of that worked and it never became obsolete. They are still even in plug-ins and everything else there. Nothing changed in 40 years, nothing, other than the speed in which you work and the amount of those pieces of gear. You might have 20 of those in a rack. Economics forced you or the studio to add this stuff, and it became almost mandatory in your thinking as a producer, "I need a couple of racks." Now do you build them yourself or sublet them from the studio to yourself? You know, there were so many extra formats you had to come up with. And I wasn't afraid because I loved Rupert Neve, I met him in the early '60s and I loved his consoles. And, I liked his television and radio consoles; just the way he had thought them out. I think to this day, considering that I sat there one day with Evelyn, his wife, and she said, "You know, you guys are not letting my husband work because he should be making new stuff. He's still a designer; he still creates." I said, "I absolutely agree with you, I said, "It's like somebody saying, 'I want to drive a 1960 Rolls Royce or 1970 Mercedes.' I said, "There's that element of people, the trust." And that, "None of these parts were designed to work this many years without rusting out or becoming aware of what could go wrong."

So I think the modular console was well on its way. API, and there were so many inventive people who had worked a lot in the film business. Bob Fine did both. He was recording on film for the quietness and the width of the tracks. Nobody stopped in their tracks and said, "This is all there is." Nobody did. And yes, there were more manufacturers in all fields of audio. And the PA companies were still doing what they could. I had to do a show with Barbara Streisand in the park. This was right before Woodstock, and I had JBL make me these long throat horns because I was nervous that we would lose some of the audience. I thought, "We may have as many as 20,000 people." Well guess what? It was almost 50,000. And I put in delay towers. I said, "Did I know they were going to work?" No, I knew scientifically that if I delayed a tower I could make it get rid of the time delays. But I didn't know how far that song would travel and how many feet. I knew what it said, but then when speaker manufacturers came out at Woodstock, they followed with the same thought. They did very much agree. We all talked to each other because it was way bigger than anybody had ever thought it would be or could be. You know race tracks and other things weren't even in existence. But whether the guy in the 30th row heard wasn't really a problem. And I dealt with PA systems in the early '60s for galas like presidents, you know, that kind of stuff. And, I thought, "You got 10,000 people, what, we're not going to cater to them?" They came here to hear this. And hear it over the reflection of the building? No, no, no, no, no.

And I felt I could get manufacturers interested because we were doing spectacular stuff. But it was the change of the era, it was the biggest change, the mid-60s, even the early

'60s. Things were not going to be the same. The speakers weren't going to be the same. The 604s in a box, a gray box, 14 cubic feet, all that wasn't going to stay on. We needed to get some bottom. We needed to know that it wasn't up against the glass and there were speakers next to you. No room for the clients.

I remember building our first control room. I knocked the wall out behind us and eventually, I put us there and put the clients in the front, like theater seats. You say, "What am I doing here?" They're used to movie theater seating, they're used to television control rooms, I worked in all of those places and realized what the discomforts were and what the comforts were, so maybe I should think of asking guys to build something for us. At Colombia, but particularly CBS, they could have gear built for them because they had their own labs. And that helped tremendously because they could requisition an idea, they'd fill four boxes, and put a name on it for now. Whatever that was, a delay unit, whatever. The only delay units that I could find were made by Philips in Europe. And I said, "Okay, I'll have one of those." Let me see what I can do with vocals and how to make instruments sound twice as big by looping and doing stuff. That's how you learn. It felt like, "If I'm going to do this, why can't I put this on a small motherboard?" Create the same technology and have somebody do it. You know, once you started to get to a 3/4-inch on center idea for each fader you started to make, I built either 36 or 42 faders on a board. I mean I had them built, and people weren't sure they wanted sliders or knobs. We had to go through that transition. So, do you want everything in line? Ehh... Could be problems. Too many choices in the same place. How do you choose which weapon you're going to use, whether it's a slider or a rotating knob? And kind of never look like you're so nervous that something's going to go wrong in front of anybody, which is always a big thing in our business. It's like a surgeon, I've always said, "What's that thing I use? I need, you know, a ratchet". Who wants that in a brain surgeon's hands? Thank you. Later.

Anything I have now that I wish I had then? Oh sure...gates, parametric EQ. In general everybody, SSL, everybody came up with something. I mean I worked on a console that was a complete disaster but the thought pattern of what the designer had in mind was that every fader had compression, EQ, gates, limiters all on one. This was before SSL, and by the time he built 24 of them into a row it was a lot. The thing just budged out all the time. And it took the guys who would build SSL, I mean theirs had problems but it didn't have anything like this. And, you know, Quad Eight had a simple board, the Coronado.

When Bob knew he was going to lose the Great Northern Hotel in New York, he came to work for me at A&R. He said, "I'm gonna give you three or four of the best film and audio technical guys you'll ever meet." You know, we had a full-time shop. I never reached outside. I said, "Build me four equalizers and let me hear that. No, take the broadband and make it broader, make it imitate a Neve, but then I want the shelf that an API has." So we built a lot of it to our own specs. Well you know, if it really worked, somebody asked, "Can we borrow that idea?" It was pretty competitive, but not destructive. Bob Lifton was a really good designer. Bobby had a studio called Regent Sound, and we, as studios, weren't competitive. Alan Merchin was a really good engineer, but he also sang jingles, so he kept himself in good supplies and was a really good mixer. He didn't have to be all compression, it all had to be how you mixed. Putting a little bit of compression on the bass and a little bit on the kick or something like a guitar solo that was getting out of hand. Al Schmitt and all these guys came from the school using their hands. That's what the word "mixer" meant to us.

So not putting something in mind just because it could be automated—automated levels were what I wanted. Some of that gear moved so rapidly through the '80s and '90s. I had my first automated Neve board in New York, and then, a couple of others, Ragavoy, the Hit Factory, and other people got automated boards. It was a big deal because Allison Research had built a copy track 1–16 that kept overdubbing, and then had the information stay, and when it shifted you were dead.

There were so many inputs that could be nullified of what you did before, and then you'd put up a room sound and then you'd laugh. I know I did because at the time you'd try to mix both with so many out-of-phase, in-phase conditions. You can put too many engines in a car. You just can. If you put a tuned-up idea and you kick it and say, "This is what I'm driving and I'm going to drive as fast as I know how", you'd be amazed at how much good you can do. Because otherwise, you look at two or three mics that are in a row next to each other, one being four inches higher than the other. Some of the scientists can argue for and against all of them, but we're in a commercial business, and I think, like in the cockpit of a plane, if you can duplicate it twice, that means it would really work as a one-man operation. I didn't like the idea of splitting consoles to the point that you had an assistant all over your first set of 64 faders, and you're not riding any of them.

I knew sound designers and all of the different points of view. I wanted it to be in hard disk format. I didn't mind digital. I really didn't love 16-bit. I made some good records on 16-bit, as I did on tape, but I think the ultimate was to get to where we are now, you know, in the 24/96 or whatever you want to do, 192. The questions are still about your music and if it slows down the process, the immediacy in tracks, all that helps. Being able to punch in and not have to be that careful. It's taught us a lot of good, but a lot of bad habits: a habit you may not have employed much. You know, a bad kind of a punch and it was no more and that person had left the room. Your job would be at stake, or your feelings about having to call them and say, "Can you come back and just sing the word?" My first big digital date went down in flames, where the whole orchestra was there, and at the end of a Streisand piece, it's the last 16 bars, and the machine decided to add thumps. When we played the safety, which was not digital, we couldn't even get close to the quietness of the other tape. Now if I'd had Dolby on that I might've been able to fudge it, but not with Streisand's ears or mine. We spent two and a half days, I demanded that they fly over from Japan, and they had all the excuses. You know, six months later they got out the thumps, but the record was the number one record. They said "Well, we accomplished what you wanted," and I said, "No you don't understand, you had the Titanic in the room. It's not what you did, your intent wasn't to fail, but you had no fail safe".

The tune was "Papa, Can You Hear Me" from Yentl. She had done a lot of the score and loved it. When they re-scored it on Sony tape machines, and we mixed the analog with the digital because she said, "I like the way you played it over here." There's noise, there's cameras, there's people. Forget the challenge, the key to it was that nothing was actually wrong except what I saw, and what I found was the warning system, where the lights go on and off and tell you there's an error being committed, was in the actual trunk case that the machine sat in.

I said to them, "You got to put that on a series of meters." That was the Sony 3324. They didn't want to do it. It wasn't a matter of them paying for it. They couldn't possibly pay for bringing back the string section, that would've been obvious they didn't. Nobody wants to do that. The point of a fire alarm is to see it and hear it. They might have structured it badly, but they're really good people. They understand that I don't do this to destroy anything. But I must have some light that comes on that says, "Your landing wheels aren't down, you better stop." I said, "Yeah, I'd get pissed off if the lights went off. We have to do another take. We're gonna go a half hour over? Better that." I can't tell you the lack of sleep and the nerves and what that does to you. The first 3M machine did the same thing—it blew up from the heat. It didn't really blow up, the first 3M digital machine. I'm on the road with Billy Joel and I couldn't mix with it because the temperature would change and then the sound would change.

I tend to get invited to do these things. The night we did the three-network live one hour Standing Up To Cancer they put in a brand new video truck too. Audio and video. Brand new Calrec console. You say to yourself, "Am I subjecting myself to the craziest thing in the world?" The guy said, "If something fails," which happened at dress rehearsal with EQ, and all the memory of the limiters and stuff went out, he said, "Well you can fix it during the commercials." I said, "There are no commercials. None. It's 59 minutes and 35 seconds to roll from the first title."

You say to yourself, "This is not the way I was brought up to work." So, with all of these vast improvements, you know, warning lights, everything else that you want, you can't look at 160 inputs. You know, the other one that you never can tell is that unless you're soloing everything and you don't have a lot of reverb on it, you may have distortion on one track, completely destroy your work.

An important part of what we do is we make decisions. My brain, and my eyes, and ears work as a team. The tendency to get lazy is to say, "Don't worry, it's on a separate track by itself." That's not true. On a large stage or in a large theater if the trumpet mic is totally destroyed, the leakage on the violin mics might be your only source. That's not an answer. How do you know, how do you meter it? You're supposed to hear it in the composite, hopefully. There are distractions. You know, punching in and fixing and all that stuff: You can do it in a studio, but not always. Nobody designed this art to have all of the toys available to you and have them all work perfectly in concert. It's pretty hard to ask. I still marvel and ask myself, when they built the Twin Towers did they implode it in their brain? How do you calculate the two airplanes hitting it? How did they implode inside rather than explode? How did it fall straight down? Architecture is all about calculations that should help you. In earthquakes, you see some buildings totally survive. All of that, not that what we do musically doesn't feel like that sometimes when you're in trouble. The pressure is to be great and to make it as comfortable as possible for somebody. So it shouldn't be a gear record. The ones that are sentimental are using old gear and asking for it in a way, by relying on something that's 40 or 50 years old. They do have tubes in them.

Well, you know the good thing about a limiter or compressor, the tube type, is that it would take all of the guts you could give it and then it would crack and distort. A lot of the digital stuff doesn't show its face until, whoops… I guess I recorded it that way. How do you monitor this? I mean there's a way if you want to use a mixer who's in another truck, feeding you only information. His job is not to mix. We did it once with Elton John. We had a 70-piece orchestra and a 60-voice choir and his band and the audience and the cameras, all of that. We decided to put the orchestra in truck 2 and the rhythm section in truck 1, so we knew upfront that Elton John and his rhythm section sounded good. If there was any problem in the sharing of mics and the little bit of Plexiglas around some stuff, it was flying within Radio City. The height of the platforms helped, the band was coming back at full force, so having almost a light Plexiglas curtain helped us cut it down maybe 10 percent or more. What is that in dB, could be 10–15 dB, which is a lot against your original source. We did it that way so that the guy in truck A was really making sure that every track that he heard was only the strings. He was not listening to the rhythm. All he had to do was feed it to us. And we fed it on two faders.

I think the most important philosophy in that sense is to have the gear work for you and make it convenient to yourself, so that you question yourself as you work with anything else. You don't want to climb on top of a car and not know what it feels like to accelerate, to brake, to steer. I mean, there'll be a day when you will not have to do that, but I think you start to learn why things go wrong. You automate beyond the point that you need to automate. So you need some things in your hands, or the engineer that you choose, because producing, the assignment is to make that performance count. I think we tend to screw up, not slacking because there are several great engineers who people come to.

I like records too, which is the rhythm section and the singer, and you can hear if it's a good mix. I think you should always hear the final product in your head and go for it; not sitting around and saying, "Oh well, I could've done that, I should've." Should've/could've is not a good move. I think the attitude helps you because you come in to work with a real goal in mind, a purpose, and sometimes you say I don't know whether I'm gonna get three hours or 23 hours or 63 hours to do this, whether it's time to fix the vocals or tuning and mixing or whatever the composite is, but if you can make everybody come to a standard, I think it's like saying how do we get 60–70 people in the orchestra to play the repertoire they played two weeks before with a young talented kid out of Venezuela or a great German or Englishman conductor. The attention of how they played is purely about performance.

I think our job is to know your role, "check your ego outside the door", Quincy Jones' famous phrase. But the producers have to do that, too. Because you're there to inspire, to perspire, settle on nothing, and make the gear work for you rather than always saying, "Well, it never did this before." Give it a break, you know? I don't curse at computers because I think they hear when you're irritable. That says it all, pretty much.

Index